HOUSEHOLD CHOR

HOUSEHOLD CHOIC

MW01037128

HOUSEHOLD CHORES and HOUSEHOLD CHOICES

Theorizing the Domestic Sphere in Historical Archaeology

Edited by
KERRI S. BARILE and JAMIE C. BRANDON

THE UNIVERSITY OF ALABAMA PRESS
Tuscaloosa, Alabama

Typeface: Minion

∞

The paper on which this book is printed meets the minimum requirements of American
National Standard for Information Science–Permanence of Paper for Printed Library
Materials, ANSI Z39.48–1984.

Library of Congress Cataloging-in-Publication Data

Household chores and household choices : theorizing the domestic sphere in historical
archaeology / edited by Kerri S. Barile and Jamie C. Brandon.
      p. cm.
   Includes bibliographical references and index.
   ISBN 0-8173-1395-8 (cloth : alk. paper) — ISBN 0-8173-5098-5 (pbk. : alk. paper)
   1. United States—Antiquities. 2. Historic sites—United States. 3. Material culture—United
States. 4. Landscape—Social aspects—United States—History. 5. Households—United
States—History. 6. Family—United States—History. 7. Sex role—United States—History.
8. Archaeology and history—United States. 9. Feminist archaeology—United States.
10. Archaeology— Methodology. I. Barile, Kerri S. II. Brandon, Jamie C.
   E159.5.H68 2004
   640′.973—dc22

                                                                        2004001019

Contents

Figures

Tables

Acknowledgments

As editors, we would like to thank Maria Franklin and all our colleagues in her graduate seminar in household archaeology at The University of Texas at Austin, as well as all who participated in the symposium at the 2001 meeting of the Society for Historical Archaeology in Long Beach, California, from which this volume has grown. Not all who gave papers could contribute to this volume, unfortunately, but all have in some way shaped our dialogue about households.

We would like to express our gratitude to Laurie Wilke and Amy Young, who read early drafts of this volume and provided us with invaluable advice and thought-provoking comments, and Mary Beaudry, for belatedly joining the volume and adding her insightful contribution. Judy Goffman, our technical editor, smoothed out all of the final wrinkles. Personally, we would like to thank Sean and T.J.—for putting up with the weekends spent at work and the "archaeology talk" at the dinner table.

Foreword

Maria Franklin

The social unit that we refer to as the "household" has been the subject of intensive study within anthropological archaeology, most notably since the 1970s, and particularly within prehistory (for example, Flannery 1976; Gero and Conkey 1991; Wilk and Rathje 1982). For archaeologists, the household is often the most basic social unit of analysis "accessible" through the archaeological record, typically via residential structures and activity areas. The focus on households, however, cannot simply be reduced to the issue of archaeological "visibility." Unpacking the household archaeologically may be as close as any of us gets to comprehending the experiences of past individuals and as far as we may go in revealing the intimacies of their lives. Moreover, its influence regularly transgresses the domestic, as the household is both a microcosm of society and an active agent instituting change within that society. As James Deetz (1982:724) once wrote, "Whether a structural, functional, or evolutionary approach is taken to obtain this information, the household reveals relationships of thought and substance that can aid immensely in understanding the past."

While it is certainly true that historical archaeologists have greatly concerned themselves with the "domestic" since the discipline's emergence, it also holds true that we have yet to develop a substantial theoretical body of work concerning historic households. Mary Beaudry's (1989a:84) observation still carries weight today: "if one uses the anthropological definition of households that stresses the dynamics of this highly variable social grouping as the yardstick for evaluating what has been done, it is clear that domestic sites of the historical period have seldom been examined from what can truly be called a household-oriented perspective." We typically fail to even define "household" while we regularly employ the term. The end result is often an uncritical imposition upon the past of our contemporary notions of the household. Since the dominant American household norm, or "domestic" realm, relies heavily on the intact, nuclear family for its definition, many of us presuppose that the family does the same work as the household, then as now, and regardless of place.

The authors presented in this volume make no assumptions about the nature of households. As each chapter unfolds, it becomes apparent that just as it is ubiquitous, the household defies singular definitions and lays claim to a multiplicity of forms, functions, and meanings. The fluidity and vibrancy of the household is underscored as its life cycle is inextricably tied to the births, marriages, departures, and deaths of its members, whether living on a Spanish colonial rancho in the Rio Grande Valley or on a plantation in the Bahamas. The household as a social network instrumental to the formation and resilience of subjugated communities is highlighted in works concerning African Americans owned by Andrew Jackson and those establishing new lives in post-emancipation Texas. The household is deeply implicated not only in biological reproduction, but in the social reproduction of individuals where racial, class, and gender identities are constructed worlds apart from within a Colorado coal camp to a home in the Old South. The essentialized household as a cozy, safe, and peaceful domestic haven is challenged by research in Arkansas and South Carolina, where householders divided by race and slavery illustrate that household relations could be highly discordant. Yet we are also reminded of the household's role in reproducing and perpetuating naturalizing ideologies. In Massachusetts, where women's coalition-building threatened to disrupt Victorian gender norms in part by violating men's public spaces, paternalism worked to diffuse women's attempts to create a woman-centered, community-based household. Eight decades later in a California logging camp, we find company management using paternalism in the guise of the metaphorical family to maintain order and discipline over laborers (particularly single males), largely through household structure and organization.

From front to back, there is no shortage of concrete archaeological and historical analyses, rigorous theorizing, socially relevant questions, or political consciousness centered on the household within these pages. In their introduction, editors Kerri Barile and Jamie Brandon provide one of the very few historical perspectives and surveys of the study of households within historical archaeology. The volume is further strengthened by commentaries from two leading scholars of the discipline, Mary Beaudry and Suzanne Spencer-Wood. Each has been instrumental in advancing household-level research and social theory in archaeology, advocating in particular for contextual and interpretive approaches and feminist and gendered analysis.

To close, all of the authors are to be commended for their collective endeavor in revealing the productive potential of a household-oriented perspective. Given the diversity of case studies and approaches, *Household Chores and Household Choices* represents a critical step toward building a corpus of theories of households that is so direly needed in historical archaeology.

HOUSEHOLD CHORES and
HOUSEHOLD CHOICES

1

Introduction

Household Chores; or, the Chore of Defining the Household

Jamie C. Brandon and Kerri S. Barile

The household is a school of power. There, within the door, learn the tragicomedy of human life.

> Ralph Waldo Emerson, 1883

A comfortable house is a great source of happiness. It ranks immediately after health and a good conscience.

> Sydney Smith, 1843

Home is a name, a word, it is a strong one; stronger than magician ever spoke, or spirit ever answered to, in the strongest conjuration.

> Charles Dickens, 1844

"Home" is any four walls that enclose the right person.

> Helen Rowland, 1903

Home is the girl's prison and the woman's workhouse.

> George Bernard Shaw, 1903

Reflecting upon the quotations that open this chapter, it can be no surprise that archaeologists and historians have a great deal of trouble untangling the terminology and meaning surrounding the words *house, household,* and *home.* These terms can point to a simple building, a more ephemeral place (geographically specific or general) connected to emotion and feeling, a "school of power" (as in the Emerson quotation), a terrain upon which culture is learned, a gendered space, shelter against nature, and the sum of its contents (the listing phenomena exemplified by both probate inventories and the "House that Jack Built" nursery rhyme). A household can elicit some of these images or all of these things at once. Above all, house and home can be used as metaphors for almost anything one can imagine—a fact that points toward the all-pervading nature of the term and the importance of unraveling its multiple meanings in order to understand the past(s).

Although it is a problematic concept, archaeologists have given a lot of thought and effort to households, recognizing almost from the discipline's inception the importance of house and hearth to understanding the past. Likewise, there have been many attempts to deal with this domestic rubric and to untangle that maze of strands that render past households difficult to discern clearly through the historical and archaeological records.

HOUSES, HOUSELOTS, AND HISTORIC HOMES: ROOTS OF HOUSEHOLD APPROACHES FROM ARCHAEOLOGY AND HISTORIC PRESERVATION

Within the historic preservation movement, interest in *houses* was a paramount founding focus. In the United States, it is in the early roots of the preservation movement where "Americans developed their own distinctive version of historic preservation while Europeans were restoring their churches and castles or gathering vernacular architecture and folk objects into outdoor museums" (Alexander 1996:88). Alexander is referring to the historic house museum—a single dwelling or group of buildings, surrounded by a house lot or extensive acreage, with historic significance (once inhabited by a famous individual or family; representative of an architectural style or architect; or, signifying a particular historic event). The first historic house museum, the Hasbrook House in Newburgh, New York—Washington's headquarters during the Revolutionary War—was established in 1850. In 1856, Ann Pamela Cunningham began the fight to save Mount Vernon, Washington's plantation on the Potomac River. Her preservation work, and the ensuing creation of the Mount Vernon Ladies' Association of the Union, was to become the model of household preservation in the United States for the next 100 years (Alexander 1996:89).

Like Mount Vernon, early-twentieth-century projects that involved historical research and archaeology were framed around homes and the "enshrinement of home sites and landscapes belonging to the nation's 'founding fathers'" (Sanford 1999:7), thus bounding the definition and assumed function of the household by gender, race, and status. For example, archaeological and historical research at Stratford Hall Plantation in Westmoreland County, Virginia, home of the Lee family and birthplace of Robert E. Lee, began in 1929 with the creation of the Robert E. Lee Memorial Foundation, a group modeled on the Mount Vernon Ladies' Association. Archaeological excavations concentrated on the area surrounding the Great House in an attempt to reconstruct the outbuildings and landscape built by, and modified by, the Lee *men* and, moreover, to establish Stratford as "a civic shrine" dedicated to Robert E. Lee (Sanford 1999:7).

Certainly during the mid and late nineteenth century, as modernity solidified and industrialization progressed, "tokens from the nation's childhood" became symbolic of a dying past that needed to be preserved, catalogued, and recorded "to bolster the mature and rational evolution of the Bourgeois and bureaucratic state" (Boyer 1994:378). Part and parcel of the nation's new concern for remembrance is its obsession with forgetting and erasure (Flores 2002:20–25; Trouillot 1995). Historic homes, along with battlefield sites, became the perfect venue for both remembrance and erasure. Such strong focus on the white, wealthy male individual (such as Washington, Lee, or Andrew Jackson at the Hermitage in Tennessee) easily created an aggregate household completely subsumed under what the public identified as the "head of household." Any evidence that might complicate this picture of a harmonious household is "silenced by the weight of its structure" (Flores 2002:21), and the past was presented with idyllic, innocent charm.

Early-twentieth-century household archaeology and historic research was not limited to large-scale plantations and homesteads but also extended to the creation of some of the first historic districts in the country. Even these districts, however, remained focused on the "household as architecture" idea first established in the mid-1800s, one that was directly tied to the "great men of history" myth. The first historic district in the nation was created between 1928 and 1931 in Charleston, South Carolina (Howard 1987:115). Throughout the first quarter of the twentieth century, prominent local citizens of Charleston witnessed the slow demise of large portions of the historic downtown area. The automobile and the creation of new commercial venues caused the widening of roads, the removal of streetside landscaping and ornate ironwork, and the outright destruction of several historic homes once belonging to the Charleston elite. The Charleston Historic District was thus designed to protect both the house structure and house lot from destruction or alteration. (See Brandon's chapter in this volume for the gendered implications of the Charleston historic preservation movement.) The establishment of local preservation legislation and the protection of household structures soon spread to other American cities, such as New Orleans in 1936, San Antonio in 1939, Winston-Salem, North Carolina, in 1948, and Natchez, Mississippi, in 1951 (Howard 1987:115). Archaeologically, this period is certainly marked by the assumption that investigations into the architectural remains of a dwelling lead to an understanding of domestic behavior in the past (Allison 1999a:4).

From the late 1960s into the 1980s, however, anthropology and prehistoric archaeology attempted to move away from the static concept of household as architecture and began to address questions beyond the physical fabric and layout of the home and house lot. Simultaneously, these disciplines struggled to achieve a "greater degree of precision" by separating the "two phenomena [encapsulated within the concept of household] that are logically distinct and vary somewhat independently: co-residence and domestic function" (Bender 1967). This distinction between structure and function was sought to "bridge the existing 'mid-level theory' gap" (Wilk and Rathje 1982:617) and "replace a culturally defined unit with one that is more based on observation and can be more readily compared across cultures" (Wilk and Netting 1984:1). Here, the "household" became "the most common social component of subsistence . . . [a] strategy to meet the productive, distributive and reproductive needs of its members" (Wilk and Rathje 1982:618), and inevitably households were primarily seen as the basic "measurable socio-economic unit" through which archaeologists could generate understandings of the past (Allison 1999a:1). Yet the conflation of the two "logically distinct" aspects proved difficult to evade, as households were still commonly grouped "on the basis of what kind of family lies at the core" (Wilk and Netting 1984:3).

Historical archaeology, suffering something of an identity crisis at the time (e.g., Honerkamp 1988), saw the deployment of many permutations of the aforementioned approaches. For instance, some researchers continued to "define the household in terms of the household head and his relative rank in society" (Beaudry 1989a:84), while others joined prehistoric archaeologists in attempting to refine definitions and separate function from form—although often falling right back upon the convenient conflation of terms when interpretations are sought (e.g., O'Brien 1984:26–27).

Stanley South's influential *Method and Theory in Historical Archaeology* (1977) is a convenient example of processual thinking on households within historical archaeology. He states that each household "represents a system within a much larger system imposing on each household a degree of uniformity in the relationships among its various parts" (1977:86–87). For South, this uniformity was the basis for the generation of "household patterns" of material culture that could be used to attain his final goal—a clearer understanding of the broad processes of cultural evolution (1977:2–5). Similar sites should produce statistically similar patterns, while unusual sites will have patterns that deviate from the norm.

So it seems that processualists also saw the past as inhabited by "aggregate" households. These households were not necessarily conflated with individuals but rather were (when deployed ideally) entities unto themselves. That is, the processual household is an abstract "unit," usually a unit of production or consumption that makes rational choices about behavior within its worldview. Unfortunately, although South's approach was admirable in its attention to site structure beyond architecture and its emphasis on contexts, the vast majority of those who flocked to his methods "used pattern analysis as if it were an end in itself" (Beaudry 1989a:85; South 1988:27), resulting in many sites being pigeonholed into patterns and a multitude of newly formulated patterns that threatened to outnumber the sites to which they were assigned.

Parallel to these processual approaches stressing artifact patterning is the structural approach to symmetrical patterning in architecture and other material culture advanced by researchers such as James Deetz (1977, 1982) and Henry Glassie (1975). Although Deetz (1982:720) was quick to point out that "households and houses are neither isomorphic with each other, nor with families," he quickly returned to the idea that *houses* (or the remains of dwellings) are "powerful mirrors for the way in which . . . [people in the past] saw themselves and their world and expressed the values of their culture in substance." Although he was often defensive of his structural approach (as "non-provable" and "non-predictive"), Deetz's goals have much in common with the processual approach of South and others. These goals include the positivistic idea of "reading" a knowable pattern "encoded" into material culture (and its patterns) which, in turn, point toward shifts in the larger worldview/belief systems of past peoples. Aside from the "essentially passive, reflective view of style" advanced here (Dietler and Herbich 1998:239), it has been pointed out that the vast majority of individuals will not build the house in which they will dwell (Allison 1999a:4), a problem that plagues both the strict structural approach and the return to houses and the "key" to past household behavior.

THE HOUSEHOLD PERSPECTIVE IN HISTORICAL ARCHAEOLOGY: HOUSEHOLD CORES AS PRACTICE

Given the long associations outlined, it may seem ridiculous to say that "household analysis" has been implemented within historical archaeology only since the mid-1980s, but that is indeed the case (Beaudry 1989a). At that time, historical archaeologists began a critical assessment of the definition of *households* (e.g., Beaudry 1984, 1986, 1989a; Mrozowski 1984; Stewart-Abernathy 1986a). Although somewhat distinct owing to intellectual traditions, these studies did seek to bring a "household oriented perspective" to historical archaeology, but the emphasis was on a "holistic, contextual approach" (Beaudry 1989a:84–85)— one that did not hinge solely on architectural or subsistence remains but employed dynamic, historicizing methodologies. Incidentally, Beaudry's formulation was set off alongside the idea of artifacts as "active voices" or the material manifestations of social discourse (Beaudry 1996; Beaudry et al. 1991; Yentsch and Beaudry 2001:226). Although it bears the difficulties of using a textual metaphor for material culture (cf. Dietler and Herbich 1998:243–244), this formulation has more to offer than many of its predecessors, as it enables multiple, contradictory meanings within material culture, stresses contextualization, and represents the people who give material culture meaning in different situations.

A plethora of other theoretical forces impacted household archaeology (both directly and indirectly) throughout the 1980s and 1990s; they included consumption, consumer choice (Miller 1991; Spencer-Wood 1987a), feminist issues (e.g., Lawrence 1999; Spencer-Wood 1991a, 1996), and Marxist approaches, often combined with structural positions and utilization of consumer behaviors (Leone 1984, 1995; Leone and Little 1993; McGuire 1992; McGuire and Paynter 1991; Orser 1988, 1996, to name a few). More recent archaeological studies have attempted to look beyond the aggregate household—a view stressing economic production or belief systems painted with a broad brush—toward "the practical actions of daily life" (Pader 1993:114). For example, archaeologies influenced by Bourdieu's practice theory have become commonplace (e.g., Allison 1999b; Dietler and Herbich 1998; Wilkie 2000a; also see Battle and Stewart-Abernathy, this volume).

THIS BOOK AND THE LIST OF HOUSEHOLD CHORES

Discussion of an explicit "household perspective" seems to have receded somewhat in recent literature in historical archaeology (with some notable exceptions, such as the papers in Allison 1999b). Its most likely successor seems to be studies employing the "landscape perspective," which have become ubiquitous of late (e.g., Ashmore and Knapp 1999; Shackel 2001a; Stine et al. 1997; Thomas 2001; Yamin and Metheny 1996; Young 2000). Although landscape archaeology, in our opinion, provides a productive ground for understanding past power relationships and ideology, it must be said that many landscape analyses, as well as other recent works dealing with race, class, and gender in a more general way, still rely on household data or have households deeply embedded within their matrices.

The analytical move to landscapes, in fact, opens up interesting possibilities for household analysis—the household as "small" landscape. The same theoretical underpinnings are at work on the household level, no matter how one parses the definition. Practice theory, power relations, gender constructions, and many other subjects that have been treated successfully via landscape analysis beg to be applied in similar fashion to the household. This approach is, no doubt, influenced by Henrietta Moore's (1988, 1994, 1996) stressing of the symbolic uses of space and the reading of the complete "text" of households and their articulation with gender constructions.

Some of the authors in this volume move toward a landscape perspective, such as Barile's discussion of plantation *household complexes* and the use of spatial alteration as the response to the fear of insurrection, Battle's focus on exterior, communally used areas, Pappas's interrogation of house plans in logging camps, and Stewart-Abernathy's keen observations about detached kitchens.

In a similar vein, although not overtly spatial, Wood's contributions utilize feminist, Marxist, and practice theory approaches in ways akin to those perusing landscape studies (e.g., papers in Ashmore and Knapp 1999 and Delle et al. 2000).

In addition, while gender is certainly prominent in these papers, we attempt here to see households as not *solely* the locus for an engendered power struggle (although it is certainly an important aspect of household analysis). To be sure, some authors confront gender constructions in the household (Spencer-Wood and Wood), while others examine the intersection of multiple identities in the household (Anderson and Brandon) or address gender in more subtle ways (Davidson, Galindo, and Stewart-Abernathy). Still others eschew gender as a category altogether in favor of other analytical registers (Barile and Bonine).

This book is, then, both in the "household perspective" tradition (as outlined in Beaudry 1989a) and a break with it. Like Allison (1999a:5), we feel that it is important to break free from a household archaeology dominated by architecture-oriented approaches. Further, we feel that we must problematize notions that behaviors of the past are simply "coded" in material culture and their patterns that can be easily "read" by archaeologists. Such notions often lead to disappointment in archaeology's abilities to answer social questions (cf. Allison 1999b; Dietler and Herbich 1998; and papers in Laurence and Wallace-Hadrill 1997), as well as overly simplistic and reductionist explanations of household analyses, which deny that cultural production is accomplished by "socially situated subjects with different cultural competencies and different, often contradictory, interest" (Dietler and Herbich 1998:239).

A variety of papers are included that, in varying ways, grapple with the meaning of household on their own terrain—the only place we believe these meanings can be clarified. We do not believe in a single, universal definition or approach to the household. Rather than presenting one definition of the household, the authors critically examine the concept within their own parameters. This move to the particular enables them to attempt to understand the workings of "house" and "home" in their own terms and the terms of their own data. This approach leads to the most promising and, we believe, the strongest facet of this book: each author first develops a context for his or her project and an understanding of the needed research questions, then attempts to define and analyze the household based on this framework.

In the United States today, there are many definitions of household. According to the U.S. Census, a household includes all those living within one space, at one postal address. This definition disregards kinship and economics in favor of a spatially based analysis. The Internal Revenue Service, however, believes a household is based on the economic unit and includes all those linked by finances, as well as by kin relations. This system is judged on economic "dependents." Certainly, most people not only define their own household beyond the categories of these government agencies, but, more significantly, change their definition of a household several times throughout their lives. Is the definition of their household at eighteen years of age the same as at age fifty? Likely not.

With this in mind, the authors here recognize that, while they cannot impose modern concepts on their understanding of the past, the household in the past probably had many definitions, as it does today, and, moreover, the boundaries of that household remained fluid through one's life span. The authors clearly establish a context for their projects based on the social and cultural background of the occupants, temporal association of the site, geographic location, social context for which the site(s) was developed, and even the circumstances surrounding the present-day research and excavations. The "household" is then defined based on this context and the research questions are developed accordingly.

This approach seems to agree with Julia Hendon's assertion that "*what* households do [should be] a matter to be investigated rather than assumed *a priori*" (Hendon 1996:46, emphasis added; also see Yanagisako 1979:164). Some authors in this volume do go as far as to say that households are the basic unit of production and reproduction in a given community, but production and reproduction do not stop at the vulgar Marxist conceptions of "producing surplus value" or "reproducing the worker" (Hart 1992, cf. Smith 1978). Here, households are to be seen as the nexus of *social* reproduction and production in the form of practice (Bourdieu 1977). At times, these household activities serve to "produce" material things (such as food, clothing, and shelter), but they do these things in a way that both reifies and transforms the social structure— along with such things as gender constructions and power relations—which, on a grander scale, are shared with the larger community. To evoke the words of Hendon (1996:47) again, we see a household as a "symbolically meaningful social group that forms the next bigger thing on the social map after an individual." In short, it is one of the most basic venues for the sharing of culture (Tringham 1988).

The broad framework outlined here alleviates the need to shoe-horn definitions into universal categories. The reader will note a wide array of definitions and influences in play. Some approaches to households here stretch and make problematic the definitions to include communal households (e.g., Pappas and Spencer-Wood) or entire plantations (e.g., Anderson and Barile), and some attempt to clarify and intensify more traditional approaches (e.g., Bonine,

Davidson, Stewart-Abernathy, and Wood). Not all of these authors separate the structure and function of households, as do economically based approaches, but this entanglement is, in fact, part and parcel of the concept of households, and separation may obscure more than it illuminates.

Finally, while not all of these papers are specifically archaeological in the traditional sense, all approach specific households (in time and space) from an archaeological perspective. Some authors marshal excavated data to discuss households, as Stewart-Abernathy and Wood have done; others have relied on limited excavations (e.g., Battle and Davidson), landscape analysis (e.g., Barile and Pappas), reanalyzed existing collections (Bonine), or utilized the archival record to shed light on little-examined aspects of households (e.g., Anderson, Brandon, Galindo, and Spencer-Wood).

PLACE, SPACE, AND BEING

There are many ways that a volume such as this one can be organized: chronologically, regionally, or topically. After experimenting with many possible permutations, we have settled on an organization based around the subtle and fluid distinction between senses of place, space, and being. Taking our cue from humanist geographers, we regard a "Sense of Place" as the cultural textures that attach themselves not only to "surfaces, processes and structures but also communication acts and the multiple contexts" that create and are constituted by a particular locale (Adams et al. 2001:xiv). For example, Whitney Battle's chapter is an examination of an enslaved community living within the First Hermitage, a portion of Andrew Jackson's Hermitage plantation in central Tennessee. She points out that researchers have often concentrated on enslaved families or slave dwellings, but that concrete evidence of shared household space, such as outdoor spaces, has not often been investigated in its role of creating community and giving the enslaved "a place of their own."

Stewart-Abernathy in "Separate Kitchens and Intimate Archaeology" follows a vein similar to Battle's by foregrounding the detached kitchens of Old Washington, Arkansas, as places where daily practice and physical separation could create a brief refuge from the intimacy and inherent power relationships at play within the southern urban farmstead. He points toward the little-studied detached "kitchen" as being much more than a place for food preparation in the eyes of the enslaved African Americans who worked, slept, and lived much of their lives in that setting.

James Davidson examines this "sense of place" on a much larger scale—the urban cityscape of Dallas, Texas. He carefully follows the way in which the constantly shifting urban landscape impacts historical memory and the meaning of place. After outlining the transformation and loss of a historical Black

Dallas, he turns toward household-level analysis and urban archaeology as one method that may help expose modern and historical racism at work in our current landscapes.

Finally, Mindy Bonine's analysis of two dwellings excavated in 1949 and 1950 in the borderlands of Starr County, Texas, is bold in its attempts to separate the concepts of family and household using excavated data more than fifty years old. Despite the limitations of her dataset, she manages to pose important questions about family, households, and the limitations of the investigations of activity areas and the aggregate household.

Authors with papers under the heading of "A Sense of Space" actively examine the physical landscape in dialogue with social construction and transformations. Nesta Anderson extends Battle's line of reasoning by questioning the underlying assumptions that the scale of spatial analysis and its reliance on prescribed boundaries that, in certain circumstances, obscure as much as they reveal. She deploys the notion of nested household as an alternative definition of household when working on Bahamian plantations. Her case study suggests that researchers should situationally use different scales of landscape analysis when examining multiscalar cases, such as the plantation household. More important, in these situations one must always keep in mind the fluid boundaries between often-fixed concepts such as "house yard" and "slave quarters."

Kerri Barile uses Anderson's "plantation as household" model in her analysis of plantation landscapes and their response to real and imagined threats of slave insurrection. With Middleburg Plantation in South Carolina as her backdrop, she follows plantation layouts through time—particularly following the Denmark Vesey conspiracy of 1822. The culture of fear and the desperate need of secure hegemony are clear in her depictions of white plantation owners.

Suzanne Spencer-Wood, in her chapter on the Cambridge Cooperative Housekeeping Society, provides us with a good example of a situation that confounds traditional definitions of the household. Here, domestic reformers attempt to transform chores commonly classified as "private" and associated with the "household" into "public" and professional activities. While this work could have easily been classified into our "sense of being" section (Part IV) based on the conscious attempt to change the oppressive gender structure of Victorian America, it is Spencer-Wood's examination of the spatial map of the society's activities that places the piece squarely in our "sense of space" section. While many researchers, especially Spencer-Wood herself, have explored the ideological entanglements of feminist thought and domestic reform, it is unusual to encounter a physical mapping of reform-oriented sites. Moreover, Spencer-Wood posits two interesting twists regarding the demise of the cooperative. Male domination within individual households (the realm often deemed the woman's purview in Victorian ideology) along with the spatial location of these cooperatives are credited with their eventual demise.

Efstathios Pappas provides another unconventional household case study—the Soap Creek Pass logging camp in the Sierra Nevada Mountains of California. Here, he attempts to understand variation in the spatial layout of company housing at the camp by examining the interplay between company paternalism and the agency of its employees. The result is an interesting addition to the "archaeology of capitalism," juxtaposing family-oriented housing with the housing of single male workers, where the company itself takes the place of family—creating a large "household" consisting of labor "children" and management "fathers."

Papers under the heading of "A Sense of Being" are centered around the more abstract cultural framework sometimes referred to as a "structure of feeling" (Williams 1973, 1977:128–135) that defines the lived experience of people *and* a set of productions (such as strategies of representation) that reflect upon, speak to, or attempt to transform those experiences (Mitchell 2000:13). Jamie Brandon's chapter, for example, attempts to get at the nexus of gender and race construction in the postbellum South by looking at various practices, strategies, and discourses that center around the southern household and enable it to be a locus for resistance while simultaneously feeding into the "strategies of containment" advanced by both Victorian and modern social structures.

Likewise, Margaret Wood's chapter combines perspectives on labor, culture, and gender to examine how failed attempts at antilabor social engineering backfired on the Colorado Fuel and Iron Company by allowing women, in particular, to make friends and take in boarders across ethnic lines. Thus, at the town of Berwind, it was social relations built at the *household level* that enabled the collective action of the mineworkers—an aspect of the Ludlow Massacre that historical literature has erased.

Mary Jo Galindo marshals an impressive set of data from local historians, oral traditions, and archival data to outline an expanded definition of the Spanish colonial household in Nuevo Santander. In her case study of the application of household theory, she surmises that archaeologists concentrating on the ranchos would only understand a part of the household activities, and the remainder of the household tasks took place at a second dwelling spatially removed from the rancho—in town. She follows a complicated network of kinrelationships and landholdings to reveal that these families were certainly joined by all of the criteria used by traditional archaeologists to describe the household. They were economically a unit, and they were related through kinship or fictive kinship, but they lived spatially distinct lives.

The volume concludes with commentaries by two researchers who have done much to advance the notion of an explicitly household-centered archaeology, Mary Beaudry and Suzanne Spencer-Wood. These summary essays contextualize and critique the case studies included here and stress that this volume "further relates household inequalities to inequalities socially constructed, ideologically justified, and structurally enforced between social groups in the culture as a whole" (Spencer-Wood).

Spencer-Wood examines the papers in this volume for their implicit or explicit reliance on feminist theory. She has shown, in great detail, how different social standpoints are embedded in the different levels of household definitions and that feminist theory has influenced much of the research on power dynamics here. Beaudry's concluding commentary, on the other hand, parses the volume into three themes (Intimacy and Separation; Patriarchy, Spatial Ordering, and Power Relations; and The Subversive Poetics of Housework), and she deftly points to many of the strong points and weaknesses of each of the chapters within these themes.

A careful reading of these concluding commentaries will show that these authors do not always agree with the other authors in the volume or with each other, but they both feel that "the household is a critical social unit and vital medium for understanding innumerable aspects of social life" (Beaudry). These commentaries, and the case studies they summarize, open a dialogue about how these different approaches and definitions affect our understanding of the past(s). The key here is that a household perspective sensitive to changes in context and structure through time and space is an important framework for historical archaeologists and historians—one whose interpretations will, no doubt, be explored and debated for some time to come.

Part I
A Sense of Place

2

Analysis of Household and Family at a Spanish Colonial Rancho *along the Rio Grande River*

Mindy Bonine

INTRODUCTION

There have been several discussions in recent decades about the concept of households, how they can be seen in the archaeological record, and their value in observing larger social issues. This scale of analysis is particularly useful in studying the Spanish Colonial rancho, a small-scale, family-owned cattle ranch established in several locations in New Spain. One such location was the area around the Rio Grande, now divided into South Texas and Northern Coahuila, Nuevo Leon, and Tamaulipas, Mexico. This area was not inhabited by those representing large institutions—no administrators, clerics, or military personnel— but comprised civilians trying to make a living in an inhospitable territory. Archaeological evidence of these people and their efforts can be found only at the household level.

Initially, since households were believed to be a core social attribute, the "most common social component of subsistence, the smallest and most abundant activity group" (Wilk and Rathje 1982:618), definitions based on cultural and cross-cultural attributes were attempted. However, an exception to the rule was usually found that gave the definition less weight (see Tringham 1991:100). For example, in our society the nuclear family unit in a single residence usually signifies a household, but of course there are many households that do not conform to this ideal. To get a better sense of this diversity, several archaeologists have defined the household based on the activities performed there rather than on the physical structure where the activities are conducted or on the kinship structure of the inhabitants (Blanton 1994; Hendon 1996; Meadows 1999; Wilk and Netting 1984; Wilk and Rathje 1982). Houses and families were not left out entirely from the definition, but they were heavily de-accentuated (Wilk and Netting 1984:1–3; Wilk and Rathje 1982:618).

HOUSEHOLDS, FAMILIES, AND OTHER SOCIAL GROUPS

Early on in discussions about the structure of households and how they can be seen archaeologically, a division was made between the household and the family. Although households and families often go hand in hand, particularly in cultures that promote the nuclear family ideal, the wide variety of actual home life situations prompted several archaeologists to argue that the household should be defined by propinquity and activities (functional) and families as a social group based on kinship (structural and organizational) (Bender 1967; Kramer 1982; Laslett 1972). This separation of ideas was done to avoid automatically linking households and families together in a set of predetermined relationships (like our own relationship between household and family), regardless of evidence for more variability in a society or different sorts of relationships (Kramer 1982:664; Wilk and Netting 1984:1). The separation is not comfortable, and many of the activities talked about, including domestic functions, co-residence, economic ties, food preparation, and socialization of children, arguably can be applied to either term, depending on the perspective (Bender 1967; Yanagisako 1979).

Later in the discussion about households, the emphasis on the function of the household was criticized for trivializing the composition of households and the relationships among their members (Allison 1999a:2; Henden 1996:48; Tringham 1991:101). Household studies concentrated too much on what households did as a single social unit and not enough on the individuals within the household who did the work. This approach treated all households as having the same internal composition and failed to explore the various dynamics among household members, including factors that would impede the successful "running of the household," such as conflict and strife. Although these authors were discussing this phenomenon in terms of gender relations, they also included class and ethnicity (Hendon 1996:46). I argue that family should be included in this list as well, for socially defined familial relationships, including non-kinship age-rank relationships (for example, see Pappas, this volume), structure how household members interact with each other throughout their lives, and are intimately tied with gender, class, and ethnicity.

Because, like the household, the family is a social unit, it cannot be analyzed in any depth without talking about other social categories, which, in turn, say a great deal about what the family means in a particular culture. I believe that the family, whatever its particular cultural definition, shapes the life of an individual in such a profound and personal way that it would be difficult to ignore in a microscale analysis, such as household archaeology. Even if kin members do not cohabitate or share in household functions, they do have an effect on the household through the household members themselves.

Examining households solely in terms of function is productive, but it is also a matter of convenience. It allows archaeologists to link a collection of physical structures to social activities, and in turn to larger social processes, without having to determine exactly who is participating in those activities. In circumstances where finding household composition is difficult, such as areas of research that have little comparative information, this concept works very well. Further attempts to associate functional categories from the artifact assemblage to groups or individuals most likely to perform those tasks would be a shot in the dark. However, in situations where more can be known about the inhabitants of these physical structures, for example, through extensive archaeological excavations or ethnographic or textual information, a functional analysis of households is not enough. Information concerning gender, class, family, and ethnicity, attributes of the individuals who lived and worked in these households, are left out of the equation (see Lawrence 1999:122–123). This absence limits what can be said about variation between and among households, issues of conflict between and among household members, exploration of identity formation and maintenance, and an individual's relationship with the physical environment. If multiple lines of evidence exist and, most important, contextual information concerning archaeological data exists, then the relationship between household function and household composition can be explored with rigor. The arguments that were used to separate household and family are still valid (i.e., an awareness of the biases generated from modern cultural perception of families and households that might be placed on the past); however, a recognition that households are not all the same (or even the same over time) should make the dangers avoidable.

In my research concerning civilian Spanish settlements along the Texas/ Mexico border in the mid- to late eighteenth century (Bonine 2001), I had initially welcomed the idea of separating the household and family because I did not have to worry about associating certain groups of people with the structures that were excavated. As a focus of my research, I could relate the activities of the households to other Spanish colonial settlements in the area, particularly missions and presidios, and remark on the similarities and differences between them. However, I kept wondering about who really lived there and why they were willing to risk so much to settle in an inhospitable land so far from "civilization." I decided to change my direction to include questions about household composition as well as household function to try to understand these civilian Spanish settlers. I will briefly describe the investigation of a Spanish Colonial rancho site along the Rio Grande and discuss the possible connections between the archaeological and architectural evidence, which provides data about activities and use of space, and the historic evidence, which provides some information on the people who lived there.

TWO SITES, ONE RANCHO

In 1951, construction of the Falcon Dam in Starr County, Texas, was completed along the Rio Grande. Upstream of the dam, a large reservoir was created that covered two small towns along the riverbank, as well as numerous archaeological sites. While Falcon Dam was under construction, several people became concerned about the archaeological and historic resources that would soon be underwater and scraped together some funds to travel down to the banks of the Rio Grande and conduct archaeological surveys (Krieger and Hughes 1950). Fifty-five sites were recorded along the entire length of the proposed reservoir, but archaeologists concentrated on the town of Zapata and the dam spillway construction site that was being bulldozed at the time. In 1951, the River Basin Surveys at the Smithsonian Institution conducted emergency excavations of three historic sites, two of which appeared to have an interesting relationship (Hartle and Stephenson 1951).

Two Spanish colonial sites were among the sites recorded and partially ex-cavated in 1949 and 1950, before the dam and reservoir were completed. Each site contained ruins of one-room stone buildings situated close together, along with domestic trash middens (Figure 2.1). The buildings appeared to be domes-tic structures associated with a Spanish rancho operating in the mid-eighteenth to mid-nineteenth centuries. However, only two small survey and excavation reports were written about the sites, and only one of the reports was available to the public. No further analysis of artifacts or archival work was done on either site. The artifacts and excavation notes were housed at the Texas Archeo-logical Research Laboratory at the University of Texas at Austin for 48 years. Fortunately, interest in Texas's Spanish Colonial history has been revived, and archaeologists and historians are conducting more research in this area (e.g., Alonzo 1998; DiPaolo Loren 2000; Galindo, this volume; Jones 1996; Monday and Colley 1997; Perttula et al. 1999; Tijerina 1998; Williams 1982). However, archaeological investigations into Spanish ranchos were still sparse, and an analysis of material recovered from Falcon Reservoir was considered an impor-tant addition to this area of research.

Site 41SR39 is located approximately 300 feet north of the dam along the Rio Grande valley, less than 100 feet from the water's edge (Hartle and Stephenson 1951). The site contained two one-room stone ruins, consisting of concentrated rock piles over the remaining walls, and a trash midden only a few inches deep (Figure 2.2). One building had a fire pit in the center of the room. The other building measured 16.8 feet × 11 feet and contained a sealed 41-inch-wide door. The artifact complement for both buildings was noticeably similar.

Site 41SR43 was recorded as 675 feet from the dam site and about 350 feet from the river. This site is quite a bit larger than 41SR39, with four one-room

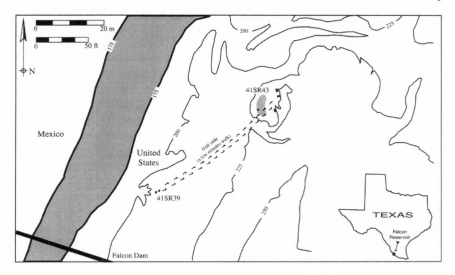

Fig. 2.1. Map of Falcon Dam and Sites 41SR39 and 41SR43.

structures, a possible well, and a large trash midden (Figure 2.3). The site as a whole seemed to be in worse condition than 41SR39; rather than discrete piles of rubble, the sandstone blocks were scattered around the ground, with the walls of the buildings just visible on the surface. One building was almost entirely washed away by erosion.

All the buildings were constructed in the same manner at both sites: cut sandstone chinked with smaller stones and remnants of adobe plastered on the walls. No floors were found in any of the buildings; however, evidence of thresholds, the only openings in the buildings, was found at the level of the modern ground surface. This led the investigators to think the floor was already washed away, and they were excavating below the floor. Recovered artifacts were also similar between the sites. Later investigation into property ownership showed that both sites were on the same *porcion,* or land grant, drawn up by the surveyors of the José de Escandón expedition in 1767. Also, the sites were in close proximity, only a five-minute walk apart. It was likely that the two sites were actually part of the same rancho complex.

RECOVERED ARTIFACTS

At first examination, the artifacts recovered from each group of buildings within the rancho were similar, but on closer inspection there were interesting differences in the type and quantity of the artifacts recovered. Although the sites were not excavated in their entirety, particularly site 41SR43, and there is

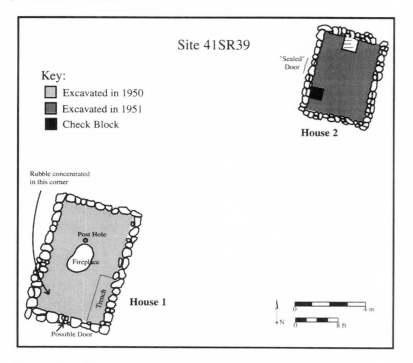

Fig. 2.2. Site 41SR39.

a danger in making conclusions based on incomplete excavation data, the artifacts that were recovered can hint at some of the activities conducted at this rancho, as well as the identity of the inhabitants.

Unfortunately, there are excavation sampling issues that influence the artifact analysis of these two sites. The buildings were either excavated in large areas that covered the entire interior space of the building, or narrow trenches were dug on the interior side of the walls. The only exception to this was House 2 at 41SR43, where a square was laid out and the interior was excavated in blocks. If there was any vertical distribution of artifacts inside the structures, it was not recorded by any of the excavators. Vertical distribution was a little more controlled in the excavation of the test units at site 41SR43, consisting of two levels, one 0 to 6 inches and the other 6 inches to 1 foot. Horizontal distributions of artifacts were very broad in most areas for both sites. The information recovered does not lend anything to an investigation of possible activity areas within the buildings, the relationship between the interior and exterior habitation areas, or the vertical distribution of artifacts that might help identify a floor or floors. Therefore, the discussion will concentrate on the differences and similarities between the buildings themselves and on the trash midden.

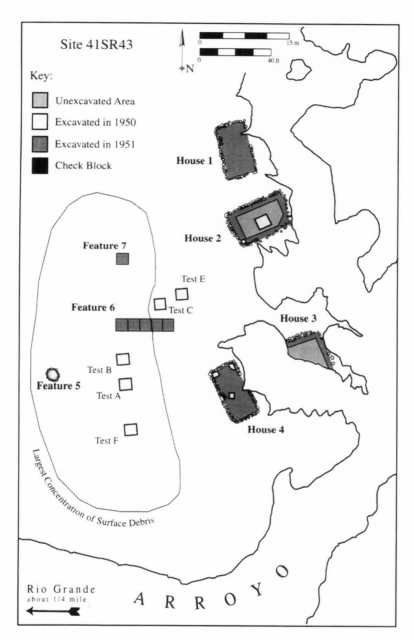

Fig. 2.3. Site 41SR43.

Perhaps more worrisome is the existence of large quantities of artifacts that, through mistakes in excavation, transport, or analysis, have lost all provenience save for the site they came from. Several of these artifacts are interesting and should not be left out of the discussion, but what can be understood about them will be more limited. That said, it is still a valuable exercise to reanalyze cultural material housed at curation facilities, as will be demonstrated.

Site 41SR39 Artifacts

Despite the fact that only two one-room buildings were excavated at site 41SR39, several attributes of the recovered artifacts are significant. Of the total number of artifacts (n = 3,441), over 96 percent (n = 3,310) were ceramics. Bone (2.2 percent, n = 78), lithic material (.8 percent, n = 29), and glass artifacts (.5 percent, n = 18) comprised the remainder, along with three metal artifacts and three shells.

House 1 contained the most material (n = 2,583), and a vast majority of the ceramic sherds were reconstructed into semirestored vessels. The vessels consisted primarily of storage jars (*ollas*) of a shape similar to an olive jar. Small, flattened bases widened to an oval-shaped body and narrowed down to a short neck and mouth. All were unglazed; the mouths were not as small as an olive jar's and were thin-lipped. Other completed unglazed forms included small bowls with slightly flattened bases and lips that turned slightly outward. All of these storage vessels were handmade and consistent with the Mier Plain category of unglazed coarse earthenware (Perttula et al. 1999). Several glazed and wheel-made vessels were also found in House 1, including two "mixing bowls," large curved coarse earthenware bowls with no foot, a wide mouth, and decorative edges. These bowls showed evidence of heavy use, as the green glaze on the interior had been almost worn off. Two majolica *platos* (San Luis Polychrome Variant) were reconstructed from sherds, and at least two *chocolateras* were present. The restored ceramic vessels were so numerous that the 1950 survey team, which excavated House 1, identified 25 complete and partially complete vessels. Upon further observations, the number of identifiable vessels was somewhat less, but the fact that so many existed is still significant. The only glass and metal artifacts at site 41SR39 were also found in House 1, as well as one metate fragment and two bone buttons.

Compared to House 1, House 2 contained little cultural material, only ceramic sherds (n = 250) and bone (n = 13). One chocolatera was found there (Figure 2.4) and a few glazed sherds, but most of the material was unglazed coarse earthenware. About 595 artifacts did not have any provenience information included. Some of these materials were surface collections, including five bifaces and a thick iron plate, and a collection of 19 bifaces and cores could be

Fig. 2.4. Semirestored Galera Polychrome chocolatera vessel from Site 41SR39.

traced to either House 1 or House 2. A clay whistle was also found in an unknown location at the site.

Site 41SR43 Artifacts

Considerably more artifacts were recovered from site 41SR43. The site was larger than 41SR39, and several test units were placed in the trash midden, leading to both larger artifact counts and more variety of artifacts. Of the total fragments of cultural material recovered (n = 5,102), 89 percent were ceramics (n = 4,544), 4.7 percent were stone objects (n = 255), and 4 percent were bone (n = 205). Shell (n = 61), metal (n = 21), and glass (n = 5) made up the rest of the material.

Of the four structures located at site 41SR43, House 1 contained the largest amount and widest variety of material. The ceramic artifacts included Mier Plain sherds (n = 81), Galera Polychrome (from chocolateras) (n = 65), and Green and Brown Glazed Utility Ware (n = 18). Majolica, totaling 15 sherds, included Aranama Polychrome, San Elizario, Pueblo Blue on White, and Plain.

Mexican Red Painted Ware and an unusual glazed earthenware, designated "Orange Glazed," were recovered. The only piece of olive jar was found in House 1, as well as the only pieces of native ceramics (n = 5). Another unique item was a very small Mier Plain pinch pot, only 3.25 inches in diameter, marked with an "X" in the center of the bowl. Other cultural material included a broken metate, a biface, two tubular-shaped chert stones, one copper plate with a wire attached, one piece of bottle glass, two whole oyster shells, and lithic flakes (n = 22).

House 2 also contained a variety of ceramics, including Mier Plain (n = 50), Green and Brown Glazed Utility Ware (n = 4), Aranama Polychrome, San Elizario, and Plain majolica (n = 3), and Galera Polychrome (n = 2). Two unfamiliar types of ware were also found in the assemblage of House 2, and they are designated here as Burnished Ware (n = 2) and Green Slipped Ware (n = 14). Three pieces of bone, nine lithic flakes, and six complete or mostly complete oyster shells were also recovered.

House 3 was almost completely destroyed by erosion so very little of the interior was excavated and not much was recovered. No Mier Plain ceramic sherds were recovered, and only one piece of Brown Glazed Ware, two pieces of Green Glazed Utility Ware, and one Plain majolica sherd were found. Three bone fragments and three lithic flakes were also found. Interestingly, two clay marbles were included in the assemblage from House 3, measuring $9/16$ inch and $7/8$ inch in diameter, made apparently of the same clay as the Mier Plain ceramics.

Ceramic sherds found within House 4 include Mier Plain (n = 48), Green Glazed Utility Ware (n = 3), Mexican Red Painted (n = 10), and one Plain majolica sherd. Several Mier Plain sherds (n = 12) were unusually thin ($1/16$ inch) and dark pink in color, probably from a small bowl. The most bone inside a building was found in House 4 (n = 32), consisting of bird, horse, and cow remains, as well as one copper tack, one biface, and 48 lithic flakes.

Not surprisingly, the largest amount of cultural material was uncovered in the trash midden. About 2,815 ceramic sherds were located there, representing 23 different ceramic types. Bones of sheep, cow, and *tayassu* (a wild pig) were also recovered, totaling 167 bones or bone fragments. Five flat copper pieces, two metal buttons, a ½ *real* Spanish coin dated 1778 (Figure 2.5), and one decorative copper pull or *higo* ("jingler," a saddle trapping) were found, along with several oyster shells (29 whole, 19 partial), 1 gunflint, 4 bifaces, 36 lithic flakes, and 14 small rounded chert stones.

Unfortunately, there were about 1,501 artifacts that had no provenience. Included in this category were several unique ceramic sherds, a clay whistle, two manos, one metate fragment, several pieces of thin copper plate, a blue glass gem, bottle glass, and large wood chunks.

Fig. 2.5. Close-up of Spanish ½ *real*, dated 1778, recovered from Feature 6 at Site 41SR43.

ARCHITECTURE

Each of the buildings was a one-room structure made of sandstone blocks, stacked with little or no mortar and chinked with smaller stones for support. A lime-based slurry coated the interior and exterior walls like adobe. All of the walls were rubble piles by the 1950s, some discrete piles of debris (41SR39) and some scattered around the ground (41SR43). The roofing on the structures is unknown, but some large wood fragments suggest that at least some of the roofs may have had wooden rafters. Doorways were not obvious, and since several sections of many houses were washed away, it was assumed that the doorways may have been located there. Additionally, the investigators were not able to find floors in any of the buildings; artifacts were scattered throughout the top 6 inches, giving no clue to a level habitation surface, although there were some changing soil characteristics that may have indicated a dirt floor. The same characteristics were found at Area 1 at Cabaseño Ranch, just north of this rancho, indicating the use of similar building techniques all along the Rio Grande in the late eighteenth century (Perttula et al. 1999).

Eighteenth-Century Architecture along the Rio Grande

In 1962, Eugene George conducted an architectural survey of the Falcon Reservoir area, concentrating on the part just north of the dam site. He used archival descriptions of buildings, especially Joe Carson's field notebooks of work conducted in 1952 (George 1975:5), historical photographs, and modern ruins to describe the architectural style of Spanish ranches in South Texas. Many of his observations coincide with elements at the ruins of this rancho. Later investigations helped to refine rancho architecture further (Fleming 1998; Fleming and Perttula 1999).

Two general types of building styles were prevalent in the area, the *jacal* and the stone house. The jacal was an easily assembled wooden structure that was made by placing posts (palisades) upright in a ditch, supporting them with horizontal sticks and lashing, and plastering them with adobe. A thatched roof supported on a network of tree limbs topped the structure, and the floors were made of compact dirt that was swept daily. At times, the adobe plaster covered both sides of the walls, but most often the outside was left unfinished, showing the wood "frame" (George 1975:28–30). In the construction of jacals, whatever material was available was used, and in the Falcon Reservoir area, mesquite and cypress were the only available woods.

Stone houses were built in several forms, and their characteristics can be divided into three general time periods (Fleming and Perttula 1999). From 1750 to 1848, the basic stone house consisted of worked sandstone blocks, chinked with lime concrete and smaller stones. All decisions concerning style were based on defense issues. Both inside and outside walls were plastered with lime-tempered concrete to make them flame-resistant. The buildings were usually one room, with no openings at all except the door or a series of *troneras,* small holes in the outside of the building just large enough to stick a musket muzzle through (Fleming and Perttula 1999; George 1975). Stone houses had, at first, thatched roofs, much like jacals, but because of the threat of burning caused by Native American attacks, roofs were quickly adapted to thatch covered with a concrete made of lime mortar and small stones, or the building's roof was flattened, covered with lime concrete, and the walls extended up to give cover under fire. Floors were usually covered with clay, limestone, or flagstone and were set below grade, so a person would have to step down to enter the house. After the native attacks, the War for Mexican Independence, and the battles between Texas and Mexico from 1836 to 1848, houses were not styled for defense. Fortified houses were still built, but additions of decorative elements to the homes marked a change in style. At the end of the nineteenth century, the area had enough political and social stability for the inhabitants to feel safer, and windows appeared in new constructions. Two-room structures appeared by this time, either by new construction or by additions to single-room buildings.

Both jacales and stone houses had a patio, or covered outside space, where fresh water was located, items were placed for temporary storage, plants were arranged, and general household activities were conducted (Tijerina 1998:28–31). This space was the most frequented living area of the rancho.

In his study of architecture at Falcon Reservoir, George (1975) found three basic types of cooking facilities. There were massive fireplaces attached to the outer wall of a house and covered with lime plaster. He also noticed fireplaces freestanding in the center of the structure but adjacent to an inner wall or corner of a structure of two or more rooms. In addition, he found large cooking areas located outside of the structure under a freestanding awning; these were called a *ramada* or a *gallería,* and dining was outside when this type of fireplace was used. Another outside cooking feature was the *horno,* an outdoor cooking oven with a square base and dome-shaped top. It could be separated into sections and used by several different people at once.

Rancho Architecture at 41SR39 and 41SR43

A comparison between the buildings found at sites 41SR39 and 41SR43 and those researched by George (1975) and Fleming and Pertulla (1999) leads to interesting parallels and differences. All of the buildings were similar in size and shape to other one-room houses in the area, and the amount of rubble indicated a one-story building. Because the sites discussed here were occupied from the late 1760s to the early nineteenth century, they likely followed the common practices of defense-minded architecture: a flat or reinforced thatch roof, a single entry, and no windows.

No courtyards, patios, irrigation systems, gardens, outside cooking features, fences, or jacals were observed by the survey or excavation team at either site. However, there was evidence for a firepit in the center of House 1 at site 41SR39, as well as a posthole off to the side. No other structure had these features, and this one might have a more specialized purpose. It was on the portion of the site that contained artifacts that were reconstructed into several semi-restored vessels, so it could have been the primary kitchen or a smokehouse, perhaps with an opening in the roof to allow smoke to escape and a post for extra support. No such situation appeared at site 41SR43, and it is possible that the kitchen served all those who lived in the immediate area or that the kitchen facilities for the four remaining buildings were destroyed by earth-moving activities. It is also possible that an outdoor cooking facility, an open-air fire pit, was used to feed the inhabitants of the rancho.

HISTORY AND LAND USE

Based on the architecture of the one-room buildings and recovered Spanish artifacts, the inhabitants were probably members of a colonizing effort in 1753. José de Escandón led a Spanish expedition to settle the Province of Nuevo Santander in the north, a portion of land uninhabited by the Spanish located north of Nuevo Leon and incorporating the Rio Grande as its southernmost river (see Galindo, this volume). The expedition was to be the first civilian-only settlement in Texas. Escandón handpicked the locations for the new colonies, which consisted of civilian cattle-ranching *haciendas* (headquarters), *villas* (towns), and *lugars* (settlements). One of the lugars established was Mier, located at the confluence of the Rio Grande and the Rio Alamo (Alonzo 1998; Galindo 1999:4; Graham 1994:19; Jones 1996).

Mier was founded to be the central settlement for a series of ranchos that occupied the land surrounding the town. Thirty-eight families were brought up from Cerralvo, Nuevo Leon, to join 19 families already in the area (Alonzo 1998:30; Galindo 1999). Each settling family was awarded a porcion, or land grant, that consisted of a thin strip of land containing 0.5 to 1 mile of riverfront property and extending about 14 to 15 miles away from the Rio Grande. Each landowner was also given property in town to build a residence (Alonzo 1998; Galindo 1999). Many of the buildings on each porcion were placed near the Rio Grande, just far enough away to avoid flooding, and the rest of the land was used to herd sheep, goats, and cattle. No fences were used, and cattle (whose brands designated ownership) could roam as they pleased across porciones. In 1757, Tienda de Cuervo described Mier as having 39 families living in mud huts, totaling 274 people, and 44,015 head of livestock (Jones 1996:67–69).

The rancho containing archaeological sites 41SR39 and 41SR43 was located on Porcion 55, the westernmost porcion on the northern side of the Rio Grande. Its western boundary marks the line between Starr and Zapata Counties. Juan Antonio Leal was awarded this porcion of 5,783.6 acres, about average size, in 1767. The porciones were reassessed and incorporated into the Texas land-grant system once the area became part of the United States.

HOUSEHOLDS AND CATTLE CULTURE

Little direct historical evidence remains, other than censuses and the chronicles of Escandón's mission, to profile the lives of that expedition and subsequent settlements. Very little information is available about the social structure, ethnic backgrounds, gender roles, economic prosperity, and general lifeways of communities like Mier or of the ranchos themselves. Therefore, evidence concerning ranchos in Northern Mexico can be tapped to find out more about these settlers, since they emigrated from that region and would likely try to set up their social and economic systems similarly.

Cattle-raising operations in Northern Mexico fell into two general categories. The hacienda was a large, rural, self-sufficient estate that was involved in cattle raising, sheep and goat herding, agriculture, or mining, anything that could be produced and sold for a profit. The hacienda could sit on hundreds of thousands of acres and contain tens of thousands of cattle. The rancho, on the other hand, was a small rural estate that was worked by the owner and his family and was usually associated with an urban center (Jones 1996:3; Monday and Colley

1997:xvi; Myres 1969:22; Williams 1982:2–4). The majority of the livestock was cattle, but sheep, goats, and horses were also raised. The general social hierarchy of a Spanish hacienda in central and northern Mexico consisted of a landowning class (*patrón*) and a laborer class (*peón*). Even though these colonies operated under the Spanish crown, that level of government had little influence on the edges of New Spain; the estates were run by the powerful landowning class much like a feudal state (Dary 1981:29–30; Graham 1994:25; Robinson 1979:126). This system was most often found at the hacienda, where the peón class, including *vaqueros* (cowboys), was bound by debt to the landowner.

Homes were also a visible sign of class division. The peón class typically lived in jacales, but the patrón class usually lived in two-room stone structures (or larger) that offered more protection (Graham 1994; Williams 1982:31). This same visual sign of class division could be seen at the King and Kenedy Ranches in South Texas, which modeled their operations after the hacienda system (Monday and Colley 1997:xvi; Tijerina 1998:14). Most of the ranch workers lived in jacales until the early twentieth century, when wood-framed houses were provided for them (Monday and Colley 1997:126–128).

The small family-owned rancho and surrounding community provided a different scenario than the hacienda system. The classic peón/patrón system did not apply, and in fact the settlement was designed to be more "middle class." José de Escandón was intent on finding tough, hard-working colonists from the surrounding areas and "refused to include parasitic bureaucrats, aristocrats, and high-ranking military officials" (Cárdenas 1999:75). This would lead one to believe that members of the patrón class of the haciendas south of the Rio Grande, who were extremely wealthy and powerful, were not invited. Although there were class divisions among the settlers (servants were among those who traveled), it was not composed of the small upper class and the large lower class that was present at the hacienda. The inhabitants of the area did expand their holdings through marriage with their neighbors as an economic strategy (Galindo 1999, this volume), and families like the Guerras and Garzas became wealthy and powerful, but even their holdings did not come close to the self-sustaining haciendas to the south, nor did they have the nonfamilial labor pool necessary for the peón/patrón system.

DISCUSSION

The archaeological, architectural, and historic evidence points to several activities that were conducted at the rancho, but all were performed to reach one goal. The primary motivation for settlers to move to the banks of the Rio Grande, in "untamed" and hostile territory, was economic. They were there to produce a profitable commodity, cattle, which provided meat, hides, and tallow, as well as other domesticated animals, including sheep, goats, and horses. How successful the ranchers were at breeding, raising, and transporting to market determined how profitable their enterprises were.

Cattle ranching was labor intensive, especially during certain parts of the year, but after an initial investment the costs were minimal, as the cattle fed and reproduced themselves on the open range. Sheep and goats were probably less labor intensive overall but needed more consistent observation and care. Those who were not involved in the maintenance of the commodity supplied supporting roles: domestic duties (cooking, serving, washing, household maintenance, etc.); producing, raising, and educating children; trading and purchasing goods; keeping accounting records; maintaining defense; and building a connection with the community at large (through church services and special events).

Family dynamics were also influenced by life on the rancho, as strategies for the successful continuation of ranching activities affected marriage and residence practices among different families (Galindo 1999). Land acquisition and marriage-based alliances were methods used by the ranch holders to maintain and expand their profit base. If family members or extended family members, especially males, were not available to do the work, vaqueros were hired to supplement the labor pool. These were men who may have also brought their families to the ranch to live and work for the landowners. Wealthier families may not have worked the rancho at all but could have afforded two residences (one in town, as well). The women and children would stay in town where there were churches, schools, and more security, and landowning men would go to the ranch only during certain times of the year (Galindo 1999:9; Galindo, this volume; Graham 1994:22; Tijerina 1998:21).

Given all this information, the identity of the inhabitants of the rancho at Porcion 55 could be categorized in three general ways: they could be vaquero families (men, women, and children) who worked for the Leal family; they could be the entire Leal family (men, women, and children) with or without hired hands (no one living in town); or they could be the male members of the Leal family along with hired vaqueros (all men). It is unlikely that the inhabitants were all women, since they were probably discouraged from living alone and performing ranching activities.

It is clear from the quantity of artifacts recovered from both sites, as well as estimates for the quantity of artifacts that were present but not recovered, that either a large group of people lived there for a short time, or a small group of people lived there for a long time. It is also possible that the settlement grew and declined over time, beginning with a small group of people and expanding to a larger one through marriages, children, or acquisition of hired hands. The existence of six separate stone structures, all but one apparently lived in at one point, would indicate separate socially defined groups of people inhabiting each house. Several pieces of evidence support the possibility that these groups were kin-related nuclear families, including men, women, and children. Artifacts traditionally associated with women and children (manos, metates, cookware, and toys; see Deagan 1996:149; DiPaolo Loren 2000:91, fig. 2) were present at both sites. In addition, save for the unique green glazed chocolateria found in House 1 at site 41SR39, the other recovered chocolaterias from both sites were virtually identical, probably from the same source and possibly of the same "set," indicating sharing between the inhabitants of each site. Distribution of such hard-to-obtain items was more likely to happen if the members were closely tied than if they were members of two different social groups. Most significant, however, the census data of neighboring ranchos from 1817 grouped individual members of each rancho into nuclear families, who appeared to be related by blood (Galindo, this volume). The composition of this rancho was probably similar, if smaller.

Although separated by a short distance, the two sites were likely closely interdependent (Tijerina 1998:22). Since the Leal family did not appear on any surviving census of the area, how long the family stayed at the rancho could not be determined historically, but artifactual evidence suggests a terminating date of about 1800 (Perttula et al. 1999), making a total habitation period of around 33 years. Whether the Leal family had a house in Mier, where some members of the family resided all or part of the year, remains unclear.

CONCLUSION

Several books have been written that trace the Spanish influence on cattle ranching in Texas (e.g., Alonzo 1998; Dary 1981; Graham 1994; Monday and Colley 1997; Myres 1969; Poyo 1996), but while much has been written about political battles with the Spanish government, cattle drives, cowboy gear and techniques, and various wars, not much has been written about daily activities and general lifestyle. It is unclear in several of these texts whether cowboys even had wives or children (see Monday and Colley [1997] for the exception). An archaeological analysis of Spanish colonial household sites based on daily activities would lead to a more comprehensive understanding than we now have of ranching operations and their role in the wider Spanish colonial enterprise on the northern frontier. In such an investigation, a separation of household and family would be helpful in this research. However, some of the more interesting questions, I think, cannot be answered by an investigation of household activities alone. Bringing in questions about gender, family, class, and ethnicity —in effect, other social relationships—adds to our understanding of the diversity of households, not just their role in the larger society.

ACKNOWLEDGMENTS

I would like to thank those who spent considerable time and effort conducting emergency excavations of the Falcon Dam impact area in 1950 and 1951. Their efforts only hint at the important cultural resources that have been lost because of federal projects conducted before the enactment of the National Historic Preservation Act (NHPA) of 1966. Without their contributions, we would have considerably less information concerning archaeological sites beneath Falcon Reservoir.

3
A Space of Our Own

Redefining the Enslaved Household at Andrew Jackson's Hermitage Plantation

Whitney Battle

INTRODUCTION

The expanding dialogue among African Diaspora archaeologists in the United States has moved well beyond the search for artifact patterns or African cultural continuities reflected in African-American material culture. More recent research has focused on the analysis of material culture and its relationship to social relations. I propose here that a study of the household as a social unit should be given more attention than has previously been the case. While research of domestic sites abounds in the study of plantation life, theorizing the household has not. Household-level analysis can allow archaeologists to develop a better sense of the everyday actions of a slave quarter community.

The developments of meaningful extended kin networks and collective labor and knowledge were integral parts of the enslaved experience. I will demonstrate how household theory can help to define not only the composition of the enslaved household but the function and meaning of family, household, and quarter as well.

The Project

In recent years, Andrew Jackson's Hermitage museum in Tennessee has employed a variety of methods to enhance the representation of slavery. Among these strategies are the inclusion of enslaved Africans in the central narrative of the museum, the use of visual symbols of the enslaved African population throughout the property, and increasing the number of exhibits apart from Jackson's mansion. A Hermitage brochure states that "through archaeological exploration, we continue to uncover details that change our perspective of slavery and plantation life" (The Hermitage 1999). The research presented here will demonstrate the potential of the archaeological record for interpreting the enslaved household as a microcosm of the larger enslaved community. The evidence includes archaeological data, African-American women's literature, archival sources, and oral histories from the local community of African-American descendants.

HISTORICAL BACKGROUND OF ANDREW JACKSON'S HERMITAGE

The Hermitage Plantation

The Hermitage, located 20 miles east of Nashville, Tennessee, was a nineteenth-century cotton plantation and home of President Andrew Jackson. Beginning in 1889, the Ladies' Hermitage Association (LHA) assumed responsibility for the upkeep of the mansion and immediate surrounding area. The Hermitage today is a parklike setting dedicated to telling the story of Andrew Jackson and the many complexities of plantation life. Initially, the LHA focused on preserving the legacy of the Jackson family and their home, before the mansion and surrounding land went into complete decay as a result of years of neglect. Appealing to multiple publics is a serious challenge for a museum focused on a single individual, but the Hermitage wanted a way to broaden its appeal and distinguish itself from other historical sites in the region.

Today, the Hermitage Museum consists of the Andrew Jackson Center (which contains a museum, a gift shop, and an auditorium), Jackson's Greek Revival mansion, and the original 1,000 acres (this property is shared between the State of Tennessee and the LHA), including several outbuildings and farmland. The public interpretation of the Hermitage mansion is set at 1837, the year Jackson retired from the White House and returned to his Tennessee plantation (Figure 3.1).

When Jackson initially moved to the tract of land called "Hermitage" in 1804, he settled on the highest point of the property. The "First" Hermitage is located approximately 250 yards from the brick mansion (completed in 1821); it is called the First Hermitage because it was the original center of the Jackson property, until the brick mansion was completed. The site was impacted by a variety of postbellum activities, including the use of the site by African-American sharecroppers, the slow deterioration of outbuildings from neglect, and the transition from farmland to a public museum. The LHA employed a range of methods to maintain the First Hermitage cabins, but making the site attractive to visitors and continually using the buildings for numerous events added to the deterioration of the log structures.

There are varying accounts of the property's appearance during the early stages of Jackson's occupation (for one example, see Parton 1850). According to recent historical and architectural research, there were probably six structures standing when Jackson lived at the site from 1804 to 1821 (Jones 2002). During excavation of the site there were only two log structures from this period remaining. The West Cabin (also referred to as the Farm House) was a two-story log structure that served as the main house for the Jackson family from 1804 to

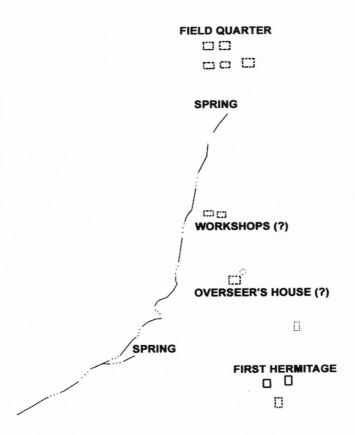

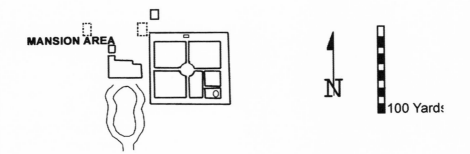

Fig. 3.1. Hermitage Plantation, general map.

Fig. 3.2. Image of First Hermitage site.

1821 (Jones 2002; McKee and Galle 2000; Remini 1977). The East Cabin was a log duplex with two end chimneys measuring roughly 20 × 40 feet (McKee and Galle 2000). This structure has also been described in written accounts, documents, and oral accounts as Jackson's kitchen quarter (Figure 3.2).

Referring to household archaeology, Mary Beaudry (1989a:85) stressed not only the significance of site structure and spatial analysis but also the need to "consider site formation as a reflection of diachronic process that can be linked to the household." The importance of these formation processes are what Michael Schiffer (1987:7) refers to as "the process of human behavior that affect or transform artifacts after the initial period of use." It is for these reasons that I considered four general time periods for interpreting the First Hermitage site. In the first, the Jackson period, the Jackson family and 10–12 enslaved Africans lived on the property. At this stage the First Hermitage resembled a large farm rather than a working plantation. The family and the enslaved workers lived less than 40 feet from each other, and the primary goal was to clear land and begin planting crops (Jones 2002; Remini 1977). The next stage of occupation is the Middle Quarter period, approximately 1821 to 1850, a time when the plantation underwent major changes. Jackson began to expand his landholdings, slaveholdings, and financial capabilities. These factors were directly reflected in how he reshaped the plantation's landscape. The First Hermitage was transformed from the center of the property and Jackson's home to a quarter occupied exclusively by enslaved families. With Jackson's removal to the Mansion, there was an increase in distance between master and enslaved. I refer to the

First Hermitage at this time as the Middle Quarters because of its location. It is midway between the mansion backyard quarters (directly behind the mansion) and the field quarters (located approximately 250 yards north of the First Hermitage site).

The post-Jackson period of 1850–1880 occurred shortly after Jackson's death in 1845. It marked the end of financial success and growth at the Hermitage plantation. Andrew Jackson, Jr., had neither the good fortune nor the business sense to maintain the plantation through lean times. After 1855 he began to break up the property by selling 50-acre plots to pay off pending debts (Jones 2002). The impact of this change on the enslaved community is still unclear, and this period has been neglected by archaeological and historical research at the museum. By combining oral history and written sources, I have been able to gather some general ideas about what was occurring at the plantation during the post-Jackson period. The fourth and final period spans from 1889 to the present. The Museum period marks the beginning of the LHA's role as caretakers of the mansion and surrounding areas. This period had the most visible impact on the First Hermitage landscape. In order to tell the full story of Andrew and Rachel Jackson, the First Hermitage site was used to show his humble beginnings before the War of 1812 and his presidency. It is in public interpretation of this site that much of the legend of Jackson as a "man of the people" began.

In order to investigate how enslaved Africans shaped and transformed the physical landscape to reflect their cultural and community needs, I chose to focus on two of the four time periods: the Jackson (1804–1821) and the Middle Quarter (1821–1850) periods, clearly the most significant in terms of their relevance to the history of slavery at the site.

Historic Context

In 1803 Andrew Jackson purchased 425 acres of land from Nathaniel Hay. The Farm House, or West Cabin, was already standing when the Jacksons moved to the property. It was a large structure containing a main hall, a "boxed in" stairway, and several private rooms for the Jackson family and their guests (Jones 2002). This two-story structure has been referred to as "rustic elegance" (Robbie Jones, personal communication 2001). After extensive analysis of the interior of the dwelling, architectural historians discovered fragments of imported hand-painted wallpaper beneath the whitewashed walls and decorated ceiling joists used as floor joists in the standing cabin (Jones 2002). The East Cabin, located about 40 feet east of the West Cabin, was constructed in approximately 1805 and served as a kitchen/quarter dwelling during the Jackson period (Brigance 1975; Jones 2002; Smith 1976).

Testing and small-scale excavations in the past have produced little information about the outbuildings described in visitors' accounts and some historical records. In the late 1970s archaeologists Samuel Smith and Jane Hinshaw conducted excavations at the First Hermitage site. Although these projects were limited in scope and focused on areas surrounding the standing structures, they provided key questions that were used to guide excavations begun in 1996 (McKee and Galle 2000). In 1975 Samuel Smith directed excavations focused on the South Cabin with some minor testing around the East and West Cabins (McKee and Galle 2000; Smith 1976). He identified a large portion of the limestone foundation and brick chimney base of the South Cabin, which was identical in construction to the brick duplexes unearthed at the Field Quarter site in 1995 (McKee 1995; Smith 1976; Thomas et al. 1995). Smith was the first researcher to investigate the material aspects of slavery at the Hermitage. Later, Jane Hinshaw conducted excavations in preparation for structural repairs to the West Cabin by testing along the eastern side of the structure (Hinshaw 1979; McKee and Galle 2000). She also excavated around the East Cabin for additional structure repairs. She identified evidence of deep ash and charcoal deposits and a pit filled with limestone chippings, two significant findings relevant to later excavations.

As stated, the year 1821 marked a profound restructuring of the entire plantation (Jones 2002; McKee and Galle 2000). According to the 1820 census Jackson owned 44 enslaved workers. In 1822, he sold his cotton plantation near present-day Florence, Alabama, and moved the majority of his enslaved workers to the Hermitage (Jones 2002). By the time he was president (1829–1837), 95 enslaved women, men, and children labored at the Hermitage (Remini 1977). With more land and a larger enslaved labor force, Jackson also increased his cash crop of cotton at a rapid rate. In 1821 the large brick mansion was completed. This property was beginning to reflect the man that Jackson was becoming, both politically and financially. With the Jackson family's move to the mansion, the First Hermitage's population was directly affected. One particular historical source indicated that once the Jacksons moved to the mansion, the West Cabin, kitchen structure, South Cabin, and possibly the Southeast Cabin all became "Negro cabins" (Parton 1850).

Subsequent alterations to the West Cabin reveal Jackson's views on "appropriate" slave housing. The top story of the West Cabin was removed when enslaved families replaced the Jacksons as residents. Evidence for this change comes from the floor joists in the single-story structure that have beaded decorations, indicating that these beams at one time served as ceiling joists when the structure had two stories (Jones 2002; McKee and Galle 2000).

DEFINING THE ENSLAVED HOUSEHOLD

This study builds upon previous research on households from archaeology and history, and this research assists in the overall interpretation of the daily lives of the enslaved. Beaudry (1989a:84) sees the shift in focus calling for a "holistic, contextual approach to the archaeology of historical households" as not only in distinct contrast to studies in the past but as essential in the quest for understanding the life-cycle of a variety of household forms. Maria Franklin (1997:46), however, still cautions about searching for the "all-encompassing, cross-cultural definition of the household."

Although the subject of enslaved "communities" is often referred to in historical and archaeological studies (e.g., Blassingame 1972; Genovese 1974; Gutman 1976a; Joyner 1984), there remains a gap in our understanding of how enslaved women and men "organized into domestic units and how that organization developed or changed over time" (Malone 1992:4). The study of enslaved domestic organization, activity, and social relationships, as well as the spaces and landscapes associated with them, is clearly important if one is interested in the experiences that were most significant to enslaved groups. It is within the context of the plantation quarter that the enslaved created social and cultural practices, taking as much advantage as possible in the absence of the slaveowner's prying eyes. It is at this junction that my definition of the enslaved household is aided by household theory. Wendy Ashmore and Richard Wilk (1988:6) see a "household as a social unit, specifically the group of people that shares in a maximum of definable number of activities including one or more of the following: production, consumption, pooling of resources, reproduction, co-residence, and shared ownership." At the First Hermitage, production, reproduction (both social and biological), and the pooling of resources are the central activities used to identify the enslaved household.

Along with family units, households developed as a means to carry out domestic activities, and, like the family, the household was meaningful to the inhabitants. In fact, both the "family" and "household" relations operated simultaneously. As noted by Laurie Wilkie (2000a:119), it is important to explore how "[enslaved] families created and presented themselves in different household community contexts, [to] achieve a more balanced and humanized understanding of the African American experience." The fluidity of enslaved social organization is underscored by Ann Malone's observation (1992:4) that enslaved African communities "were organized into fundamental units of affection and support" that were "far more diverse and adaptable than previously believed."

This research is an attempt to use household theory to fine-tune methods that can be used to define how one specific enslaved community operated within the realm of the quarter. There were more than 160 enslaved women, men, and children living on the Jackson plantation, and the typical approach has been to define them according to their position in the slaveowner's labor regimen as "house," "field" or "skilled." In using these categories, or that of "community," to discuss the details of daily life, one masks the varying forms of social structure such as family and household that existed on plantations like the Hermitage and runs the risk of creating false dichotomies between individuals working in the "field" and in the "house." One advantage of using household theory is that it allows the researcher to redefine the enslaved community, regardless of their occupations, using social units that were more meaningful to them.

Hermitage Plantation Family Structure

Family structure differed from plantation to plantation, and in the case of the Hermitage, oral history and written documents indicate that the "simple" nuclear family made up of a mother, a father, and their children was typical. Jackson's 1829 inventory alludes to his preference of an enslaved nuclear family model by listing men, women, and children by single family units (Table 3.1).

Jackson, like many other nineteenth-century planters, likely followed the advice given in southern farm journals by advocating his role in the social engineering and community planning of his enslaved workers (Breeden 1980; Faust 1982; McKee 1995). In his constant absence, Jackson often referred to his enslaved workers as "my Negroes," reflecting his concern for their safety, family life, and treatment by overseers (Remini 1977:133). However, within the sphere of the quarter, social organization likely extended beyond the single family unit to incorporate various members of families into households at different times in order to perform household-related activities (Fox-Genovese 1988; Franklin 1997; Malone 1992; Wilkie 2000a). Given the burden of enslavement on their energy and time, enslaved households formed as a strategy to complete much-needed domestic tasks (see Anderson, this volume). Household organization, therefore, relied on the cooperation of community members, both kin-related and nonfamilial.

My interpretation of the enslaved household adds a new dimension to how daily life differed from Jackson's emphasis on "simple" family units. As men and women performed household-related tasks throughout the plantation, individual families constantly shifted social divisions to meet their various needs. In doing so, the typical divisions of field, skilled, and house were not meaningful to the enslaved when it came to household performance. For example, Julia Hendon (1996:53) argued for the existence of "hidden laborers" within many forms of household activity. Hidden laborers may have been involved in Middle Quarter domestic-related activities such as gathering wood, maintaining and cultivating herbs and vegetables, sweeping yards, or keeping watch over small children and the sick. These individuals were not listed on inventories according to the occupations but were central to the well-being of their quarter sub-community. Thus, the slaveowner's records do not take into account the layers of domestic responsibilities performed by household members.

Table 3.1 Slave inventory from the Hermitage, 1846–1849.

Old Hannah (76)

  Betty (53) & Ned (53)

    Alfred (28) & Gracy (30)

      Augustus

      Sarah

  Squire (47) & Gincy (35)

      Amathus (17)

      Cancer (16)

      George (14)

      Smith

      Jim

      Hannah

      Matilda

      Molly

      Squire (born 1846)

      Tom (born 10/49)

  George (39)

Charles (52) & Charlotte (47)

  Jane (20) (no husband listed)

    Aggy

    Beatrice

    Jessy

  Maria (18) & Moses (19)

    John

    Albert Alsbury (born 12/46)

    Maria Indiana (born 3/49)

Aaron (57) & Hannah (40)

  Byron (26) & Nancy (26)

    Nancy

    William (7)

    Nelly (4)

    John (under 1)

  Charlotte (20) (no husband listed)

    Matilda (1)

  *Moses (19) & Maria (18)

    Mary & Daniel (23)

    (married in 1849)

Continued on the next page

Little Sally (32) & Ben (not listed)

Sincy (15) & Phil (19) (in Miss)

  Jenny

  Milley

  Leander

    Shadrack

  Simmon

  Kutchina

  Julius

Eady (25) (no husband listed)

  Kitty

  Anaca

  Jack (born 2/47)

Matilda

Washington

John (32) & Anny (30)

  Mary (23)

Henry (20) & Adaline (23) (in Miss)

  (Henry sold in Miss)

Polladore (57) & Sally (42) (in Miss)

  Margaret

    Marion

  Polidore

*Phil (57) & Sincey (15) (in Miss)

  Prissy (sold to Miss after inventory)

    Joannah (born 2/46)

  Smith (29) & Louisa

  Joseph

  Rubin

  Harriet

Pleasant (67) (died in 1847)

George (33)

Eliza (30) (no husband listed)

Table 3.1 *Continued.*

Ned	George
Abraham	Stephen
Martha	Daniel
Margaret Ellen	Creasey
George (1)	James

Tom (57) & Molly (47)   Nancy (26) & Byron (26)

    Campbell (39)   Jim (23)
    Malinda (31) (died in 1849)
    William (26)   Peter (67)

Grace (37) & Donelson slave   Penny (67)
(not living at Hermitage)
    Dick (19) (sent to Miss 1846) & Sally
        Florida (no husband listed)   Rachel & John Fulton (lives off
           Rinda   Hermitage)
           Larry (born 1849)   Harry
        Nan & Peter
        Jim   John 2 (sent to Miss 12/46)
        Kitty
        Letty   Washington
    Harry
    Orange
    Cornelia
    Julia
    William
    Andrew
Anny (30) & John (32)
    Randal
    *Peter & Nan
    Easco
    Philly
    Phil
Sarah (25) & Sampson (not listed in 1846)
    Sampson
    Coeff

Continued on the next page

Table 3.1 *Continued.*

1846–1849 Inventory Totals.

Category	Enumerated	Number who left the Hermitage 1846–1849
Adults (13 & older)	61	9
Children (12 & under)	11	0
Under 17 (specific age unknown)	58	3
Total	**130**	**12**

Note: Family structure taken from an 1846 inventory of slaves at the Hermitage, with additional notes added over the next several years. Inventory appears in a Hermitage memorandum book. The original document is owned by Western Reserve Historical Society (1845–1877); a copy is on file at the Hermitage.

*appear more than once on inventory.

Household Space and Meaning

Barbara Heath and Amber Bennett (2000:53) have noted that "together, house and yard form a nucleus within which the culture expresses itself, is perpetuated, changed, and reintegrated." Similarly, I argue here that the yard served as an extension of the house at the Hermitage (e.g., Edwards 1998; Gundaker 1998) and that household activities were carried out in these yard areas. This research, therefore, focused on areas exterior to houses at the First Hermitage site. I attempted not only to pinpoint various outdoor activities but to address how these activities may have been associated with a multifaceted household like that of the Middle Quarters.

The research of household activities can also lead to the interpretation of symbolic dimensions of the landscape as it is defined by those who occupy it (Bourdieu 1973). Massey (1994:154) observed, "Instead of thinking of places as areas with boundaries around, they can be imagined as articulated moments in networks of social relations and understandings. . . . Places do not have to have boundaries in the sense of divisions which frame simple enclosure . . . they are not necessarily for the conceptualization of a place itself." This view is particularly insightful when considering enslaved people's relationship to landscapes. It is easy to assume that the enslaved were simply confined to the quarter and considered their immediate environment only as a part of their world. However, it would be a mistake to give too much weight to plantation boundaries defined by structures, fences, and roads. For the enslaved, the plantation landscape was contested ground where they asserted themselves by using and defining space to suit their needs, regardless of the slaveowner's intentions.

Landscapes are loaded with symbolism and cultural value, and this fact would have been true for the enslaved. Rebecca Yamin and Katherine Methany (1996:xv) described the relationship between culture and landscapes: "landscapes are created in terms of human use through action and perception and are loaded with cultural meaning in specific historical contexts." They further argued that because the landscape embodies culture, its symbolism would vary between diverse groups. Within the plantation context, enslaved Africans would likely conceptualize the plantation landscape in ways that differed from elite slaveowning whites.

The following material is a discussion of the archaeological research of household-related activities and the landscape and spaces associated with them. Because of the location of datable deposits, it was possible to identify and distinguish Jackson's yard and house activities from those of his slaves during the Middle Quarter period. This distinction helped in comparing the transformation of household spatial use and activities over time from the Jackson period to the Middle Quarter period.

ARCHAEOLOGICAL ANALYSIS OF THE EAST CABIN AREA

As discussed, there are varying forms of social organization that were practiced by enslaved women, men, and children. Households performed distinct activities, as did families, and both often contributed to the greater good of the enslaved community. The following is an attempt to use archaeological evidence to identify and interpret these various forms of collective labor. In doing so, I hope to demonstrate that it is possible to distinguish, through the archaeological record, those social units that were integral to the enslaved community. In particular, three related archaeological features demonstrate that the social organization of a household extended beyond the bounds of a dwelling and the notion of a family unit. These features helped to address specifics about collective household labor, gender roles, and how the enslaved community restructured the built landscape to reflect and meet their needs.

During the 1997 season, excavations focused on areas between the East and West Cabins. Nonarbitrary levels were used to define the strata, which can be tied to the four major periods listed. Starting from the most recent strata, Level 1, dating to the Museum period, consisted of a dark, rich soil heavily mixed with gravel that once made up a gravel pathway for tourists. The central portion of the area was strikingly shallower than the northern and southern extremities. There was a considerable amount of mostly twentieth-century artifacts close to the surface.

Level 2A consisted of a dark, rich brown loam, with a combination of tourist and post-Jackson related material, showing that it straddled the Post-Jackson and Museum periods. Level 2B was a light sandy loam combined with a dense concentration of limestone rubble scatter. Throughout this rubble layer almost no bricks or brick fragments were recovered; this might be evidence that it dates to the end of the Middle Quarter period because there was no brick manufacturing on the plantation prior to 1818 (Jones 2002; McKee 1995). Within this level several distinct features appeared, which are discussed below. Level 2C, the fourth and final level, was a cultural layer associated with the Jackson period.

Just Outside the Cabin Door: Features 668, 688, and 705

Efforts initially concentrated on a 10-×-30-foot strip directly outside the western edge of the East Cabin (Figure 3.3). Varying frequencies of artifacts were found within each one of these features, but how they were related is the most important aspect of analysis. While excavating the third layer (level 2B) of the strip, large amounts of nineteenth-century artifacts were recovered, and four bricks in course were revealed. Following the direction of the brick formation, the remainder of level 2B was removed across five separate quadrants. The soil between the brick feature and the East Cabin was very different from the soil in other surrounding areas in that there was a considerable concentration of small animal bones, charcoal, ash, and nails. The soil on all other sides of the bricks was a smooth dark brown loam containing architectural debris and an array of artifacts commonly found in other areas along the East Cabin quadrants.

The bricks continued in course for approximately 15 feet. We began to refer to this grouping of bricks as a "patio" and designated it Feature 668. The brick patio was dry-laid and consisted of whole bricks, which was a contrast to the typical availability of building material for enslaved houses at the First Hermitage. Feature 668 was capped by level 2A, which in this case consisted of Museum period artifacts. This suggested that this brick patio was likely exposed during the Middle Quarter period and covered after approximately 1850. Feature 668 ended abruptly because of a modern pipe installed underground in the early 1990s. There appeared to be no additional bricks to the north of the feature or the modern disturbance.

Feature 705 was located just east of Feature 668. It was initially described as an ash and charcoal deposit, and I later interpreted it as a possible food preparation area bounded by Feature 668 (the brick patio). A 10-liter soil sample from Feature 705 was water-screened, and we recovered a high frequency of small animal bones, straight pins, buttons, fish scales, a bead, and various other small items.

During removal of Feature 705 a second series of bricks was discovered in a diagonal orientation that went directly up to the East Cabin's northern door. This small brick pad, Feature 688, was not connected to the bricks of Feature

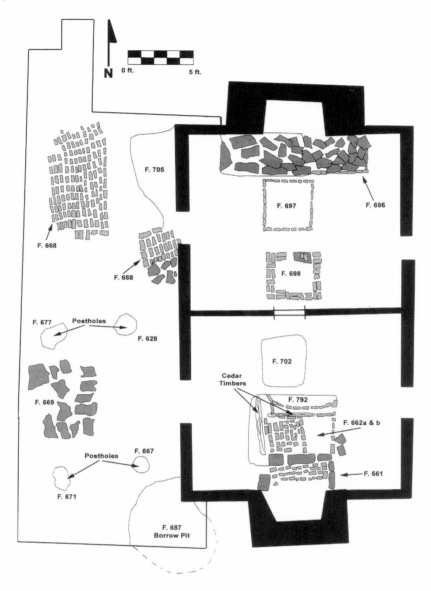

Fig. 3.3. East Cabin, feature map.

668 but seemed instead to border Feature 705. Feature 688 also stood out because two large fragments of an iron kettle or Dutch oven were found resting
on top of the bricks. This find along with the close proximity of features 705
and 688 suggested that this area was used for cooking or food preparation.

Feature 705 was likely related to food preparation or cooking activities that took place just north of the East Cabin. The East Cabin was located directly behind the West Cabin and may have served as a central meeting point in the early years of the Hermitage farm. These spaces were negotiated during the Jackson period, and enslaved women and men found ways to create social boundaries between their work life and their private lives. Women, however, would have been central to this area, often performing what Deborah Gray-White (1999) refers to as "double duty," including food preparation, laundry, sewing and repairing clothes, cleaning house, or tending to small gardens. In most of my oral interviews and discussions about yards and gardens, I learned that yards were often spaces dominated by women and children among the black community living in the area surrounding the Hermitage (Minerva Washington, personal communication 1998).

The use of outdoor spaces as an extension of the house was a practice that is visible at the First Hermitage site. Level 2C revealed a hard-packed orange clay that looked similar to soil found by Larry McKee just outside of several structures at the Field Quarters site in 1991 and 1995. He described the surface (McKee 1992a:6) as "almost certainly a cultural, rather than a geological feature . . . the compacted layer may be the result of a combination of sweeping, cleanup, and trampling across the zone of greatest activity around the dwelling." The absence of artifacts in the area between the East and West Cabins during the Jackson period points to the possibility of sweeping to keep debris away from the main house or the presence of an L-shaped extension. This changed drastically, however, once the site became a quarter. Comparing the archaeological evidence from the Jackson and Middle Quarter periods supports the idea of a gradual transformation of the physical landscape.

The enslaved community displayed very different ideas about space than Jackson may have intended. For example, the location of the First Hermitage site is significant; its siting more than 250 yards from the main house enabled the enslaved community to alter the use of exterior space. With the restructuring of the West Cabin, the First Hermitage site took on a different appearance. The cabins formed an enclosed space, visually inaccessible to the Jacksons from the main house. Here again is the example of how the sweeping of a yard and the clearing of space between the various structures were important. The central courtyard area defines how the organization of place and the symbolic parameters of the area resembled more of a house lot rather than a "standard" quartering area, with houses placed neatly in rows. Individuals participated in a number of activities that helped each member of the First Hermitage community, creating a different configuration than the Mansion Backyard Quarters.

Archaeologically, the courtyard area indicates that it served different purposes during different periods. Based on the type of hard-packed clay uncovered at the base of level 2C, it appears that the central courtyard area was kept clean at all times. The area was an active and busy part of the 425-acre farm but was still used as a reflection of Jackson's social and political role between 1804 and 1820. The idea of an L-shaped addition to the West Cabin is supported by the lack of artifacts or man-made features between the cabins at this level.

Not until the Middle Quarter period do we see examples of small-scale trash and ash deposits and indications of large-scale outdoor activities taking place throughout the First Hermitage area. Although the courtyard area was still kept clear, the presence of trash deposits and possible cooking areas indicates the change in how the central area was used. Feature 668 was constructed during the Jackson period, but its use changed when the East Cabin shifted from the main kitchen to a living space. Daily survival and an increase in privacy translated to members of the First Hermitage quarter as a space of their own.

Interpretation

Several circumstances led me to concentrate on the exterior spaces at the First Hermitage site. As the confining dimensions of each cabin forced a great deal of activity to shift to exterior areas of the quarters, I believed that the yard was more than empty space between the two structures: it was a bridge connecting several individual families. The yard was the extension of the house, a "living room," so to speak (H. Lawrencie Jones, personal communication 1997). Ywone Edwards (1998:249) further explains how "African American houses and yards also embodied complex and simple rhythms of time, space, energy, and change during slavery, as they do today." The courtyard was not only socially significant and meaningful to inhabitants of the Middle Quarters; it also served as a connection across a culturally defined landscape.

In the sense that landscape was a functional and integral component of the enslaved community, like the families of the Middle Quarters, landscape can be seen as a form of material culture and thus a part of the archaeological record. Ideologies are actively expressed in landscapes as visual symbols that archaeologists have to interpret (Massey 1994). The concepts of landscape, space, and place in relation to archaeological inquiries are complex notions. If "landscape is the stage for human action, it both reflects past activities and encodes the cultural landscape in which people's views of the world are formed. The trick is to disentangle the various strata that represent physical changes to the land or changing land-use practices in order to analyze the changing symbolic meanings of the landscape over time" (Yamin and Methany 1996:xv). It is difficult to identify individual families when the dwelling space is limited and there are many "domestic" activities that are conducted communally (Wilk and Netting 1984). In a house lot context, there are activities carried out collectively, such as outdoor cooking, food preparation, soap making, laundry, repairs to structures, gardening, or tending to chickens.

By the nineteenth century, southern agricultural journals suggested various reforms to maintaining quarters, and there was a call to promote orderly family life among the slave community (McKee 1992a). Health and housing were among the top priorities of a slaveowner, yet overcrowding was mentioned often as a main concern in several planter documents and letters (Breeden 1980). For reasons of health and happiness, masters believed that only one "family" per structure was the proper formula for success (Breeden 1980). Different people define landscapes differently. John Vlach (1993) sees them as not only visual scenes or environmental settings but also as cultural constructions. The enslaved inhabitants of these areas may not have created the way structures looked or where they were located, but they did shape the way landscape functioned.

CONCLUSION

The Enslaved Household Revisited

Occupation at the First Hermitage site spanned more than 100 years. Through those years there were several communities that influenced the landscape. During the Jackson and Middle Quarter periods there was a transformation of physical and social space that is directly linked to how household and family structures were dictated by the cultural and social needs of different groups of people.

The Jackson model of family relied on the enslaved population being grouped into small, "simple" units, yet archaeological evidence at the First Hermitage during the Middle Quarter period indicates a large amount of communal exchanges between individual families. The codependent relationship between labor and slavery meant that members of the enslaved household had to find alternative ways to complete household chores. Extended family, fictive kin, and nonfamilial relations would have most likely shared in production, reproduction, and other power relationships at the First Hermitage as well as the larger plantation community. By concentrating on three features, I was able to test how my use of household theory aids in a developmental model of the complexity of an enslaved household at one site.

The Historical Memory of Home

In *Incidents in the Life of a Slave Girl*, Linda Brent (1987) described the home of her grandmother with feelings of love, comfort, and nurturing, a place somewhat removed from the reality of slavery and domination. When I began the archaeological project at the First Hermitage, I was obsessed with learning about yards and how enslaved women and men used these spaces to reflect their own social and cultural needs. During a casual conversation with my grandmother, I learned how the yard she knew as a child was an extension of the living room, and a part of Saturday chores was to keep it clean of grass and debris. It was the center of the farm, where food was prepared, herbs were grown, games played, and people came to visit. These activities amazed me but forced me to realize that the enslaved household could not be confined to the four walls of a 20-X-20-foot dwelling.

The wealth of information provided by household theory has added a more complex level of analysis to interpreting the daily lives of enslaved populations. I realized early that I needed to dig deeper, to look beyond Jackson's prescription for a family and general categories of the enslaved community for the unspoken. The enslaved household takes on many forms at different times; it can be on the landscape, in the fields, around the main house, and, more important, within the yard outside of a structure.

The enslaved household has been marginal in the narrative of slavery. Scholars have discussed various aspects of the enslaved family, yet I would argue that our historical memories should begin to include how the emotional, spiritual, and gendered aspects of the enslaved household are connected to the complexity and fluidity of the enslaved family. The practice of social norms, passed down from generation to generation, created an alternative reading of how a household or family "functioned." As researchers of slavery, we can find new methods of examining documents, archaeological research, and oral histories by combining them with tools provided by household theory.

The First Hermitage site has provided a wealth of information about nineteenth-century plantation life. Although excavations have ended and the site has been filled in, the interpretive process is just beginning. This study was a way to participate and share in the exchange of ideas with colleagues who may have encountered similar questions and ideas about the enslaved community. A great deal of work lies ahead, yet with the use of household theory, the investigation of enslaved households at the First Hermitage site can take on new directions and be pushed to the forefront of the study of plantation landscapes.

ACKNOWLEDGMENTS

I would like to thank Maria Franklin for creating the household seminar at the University of Texas and being incredibly supportive through the different stages of writing. I would also like to thank Kerri Barile and Jamie Brandon for their diligence and patience in getting these articles together. I have to mention Larry McKee, Elizabeth Kellar, Sam Wilson, Suzanne Spencer-Wood, James Denbow, Ted Gordon, R. Steven Kidd, Peggy Brunache, and Andrea Battle-Brown for their comments and suggestions. My thanks to the Hermitage Museum staff, especially Robbie Jones, Marsha Mullin, and Carolyn Brackett, for all of their support and research help. Also, I would have never been able to work through some of my ideas without my countless conversations with community members and elders such as Mrs. Washington, Mr. and Mrs. Adams, and my late grandmother H. Lawrencie Jones.

4
Separate Kitchens and Intimate Archaeology
Constructing Urban Slavery on the Antebellum Cotton Frontier in Washington, Arkansas

Leslie C. Stewart-Abernathy

KITCHENS AND SLAVERY

Since 1981 the Arkansas Archeological Survey has conducted fieldwork at the site of several kitchen buildings in Washington, Arkansas, an antebellum county seat prominent on the Cotton Frontier from the 1820s to the 1860s. These kitchen buildings were considered to be separate structures, detached from the house and informally referred to as "out in the back yard." No such kitchens survive in Washington today.

Since 1973, much of the town has been incorporated into Old Washington Historic State Park, with a focus on the exhibition of restored houses. In other such settings, interpretive staff members have discovered that the aromas of cooking food and the various practices associated with cooking, such as gardens and wood fires, provide powerful tools for transforming static displays of furniture and bric-a-brac into a semblance of a life at least somewhat evocative of the past. With no kitchens, there are no multilayered evocations. The houses remain exhibits encased in grass instead of glass.

However, the absence of these kitchens means more than the absence of aromas, because kitchen structures were not just places where food was cooked. In antebellum Washington these kitchens embodied and were embedded in a set of meanings and practices that were fundamental to social conditions of existence. Food preparation was a daily reproduction of the divisions between those who were doing the cooking, slaves, and those who were doing the eating, owners. These kitchens are important components of the social landscape of slavery in the Town South. As a result of additional archaeological, architectural, and historical research in Washington and its environs, and the examination of landscapes elsewhere in the South, it is clear that kitchens were an integral part of the "landscape of separation and spatial discipline" (Epperson 1989, 1991).

To understand how kitchens in Washington and elsewhere could be much more than a source of nutrition and evocative aromas, one must appreciate two sets of interpretive frameworks—one is habitus, and the other the household, with special consideration of gender issues. Taken together, we can perhaps understand why there is so much confusion incorporated into the phrase "detached kitchen" and why, in spite of laws, biblical injunctions, bills of sale, and fear, the interactions of Anglo-Americans and African Americans were marked by ambiguity and contradiction. It could hardly be otherwise when they were inextricably tied together in the confines of house and house lot and when those interactions took place in a context constructed by systems of values and meanings that depended on ambiguity and contradiction.

Habitus

The forms and functions of separate kitchens in Washington are of interest today partly because the kitchens were integral to the culture of those who lived in Washington in the past; the question is, how were these kitchens integrated within that culture? The concept of "culture" itself remains one of the key contributions to the understanding of the ways in which human beings have attempted to solve the mundane and profound problems of existence, but the place of human beings in culture has always been problematic. There have been many efforts to understand how culture can, on the one hand, provide the answers to the problems of existence but can, on the other hand, allow the human beings who are the carriers and transmitters of that culture to be anything other than automatons. The debate will continue, but perhaps one body of guides to the understanding of this paradox and of its expression in architecture and households can be summarized by the term *habitus*. The concept was offered by Pierre Bourdieu (1977, 1993) and explicated by others (e.g., Calhoun et al. 1993; Fowler 1997; Johnson 1993). Archaeologists are starting to adopt the concept; one strong example is Wilkie (2000a) in her perceptive study of African Americans on Mississippi River plantations in Louisiana (and see elsewhere in this volume).

Drawing on currents in cognitive anthropology, symbolic anthropology, and structuralism, Bourdieu sought to understand how humans carry on the routines of daily life. He concluded that daily life remains routine because people do not have to think about what they do as they would if they were consciously operating within a strict system of rules (1977:72). People exist instead in a habitus, a "system of durable, transposable dispositions." The dispositions are tendencies, propensities, inclinations, and habits (Bourdieu 1977:214n.1).

According to Bourdieu, a habitus has a history because it is generated by specific conditions of existence that impose definitions of what is possible and what is not. This is done through the division of the full range of phenomena in the physical and social universe into classifications as a result of choices. Once these classifications or structures are formed or "generated," habitus is durable because it produces individual and collective practices that tend to perpetuate those same conditions, including the inculcation of children to the unthinking acceptance of the habitus and the lack of awareness of the actors that they are even operating within a system of values and meanings that are not universally held. Bourdieu (1977:91) makes a specific place for material culture in habitus, referring to "the magic of a world of objects which is the product of the application of the same schemes (of structuring) to the most diverse domains." Since one cannot directly observe those structures or classifications, one must analyze the products those classifications produce in daily life. For example, each aspect of the way a house is laid out and used represents choices (Bourdieu 1977:90–95). The structure that is built by those choices continually reminds the occupants that those choices were right.

Thus individuals and social groups make ordinary daily life possible by using things of the material world that have been given meaning, without even being aware that codes exist or that objects could carry other codes. Community members are taught through enculturation how to read the codes that objects carry. These codes are not unalterable, however, and negotiation, action, and reflection are intrinsic to daily life. There is continuity provided by the shared values, behavior, and experience, and new situations are worked through using old values. The habitus persists because it has practical value. The inhabitants of antebellum Washington were functioning within a habitus. It may have been still under construction, because Washington itself was established only in 1824 (Medearis 1976; Williams 1951). Indeed, Eli Whitney's cotton gin was still a relatively new invention when Arkansas was made a territory in 1819, putting southwest Arkansas on the Cotton Frontier.

Households and Gender

The Cotton Frontier was a landscape constructed by both Anglo-American owners and African-American slaves. There is a growing body of studies on African Americans as constructive participants in southern society rather than just objects with value or in someone's morality play. They are being recognized as participants because they were intimate parts of the household.

Archaeologists have found that the idea of the "household," defined here as a co-residential, social, or economic unit within a particular culture, may solve many difficulties in relating the evidence at a single locus to the activities of human beings who created that evidence and in understanding that locus over time (e.g., Allison 1999a; Ashmore and Wilk 1988; Beaudry 1984; Mrozowski 1984; Netting et al. 1984; Spencer-Wood 1984, 1987a; Wilk and Ashmore 1988).

In turn, the concept of the household permits connecting the scattered bits of data recoverable about individuals, from such sources as birth and marriage records, with equally scattered bits of data about larger social entities, such as censuses and tax records and archaeological artifacts and features from which those individuals were inseparable. This linking was exploited with particular success by historians of the family beginning in the 1970s (e.g., Laslett and Wall 1972).

An individual household is also dynamic, with changing numbers and roles of participants and changing types of tasks. Sources for dynamism are many, ranging from daily routine to long-term generational development. However, habitus generates stability by providing a shared framework of accepted routines and underlying dispositions in which and by which the household operates. Habitus thus both creates a setting for the activities and interactions within the household and conditions how the interactions take place.

It is becoming clear that an important element in households in the South was African-American women, as recent studies call attention to variability in slave experience based on gender (Fox-Genovese 1988; Jones 1985; Lebsock 1984; White 1985). When one looks at slavery in the domestic context of the house and kitchen, one is in fact dealing primarily with women. As Fox-Genovese and White emphasized, it was slave women who did much of the housework, as cooks, nurses, washers, and servant girls; it was slave-owning women who supervised their labor and assisted when necessary. Lebsock has pointed out that because of these shared tasks, there were probably closer ties between Anglo-American women and African-American slave women than between most Anglo-American males and African-American slave males.

In the last three decades, there have been a number of studies by historians concerned with exploring the ways in which southern Anglo-American women struggled within a complex series of roles that ranged from mother and wife to activist and victim (e.g., Clinton 1994; Coryell et al. 2000; Faust 1996; Friedman 1985; Gillespie and Clinton 1998). Archaeologists have also begun to raise questions about gender in a variety of contexts, including the urban North (Spencer-Wood 1994; Wall 1994), town and countryside in the Chesapeake (Gibb and King 1991; Yentsch 1994), and elsewhere (e.g., Nelson 1997; Walde and Willows 1991).

However, Fox-Genovese (1988) also made clear that the privileges of one set of women in the antebellum South depended on the oppression of the other set of women. They shared a world of mutual antagonisms and frayed tempers. Their world and the household was both a landscape of dominance and control and one of ambiguity, contradiction, and confusion. Ambiguity and contradiction have been present in Anglo-American and African-American relationships in household settings since the nineteenth century, when the South of myth, legend, and multiple realities began to be constructed during slavery times. Here are two examples from the South, from southwest Arkansas.

First, Mrs. C. E. Royston, looking back from 1912 to her privileged childhood in antebellum Washington, said "we Southern women feel so attached to these old family servants, especially so to those who nursed us, stayed with our parents during the war and could not be persuaded to leave them even when they were told they were free" (Royston 1912:16). Second, in April 1864, when Union troops entered Camden, about 40 miles east of Washington, a witness reported that when it came to trying to hide stores from troops, "little confidence is to be place in (Negro) servants. They betray their masters in almost every case" (quoted in Williams 1951:80, parentheses in the original).

SLAVERY IN TOWN

Contradiction, confusion, ambiguity: These examples have come from towns, a mostly neglected arena for the study of slavery until recently (notwithstanding Richard Wade's 1964 pioneering overview *Slavery in the Cities*). There are advantages to examining the contradictions within slavery in the context of nucleated settlement. The scale of slaveholding in towns and villages across the South more closely approximated the human scale in which slavery was experienced and reproduced by both owner and owned and by Anglos who did not own slaves. Unlike the larger plantations where one family might own 20–50 or more slaves, in the towns it was more often one family owning a few servants or a craftsperson.

Each plantation has only one "Big House" regardless of how plain or elaborate that structure might be. Towns were primarily "Big House" settings, particularly when many mercantile or craft activities were carried out in or adjacent to residential spaces. The life of the Big House on plantations, of African-American and Anglo-American women, men, and children coexisting intimately within the socially and spatially confined space of house and yard, was thus reproduced repeatedly on house lots and residential blocks throughout the town.

Wade's main conclusion was that the urban slave experience was unlike that of the rural field hand because of the greater opportunity and wider contacts offered to the urban slave. This conclusion has become accepted as the variations in urban slavery have been documented and explored, primarily by historians but also by archaeologists (e.g., Blassingame 1973; Borchert 1980; Goldfield 1991; Joseph 2000; O'Brien 1978; Richter 1969; Yentsch 1994). There has been, however, remarkably little concern by archaeologists with slavery in nucleated settlements in the lower Mississippi Valley, at least outside of New Orleans (Stewart-Abernathy 1999).

Moreover, much of the historical analysis of urban slavery to date may be more limited than might first be appreciated. The demographic prominence of female slaves in the Big House and in the towns was largely ignored until studies by White (1985) and Fox-Genovese (1988), who dealt primarily with the rural Big House setting. Yentsch's (1994) examination of slavery in colonial Annapolis is an important and notable exception in that she spends considerable time examining the place of female slaves.

It is crucial to remember, in the title of a recent book, that housework is *Never Done* (Strasser 1982), even on the Sabbath. Although Arkansas law, as in most states, prohibited the master to compel slaves to work on Sunday, there was the qualification "except the performance of the customary household duties of daily necessity, comfort, or charity" (Trieber 1911:177). In other words, work by the household slaves continued seven days a week, from before dawn to well after dusk (Genovese 1974:337).

To understand how people worked out these issues of slavery, gender, habitus, and household in a particular place, one needs the case studies that focus, to use Ian Hodder's words (1986:2–12), on cultural context, individual action, and historic context. The historic context here is the town of Washington. The cultural context is the construction of habitus, that enfolding symbolic and physical order and routine and habit by Anglo-Americans and African Americans—*The World They Made Together,* to borrow Sobel's (1987) title. The individuals are the people of Washington, particularly the households of the Block and Sanders families and their slave servants. It is in households that so much of society is focused, a direction some historical archaeologists have argued for nearly twenty years (Beaudry 1984, 1986; Mrozowski 1984; Spencer-Wood 1984, 1987c).

Finally, the immediate setting is the urban farmsteads of the Blocks, the Sanders, and their neighbors in Washington. "Urban farmsteads" here means the house lots that contained the house itself and necessary spaces and structures to support the household in a time when city services were minimal. The Block and Sanders urban farmsteads each covered an entire city block, laid out with four lots totaling 200 × 200 feet (61 × 61 meters). This provided plenty of space for vegetable and flower gardens, smokehouse, wells, woodshed, animal pens and sheds, and, most important, the kitchen buildings that served as the principal workplace of the slave cooks and washerwomen and as their residence.

It is in these kitchens that much of southern life was created and maintained, the habitus of daily life. It is with these kitchens, conceptually and emotionally, that also was created and maintained much of the intimacy, contradiction, and ambiguity of Anglo-American and African-American relations of today.

URBAN SLAVERY IN WASHINGTON

Formal public interpretation has been under way in Washington for over 40 years, since the creation of the Pioneer Washington Preservation Foundation in 1957, but there has been no detailed study of the documentary evidence of slavery there. Investigation of slavery in Little Rock, the largest antebellum town in Arkansas (Lack 1982), provides a useful regional transition from studies of bigger cities begun by Wade. Along with Taylor's (1958) history of slavery in Arkansas and White's (1984) study of slavery in Hempstead County, these provide the basic outline by which Washington can be compared (see Walz 1953).

Demographics

In discussing slavery in Washington, there are some demographic problem areas still unresolved, arising in part from the dynamics of growth in the region and from the imprecise boundaries of the town. Nonetheless, if one uses the 1850 and 1860 censuses of Washington, as edited to include only those who probably actually lived within the bounds of the nucleated settlement, it is possible to develop a statistical picture of the African-American population without complicating the matter with slaves who were field hands (see Tables 4.1 and 4.2).

Slaves as Individuals

Memoirs by Anglo-American owners or their descendants allow one to move beyond these numbers to some of the names and occupations of slaves in Washington (Royston 1912:17–19). For example, Aunt Aggie Royston was a cook and kitchen boss in the 1840s and 1850s. Aunt Myra Etter was a nurse and cook. In the 1850s, Mammy Rhoda was a servant, nurse, and cook. Daddy Law Lewis was a servant who also taught owners' sons to hunt and swim. Others served as house servants, maids, laundresses, ironers, and seamstresses. Anyone who did not own a servant could hire one from another owner. S. L. Slack advertised in 1853 "to hire three or four good house servants, for whom a liberal price will be given" (*Washington Telegraph*, hereafter *WT*, 5 January 1853). The next year someone wanted to hire "an able bodied negro woman, who is a good cook, washer, and ironer" (*WT*, 12 July 1854).

THE BLOCKS, THE SANDERS, AND SLAVERY

It is now time to look more closely at the slaveholder experience through two families who were prominent in antebellum Washington. These families were the targets of the first extensive archaeological work in Washington—the surviving house of the Block family dating to 1832 and the surviving house of the

Table 4.1 Slave ownership in Washington, Arkansas, 1850 and 1860.

	City of Washington		Hempstead County	
	1850	1860	1850	1860
Total Number of Owners	34	45	297	440
Total Number of Slaves	145	243	2459	5398
Average Number of Slaves	4.3	5.4	8.3	12.3
Total Owning 6 or Less	28	35	—	—
% of Total Owners	82.5	77.8	—	—
% of Total Slaves	57 (n=82)	51 (n=124)	—	—
Average	2.9	3.5	—	—

(Sources: Arkansas Slave Schedule 1850, Schedule 2 Slave Inhabitants, Town of Washington, Hempstead County; Arkansas Slave Schedules, 1860, Town of Washington, Hempstead County. Correlated lists of owners who actually lived in Washington in *Hempstead Trails* 1990, April, pp. 37 and 1991, April, pp. 16, 19; Hempstead county totals from White 1984:4–12).

Sanders family dating to about 1845. Both families were intimately involved in all aspects of the transition of their region from frontier to settled cotton country. Both families embody the high expectations of abundance and security on the Cotton Frontier and thereafter, but they achieved their expectations not in the classic southern rural setting of cotton plantations but in a town dedicated to serving the planters, the would-be planters, and the administrative and commercial infrastructure necessary to all their dreams.

The Block Family

The Blocks were prominent merchants, cotton commission agents, and entrepreneurs from the 1820s into the 1860s (Montgomery 1981a; Stewart-Abernathy 1988; Stewart-Abernathy and Ruff 1989). They were directly involved in laying down the commercial framework for Washington and its environs and in maintaining and expanding that framework for two generations.

The Blocks were intimately involved with slavery as dealers and as owners. As part of their many business operations under multiple partnerships through the years, the Blocks served as commission merchants and factors. Advertisements in the *Washington Telegraph* indicate that they repeatedly dealt in small numbers of slaves both under their own name and as agents for others (see, e.g., *WT,* 4 May 1842, 6 November 1844).

Block family patriarch Abraham was a slave owner, although the details are

Table 4.2 Slave demography in Washington, Arkansas, 1850 and 1860.

Slave Population—1850

Gender		Number	% of Gender	% of Total
Male	Black	41	71.9	28.2
	Mulatto	16	28.1	11.0
	Total	57	—	39.3
Female	Black	65	73.9	44.8
	Mulatto	23	26.1	15.9
	Total	88	—	60.6
Grand Total		**145**	—	**100.0**

Slave Population—1860

Gender		Number	% of Gender	% of Total
Male	Black	79	73.1	32.5
	Mulatto	29	26.9	11.9
	Total	108	—	44.4
Female	Black	101	74.8	41.6
	Mulatto	34	25.1	13.9
	Total	135	—	55.6
Grand Total		**243**	—	**100.0**

somewhat confusing. This confusion occurs in part because of the uncertain impacts of his long life (1780s–1859) on household dynamics, on the fact that several of the children apparently continued to live in the family home into their thirties and they owned slaves, and on the fact that households began fissioning off in the 1850s. Census data indicate that the Abraham Block household numbered 11 or 12 Anglo-Americans for much of the first half of the 1800s (Montgomery 1981a:19–23). These people certainly filled a house with only seven interior rooms and five fireplaces. Tax and census records indicate that the slaves listed under Abraham's ownership generally numbered from two to five in the 1830s and 1840s, and these were primarily females (Montgomery 1981a:19–20). By the 1850 census, Abraham Block was one of the largest slave owners in Washington with 14 (Table 4.2). In 1850, the gender ratio was equal—three adult males and four male children and four adult females and three female children. It is possible that the adult males may have been either servants or valets or may have assisted in the Block store or in some of Abraham Block's small entrepreneurial enterprises such as the sawmill in which he had interests and the tannery he owned in 1842 (Montgomery 1981a:23).

The Sanders Family

The other family, the Sanders, was directly involved in laying down the administrative, governmental, and bureaucratic framework of the Washington area and in maintaining that framework into the chaos of the Civil War, when Washington served as the capital of Confederate Arkansas in 1863–1865 (Montgomery 1980, 1981b). Simon T. Sanders (1797–1881), head of the household, was closely associated with politics and government bureaucracy in Washington for nearly 70 years. He served as bookkeeper to stores and later to planters. He was also a secretary to most civic, fraternal, and religious organizations in town. Most significant, he was Hempstead County clerk for three decades after 1838. He was always working to establish and maintain order in the very institutions of government and economics that gave county seat towns their principal purpose.

The Sanders family was also involved in slavery. As county clerk in a rapidly growing town, Sanders dealt with the bureaucratic aspects of a slave-based society on a daily basis, recording slaves as taxable property and as objects of court proceedings involving debts and crimes. He was also personally concerned as an owner of household servants, although for the most part their names and gender are unknown. His house was smaller than that of the Blocks, only five enclosed rooms on one floor, though with three fireplaces. His family was also smaller, usually no more than four or five, not counting slaves. The family usually considered only one or two female slaves necessary to support the household. At least one of those slaves was more than simply a servant.

Tax and census records show Simon owned from one to three slaves from 1839 to 1854, including a housemaid and nurse named Eliza Thomas. The 1850 census indicates two adult females and one infant female—Eliza may have been the twenty-year-old female slave. Sanders was thus close to the average of 2.9 slaves owned by 76 percent of the owners (average 4.3 overall). The number of his slaves rose to four and eventually six by 1860 (Montgomery 1980), reflecting the same increasing involvement as Abraham Block. The 1860 census indicates two adult females, one female child, and three male children including an infant, a total that surpasses the average of 3.5 slaves held by 78 percent of the owners (average 5.4 overall).

KITCHENS

Discussions of residence patterns for town slaves usually hide uncertainty behind brevity. It is not surprising that historians run into difficulty in trying to pin down slave residence, for three reasons. First, housing conditions apparently varied substantially in type and quality, ranging from separate quarters with a fireplace and windows to makeshift quarters in outbuildings or even in hallways or other-purpose spaces in the master's house (Lack 1982:265). Second, housing for anyone in town was often somewhat transitory owing to the rebuilding and updating of urban cores and the loss of outbuildings whose functions declined. Finally, vernacular urban housing in general is poorly documented.

As residence has been neglected, so has the related issue of kitchens. They are ubiquitous throughout the South, in lore, in old photographs, rarely even as standing buildings. They have been frequently excavated as part of restoration efforts in both urban and rural contexts. But they have not been the subject of thought or interpretation other than the ascribed role in cooking. It is intriguing that kitchens have been neglected, much as the entire sphere of women's work has been, in North American historiography and historical archaeology. As with most things ubiquitous, kitchens carry important meaning as conceptual and physical places. Unstated assumptions about them get in the way of observations, much the same way Bourdieu (1977:79) noted that "it is because subjects do not, strictly speaking, know what they are doing that what they do has more meaning than they know."

Wade (1964:57–62) and others do briefly mention the use of kitchens as quarters, but they do not do justice to the crucial importance of kitchens as both workplaces and as quarters. Fortunately, good documentary evidence can be found that connects kitchens and their use as slave quarters. For example, vivid examples were found at the antebellum county seat and market town of Cahawba in Dallas County, Alabama, as a result of extensive documentary research carried out by the Old Cahawba Preservation Project (Derry 1992). For example, an 1855 Cahawba Town Ordinance included the phrase "negro-house or kitchen, the same being the temporary or permanent abode of negroes" (*Dallas Gazette,* 16 January 1857).

Separation?

Perhaps "kitchen" is a metonym, wherein the name for the most important part of the structure to the Anglo-American owners provides the name for the whole that included the living spaces for their African-American slaves. Perhaps kitchens would be of more interest if they were also thought of as control measures with contradictory messages, physical structures that reflected basic doubt and uncertainty in the underlying social conditions of existence that structured the habitus. They may have been buildings that isolated the work and lives of slave women and their families. On the other hand, the intimate and necessary work that occurs in kitchens tied these buildings tightly back to the owners.

To date, kitchens in the South have been quickly dismissed as "separate kitchens" without further consideration. The key notion here is the *idea* of separateness, that these kitchen buildings were distinct from the house. That they were conceptually distinct is clear from contemporary documents. In southwest Arkansas, advertisements for the sale of plantations and farms in the *Washington Telegraph* frequently list the kitchen as a separate named entity comparable to the identity of other buildings clearly separate from the house. For example, in 1847, G. D. Royston offered his place "adjoining Washington" including "a large and commodius dwelling house, kitchen, negro houses, corn crib, stable, carriage house, and other necessary buildings" (*WT*, 21 July 1847), and in 1850 E. Nance was selling his 730-acre farm "five miles southwest of Washington . . . on which is a good Frame Dwelling House, Kitchen, Negro Cabins, &c." (*WT*, 4 September 1850).

It is difficult to find contemporary explanations for the separation. The causes offered for separate kitchens by oral informants usually are physical, the same reasons given until recently by the few scholars who noticed kitchens (Herman 1999; Jordan 1978:138–142; McKee 1992b). As Rapoport (1969) and others have noted, choosing "natural" causes is a common inclination, after all, when trying to explain problems in vernacular architecture. With kitchens these putative physical causes include problems with excess heat and objectionable odors from cooking in the subtemperate climate of the South and with flies and other insects congregating around foodstuffs stored or being prepared for consumption. There was also a real danger of fire, as when the *Washington Telegraph* reported sad news of David Block in 1862—that "a fire broke out in the kitchen building of his elegant mansion in the suburbs of town and consumed all his outhouses, including the smoke house and a large amount of meat. The residence was saved by great exertion" (*WT*, 26 February 1862).

Certainly odors, insects, and flames were substantial parts of the kitchen experience for those who worked there. However, using these physical factors as the explanation for separation collapses under closer examination. Those claiming that odors are a problem forget that the aromas produced by most foods during cooking are hardly objectionable. Even the definition of "objectionable odor" must be reconsidered given the ubiquitous presence of chamber pots containing human waste, stored underneath beds in the sleeping quarters. For that matter, insects were equally omnipresent in bedding and on the body, so one must be cautious about complaints about food and insects. Finally, the danger of fire was also present within the house itself, where every house had at least one fireplace and some houses had five or more. David Block lost his kitchen in the winter, when more fireplaces were in use in houses than in kitchens.

Moreover, although fire danger, heat, odors, and insects continued to be problems in the South into the mid-twentieth century, kitchens have long since been incorporated into other household activity within the main house. Many remedies for perceived problems were sought and offered as part of domestic reform movements far beyond the South (Beecher 1841; Beecher and Stowe 1869; McMurry 1988). The adoption of window screening of tightly woven wire in the late nineteenth century at least cut down on problems with flying insects, but other technological improvements did not necessarily provide remedies for environmental problems. Replacing the drafty fireplace for cooking with the greater heating efficiency and heat retention of the cast-iron, wood-burning cooking stove did not cool off the kitchen but actually increased the heat in the work space. The fire danger may have also increased when the thin metal stove-pipe replaced the masonry chimney stack. The stove likely offset any gains even from the introduction later of electric-powered ceiling fans. It was not until the development in the early twentieth century of oil-fired and then gas or electric stoves and the general introduction of air-conditioning in the mid-twentieth century that the heat problem was ameliorated.

However, arguments for physical causes are undercut by the a priori assumption that "separate" is a clearly defined and recognizable physical attribute. In fact, those contemporary documents could be contradictory about the physical nature of separate. According to an account in the *Washington Telegraph*, in 1851 fire struck "the frame kitchen attached to the dwelling occupied by Mr. J. G. D'Armond." The roof was burning so rapidly when first discovered that the building could not be saved. "By great exertion, the dwelling, not more than 20 or 30 feet from the kitchen was saved" (*WT,* 5 March 1851). In this case, the kitchen was "attached," but it was also quite obviously distant from the house, and "20 or 30 feet" was almost not far enough anyway.

Washington Kitchens

Instead of assertions about climate or risks, what is needed is reliable evidence about kitchens, drawn from a specific place and time. In Washington there has been a detailed reexamination of kitchens and their place on the urban farmstead. Thus, as a result of excavations in concert with informant interviews and focused documentary and photographic research, the particular places of the Block kitchen, built between 1835 and 1850, and of the Sanders kitchen, constructed sometime in the 1840s, are now relatively well known (Cande and Brandon 1999; Guendling 1992; Guendling et al. 2001, 2002; Novak 2001; Stewart-Abernathy 1982, 1986a, 1986b, n.d.). These two cases can be supplemented with data on other selected kitchen buildings in the town researched as part of architectural restoration efforts (e.g., Stewart-Abernathy 1987; Witsell et al. 1985).

It is clear that by the mid-1800s there were two different ideas as to kitchen

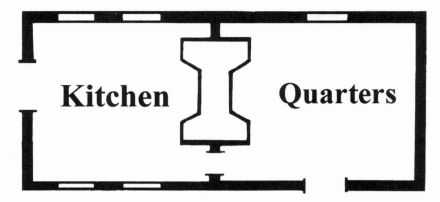

Fig. 4.1. Schematic of plan of two-room kitchens, Washington, Arkansas.

location, even though evidence exists for only one set of rules about what a kitchen was supposed to look like. And, it is also possible to suggest reasons for separation, reflecting a growing consensus that southern kitchens were separate, whether across an open portion or across the yard, not because of heat or insects but because of important needs for control and distance (Herman 1999; McKee 1992b; Stewart-Abernathy 1992; Vlach 1993).

Kitchen Form. Washington kitchens in the antebellum period closely resembled one another (Figures 4.1–4.3), at least the ones about which knowledge exists. They were one-story, two-room, rectangular structures with central chimneys, a form that likely reflected both European and West African sensibilities (Barley 1961; Ferguson 1992:63–82), and that is documented in many places across the South. Based on archaeological evidence, the Block kitchen measures approximately 14 × 48 feet (4.3 × 15.2 meters), the Sanders kitchen 14.75 × 36 feet (4.5 × 11 meters).

Based on oral history for Washington, one room was the kitchen proper, the other was a quarters/storeroom, though it was also rarely noted that the second room was a washing or laundry room. The "kitchen" was more likely to be the room located toward the public end of the urban farmstead complex. At Block this was the east room (the room closest to the house), at Sanders the north one (the room toward the main street passing through town from east to west). There was also some variation in relative room size. In the Sanders kitchen, the rooms were the same size; at Block the quarters room was smaller than the kitchen room.

A massive axial brick chimney column was located on the central dividing partition and provided fireplaces in each room. At both sites, the chimney columns had been entirely removed during demolition. One informant suggests that at the Sanders site, the hearth in the kitchen room (on the north end) was

Fig. 4.2. The Sanders kitchen as reconstructed in 1994, designed by Charles Witsell. Viewed from the rear porch of the Sanders House looking southeast (Arkansas Archeological Survey Neg. No. 956205).

Fig. 4.3. Detached kitchen behind the Page House, detail from a March 1907 photograph, looking northeast; photograph taken from the roof of the 1874 courthouse (Arkansas Archeological Survey Neg. No. 823163).

accompanied by an oven built into a shoulder or adjacent face (Wilson, personal communication 1992).

These kitchens were raised off the ground with wooden floors and a crawl space underneath. The Sanders kitchen sat on brick piers, apparently supplemented with a curtain wall. Although all known dwellings in town, including the Sanders and Block dwellings, sat on brick piers, the Block kitchen was strikingly different in that it sat on posts sunk into the ground. Along with postholes found along the perimeter and in the interior, one remnant of a locust post was found in situ, and another post had apparently been shored up with a boxed footing of brick (Guendling et al. 2002).

Other kitchen details include braced frame construction, gable roofs sheathed with wood shingles, and weatherboarding on the exterior. There was some variation in window openings and door openings depending on orientation to the house. In addition, both oral and archaeological data indicate the Sanders kitchen probably had porches along the east and west long axes and on the north gable end. (When the Sanders kitchen was reconstructed in 1994, porches were built only on the north and east facades, as a result primarily of 50 years of study of a 1907 photograph, taken after a tornado passed through the town, that includes a blurred image of the Sanders kitchen without a porch on the west facade.) The Block kitchen had a porch on the north side, also on the long axis, and connected to an open porch on the east gable end.

Kitchen Placement. Two patterns are present in the placement of the kitchen relative to the house (Figure 4.4). They reflect different statements and choices about the physical attributes of "separation" but share the social definition. The most obvious pattern is a kitchen structure located far enough from the house so that it is visually a separate building. There are no known surviving examples of detached kitchens in Arkansas, although there are unverified claims about a few kitchens that were originally detached but have since moved up to the house. A 1907 photograph showing the Sanders property confirms that this kitchen was the detached type (Stewart-Abernathy 1986a:figs. 2, 3). The "public" end of the kitchen is probably the north, because that end faces an early main road through town.

It is more difficult to say how the kitchen was oriented to the house, because the Sanders house itself is an L-plan with porticos leading to central hallways on both the north and west facades of the house. Oral history suggests that the Sanders kitchen and house were probably linked by a walkway (Wilson, personal communication 1992).

The second pattern for kitchen separation is less visually apparent, although at least the relationship of orientation is more obvious. In this pattern, illustrated by the Block kitchen, the "separate" kitchen is actually an appendage to the rear quarter of the two-story, seven-room house, giving the entire complex

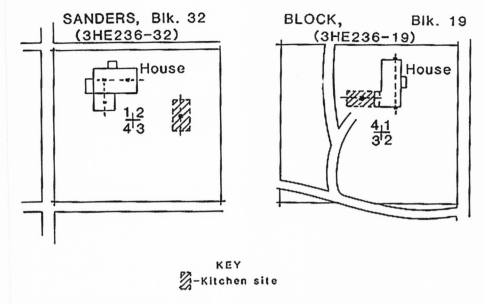

SANDERS, Blk. 32
(3HE236-32)

House

BLOCK,   Blk. 19
(3HE236-19)

House

KEY
⬚-Kitchen site

Fig. 4.4. Kitchen placement on the Block and Sanders urban farmsteads (Arkansas Archeological Survey Neg. No. 825884).

an L plan pierced by a total of four chimneys for the seven fireplaces. The distance between the house and its appendage is only the width of a porch or breezeway, but the cognitive separation is present nonetheless. And indeed the same reasons of health and climate along with fire danger were used by informants after the mid-twentieth century as explanations for why one had to cross what was only a fully open hallway to enter the appendage Block kitchen and other examples of its type no longer extant.

In the context of wider architectural developments, the kitchen as appendage belongs to the wings sprouted by Greek Revival houses on the east coast and the ubiquitous kitchen ells or tees behind I-houses across the Midwest and built throughout the South after Reconstruction (cf. Walker 1981). However, there is little to suggest that those kitchens were in any way considered separate though the form was identical.

The important distinction is thus made with modern kitchens that lie within the perimeter of the main house, rather than with how far away a building has to be before it is considered separate. There are numerous surviving antebellum and postbellum examples in Arkansas of the appendage type kitchen with a two-room center-chimney plan. One room is frequently identified today as a dining room and the other as storage, probably a linguistic mask for the cook's status as slave before the Civil War and where she might have lived.

INTIMACY AND CONTROL

Legal control mechanisms attempted in the town setting have been discussed by Wade (1964), Lack (1982), and others. Washington had its control ordinances, for example, on the duties of the patrols to monitor slaves (*WT*, 18 April 1849; see also Arkansas Slave Code laws [Taylor 1958:29–32, 202–211]). These mechanisms were apparently poorly enforced. In fact, close attention by Herman (1999:99, 100) to the testimony in the trials following the Denmark Vesey uprising in South Carolina in 1822 (see Barile, this volume) indicates that, in fact, slaves were "able to claim some measure of privacy and independence in spaces located at the very heart of the urban plantation," possessing an astonishing degree of autonomy "within the quarter and the interstices of the house, house lot, and city." Some had apparently used that autonomy to plan a revolt, the nightmare of the owning class. This insight suggests a number of opportunities for further exploration of issues of domination and resistance within the context of urban settings (Paynter and McGuire 1991). Slaves objectified as "fixtures" sometimes had surprising opportunities for concealment "in plain view," opportunities discovered only in the aftermath of active resistance (Herman 1999).

In any case, control in the intimacy of the urban farmstead could not depend on police powers or similar public expressions, given the constant work demands of a household in the days when housework and food preparation were done by hand and were carried out in the intimacy of the Anglo-American household. Certainly a casual word of warning would carry more force when both parties knew that the power of the state and the force of the whip lay behind the quiet word. However, a household controlled by the whip would be a difficult place in which to live.

Some other means was necessary to aid discipline and inculcate subservience, to incorporate control measures into the habitus of the household. That means may have been the conceptual separation of the primary workspace of the domestic slave, the kitchen. This separation limited the intimacy of interaction between Anglo-American owners and African-American slaves. Separation at least pushed the interaction out of the main body of the house to a space that was symbolically, if not physically, separate. With cook or servant in the kitchen building, connected to the house across an open porch or along a walkway, that person was both physically distant but always reachable. This separate but nearby residence not only allowed control and supervision, conferring "visual authority over adjoining spaces," in Herman's phrase (1999:99), but also imposed a physical distance between owner and owned.

The separation between kitchen and house was thus a metaphor for the structured separation between those who worked in the kitchen and those for whom they worked. The metaphor came to life when the slaves had to move from kitchen to house. It was not just food that moved from the area of preparation to the area of consumption; it was the body of a cognitively aware human being who was being forced to move from one place to another. From exclusion to inclusion, from outside to inside, from a small building conceived and named for heat and toil to a much larger building conceived and named for rest, leisure, and consumption—each place provided a separate context for interaction recognized and agreed to by all parties, at least most of the time, a stage embedded in symbol and embodied within walls and floor and ceiling, but only one actor had to make the physical journey. That actor could have also seen the journey as one from "home" to contested space.

The spatial dimensions of social relationships between Anglo-Americans and their African-American slaves in the general plantation landscape have been explored recently by a number of archaeologists and architectural historians (e.g., McKee 1992b; Upton 1988; Yentsch 1994). Vlach (1993:43–62), for example, has emphasized the importance of distancing and segregation, particularly concerning kitchens on plantations. McKee (1992b:173) noted this same phenomenon of deliberate separation regarding plantation kitchens, in this case to help explain a subtle but distinctive change at the Hermitage, Andrew Jackson's manor home near Nashville (see Battle, this volume). The house suffered a terrible fire in 1834. The original 1831 kitchen had been separated from the dining room only by a partition wall. The replacement kitchen was pushed farther away, separated from the eating area by two pantries and an open passageway. This act created an L-shaped kitchen whose separation was visible in profile by the opening between the back of the main mass of the house and the kitchen itself, but there was no actual space between the roof of the kitchen and the back of the house. A fire could easily have passed between the two buildings, but the separation was intended to be more social than physical, "another layer of social insulation between the owners and the owned" (McKee 1992b:173).

On the other hand, the spatial separation did provide some of the freedom and independence for the slaves when the Blocks, Sanders, or other owners were not looking. This slight freedom may have been a necessity as well, providing a brief refuge for the slaves who might otherwise find their own patience frayed by too close contact with their owners. (See also the experiences of Lucy Skipworth, a Big House slave on an Alabama plantation, in her own words in Miller 1990:183–263. For a contemporary archaeologist's perspective, see Garman 1995 on a New England urban setting).

Just as the kitchen buildings were much closer than symbolically conceived, the slaves who inhabited those kitchens were not as socially distant from the owners in the main house as those owners hoped or recognized. Whether on the plantation or in town, the kitchen, Deetz noted (1993:145), is the place where the world of the owners and the world of their slaves came together. In Washington, one does not have the contemporary documentary sources about household life that put Anglo-Americans and African Americans so close together. So far, there are but two hints into the intertwining of Sanders and Blocks with the human "chattel" with whom they shared their lives. First, the food bones excavated from the pit feature under the Block kitchen may speak to the close interaction of Block matriarch Frances (also known as Fannie) with her anonymous African-American cook as together they wrestled with the option of keeping a kosher Jewish household on the far edge of the Mississippi Valley frontier. Second, although the story of Eliza Thomas, housemaid and nurse to the Sanders family, is recorded in an anonymous and glowing biography of Sanders (Anonymous n.d.; Montgomery 1980; Royston 1912:19), this vivid anecdote communicates the interdependence of owner and owned, even as it reminds that one is owned and one is the owner.

At Block

In recent years there is increasing appreciation for the extraordinary role of West African traditions in the creation of classic southern foodways (Ferguson 1992:93–100; Genovese 1974:540–549), traditions imported into the South and syncretized by African-American cooks. At the Block household, cooking also created a potentially complex situation, because food preparation was carried out in the context of Jewish religious beliefs with much to say about foodways. (For detailed discussion, see Stewart-Abernathy and Ruff 1989.)

Both Abraham Block and his wife, Frances, were trained in Jewish belief and practice, he in Bohemia, she in Virginia. In 1827, by which time they were already living in Washington, they participated in the founding of the first Jewish synagogue in the Mississippi Valley, in New Orleans. However, for the Blocks, taking advantage of the social and economic opportunities that frontier Washington offered also meant that they were isolated from their fellow believers and separated from the fundamental congregational basis of Judaic ecclesiastical organization (for documentation of this separation, see LeMaster 1994).

An important component of traditional Jewish religion was the system of *kashrut,* an integration of ideology and foodways deliberately intended to move eating from the profane to the sacred, so that the daily preparation and consumption of food itself becomes a religious act. The complicated system of kashrut ranges from rules on how to butcher animals to how to clean cooking and eating utensils. The system is, however, not difficult to maintain in the middle of a thriving community of specialists and believers.

In their isolation, Abraham and Frances were directly responsible for the entire process. In fact, the foodways were specifically the responsibility of the mother in a Jewish household, so the burden fell on Frances and by close extension on her African-American slave women. In the late 1800s and on into the twentieth century, after large-scale immigration of Jewish families to the United States, it was possible in parts of the South, such as Memphis, for Jewish women to train their African-American cooks to operate according to kashrut.

Archaeological evidence suggests that the Blocks chose to set aside the system of kashrut in their household. A pit feature was found underneath the quarters room of the kitchen, filled with trash sometime in the early 1840s. The trash contained food bones representing about 89.6 kg (40 lbs) of biomass (Ruff 1985). About 12 percent of this meat came from pork, the consumption of which was prohibited by thousands of years of Judaic practice. It is unlikely that the food bones represent only slave consumption, because ritual contamination can easily come about by the mixing of fumes from cooking pots. Given the difficulties inherent in preparing prohibited foods in conjunction with permissible ones, it appears likely that the Blocks had set aside prohibitions against eating pork.

Documentary and mortuary evidence indicate the Blocks did not abandon the faith entirely, however (Stewart-Abernathy and Ruff 1989). It is apparent that the family's efforts, and Frances's in particular, to adapt their Judaism to frontier conditions led to sometimes painful results. It is perhaps no accident that their choices were closely similar to the currents and experiences that led by the mid-1800s to Reform Judaism, a formalizing of the adaptation that came about not in strong Jewish communities on the eastern coast of the United States but principally in the Mississippi and Ohio valleys. When Abraham died in 1857, his obituary noted that "a good man has fallen in Israel" (*Arkansas Gazette*, 4 April 1857). It was his wife, however, who knew with every meal that was cooked by her slave women under her supervision, in their kitchen behind the house, that in setting aside kashrut she had set aside one of the major responsibilities of a Jewish woman.

At Sanders

In 1847 Simon Sanders's first wife, Zenobia, died, leaving him with three daughters, Sarah Virginia age thirteen, Isabella age ten, and Zenobia age five, "to be cared for in the absence of a mother's loving kindness" (Anonymous n.d.:16). Fortunately, the slave Eliza was present. She saved the day and probably the next seven years until Sanders remarried, for "by the aid of a faithful old colored servant he continued to keep house and keep his children together" (Anonymous n.d.:16). If this is indeed the same Eliza who was reported still living in 1912 (Royston 1912:19), she herself may not have been much more than twenty at the time (according to the 1850 census) and "old" only when the touching if exhausting achievement was noted much later.

It is difficult to know the relationships that developed between Eliza and her three de facto daughters, but she was present during their most formative years and probably trained them. It is likely, to quote Fox-Genovese (1988:35), that "they shared a world of physical and emotional intimacy that is uncommon among women of antagonistic classes and different races." On the other hand, here may have been an apt illustration of what Fox-Genovese (1988:159–161) has asserted is the imbalance at the core of the relationships between Anglo-American and African-American women in slave society. The slave woman had the experience and skills of domesticity but no authority, whereas the slave-holding woman had authority but little experience.

One wonders then at the meanings given by the daughters and their "mother" to an emblem of childhood, a mid-nineteenth-century porcelain doll head of an African-American boy and at an act by Simon Sanders in 1853, when eighteen-year-old Sarah Virginia Sanders married Augustus Garland. At her wedding, her father, still a widower, gave faithful Eliza as a present to Sarah Virginia (Montgomery 1980:165n.18). Such a wedding gift was not uncommon in Arkansas and elsewhere (Taylor 1958:149, 194). It helped to maintain the emotional ties and to provide the beginning family with an important investment both in capital and experience. It is a reminder that there was more to the ties between Eliza and Sarah than emotion—the pupil and "daughter" now owned the teacher and "mother."

Fate of the Kitchens

Kitchen buildings represented major investments in the capital of the urban farmstead. Consequently, their treatment through time provides a good example of factors at work in the reworking of these urban farmsteads to the changing environments within the property and the community. Part of that changing environment was the transition from a slave-based to a nonslave society. The fate of kitchen buildings document that transition and provide the best clue to the contemporary meaning of "separation." In sum, when there were no longer African-American slaves or free servants, the kitchens came in the back door of the house.

Both the Block and Sanders kitchen buildings continued as separate and ostensibly segregated structures into the twentieth century, though their daily function changed. The Block kitchen still served as the primary cooking facility and as servants' quarters until after World War I. When the last African-American cook died or left, the kitchen building was demoted to storage. In the 1920s the first of several kitchen rooms was set up inside the main house, using kerosene-fueled stoves. The kitchen building was virtually abandoned, its disappearance almost unnoticed. It was torn down sometime in the 1950s as part of the early steps toward transformation of the Block house into a static old house museum.

By the turn of the century the Sanders kitchen had also declined. When the urban farmstead was remodeled by the Harkness family sometime in the 1890s, a new kitchen was built that was integral with the house, with the visual effect of squaring off the original L-shaped plan. The original detached kitchen was still used for at least part of its original purpose. From about 1900 until about 1910, the former kitchen room was a servants' quarter for two orphaned African-American girls and the other room a washhouse and storeroom. By the mid-1920s the kitchen building was gone, apparently disassembled (Wilson, personal communication 1992).

CONCLUSION

The Bondwoman's Narrative (Gates 2002), a contemporary novel apparently written by an escaped slave woman, vividly portrays the varying, intimate, and difficult relationships between a lady's maid and her successive female owners in the 1850s. In his preface to a book of letters written by slaves and freemen in the antebellum South, Daniel Miller (1990:9) noted that the "house servant stands in the shadows," still awaiting a major scholarly treatment. Historian Elizabeth Fox-Genovese (1988) went a long distance toward correcting that omission regarding women, but she did not deal with urban women.

Southern kitchens and their occupants also await detailed scholarly treatment. Because what happens in a kitchen physically, emotionally, socially, and symbolically is intimately connected with the house, kitchen buildings were originally important structures in the physical landscape of the town. It has perhaps been possible to illuminate here the lives of town women, particularly African-American slave women, by looking for the kitchen buildings around which much of the labor centered. Those kitchens were assemblages of nails, glass, wood, bricks, sweat, skill, and ideas that provided the space and place for much of the lives of those slave women.

The subservient position of those slave women, and the denigration of women's work in general, is summarized in the conceptualization of kitchens as separate. That notion of separation, more than the physical distance, provides a fine example of habitus and an interesting facet of the segregated southern household. Historical archaeological data suggest the dimensions of spatial and social distance between kitchen and house, between slave and owner, and some of the depth of ambiguity and contradiction.

In its day, Washington served the planters and would-be planters who dreamed of abundance and security in the opportunities of the Cotton Frontier and who lived their lives in close contact with other humans they owned. Many "heritages" of "slavery times" have developed over the century and a half since the Civil War, and many people today, African-American and Anglo-American, are still uncomfortable dealing with research concerning slavery. Today, the abundant data and interpretations from archaeological research at Washington may provide guides and understanding of past human experience in the opportunities and insecurities, ambiguities and complexities, through a postmodern, humanist archaeology.

ACKNOWLEDGMENTS

The field research discussed here would not have been possible without the dedicated help of members of the Arkansas Archeological Society during the Society Annual Training Programs in Washington or without the continued support by the Arkansas Archeological Survey, especially Charles R. McGimsey III, survey director from 1967 to 1990, and Hester A. Davis, state archeologist from 1967 to 1999, with help also from Danny Rankin, superintendent of the park during the fieldwork. Significant research aid was provided by Donald R. Montgomery, then park historian at Old Washington Historic State Park. Appreciation is also extended to Linda Derry, director, Old Cahawba Archaeological Park, for generously providing vivid documented examples of African-American slave women and couples living in kitchens in Cahawba, Alabama.

5
"Living Symbols of their Lifelong Struggles"
In Search of the Home and Household in the Heart of Freedman's Town, Dallas, Texas

James M. Davidson

INTRODUCTION: DALLAS'S URBAN LANDSCAPE, HOUSEHOLDS, AND THEORETICAL ISSUES

The name of a city may remain fixed throughout its existence, but much of what the city is—both physically and culturally—is fluid and constantly shifts over time. Portions are demolished, rebuilt, altered, and forgotten—their meanings rearticulated in ways almost unrecognizable when compared to what existed only a short time before (Boyer 1994).

Recognizing this fluidity, in this chapter I will broach the unrealized potential to be garnered in pursuit of an urban archaeology in Dallas, Texas, hoping to reveal, in part, the origins of modern race constructions as they are explicitly intertwined within the key concepts of power, capitalism, domination, and resistance. Further, the need to recognize the historical roots and important contributions of non-elite (and largely nonwhite) groups in Dallas will be linked to the increasingly complete destruction of the city's oldest black enclave and the absence of any accompanying archaeological investigations.

Through archaeology at the household level, it will be possible to examine the processes of community and social construction that occurred in Dallas's early African-American enclaves. This insight is especially important because these communities were formed within inherently racist societal structures, revealing at least some of the outcomes of racist concepts on the lives of individuals (Orser 1998).

HISTORICAL BACKGROUND

Founded in 1841, by 1850 Dallas had a population of only 163 and had just been permanently selected as the county seat. From such humble beginnings, this tiny agricultural community transformed itself into a major trade center with a population approaching 100,000 by 1910, emerging in the early twentieth century as one of the quintessential capitalist cities of the newly urbanizing and industrializing South (Hill 1996; Holmes and Saxon 1992:85; Kimball 1927:25).

Dallas always had a small, but significant, African-American presence. In 1859, a town census gave the population of Dallas at 775, of which 97 (almost 13 percent) were enslaved African Americans (Kimball 1927:25). After the Civil War, Dallas's black population increased as formerly enslaved peoples in the North Texas area gravitated toward town to search for separated family members and lost friends, to find employment, and to escape the reprisals perpetrated in the countryside by angry whites during Reconstruction (Prior and Schulte 2000a:64–66).

During this period, however, many freedmen and -women in the Dallas area were effectively barred entry into the town of Dallas itself owing to the passage of harsh vagrancy laws just months after emancipation, targeting freedmen with the threat of de facto slavery (imprisonment and hard labor) for up to half a year for each offense (Davidson 1999:22–23; 2000:23–24). To avoid arrest for lack of a job or a home, most blacks moving into the North Texas area did not settle in Dallas proper but instead formed their own communities adjacent to, but clearly outside of, the town. These communities came to be known as Freedman's Town (later called North Dallas), Frog Town, and Deep Ellum, among others (Davidson 1999; McKnight 1990; Prince 1993:31–32; Prior and Schulte 2000b:79, 90). Of these settlements, one of the earliest was Freedman's Town.

There is little extant documentation detailing the early years of North Dallas Freedman's Town. What can be assumed is that its population was likely far in excess of Dallas's own black population. By the end of Reconstruction, one early newspaper account gave an estimate for its population as "over five hundred Negroes living in what is called Freedmantown, adjoining East Dallas" (*Daily Herald* [Dallas], April 27, 1873). One year after this observation was made, at least a portion of Freedman's Town was incorporated into the city of Dallas as a part of the Peak's Addition (Dallas County Deed Records, vol. X, 161).

In 1890, the federal census gave Dallas's population as 38,067, with blacks comprising 21.2 percent of the whole city. By 1910, the population had more than doubled, to 92,104. This increase was also experienced within the African-American communities of Dallas. The 1900 black population of Dallas (n = 9,305) had doubled by 1910 (n = 18,024) (U.S. Federal Census 1900, 1910, s.v. Dallas, Texas). Along with the contiguous Deep Ellum, a commercial district, and Stringtown, the community "strung out" along Central Avenue (the dirt road along the Houston and Texas Central Railroad), Freedman's Town, or North Dallas as it was known by the early twentieth century, had become the largest African-American enclave in the city.

As Dallas was experiencing this rapid growth in the late nineteenth and early twentieth centuries, the simultaneous erosion of black civil rights and the rise of Jim Crow legislation was occurring nationally as well as locally. Leading historians effectively argue that, between 1865 and 1900, the nation as a whole suffered a sea change in its concept of race and in its attitudes toward African Americans (Fredrickson 1971; Woodward 1974).

HISTORIC PRESERVATION IN DALLAS: TWO EXAMPLES

Although Dallas lacked a single, overt symbol for the racialization of non-whites, such as San Antonio had with the Alamo (see Flores 1998, 2002), in a more subtle way its landscape was just as racializing. Of course, the most obviously racializing set of symbols in the postbellum landscape of Dallas is the statuary commemorating the Civil War (Butler 1989). These county, state, and often federally funded pieces of "public art," erected largely between 1880 and the 1930s, are often more about creating and maintaining modern segregation than they are about celebrating the South's lost cause (Loewen 1999:38–39; Savage 1997).

Dallas's own Confederate Memorial was constructed with funds provided by the Daughters of the Confederacy and formally dedicated on April 27, 1897, on the grounds of Dallas's City Park (now known as Old City Park) (Butler 1989:31–33). The Confederate Memorial stood there until 1961, when a highway-widening project for the R. L. Thornton Freeway intruded into a substantial portion of the park grounds and threatened to impact the Memorial. Faced with this danger, city officials decided to move the Memorial to the Pioneer Cemetery adjacent the Dallas Convention Center, where it now stands (Butler 1989:33).

The Confederate Memorial is an imposing monument containing, among other representations, life-size statues of the principal architects of the Confederacy—Jefferson Davis, Robert E. Lee, Albert Sidney Johnston, and Stonewall Jackson. It was built to remember those who fought and gave their lives for the Confederate cause, a cause that, stripped of its ideology of "states' rights" or other hollow rhetoric, ultimately was about the oppression of all people of color. To this day, it stands. True, the Freedman's Cemetery Memorial (erected piecemeal between 1998 and 2002 and still not completed) now stands as its counterpoint, but what of those who actually lived and died under the shadow of the Confederate Memorial when it was freshly minted? What of those who lived under the milieu that produced it?

There are echoes of them in a shotgun house, once standing at 2807 Guillot Street near the center of what was the North Dallas Freedman's Town (the modern-day State Thomas neighborhood). In the 1980s this simple home (one of dozens that once existed in North Dallas) was moved out of the path of construction of Woodall Rodgers Freeway and placed on the grounds of Old City Park, now a heritage village composed of 38 historic homes and other structures relocated onto 13 acres over the past 35 years.

Built in 1906, just nine years after the Confederate Memorial was dedicated, this little three-room house was occupied by a series of working-class Black families throughout the first half of the twentieth century (Hazel 1982; Smith 1986:22). It was moved and preserved, in one sense, just as the Confederate Memorial was moved and preserved, but Dallas's Confederate Memorial is vastly different in one important sense: its preservation was total, just as what it represents was totalizing—a dominant racist and class-based ideology.

The construction of the Confederate Memorial, as a symbol, had everything to do with providing a physical personification of late-nineteenth-century racial dominance (and a commensurate oppression). Societal structures, as well as countless physical structures on the landscape, so loudly proclaimed a white dominance and its corollary, a marginalized African-American population, that the Memorial's construction was merely a showy finial or capstone to a massive, racist societal structure.

Save for communally owned churches and a tiny handful of commercial businesses, there were no comparable monuments in Dallas's cultural landscape erected by African Americans or expressing Black achievement, wealth, or competence in the period between 1841 (Dallas's founding date) and 1936. In that year, the Hall of Negro Life was built at the Texas State Fair grounds for the Texas Centennial, though it was torn down immediately following the celebration in a transparently racist act (Sirigo 1936:72–73).

There are several historical associations in Dallas, all working to preserve the knowledge and landscapes of Dallas's past. Black Dallas Remembered, Inc., the black historical society founded in 1983, has served the community by collecting and publishing family and community histories (e.g., McKnight 1990) as well as by championing the cause of some key sites and historic buildings in the city, such as Freedman's Cemetery (Peter et al. 2000) and the Knights of Pythias Building on Elm Street. The preservation efforts of such groups have focused almost entirely on standing structures or historical research conducted through archival records or oral histories; but, if the only physical elements of African-American history worthy of attention are the handful of extant buildings from the nineteenth and early twentieth centuries, the final legacy is slight indeed.

Without such monuments or impressive and ostentatious displays of wealth as the Confederate Memorial, the only *physical manifestations* or reminders that these African Americans lived were their homes. Certainly the Guillot shotgun house, now restored with period furnishings, is a tribute to the memory of African-American survival and endurance. But, in a very basic sense, it still does not fully represent the inhabitants who once lived within its thin walls. By ripping it from its foundations on Guillot Street and removing it from its context, the hidden story, and perhaps a truer story of those men, women, and children, is lost, and it is evocable and recoverable only through archaeology.

An urban archaeology of the nineteenth and early twentieth centuries can expose modern race constructions through their relationships to both the consumption of material goods and landscape production. Like other recent researchers, I see material consumption as an important mechanism on both sides of the race coin—consumption served both as a racializing marker and as a large part of attempts by the turn-of-the-century African-American community to obtain equality (Hale 1998:121–197; Mullins 1999b:18, 31–32). Analysis of the community at the household level has the potential to reveal a great deal about the lives of the women, men, and children of turn-of-the-century Dallas. We hope that it will enable us to get at daily practice and how such practice both followed and changed the racial and gender structures of the community, the neighborhood, the city, and the region.

To make definitions clear, I see the household as a "task-oriented, co-resident and symbolically meaningful social group that forms the next bigger thing on the social map after an individual" (Hendon 1996:47). In short, it is one of the most basic venues for sharing culture. Of course, the archaeological study of households in an urban context (in the above sense) is a challenging endeavor. The transient nature of urban populations, the variability of depositional activity, and the complex formation processes inherit in urban areas make the connection of artifacts with specific inhabitants difficult at best. The study of nineteenth- and early-twentieth-century urban households, however, holds a very real potential to add to our understanding of the genesis of the modern concepts of class, race, gender, and ethnicity. Indeed, the roots of modern America lie within the remains of nineteenth-century households, for it is during this temporal period that the country transformed itself from an agricultural and small-scale mercantile society into an industrial-based capitalist market economy (Spencer-Wood 1987a:1–2).

Urban Development, Loss of Cultural Identity, and a Call for Urban Archaeology in Dallas

Urban archaeology has come into its own in the United States over the last two decades (e.g., Dickens 1982; Gums et al. 1998; Mayne and Murray 2001; Schuyler 1982; Young 2000). With rare exceptions (Brown 1990; Clark and Juarez 1986; Thomas et al. 1996), however, few historical archaeological investigations of urban landscapes have been conducted in Texas.

The city of Dallas, the focal point of this study, has seen a few historical archaeological projects, but almost all have been excavations in cemeteries (Cooper 2000; Davidson 1999; Peter et al. 2000). As invaluable as these studies are, the almost complete lack of urban archaeological investigations in Dallas at the household level is difficult to understand, especially when one considers the number of past and ongoing construction projects using federal and state funds; these projects subject the construction properties to Section 106 of the National Historic Preservation Act of 1966 and the Antiquities Code of Texas.

For example, the Federal Reserve Bank of Dallas, at 2200 North Pearl Street, was a large-scale, federally funded construction project, completed in 1992. The bank is massive, covering an entire city block with 1,050,000 square feet of office space, yet no archaeological assessment of the project was conducted, in spite of the law (Texas Antiquities Code; Anonymous 2003). To date, only one archaeological investigation of a nineteenth-century urban habitation site has been *professionally* excavated in downtown Dallas, on the grounds of the Dallas County Administration building and Book Depository/6th Floor Exhibit. Dictated by construction demands, these excavations were necessarily limited in spatial extent, cutting across only small portions of five house lots. Consequently, the resulting report of investigations was limited, heavily descriptive, and offered scant interpretation (Jurney and Andrews 1994).

Large-scale right-of-way surveys have been conducted in downtown Dallas and especially the North Dallas Freedman's Town area (e.g., Jurney et al. 1987; Peter 2000:3–4). For example, in 1985 the Texas Department of Highways and Public Transportation (now the Texas Department of Transportation) performed an assessment of historical properties that fell within the expanded right-of-way of North Central Expressway. Although North Central runs through the center of North Dallas Freedman's Town, the only property along this five-mile route identified for further archaeological assessment was Freedman's Cemetery, a property whose protection was already guaranteed by state cemetery laws (Austin 1990; Peter 2000:3–4).

The haphazard enforcement of federal and state antiquities laws in Dallas is puzzling at first glance and, on second reading, troubling, especially when one considers both the location and extent of Dallas's most intensive wholesale demolition and construction efforts of the past 30 years—namely, the downtown Arts District, "City Place," and State Thomas areas. All three are contiguous areas that, together, once constituted the largest African-American enclave in the city, the historic North Dallas Freedman's Town.

North Dallas Freedman's Town:
Issues of Gentrification and Cultural Identity

While not the geographical center of North Dallas Freedman's Town, Freedman's Cemetery, lying between the newly designated "City Place" district and the State Thomas neighborhood, is certainly the metaphorical heart of Dallas's African-American community. Freedman's Cemetery served as the primary burying ground for Dallas's people of color between 1869 and 1907. In the early 1990s, Freedman's Cemetery became the focal point of one of the largest archaeological investigations of a historic cemetery ever conducted in North America. Between 1991 and 1994, the remains of 1,157 men, women, and children were exhumed archaeologically (Condon et al. 1998; Davidson 1999; Davidson et al. 2002; Peter et al. 2000).

Now, this sacred site is marked with a beautiful memorial of bronze figures and commemorative plaques, erected to honor those who suffered the inhumanity of enslavement. The archaeology of Freedman's Cemetery has breathed new life into the exploration and preservation of Dallas's African-American heritage by bringing old memories to the surface (some quite painful). Although the cemetery had suffered repeated injuries over the years—in large part by having one-quarter of the four-acre burial ground paved over by the city of Dallas and Texas Department of Transportation—the archaeological investigation, mandated by state cemetery laws, was a success. Unfortunately, the surrounding North Dallas Freedman's Town has also suffered tremendous injuries—in the loss of population, of homes and businesses, and finally, of archaeological integrity, the last owing to massive construction efforts employed with a total disregard for the hidden story of this once-vibrant community.

When I joined the Freedman's Cemetery Archaeological Project in the spring of 1992, the community surrounding the cemetery was a strange mixture of ostentatious new wealth and urban decay. The gleaming City Place Tower, headquarters of the Southland Corporation, stood just across North Central Expressway to the northeast, while the State Thomas historical district stood marking the southern boundary of Freedman's Cemetery.

Hall Street, forming the northern boundary of the State Thomas area, once contained much of the North Dallas Freedman's Town business district of the 1920s through the 1950s. Some of the businesses once located along this stretch of Hall Street included the Harlem Tavern, the Hall Street Recreation Club, North Dallas Taxi Cab Company, the State Beauty Shop, Papa Dad's Barbeque, the McMillan Sanitarium, and the State Theater, all black-owned businesses (Dallas City Directories, 1930, 1937). Now, not a single structure remains. Dr. Robert Prince (1993), a local avocational historian and author, has written and spoken on the vitality that once existed there.

The first substantial impact to the North Dallas/Freedman's Town community came in the early 1940s through the efforts of the Dallas Housing Authority. To mitigate community demands for better housing and simultaneously to bolster collapsing segregation efforts in Dallas (by offering an alternative to black families who were attempting to settle in hostile white neighborhoods), an exclusively black low-income housing project, Roseland Homes, was proposed. This project was quickly constructed in the North Dallas neighborhood, despite local protests. Completed in 1942, Roseland Homes covered several blocks and destroyed over 100 private homes, replacing them with 650 residential "units" (Sanborn Fire Insurance Company Maps 1921, 1942; Schulte and Prior 2000:193–195).

Additional impacts on the Freedman's Town community came in the 1940s with the construction of North Central Expressway (or U.S. Highway 75, adjacent to Roseland Homes), which replaced the old Central track of the H&TC Railroad with a multiple-lane concrete barrier running through the middle of, and ultimately dividing, the African-American enclave. This construction destroyed the private homes of some 1,500 people (*Dallas Express,* October 5, 1946; Davidson 1999:83–86). In an editorial on the construction of Central Expressway (or Central Boulevard, as it was known in the 1940s), the weekly black newspaper in Dallas painted a vivid picture of the personal loss and misery it caused:

> Questions are coming fast and furious from the many long time residents who must move as their homes must be torn down to make way for the Central Boulevard expressway. Where are we going? What are we going to do? Are they planning on building a project for us? What of my family? These are typical of the questions coming from families as they search frantically from (sic?) someone, anyone who is capable of answers. The city has stated that October 15th is the final date for occupancy for a section that houses 1500 persons. With winter just a few months away, their eviction notice just a few days away, no place available for them to rent and no housing construction for Negroes underway, these persons are facing a crucial time. Already the overcrowded conditions and housing problems are puzzling the nation but with the building of the expressway here, this problem takes on an added headache for Dallasites. Many of the inhabitants are lifelong residents of their particular homes. Their homes are living symbols of their life-long struggles and have been in their families for generations. (*Dallas Express,* October 5, 1946)

Yet another highway construction decimated the community in the early 1960s, when city officials, by right of eminent domain, bought up the right-of-way for the eventual construction of Woodall Rodgers Expressway, a large elevated freeway built piecemeal between the late 1960s and the 1980s (Davidson 1998). The expressway also divided the community and destroyed many historic sites in the process, including private homes and the Boll Street M.E.

Church (Sanborn Fire Insurance Company Maps 1899, 1905, 1921, 1941; Dallas County Deed Records, Plat Maps—Blocks 302, 303, 304, 305; Prior and Schulte 2000b:89; Schulte and Prior 2000:195–196).

Finally, in the late 1970s and early 1980s, multiple "upscale" commercial and residential projects, including the City Place high-rise and its associated developments, began to nibble away at the remaining portions of the historically black North Dallas community. All of the buildings in the State Thomas area, bordering Hall Street and extending southward in a swath three blocks by three blocks, were quickly and systematically moved or razed by real estate speculators gobbling up aging properties. The once-vibrant businesses and hard-won private homes were gone—bulldozed away—while the street signs, sidewalks, and driveways that led to nowhere remained (Flick 1995; Hughs and Fridia 1990:23).

The State Thomas neighborhood was ostensibly assigned protective historic district status in 1984 by the City of Dallas, though only after virtually all of the housing that once belonged to African Americans had been leveled. In 1989, the Dallas City Council designated this area as the city's first "Reinvestment Zone." Reinvestment zones are areas of the city believed to be in need of redevelopment or revitalization; private developers working in these areas have the advantage of tax breaks and other financial incentives (Dallas, City of, 2001; Hughs and Fridia 1990:23).

Owing in part to these incentives, the process of gentrification in the State Thomas neighborhood began in earnest. The first year of the program was 1989; by 1990, a 135-unit apartment complex was completed. Between 1990 and 2002, a total of 16 residential developments with a combined 2,477 residential units (a mixture of townhouses, condos, and apartments) have either been completed or are currently under construction within the State Thomas district (City of Dallas 2001). In the best Disneyland fashion, these condominiums display facades that attempt (and fail) to mimic nineteenth-century architectural styles, as if somehow to justify the historic district designation. In sum, these developments cost an impressive quarter of a billion dollars to construct, of which $18,226,269 was reimbursed to the developers by the City of Dallas through tax relief (Dallas, City of, 2001).

None of these developments are designated as low-income housing. Rather, virtually all of them are luxury apartments and condominiums, with prices for one *mid-range* property (the Gables State Thomas Town Homes) starting at the "special introductory" price of $1,350 a month for a one-bedroom apartment to $2,300 for three bedrooms (*Dallas Morning News* classifieds, January 25, 2002). From the 1990 census, the median household income for residents at Roseland Homes, the World War II–era black housing project, was a mere

$8,875, while the median income in adjacent upscale developments (those that impacted the historic North Dallas Freedman's Town) was over five times as much—$47,344 (McCarthy 2002).

As predominately white middle- and upper-class residential development takes over much of the North Dallas Freedman's Town community, the remaining African-American presence is rapidly declining. For example, Roseland Homes was labeled progressive in its day but by the 1990s was called dangerous, drug-filled, and in need of the wrecking ball (Lyons 1992).

Whether this description was accurate or not, in 1998 the Dallas Housing Authority announced it had received funds from the U.S. Department of Housing and Urban Development (HUD) in the amount of $34.9 million for the demolishment (and only partial replacement) of much of the venerable Roseland Homes (*Dallas Morning News,* September 15, 1998). Every element of Roseland Homes, save for the administration building and two of the 62 red-brick housing units, has been demolished and replaced with "259 public housing units, 40 low cost houses, 100 apartments for low income elderly residents, and 87 market rate apartments. . . . An additional 212 apartments will be erected" on adjacent vacant lots (*Dallas Observer,* February 24, 2000). A federal agency, HUD, is responsible for the demolishment and refurbishment at Roseland Homes, and compliance with federal antiquities law has been followed in this one case: the environmental firm of Geo-Marine, Inc., conducted limited archaeological investigations amid the demolition zone.

Only a handful of vacant lots or areas without ongoing development are currently extant in the North Dallas Freedman's Town area. In the spring of 2002, a survey of the area found fewer than 20 vacant house lots, robbed of their former homes but still left untouched by development, though virtually all of these have signs announcing planned developments in the immediate future. With all of this development in the North Dallas/Freedman's Town area, issues of gentrification have been raised. Certainly there are strong feelings about this issue on the local level (Flick 1995; McCarthy 2002). On a recent visit to the area, I witnessed small billboards advertising an upcoming luxury apartment complex with grafitti of such epithets as "Zoned for Yuppies" and "Yuppies Go Back to The Suburbs."

Representation and Racism

All of this development within what was once the heart of Dallas's Freedman's Town is troubling for several reasons, both past and present, but all interrelated. Working-class African Americans are being forced out of historically black neighborhoods because of upscale development, resulting in rising property values and a continually shrinking base of affordable housing. What is also lost is a critical cultural identity for the African-American community and, finally, there occurs the wholesale destruction or erasure of the "roots" of this community owing to the destruction of the material remains of the Freedman's Town itself. Even the name of the neighborhood has changed. Originally known as Freedman's Town, by the early twentieth century this area was more commonly known to its inhabitants as North Dallas (or "Short North Dallas") and later still the "Hall and State" or "State-Thomas" Neighborhood (Prior and Schulte 2000b:69–79). Stripped of its historical precedence, the current name given to this same area is "Uptown" or the "Citiplace Neighborhood." When even the name of this historically African-American enclave is erased, what then will remain? The ground itself. Surely archaeology can recover what has been lost. But can it?

In 1999, the Texas Historical Commission (THC), the entity responsible for the management of the state's cultural resources, published guidelines for the treatment of late-nineteenth- and early-twentieth-century sites, stating, in general, that such sites would not be considered for inclusion in the National Register of Historic Places and, therefore, would not as a rule receive any archaeological investigation (Denton 1999:13).

Those few historic sites in the state that have proven the exception to these guidelines are typically those with extensive architectural remains (usually in the form of brick or stone masonry), large quantities and varieties of artifact types, or association with a famous individual—usually white, wealthy, and male. Historical archaeologist Kerri Barile examined the ramifications of such policy decisions in a recent and important study of 436 sites in 15 southeastern counties in Texas. Within this large sample, Barile (2004) found that the criteria the THC is stressing, such as large artifact densities and architectural remains, were inherently racist. In her sample, where the race of the former occupants was known, only 6 percent of sites occupied by blacks were considered eligible for inclusion in the National Register, while 77 percent of the white-occupied sites were considered eligible.

The THC guidelines justify the failure to investigate late-nineteenth- and early-twentieth-century sites at any level of the 106 process (i.e., beyond survey) by observing that "archaeological reports are being filled with increasingly redundant data and interpretations on late nineteenth and early twentieth century sites" (Denton 1999:13). So, where are the archaeological reports filled with redundant data that document the late-nineteenth-century African-American experience in Texas and, more specifically, that document excavations of urban households within the North Dallas/Freedman's Town area? In the case of Dallas, suffice it to say there isn't a single report, let alone volume after redundant volume.

To mitigate, at least partially, the lack of excavations within the historic boundaries of the North Dallas Freedman's Town, the work presented here is a necessary first step toward broaching a household archaeology of the nineteenth-century African-American community in Dallas. Available historic documentation was reviewed in order to have a fuller understanding of household composition, income, transience, and cycles. The necessity of such a study is clear: before the last vacant house lot in the historic African-American enclave of Freedman's Town is bulldozed and paved over, it might behoove us to examine just what would be irrevocably lost in the process.

Case Study in the Heart of Freedman's Town: Juliette Street

The street in Freedman's Town/North Dallas once known as Juliette no longer exists (Figure 5.1). It suffered a name change in 1932 to Munger Avenue, and what vestiges of Juliette that do remain lie either beside or beneath the Woodall Rodgers Freeway, the downtown expressway constructed piecemeal between the 1960s and 1980s (Davidson 1998:181–183). Since it was known as Juliette Street at its founding (and for much of its formative history), this name will be used for the street throughout this study.

Although Juliette Street was once several blocks in length, the focus of this study is a single block bounded by Routh (earlier known as Good or Burford) and Boll Streets (Dallas Sanborn Insurance Maps 1899, 1905, 1921, 1941). This portion of Juliette Street was officially abandoned by the Dallas City Council on December 6, 1982 (Dallas City Council 1982). It now consists of a grassy vacant lot, the houses and other buildings once present there razed during construction of the freeway. The area is still undeveloped and, therefore, potentially available for further excavations.

The choice of locale for this study was fortuitous, steered by the existence of a "surface collection" of nineteenth- and early-twentieth-century artifacts recovered in the early 1990s from the Juliette Street area by two individuals, Alexander M. Troup and Tracy Hicks. Mr. Troup, a historian and avocational archaeologist, has for the past 30 years spent much of his spare time researching the early history of Dallas while simultaneously collecting artifacts from construction sites throughout the city (Barbassa 1998). One of the sites from which he made collections was the former Juliette Street, then (as now) a vacant lot adjacent to the YMCA "Field of Dreams" sports complex. At least some portion of this surface collection, in addition to historic artifacts collected from 30 other sites in Dallas, was donated by Troup in 1999 to Texas's primary archaeological repository, the Texas Archeological Research Laboratory at the University of Texas at Austin. Local artist Tracy Hicks, who once kept a studio on Routh Street (and near Juliette), also collected surface artifacts from this field in the early 1990s, later to be used in a "found art" installation entitled "Freedman's Town." Both the Troup and Hicks collections are available for analysis.

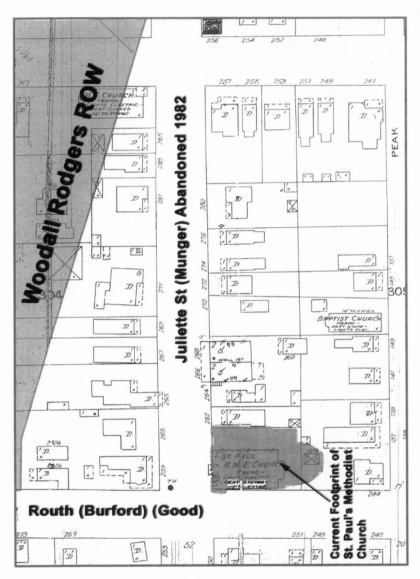

Fig. 5.1. 1899 Sanborn Insurance map of block of Juliette Street, Freedman's Town, Dallas (original maps on file, Dallas Public Library).

Juliette Street lies within the boundaries of the North Dallas/Freedman's Town neighborhood (McKnight 1990; Peter et al. 2000) and was incorporated into the city of Dallas in 1874 as a portion of the Peak's Addition (Dallas County Deed Records, vol. X, 161). From its beginnings, the residential street of Juliette had an African-American presence. For example, as early as 1874, Aaron Cobb, a freedman, purchased for the sum of fifty dollars one-third of a lot located between Cochran and Juliette Streets (Dallas County Deed Records, vol. R, 620). From what can be discerned from archival records, at least this portion of Juliette was always exclusively African-American.

It is possible to reconstruct on paper the simple outlines of this single block of Juliette and its inhabitants through Dallas's city directories, Sanborn Insurance Maps, U.S. Census data, and other archival sources. For this study, the occupants of Juliette will be examined principally between the years 1900 and 1910, an 11-year interval. This time span is in part predicated on the lack of a formal street directory in Dallas's City Directories until 1901. Indexed by street name and individual address, street directories list heads of households for every residence in Dallas. The year 1900, with the detailed information derived from the federal enumeration, will establish a baseline for the block, and city directory data will fill in the gaps between 1901 and 1910.

Street Composition. This block of Juliette was primarily residential in character. Sixteen formal residences were located there between 1900 and 1910 (Figure 5.1). Two African-American churches were also located on this portion of Juliette, one anchoring the block at either end. The Saint Paul United Methodist Church was (and is) located at the corner of Juliette and Routh and the Evening Chapel Methodist Episcopal Church at the corner of Juliette and Boll. Saint Paul's Church was founded on its present location in the summer of 1873, with services first held in a simple brush arbor. A year later, a frame building was moved onto the same lot. The present-day Gothic-style brick structure, begun in 1901, was finally completed in 1925. Of all the structures that once lined this block, St. Paul's is the only survivor, and its congregation and ministry are still very active (DeVaughn 1987:16–17; Prior and Schulte 2000b:91, 104; Sanborn Insurance Maps, Dallas, Texas, 1899, 1905, 1921, 1941).

Other nonresidential entities located on this block of Juliette included key retail businesses. At least one grocery store was present as early as 1886, and by 1891 a second grocery store and meat market was established. Both were owned by African Americans and were in operation during the 1900–1910 study period (Dallas City Directories).

At times, other retail businesses briefly existed on Juliette, both in association with the Rowen grocery store (266–268 Juliette). For example, Leoma Rowen's millinery and fancy goods shop was established in 1906 at 266 Juliette, where the Rowen meat market was formerly located. By 1910, this millinery shop was gone, and Israel Townsend had opened a tailor shop in its place. This latter business had failed by 1912. Besides the retail shops, several people worked in their homes; between 1901 and 1910, six heads of household (all women) were laundresses working out of their own homes (Dallas City Directories).

Household Demography. At the time of the 1900 federal census enumeration, a total of 71 individuals lived in the 16 residences on this block of Juliette (Table 5.1). Ages ranged from babies almost a year old to seventy-year-old Mahala Pruett, a woman born in 1830. In 1900, at the dawn of the twentieth century, almost a third of the block's residents (n = 26) had been born prior to emancipation and almost certainly had experienced the horrors of slavery. The average age of all the people living on this block was twenty-four years.

The smallest household consisted of only two persons, while the largest contained eight. Virtually all of the households on Juliette Street were composed of individuals interrelated by kin ties. That is, each household, at its core, contained a complete (or remnant) nuclear family, consisting of at least one parent and children (some fully grown). Eighty-one percent of the households on Juliette contained a husband and wife (n = 13), while only three were composed of a single parent (in all cases, widowed) and children. This differs remarkably from household organization in Dallas just twenty years before. An analysis of the 1880 federal census found that within Dallas's African-American community, over one-third of the heads of household were women, likely owing to the combined disruptions of enslavement, the war itself, and finally the horrors of Reconstruction (Engerrand 1978:206–207).

Most couples had offspring living with them at the time of enumeration, and three households contained a single grandparent. Thus, 12 of the 16 households held two generations (75 percent), two held three generations (19 percent), and one (281 Juliette) contained only a single generation (a husband and wife without any offspring resulting from the marriage). Only four lodgers (in three houses) were noted on Juliette in the 1900 census.

As historian Herbert Gutman (1976a) established through extensive research, despite much rhetoric to the contrary, the American black family did not "disintegrate" following emancipation, and it did not falter with migration to urban centers in the late nineteenth century. Gutman (1976a:433) readily demonstrated that no matter the time period or the setting, the typical black household contained two parents. His findings correspond with Juliette Street; in 1900, households composed of two-parent nuclear families (in some cases with additional persons, such as lodgers, older parents, etc.) were known in every case, save for three cases of single-parent households resulting from the death of a spouse.

Housing. Although no aboveground architectural elements remain on Juliette Street, it is possible to examine archivally some aspects of the structures that

Table 5.1 1900 Federal census enumeration for Juliette Street, Dallas, Texas (abridged).

Street Number	Last Name	First Name	Relation	Color or Race	Sex	Year of Birth	Age (at Last Birthday)	Marital Status	Years Married	How Many Children	Children Living	Place of Birth	Occupation	Can Read	Can Write	Home – Owned or Rent
259	Johnson	Starling R.	Head	B	M	1860	39	m	5			unk	porter	yes	yes	owned
259	Johnson	Lula	wife	B	F	1872	27	m	5	2	2	Texas		yes	yes	
259	Johnson	Starling R. Jr.	son	B	M	1896	4	s				Texas				
259	Johnson	James A.	son	B	M	1897	3	s				Texas				
260	Collins	Henry?	Head	B	M	1862	38	wid		2	2	Texas	cooking (private family)	yes	yes	owned
260	Jones	Henry	son	B	M	1879	20	s				Texas	day laborer	yes	yes	
260	Jones	Mary	dau	B	F	1881	18	s				Texas	nurse	yes	yes	
262	Cole	Thomas	Head	B	M	1861	39	m	20	4	4	Texas	day laborer	yes	yes	owned
262	Cole	Nora	wife	B	F	1864	36	m	20	4	4	Texas		yes	yes	
262	Cole	Della	dau	B	F	1884	15	s				Texas	attends school	yes	yes	
262	Cole	Sallie	dau	B	F	1888	12	s				Texas	attends school	yes	yes	
262	Cole	Viola	dau	B	F	1889	10	s				Texas	attends school	yes	yes	

No.	Surname	Given	Relation	Race	Sex	Birth	Age	Marital	Yrs. Married	Children Born	Children Living	Birthplace	Occupation			Own/Rent
263	Edmondson	Aron	Head	B	M	1850	50	m	20			Tennessee	laborer (gravel roofer)	no	no	owned
263	Edmondson	Mary	wife	B	F	1860	40	m	20	5	4	Tennessee	wash woman	no	no	
263	Edmondson	Clarence	son	B	M	1877	22	s				Texas	porter (whole-sale drugs)	yes	yes	rent
263	Edmondson	Roberta	dau	B	F	1881	18	s				Texas		yes	yes	
263	Edmondson	Beaulah	dau	B	F	1884	16	s				Texas		yes	yes	
264	Sparks	John	Head	B	M	1877	23	wid				Texas	coachman	yes	yes	owned
264	Allan	Sam	Head	B	M	1875	24	m	3			Texas	laborer (city park)	yes	yes	rent
264	Allan	Annie	wife	B	F	1880	20	m	3	1	1	Texas	wash woman	yes	yes	
264	Allan	Nellie D.	dau	B	F	1899	1	s				Texas				
265	Hamilton	Lucinda	Head	B	F	1861	39	wid		5	4	Texas	grocery store owner	yes	yes	owned
265	Hamilton	Almeda?	dau	B	F	1882	18	s				Texas		yes	yes	
265	Hamilton	Jesse	son	B	M	1883	16	s				Texas		yes	yes	
265	Hamilton	Stillawell	son	B	M	1890	9	s				Texas				
269	Johnson	Denzel?	Head	B	M	1860	40	m	1			unk	farm laborer	no	no	rent
269	Johnson	Susie	wife	B	F	1864	35	m	1	2	2	Texas	wash woman	yes	yes	
269	Abrom	Callie	step dau	B	F	1883	17	s				Texas		yes	yes	
269	Abrom	Ella	step dau	B	F	1885	15	s				Texas		yes	yes	

Continued on the next page

Table 5.1 *Continued*

Street Number	Last Name	First Name	Relation	Color or Race	Sex	Year of Birth	Age (at Last Birthday)	Marital Status	Years Married	How Many Children	Children Living	Place of Birth	Occupation	Can Read	Can Write	Home – Owned or Rent
269	Johnson	Clarence	son	B	M	1891	9	s				Texas				
269	Pruett	Mahala	m-in-law	B	F	1830	70	wid		11	1	Missouri		no	no	
270	Wadkins	Richard	Head	B	M	1858	41	m	5			Texas	laborer (R.R.)	yes	yes	rent
270	Wadkins	Ella	wife	B	F	1864	35	m	5	1	1	Texas	wash woman	yes	yes	
270	Rhine	Bessie M.	step dau	B	F	1887	13	s				Texas	attends school	yes	yes	
271	Rowen	Doc	Head	B	M	1860	40	m	21?			Alabama	grocery store owner	yes	yes	owned
271	Rowen	Nannie	wife	B	F	1861	38	m	20	6	6	Tennessee	grocery store owner	yes	yes	
271	Rowen	Lena	dau	B	F	1882	17	s				Texas	attends school	yes	yes	
271	Rowen	Fred	son	B	M	1883	16	s				Texas	deliveryboy (grocery store)	yes	yes	
271	Rowen	Ray	son	B	M	1889	10	s				Texas	attends school	yes	yes	

271	Rowen	Mozella	dau	B	F	1890	9	s				Texas		no	no	rent
271	Rowen	Jerome	son	B	M	1895	5	s				Texas		yes	yes	
271	Rowen	Doc	son	B	M	1897	3	s				Texas				
272	Reese	Jane	Head	B	F	1858	41	wid		3	3	Texas	wash woman	yes	no	
272	Reese	Iberfield ?	son	B	M	1881	18	s				Texas	bottler (soda water)	yes	yes	
274	Wilkerson	Elvis ??	Head	B	M	1840	60	wid		15?	7	Kentucky		yes	no	rent
274	Wilkerson	Henry	son	B	M	1875	25	s				Texas	move wagon driver	yes	yes	
274	Wilkerson	Calvin	son	B	M	1878	22	m	11/12			Texas	farm laborer	yes	yes	
274	Wilkerson	Lula	d-in-law	B	F	1879	20	m	11/12	1	1	Indian Terr		yes	yes	
274	Wilkerson	Christin	grand dau	B	F	1899	6/11	s				Texas				
276	Anderson	Randal?	Head	B	M	1879	21	m	5			Texas	cook (private family)	yes	yes	rent
276	Anderson	Roena	wife	B	F	1874	25	m	5	2	2	Texas		yes	yes	
276	Anderson	James S.	son	B	M	1896	3	s				Texas				
276	Anderson	Benny	son	B	M	1899	11/12	s				Texas				
276	Moss	Willie	lodger	B	M	1879	21	s				Texas	waiter (restaurant)	no	no	

Continued on the next page

Table 5.1. Continued

Street Number	Last Name	First Name	Relation	Color or Race	Sex	Year of Birth	Age (at Last Birthday)	Marital Status	Years Married	How Many Children	Children Living	Place of Birth	Occupation	Can Read	Can Write	Home – Owned or Rent
280	Staples	Sam (?)	Head	B	M	1856	44	m	25			Mississippi	janitor (church)	no	no	rent
280	Staples	Lou (Louise?)	wife	B	F	1859	41	m	25	7	4	Mississippi	sick nurse	no	no	
280	Staples	Staples	son	B	M	1881	19	s				Texas	coachman	yes	yes	
280	Staples	Arthur	son	B	M	1885	15	s				Texas	attends school	yes	yes	
280	Readolick ??	Rightney??	lodger	B	M	1880	20	s				unk	cook (B-house)	yes	yes	
280	Holiness?	Willie	lodger	B	M	1883	17	s				unk	coachman	yes	yes	
281	Canard	Andy	Head	B	M	1850	50	m	25	0	0	Tennessee	farm laborer	no	no	owned
281	Canard	Carrie	wife	B	F	1853	46	m	25	0	0	Texas		no	no	
283	Cooksey	Doc (Lex)	Head	B	M	1865	34	m	11			Texas	cook (private home)	yes	yes	owned
283	Cooksey	Sophronia (?)	wife	B	F	1864	36	m	11	5	2	Texas	wash woman	no	no	
283	Cooksey	Crayborn D.	son	B	M	1896	3	s				Texas				
283	Cooksey	Louise?	dau	B	F	1899	11/12	s				Texas				

283	Burton ?	Amanda	m-in-law	B	F	1844	56	wid		9	6	Mississippi		no	no	no
283	Akin	Kate	lodger	B	F	1855	45	wid?		1	1	unk	cook (private family?)	no	no	no
285	Bolden	Richard	Head	B	M	1860	39	m	10			Texas	teamster	yes	yes	yes
285	Bolden	Susan	wife	B	F	1860	40	m	10	1	1	Virginia		yes	yes	yes
285	Bolden	Margarett	adopted dau	B	F	1896	3	s				Texas				owned

Table 5.2 Estimated square footage of residences on Juliette Street.*

Street Number	Square Feet*	Adults (16+)	Subadults (15 or Younger)	Total No. of Individuals	Square Footage per Person
259	1100	2	2	4	275
260**	—	—	—	—	—
262	500	2	3	5	100
263	630	5	0	5	126
264	380	3	1	4	95
265	750	3	1	4	188
269	525	3	3	6	88
270	375	2	1	3	125
271	800	4	4	8	100
272	300	2	0	2	150
274	600	4	1	5	120
276	600	3	2	5	120
280	630	5	1	6	105
281	400	2	0	2	200
283	525	4	2	6	88
285	600	2	1	3	200

average square feet of residences = 581
average square footage per person = 139

*All calculations derived from the 1899 Sanborn Insurance map of the block.
**Listed in 1900 census, but is not demarcated on any Sanborn map.

once stood on the block. First, all of the houses on Juliette were single-story frame buildings (1899 Dallas Sanborn Maps). In addition, following the outline of the architectural footprint for each house on the 1899 Dallas Sanborn map, the approximate square footage for each of the residences was calculated (Table 5.2). The largest home was approximately 1,100 square feet, the smallest a tiny 300 square feet; the average residence was a scant 581 square feet, or an average of a 10-×-14-foot space per person.

There was a minor correlation between the number of individuals within a household and the size of the house itself; only two people lived in the smallest house, while the largest household resided in one of the larger houses on the block (271 Juliette had eight individuals living in 800 square feet). This house belonged to Dock Rowen, a prominent businessman and owner of the adjacent grocery store.

Home Ownership/Household Stability. One basic variable established during archival research was a relatively high degree of instability of residence for families in Dallas at the turn of the century. Certainly, a select few of the 16 residences contained families who had lived in those homes for decades. For example, Starling Johnson, living at 259 Juliette Street in 1886, was still residing there in 1910. In contrast, at 274 Juliette, over a ten-year interval, there were seven different families (or single men) living there. For this block of Juliette as a whole, the average stability of residence measure was 26 percent, calculated over a ten-year interval (see Table 5.3). These figures mean that, on average, a family living on this block of Juliette would vacate their home and a new family would move in every 2.5 years (Dallas City Directories). Household stability is, in large part, a reflection of home ownership (Table 5.1). Of the 16 households on Juliette, 10 owned their own homes (62.5 percent), with only one of these mortgaged in 1900 (U.S. Federal Census, Dallas, Texas 1900). Of the rental properties, five of the six (83 percent; see Table 5.1, Figure 5.1) were located together in a single "block" on the southeast side of Juliette.

The transience exhibited on Juliette is somewhat mitigated by a study done in the 1970s. Engerrand (1978) examined the stability of residence for African Americans living in Dallas between 1880 and 1910. He revealed that their persistence rate (32 percent), by continuing to reside in Dallas over the course of 30 years, exceeded that of whites by about 10 percent. Thus, while movement of families from residence to residence within Dallas may have been a common occurrence, complete migration out of the city was not.

Occupations. Another variable that could change over time within a single residence was the principal occupation of the head of household. While occupations could be highly stable (e.g., Starling Johnson at 259 Juliette, who worked as a porter for the same employer for at least 10 years), it was also not uncommon for an individual to change jobs from year to year. For example, between 1903 and 1910, James Thomas (at 264 Juliette) was, depending upon the year, a common laborer, a buggy washer, a hostler, a driver for a transfer company, a porter, or a watchman (Dallas City Directories).

Even individuals who were highly stable in their residence (e.g., Jane Reese, who resided at 272 Juliette for at least 15 years) could still change not only their jobs but also the basic kinds of work that they performed from year to year. Jane Reese's occupation was most often given as a laundress, but occasionally, she was listed as a domestic and a cook. The rapid change of occupations that

Table 5.3 Juliette Street stability of residence {% of change over 10-year interval (1901–1910)}.*

Number	Street Address	Percentage
1	259	0
	260 (listed only 1 yr)	
2	262	10
3	263	30
4	264	10
5	265	0
	266-68 (store)	
6	267	30
7	269	50
8	270	40
9	271	0
10	272	0
11	274	60
12	276	50
13	280	30
14	281	40
15	283	40
16	285	30

Average Stability Rate = 26.25%
or, on average a new family moving into a residence every 2 and 1/2 years
*(e.g.; same resident (or surname) for 10 years = 0%; new resident every year = 90%)

occurred in some of the households on Juliette may have been a contributing factor to the noted household instability. It also likely had direct consequences on the economic levels of the household.

Social Class/Socioeconomics. The study of socioeconomics (class or status) is commonplace in historical archaeology (e.g., Spencer-Wood 1987a). As pointed out by Singleton (1999a:2–4), however, specifically in African-American archaeology, problems of ethnicity and race have dominated the field, while studies of social class or economics have received less emphasis. She believes that this is owing to an a priori assumption that African Americans would naturally occupy the lowest tiers of any social system.

Obviously, social class or status is, at all times, situational. Given this, complete success in measuring status would be virtually impossible to achieve, primarily because of the fundamental problem of delineating and describing something that is constantly in flux and is profoundly influenced by race, ethnicity, age, gender, marital status, location, and life cycle, as well as by income.

In an attempt to establish at least a simplistic understanding of the socioeconomic levels of the residences on Juliette Street, information was compiled denoting the occupation of each individual head of household (as well as others living in the house who were discernible in the directories) between 1901 and 1910. To this list were assigned average annual incomes, based on an estimated average calculated for the United States in 1900 by Preston and Haines in their 1991 work *Fatal Years, Childhood Mortality in Late Nineteenth-Century America*. Given the crudity of these estimations (which exclude the possibility of others contributing funds to the household, known to be true for some households from the 1900 census, and do not account for local economic conditions), the resulting estimated annual incomes must be considered only as a relative scale and not a true measure.

On Juliette Street, what was immediately apparent was the extreme variability of incomes at any given time. The greatest estimated salary was $1,100 per annum. Two people were assigned this salary—Dock Rowen and Lucinda Hamilton, who owned the block's two grocery stores. The lowest annual wages belonged to the women who listed their occupations as laundresses. In 1900, the average annual wages paid for laundry washed by hand was a mere $209 (Preston and Haines 1991:212–220).

Spatially, the few relatively affluent households were not isolated from the less affluent households. For example, Dock Rowen, the richest man on the block (and one of the richest black men in Dallas), owning both a large home and a thriving grocery and real estate business, lived immediately across the street from one of the poorest households on Juliette (occupied by Jane Reese, who most often gave her occupation as laundress).

While it was apparent on Juliette that economic levels could vary widely among households, it was also revealing that they could vary for a single family or head of household. For example, between 1903 and 1910, James Thomas, residing at 264 Juliette, held six different kinds of jobs with estimated annual salaries ranging from a low of $373 to a high of $592 (Preston and Haines 1991:212–220).

Finally, because the 16 residences on this block of Juliette had, on average, a new family residing within them every two and a half years, the economic levels observed within a single residence (i.e., structure) through time could vary widely, depending upon the family. In households with a married couple, in addition to the men's employment, wives worked outside of the home in just over half the cases (7 out of 12, or 58 percent), with a very narrow range of jobs typical of the period (five washerwomen, compared to only one "sick" nurse and a grocery store owner) (U.S. Federal Census, Dallas, Texas 1900).

It is likely that within Dallas's African-American community, Juliette Street was considered a highly desirable place to live. Individuals of apparent high social status lived on Juliette or in its immediate vicinity as early as the 1870s. For example, in 1880, of the eight officers and founding members of the first African-American Masonic lodge in Dallas (Paul Drayton Lodge No. 9, founded in 1876), three lived on Juliette Street and an additional member lived one block away (1880–1881 Dallas City Directory). In addition, the Masonic Lodge Hall was itself located on Juliette, one block to the south. Fraternal orders and secret societies were an important aspect of nineteenth- and early-twentieth-century American life. Beyond the sheer utility of such organizations (e.g., health and death benefits), membership in one or more lodges brought with it a certain social distinction, helping to establish for its members a high level of status within Dallas's African-American community.

Household Cycles. Certainly in these sixteen residences, family cycles were played out; people got married, children were born, people changed jobs, people grew richer or poorer, aged, and finally died. While the marriages and births that occurred on this block of Juliette Street have yet to be established, it is possible at least to delineate the occupational changes that occurred to the various heads of household. In addition, for research associated with the Freedman's Cemetery Project in Dallas, I compiled a database of all known African-American deaths occurring in the city between 1900 and 1907. This database contains 1,514 individuals. For several hundred of them, it is known where death occurred or where the deceased were living at the time of death. For only this block of Juliette Street and these 16 residences, between 1900 and 1907, at least five individuals died. These deaths ranged from a three-year-old girl dying of pneumonia to 100-year-old Charles Spears, who succumbed to the effects of old age. Obviously, a death in the family can be emotionally exhausting, financially draining, and disruptive to the lives of the survivors for years.

AFTER FREEDOM CAME: THE HEART OF THE MATTER

For all intents and purposes, Reconstruction ended in Dallas in November 1872, a time that saw the first general elections since military rule had been imposed (Cochran 1928:221). It was also in 1872 that the Freedman's Bureau ceased to exist (Bergman 1969:271). Without the backing of armed federal troops, local blacks attempting to exercise their voting rights (or most of the rights granted them during Reconstruction) would have run considerable personal risk. Statewide, Reconstruction ended during the years of 1875 and 1876, when the Texas

State Constitution was rewritten and ratified by white Democrats, who rejected outright the previous constitution framed in 1869 by a Republican-dominated Congress (Barr 1996:70–71).

Reconstruction came to a close with the restoration of local (and white) political autonomy, with recently freed blacks once more relegated to a relatively powerless and subservient position. Simply put, the previously known paternalistic model of race relations, as practiced by whites over blacks, had been largely restored by 1874. Without the power to challenge this loss of political and legislated freedoms directly, freedmen and -women had to find other ways to chip away at the white viewpoint—namely, an inherent social and racial inferiority—regarding them. One fundamental way to extend the limits of their freedoms was through economic advance and subsequent consumerism, in part by the purchase of decent housing.

The necessity and desire for a home was paramount in the minds of many African-Americans in Dallas. On September 2, 1900, in an address to a large crowd in attendance at the "Colored Fair" in Dallas, the Reverend A. S. Jackson, pastor of the New Hope Baptist Church, said that "if he were asked to name, in a word, the greatest need of the negroes, he would say that that need was 'homes'" (*Dallas Times Herald*, September 2, 1900).

The homes that Reverend Jackson spoke of in 1900 were built by the hundreds in North Dallas, lived in for decades, and are now all but gone. Even the memory of their presence is fast fading. In this chapter, no mean amount of space has been spent discussing the limited aspects of some sixteen of these homes, as well as the families that resided in them—at least as they are discernible from the archival record between 1900 and 1910. As shown, some of the story of Freedman's Town is recoverable in this manner, though, save for a name in a city directory or a birth year in a census enumeration, little more can be gleaned from conventional sources, which are almost inevitably biased toward the dominant society.

As an end in itself, then, this archival study is frustratingly limited, sketching only the dim outlines of the players involved and the physical confines wherein they lived their lives. In 1900, one-third of those who lived on Juliette Street were born prior to emancipation and experienced the inhumanity of enslavement, while the rest were the children of formerly enslaved peoples. Certainly the final outcome of many of these lives is discernible from the Freedman's Cemetery excavations and analyses (Davidson 1999; Davidson et al. 2002; Peter et al. 2000). But what of the space between birth and death, what of the insights into their personal lives, their joys, and hard choices?

Frustrated by the lack of household archaeology in Dallas, researchers from the University of Texas at Austin (UT) (Dr. Maria Franklin, Jamie Brandon, and myself) have recently sought the answers to these questions by broaching an urban archaeological study in downtown Dallas. Between June 5 and July 15, the 2002 UT Archaeological Field School was held in the city; its focus was the North Dallas Freedman's Town area. We worked in a community partnership with the staff and congregation of Saint Paul United Methodist Church (the only survivor on Juliette Street) and directed our efforts at the now vacant house lot adjacent to, and owned by, the church (originally 262 Juliette, later known as 2606 Juliette).

During the 1900–1910 period, this simple house was the residence of Thomas Cole, his wife, Nora, and their four daughters, Henrietta, Della, Sallie, and Viola. Thomas Cole was, depending upon the year, a day laborer, carpenter, and one-half owner in a feed and fuel enterprise. The entire family were members of St. Paul's, and Thomas Cole served as a trustee for the church. A house was present on this lot, and a series of working-class African-American families resided on the property from its initial purchase in 1880 to 1962, when the structure was razed and the lot purchased by the church (Dallas City Directories).

Some insight into the choices made by the Cole family and others who lived there after them are observable in the artifacts recovered during the field school's excavation. They include household ceramics, food refuse (e.g., animal bone, oyster shell), bottle and table glass, elements of clothing (e.g., buttons, buckles), tools, toys, personal items, and such household decorative items as ceramic figurines and other kinds of bric-a-brac.

Paul Mullins (1999a, 1999b, 1999c, 2001), who has written extensively in regard to African-American consumerism during the Victorian age, views the purchase of such decorative objects as especially telling. Mullins argues persuasively that during the late-nineteenth- and early-twentieth-century period, consumerism was perceived as a key means by which blacks might cast off their white-imposed mantle of inferiority and achieve a measure of equality through judicious consumption. Such acts of consumerism may have been perceived as one of the steps toward equality, but salvation through consumption could also be a trap, a game played on an uneven playing field with a set of rules that, as defined by the dominant class, was constantly changing.

Think of it: out of a seemingly endless variety of mass-produced goods available for purchase in this period, what did a formerly enslaved family choose to own? Conceivably, each individual purchase of food, clothing, plate, and cup was charged with important and involved meanings, all contested and virtually invisible without the aid of archaeology.

Other artifacts may be less contentious but no less powerful as symbols. For example, several common sad irons of various sizes were recovered in the 1990 surface collections. Their number and variety suggest a direct association with the women who once lived on Juliette and made their living by taking in washing and ironing at home; six are known from the period 1900–1910—Emma

Fig. 5.2. African-American cosmetic compact: "High Brown Face Powder" (ca. 1911–1930).

Hicks, Jane Reese, Mary Revis, Maria Nelson, Izlia Jackson, and Callie Cunnard (Dallas City Directories).

These women were not alone. By the turn of the twentieth century, over one-third of working African-American women in Dallas labored as laundresses, and such labors had their costs. From a bioarchaeological analysis of the remains recovered from Freedman's Cemetery, of those individuals interred during the time span of the Juliette archival study, one-third of the women displayed signs of moderate to severe osteoarthritis in the shoulder and elbow joints (Davidson et al. 2002). This degenerative joint condition is entirely consistent with the monotonous action of scrubbing and ironing countless loads of laundry. The recovery of a sad iron from an abandoned block in the old North Dallas Freedman's Town, an artifact type whose presence in the past could be predicted from archival records with something approaching a 100 percent certainty, still has the power to evoke the life of those who labored there.

Another artifact, this one recovered from the 2002 field school excavations of the Cole House, also evokes the daily practice of women in North Dallas Freedman's Town. The artifact is a round, brass cosmetic compact (Figure 5.2). Embossed on its lid is a miniature depiction of an African-American woman, framed by the words "High Brown/Overton/Chicago." The compact was recovered from Feature 10, a shallow rectangular trash pit located in the backyard of the Cole House lot.

The compact was a product of the Overton Hygienic Manufacturing Company, a firm founded by African-American entrepreneur Anthony Overton in 1898 in Kansas City, Missouri. Originally specializing in the manufacture of baking powder, by 1903 Overton had switched to the manufacture and sale of a line of cosmetics especially designed for women of color. The compact recovered from Feature 10 likely contained High Brown Face Powder and necessarily dates to 1911 or later, since it bears the "Chicago" mark, reflecting the move the company made to that city in that year (Anonymous 1997; White and White 1998:185).

This compact is small but hardly insignificant. Like the sad irons, its existence marks the presence of women within the household. But its presence also marks something else. In late-nineteenth- and early-twentieth-century America, a myriad of cosmetic products was produced exclusively for African-American women. Some of the most common types of products on the market were hair straighteners and skin "lightening" agents (White and White 1998:169–172, 187–188). Advertisements for such products were commonplace in turn-of-the-century Dallas. For example, the local black weekly newspaper carried ads for Scott's Magic Hair Straightener and Scott's Face Bleach and Beautifier (Dallas Express, January 13, 1900). Such products have been interpreted as signifying attempts made by African Americans to emulate white conceptions of beauty and acceptability, motivated by an internalized white racist viewpoint regarding their own appearance (White and White 1998:169–172, 187–188).

Significantly, the compact recovered from the backyard area of the Cole house lot contained not a preparation designed to make one more "white" in appearance but rather was specifically formulated to enhance the natural beauty of women of color—a subtle difference but an important one, and one not recoverable save for archaeology.

HOUSEHOLD ARCHAEOLOGY: THE NEXT STEP

This work is just the smallest step taken toward the goal of understanding some of the societal processes that African-American families both experienced and created in the earliest stages of building a life for themselves after enslavement. Detailed analyses of the 2002 field school materials will aid in this process, and it is hoped that work on the remaining portions of Juliette Street will be possible in the near future. As shown through the archival record, with a predominance of single-family households, a minimum of two retail businesses, and two churches, this single block of Juliette could serve as a proxy for the whole of Black Dallas. With its 18 structures, it encompasses nearly the full economic range, from Dallas's black elite (Dock Rowen) to its working poor (Jane Reese), and contains virtually every aspect of daily life—home, commercial, spiritual, and social.

Unfortunately, this last intact portion of Juliette Street, which is itself the most intact remaining portion of the earliest Freedman's Town area, is facing complete destruction in the immediate future. The City of Dallas has plans to expand greatly its Arts District, which lies immediately to the south and east of this former block. Specifically, the Dallas Museum of Natural History has plans to build an annex museum on the property, which would in the process destroy with utter finality one of the last remaining vestiges of this city's Freedman's past.

Controlled excavations within the rest of Juliette Street—before construction is allowed—of features such as house foundations, yard activity areas, privies, and wells/cisterns would allow us to assign recovered materials to known households and to delineate different levels of socioeconomics or class within the African-American families that once lived there. The extant surface collections allow insight into race (and its consequences) only in a general sense, while the controlled excavations of all of Juliette Street would allow us even greater insight and the ability to discern differences based on race, class, and gender.

The Juliette Street archaeological materials are of enormous value, representing, as a whole, the economic levels and consumer choice of a single racial group in nineteenth- and early-twentieth-century Dallas. Because it does not restrict itself to a single, narrow temporal frame or a single topic and methodology, the Juliette Street Study would encompass virtually the entire history of the city of Dallas from Reconstruction to the present day in miniature, especially illuminating the lives of African-American families as they struggled and overcame great adversity to form the nucleus of a middle class.

ACKNOWLEDGMENTS

Thanks first must go to Jamie Brandon, who offered sage advice and helped get the Dallas project off the ground. My wife, Lydia, assisted me throughout the research and writing process. I am also indebted to both Alexander M. Troup and Tracy Hicks, who in the early 1990s salvaged artifactual materials from the Juliette Street area that would otherwise have been lost and made both their collections accessible for research. Their actions brought my attention to the Juliette Street area. Certainly my advisor, Dr. Maria Franklin, has assisted me in many ways, in large part by conducting the 2002 University of Texas field school on Juliette Street. Thanks are also extended to all of the field school students, who labored long and well under the hot North Texas sun. Finally, I would like to thank Ms. Leah Parker, Mr. Ingram, Reggie Smith and Eva Cox (both relatives of Thomas and Nora Cole), Mrs. Dolores (Hoover) Love, Mrs. Eva McMillan, the Reverend Sharon Patterson, and the rest of the staff and congregation of the St. Paul United Methodist Church, Dallas, Texas. These good people allowed the UT field school to excavate the former Cole House lot and in their kindness shared old photographs, memories, time, and energy.

Part II
A Sense of Space

6

Finding the Space Between Spatial Boundaries and Social Dynamics

The Archaeology of Nested Households

Nesta Anderson

INTRODUCTION

The concept of space is essential to the archaeological study of households. However, archaeologists are aware that spatial analysis requires boundaries, which often leads to their viewing the social concept of household as a bounded unit. Although this is difficult to avoid, sometimes in creating these bounded categories for initial discussion, we lose sight of the dynamic human interaction that creates the household. The dilemma is that boundaries are necessary for coherent analysis, but a fluid definition of household is also necessary to avoid a static analysis of social relationships within and between households.

In this chapter I present a discussion of the concept of household and attempt to define household in a way that is both spatially bounded and socially fluid. An application of this definition focusing primarily on the African-Bahamian population during the period of enslavement in the Bahamas follows this discussion.

EXISTING DEFINITIONS OF HOUSEHOLD

Among the numerous definitions for the concept of household, many scholars agree that co-residence is a necessary criterion, although some argue there are degrees of co-residence (Wilk and Netting 1984:19). Also, the ideal living arrangement, for example the nuclear family in our society, is not always attained (Bender 1967:493). Other definitions focus less on co-residence and concentrate instead on relationships among household members (e.g., Goody 1972; Hammel and Laslett 1974; Kramer 1982). Often this focus results in the equation of the concepts of family and household, which causes confusion when exploring the relationship between non-kin co-residents or in a situation involving fictive kin.

Spatial dimension is implicit in the concept of co-residence. If people are living together, they are sharing space. In different contexts, the residential area will occupy different spaces. In some instances, residential space may include more than one building, such as houses, detached kitchens, privies, etc. This idea is an extremely important consideration when one is excavating the spatial component of a household, as spatial patterning is a primary source of information in archaeological research.

Another criterion of household that may be related to space archaeologically is the idea that household members engage in productive activities to maintain the household's existence. These activities may be concentrated in specific areas and may leave artifact concentrations that archaeologists investigate as "activity areas." Wilk and Netting (1984:6) define production as "human activity that procures or increases the value of resources. We include housekeeping and domestic labor of the kind stereotyped as nonproductive in our society." Although the roles of noncontributors (such as children or the elderly) may be questioned, they may be seen as part of the process of reproduction. In this sense, children will be future producers, and the elderly may be seen as teachers of behavior that reproduces societal norms and values.

Reproduction of culture or society leads to the idea of the household life cycle (e.g., Donley 1982; Hugh-Jones 1995; Tringham 1990; Waterson 1995). Households change over time as members are born, die, leave, or marry. However, in studying a household, it is necessary to impose boundaries on the process of household formation and decomposition. Usually, this definition involves focusing on one or two people who head the household from the time they establish it until their death, which often signals the death of the household. The idea of household life cycles are especially important to archaeologists, as the archaeological record often shows multiple households at different stages in the household life cycle.

FACTORS AFFECTING HOUSEHOLD COMPOSITION

In addition to the criteria needed to define a household, there are several factors that may influence who comprises a household and affect how that household functions. Kinship relationships, gender, age, ethnicity, and race can affect household composition and division of labor. Gender is one of the most frequently discussed influences on a household's division of labor, especially in how a gendered division of labor relates to space. Many studies critique the equation of women with the household and men with the public sphere (e.g., Brumfiel 1991; Fox-Genovese 1988; Lawrence 1999; Spencer-Wood 1999a).

Age is another important factor in the context of production and division of labor, as the very young and the very old may not be perceived as active producers. Also, since social reproduction is an important component of the household, age factors significantly in how relationships are organized among household members.

Ethnicity is especially important in contexts where kinship is absent or irrelevant, such as among enslaved peoples who were sold away from family. By ethnicity, I refer to a group identity defined primarily through shared traditions, experiences, and behaviors in a context of power and domination by communities with differential access to power. This should not be confused with racial identity, which the dominant class imposed on all groups of society based on skin color and perceived biological characteristics (for further discussion of race and ethnicity, see Brah 1996; Gilroy 1993; Gordon 1998; Wade 1997). The idea that ethnicity can be defined by oppressed or marginalized groups shows that within a situation of domination, people actively create their own ethnic identity. For example, in these situations, a household that has boarders or an institutional household may be organized along ethnic lines (see Spencer-Wood, this volume; Wood, this volume).

Like ethnicity, race becomes a significant factor in situations of power. For example, during and after the collapse of slavery in the Americas, race affected social and economic advancement, which sometimes caused lighter-complexioned African Americans to disassociate themselves from their darker-complexioned friends and relatives and to establish their own households in order to improve their economic or social status. Although in these situations people are choosing to have a certain racial identity, they are limited by the dominant class's definitions of race.

WHAT IS A HOUSEHOLD?

The definition of household that I use here makes a distinction between the concept of family and the concept of household. The family is a group of kin-related people (including fictive kin) who may or may not reside together and whose primary function is to reproduce its members biologically (although this may be achieved through adoption). A household is a person or a group of people who live together in one or more structures, who carry out daily activities necessary for the maintenance and social reproduction of the group within a specific space associated with the residence, and who interact with other households. These activities are the necessary daily maintenance activities that sustain members of the household and their shared space, including food preparation, refuse disposal, raising children, growing food provisions within the yard, cleaning, bathing, doing laundry, and socializing. Also, these activities include working in some capacity to provide basic necessities for life, which may not occur within the household space. The fluidity inherent in this definition is also an important factor in studying the household.

The household is established by one or more individuals, and the division of labor within the household may be influenced by a number of factors. The people who form households may be influenced to do so according to their kinship relations, gender, age, ethnicity, race, or socioeconomic status. The life cycle of a household is tied to the life cycle of its establishing members. When they die, the household dies, and a new household is established, possibly by one of the previous household's members within the same structure. People can be members of more than one household, and in certain instances there can be different levels of households. Ashmore and Wilk (1988:6) explain this idea in their distinction between a household and a co-residential group, noting that "people often live in the same building . . . without sharing in the activities that normally define a household. A co-residential group can contain more than one household or it can be a component part of a larger household." This idea of *nested households* allows for a more fluid definition of the household and applies very well within a plantation context.

INFLUENCES ON HOUSEHOLD FORMATION IN THE BAHAMAS

In the application of this concept to the plantation period in the Bahamas, a brief discussion of the historical context of the Loyalist period (1783–1834) provides information that is essential in understanding the complexity of social relationships there. This discussion is intended to provide insight into existing social relations that may have affected household formation on all levels. This discussion will also note that the geography of the Bahamas influenced household formation; as an island collective, social relationships varied from island to island. The more isolated islands, or "Out Islands," were less populated and more rural than Nassau, the capital of the Bahamas, located on the island of New Providence. The primary purpose of this discussion is to explore the ethnic and social diversity among enslaved Africans in order to understand how it may have influenced the types of households they established.

In the 1730s and 1740s, many Spanish and French Creole slaves were brought to the Bahamas as a result of Britain's wars with Spain and France. However, many white Bahamians preferred to buy African slaves because they were said to be "easier to control." By 1741, the Bahamas had imposed a heavy duty on slaves from Spanish or French colonies (Craton and Saunders 1992:151). Both groups of enslaved people were probably employed in an urban context in Nassau or in a smaller plantation context rather than in the large-scale chattel slavery that accompanied the Loyalists' establishment of plantations.

In 1783, people loyal to Britain fled the independent United States to take advantage of available land grants in the Bahamas, where they subsequently established cotton plantations. Many planters brought their slaves with them from East Florida or New York. Free blacks also immigrated during this time (Craton and Saunders 1992:183). Within five years of the Loyalists' arrival in the Bahamas, 128 plantations with 10 or more slaves had been established (Albury 1975:115). The total immigration from the United States reached 1,600 whites and 5,700 enslaved and free blacks (Craton and Saunders 1992:179).

By 1788, most cotton plantations were failing because of the chenille bug, which feeds on cotton, and because of the erosion of the already sparse soil (Craton and Saunders 1992:196). Although the cotton industry in the Bahamas continued through the early part of the nineteenth century owing to high wartime cotton prices and the invention of the wind-powered cotton gin (Craton and Saunders 1992:197), planters were eventually forced to turn to subsistence farming to avoid bankruptcy (Saunders 1983:41). Some planters also began producing salt, but this option was available only to those who owned salt ponds and who could afford the hefty export duty that was imposed on salt in 1789 (Saunders 1983:42).

During the brief period of cotton's success, more enslaved Africans from many different ethnic groups began to arrive from West and Central Africa (Dalleo 1982, 1984). Ships of varying nationalities brought their slave cargoes through the Bahamas. Many ships en route to Havana first stopped in the Bahamas, allowing planters there to purchase enslaved Africans directly off the ship (Saunders 1991:26). Presumably some of these purchases were illicit, because unless the ships went directly into Nassau, these slaves would not have gone through the formal auctioning process (with accompanying taxes) at the Vendue House. The Vendue House served as the formal site for slave auctions and where the government assessed and collected taxes from people buying slaves. Illicit purchases might have been very common on strategically situated islands such as Turks, located at the Windward Passage between Cuba and Hispaniola (Williams 1971:90), or Exuma, an island located far south of New Providence, with its deep harbor. This harbor may have encouraged captains of slave ships to stop for provisions and to unload some of their human cargo on the way to another Caribbean port.

Economically, the failure of the cotton crop in the Bahamas created a serious problem for the planters, but the social repercussions were even greater. With their major cash crop gone, many planters had far too many slaves to work on crops that needed less maintenance. Instead of freeing their slaves, planters allowed them time off to work on their own provision grounds. By doing so, they lifted some of their burden of feeding the slaves and also kept the enslaved people busy. Planters thought enslaved people would be busy with their own crops as well as the planters' and would have little time to plan organized resistance. Although enslaved people still had to work around the plantation infrastructure, this extra time may have significantly affected household composition, as they had more time to invest in their own household activities, which may have meant a reorganization of duties among household members. This change could have resulted in the formation of a larger household that combined the efforts of one or more smaller households, or the reverse, in which a larger household broke up into several smaller households.

Another factor that influenced household formation and composition among enslaved people was the presence of a free black population. Initially, the Loyalists attempted to promote dissension between slaves and free blacks by establishing a mandatory militia in which free blacks were responsible for capturing runaway slaves (Craton and Saunders 1992:190). However, their willingness to hire free blacks to work on their plantations and to allow their slaves to hire out for work in both agricultural and domestic contexts ensured interaction between free blacks and slaves (Johnson 1991:12).

This situation was further complicated when a new group of Africans began to arrive in the Bahamas after Britain abolished the slave trade in 1807. At this time, if a ship carrying enslaved Africans was shipwrecked or captured by British soldiers, the Africans were brought as free Africans to the nearest British port (Williams 1979:2). When that port was the Bahamas, the white inhabitants established "liberated African" villages away from Nassau so that there would be little contact between themselves and the new arrivals (Department of Archives 1991:11).

Although liberated Africans had little contact with whites, they often worked on plantations as apprentices, which promoted sexual liaisons between free African men and enslaved African women (Johnson 1991:36–38). These relationships could have resulted in female-headed households that included males who did not always reside there. Liberated Africans worked on both New Providence and the Out Islands (Johnson 1996:76), but Dalleo (1984:18) reports that they preferred to stay in Nassau because of an imbalance in the sex ratio. This suggests that on the Out Islands, households might have been organized according to ethnicity or gender, which did not follow the nuclear family household model that white planters tried to impose on enslaved people.

A CASE STUDY OF NESTED HOUSEHOLDS

In order to illustrate the idea of nested households, I will use the example of the Kelsall family who lived on one of the Out Islands. This family immigrated to the Bahamas from Georgia in the late eighteenth century and purchased 1,100 acres of land on the island of Exuma. On this land, the family established three adjoining plantations: Pinxton, the Hermitage, and Sabine

Fields. Different family members occupied each plantation, and each family member owned slaves. Roger Kelsall, his son, John, and daughter, Anne, lived at the Hermitage; Roger's brother, William Kelsall, his wife, Mary Elizabeth, and their four daughters occupied Pinxton. Roger's aunt, Anne Bellinger-Wilkins, her children, and Roger's sister, Amelia, occupied Sabine Fields (James 1988:28–29). These discrete family units suggest nicely bounded spatial areas, but household analysis demonstrates a great deal of fluidity.

On a plantation, many different situations can influence the definition of a household: house slaves perform daily chores for the planter's family, field slaves perform daily activities for themselves, planter families reproduce their society, etc. However, if these different interactions are viewed as part of a series of nested households, a series of more discrete household units with fluid boundaries becomes apparent.

In the sense that all members engage in some aspect of production, co-reside in more than one structure, and reproduce socially, every person living on the plantation can be envisioned as part of one large household. Enslaved people are forced to engage in production for the planter, both groups reproduce socially (each attempting to maintain a separate group identity), and everyone lives in the same area. Enslaved people are also forced to perform daily maintenance activities for the planter family in addition to performing their own. The entire system was designed to reproduce itself. However, this does not mean that either planters or enslaved people considered themselves part of this level of household; rather, this is one level of analysis or an overall framework within which to look at how different groups interacted.

As we begin to analyze smaller groups, we can see other households nesting within the plantation household. For example, the Kelsalls owned more than one plantation, with different family members living at each place. These different residences, tied together by kinship and ethnicity, can be viewed as a household within the larger plantation household that includes enslaved people. They all engage in the same production, they reproduce socially, they pool their resources, and they interact with one another. The situation among the enslaved African population living at these plantations is nearly the same. Although there is little information available on living arrangements among slaves, such as what factors influence co-residence (and whether kinship was a factor) and to what extent resources may have been pooled, other factors demonstrate the existence of a large slave household. That is, because the slaves are tied together racially and forced to co-reside, because they reproduce socially, and because they interact with one another, the entire slave population may be seen as one household within the larger plantation household that includes the Kelsalls. However, this does not mean that enslaved people considered themselves part of such a household, or that any of these household relationships were harmonious.

Within these two groups, even more households can be found. Each of the residences of the planter families (Pinxton, the Hermitage, and Sabine Fields) can be isolated as a household according to the same criteria as above with the possible exception of pooling their resources. At this level, we can also see the life cycle of the household and the influences on household composition. For example, the household founded by William and Mary Elizabeth Kelsall does not end with William's death because Mary Elizabeth is also an established member of the household. Instead, it reorganizes as an all-female household until Mary Elizabeth leaves the plantation, and then the household dies. The reorganization of this household also has interesting implications for other households, as the social relationships among household members change.

Although this household seems to be a bounded unit, boundaries blur when deciding whether to include children born to a planter and a slave or whether to include house slaves. Roger Kelsall's mulatto daughter, Portia, whose enslaved mother was Roger's mistress, might be included in the household based on kinship ties, social reproduction, and social interaction but may be excluded on the basis of race and ethnicity. Portia may have been simultaneously included and excluded from this level of the household depending on the perspective of other household members. Also, she may not have considered herself a member of this household. Portia becomes a liminal figure representing the constantly changing household boundaries and points to the complexity of this concept and the power inherent in who is able to define a household.

Like the planters, enslaved people can be seen as having many different households according to who performs daily maintenance activities and lives together. It is more difficult to reconstruct slave households at this level, because existing documentation on slave households is rare. However, once again, Portia's situation is relevant, because we do not know whether she was considered a member of one or more slave households or if, because of her familial or racial status, she may have been excluded from the slave community. Again, the question arises of who has the power to define what a household is and who should be included. Multiple households coexist, nested within one another, and are simultaneously defined differently by different groups of people.

The overseer fits into at least two categories of household. Obviously, he is part of the plantation household in that he oversees production and his daily maintenance tasks involve reproducing the status quo. He is also part of the smallest level of household in that he would have lived in his own house and performed daily maintenance activities necessary to his household. It is possible he could also have been part of another level of household if there was more than one overseer and they interacted socially with one another.

THE HOUSEYARD AS AN ARCHAEOLOGICAL
COMPONENT OF HOUSEHOLD

With such a fluid conceptualization of the household, it may seem impossible that plantation sites could be excavated successfully on a household level. Which household would be represented? Historical, ethnographic, and archaeological records help define a more bounded space that would indicate the smallest unit within a nested household. Among people of African descent in the Bahamas, this space is called the houseyard.

The houseyard consists of a house and its associated yard, and it is an important center for daily activities. The yard area is an extension of the house, where daily activities such as cooking, cleaning, and socialization occur. As such, it is also a focal area for cultural reproduction; Sidney Mintz (1974:232) writes, "Together the house and yard form a nucleus within which the culture expresses itself, is perpetuated, changed, and reintegrated."

Houseyards are found primarily among people of African descent who live in the Caribbean and the American South. Many travel accounts of West Africa dating from the eighteenth and nineteenth centuries describe the area around the house with its associated plants and trees as an enclosed compound where livestock was kept (Westmacott 1992:9). A distinction was made between this area and those used for agricultural purposes (Westmacott 1992:9). This distinction was also present in the Caribbean during the period of enslavement and continues to be found in some areas of the Caribbean today (Pulsipher 1990, 1994). Examples of similar arrangements have also been recorded in Jamaica and Montserrat (Mintz 1974; Pulsipher 1993a), as well as in the southern United States (Westmacott 1992).

As an element of household space, the houseyard has been analyzed in terms of production via division of labor according to gender. Ethnography in the Caribbean shows an association between women and the houseyard (Pulsipher 1993a, 1993b; Wilkie 1996a). However, this should not be seen as a reification of the male/female–public/private association, as the typical household in the West Indies is headed by a single female. Also, it is possible that although the space may be associated with women, both men and women have designated activities within that space. In my own research, I have found that children of both genders as well as women had different tasks within the houseyard space (Anderson 1998). Children of either gender were responsible for retrieving water from a communal well, cleaning the kitchen with sand, or sweeping the yard with palm fronds. The types of activities assigned to each child would change with age. Children also played in the yard area, shooting marbles or playing with homemade dolls.

Archaeologically, this space might yield concentrations of artifacts associated with specific household activities, such as food preparation, refuse disposal, or socializing. For example, food preparation might be reflected by a hearth area, a concentration of faunal or ethnobotanical remains, or cooking vessel fragments. Socialization may be represented by an area containing tobacco pipe fragments or children's toys. As for refuse disposal, a midden or evidence of yard sweeping would show household patterns. For examples, see Heath and Bennett's Poplar Forest study (2000) and Anderson's Clifton Plantation study (1998).

ARCHAEOLOGY OF THE HOUSEYARD

In the Bahamas, houseyards are central features of the landscape in communities formed by people of African descent. These areas have been important as a space for daily activities since the period of enslavement. Not only are modern houseyards visible, but enslaved African houseyards are also visible archaeologically in the spatial patterning of activity areas (Anderson 1998).

The houseyard is a bounded spatial unit that can serve as a basis for examining the household at its smallest level. From this level, we can begin to understand how other households on the plantation grew more complex and reflect enslaved African positioning within the social context of slavery. One way to begin to understand other levels of household is to analyze the spatial relationships and artifact assemblages of the different living areas on the plantation.

Spatial relationships can be investigated at several different household levels by using the houseyard as a basis for comparison with other living areas within the plantation landscape. By comparing artifact assemblages from more than one houseyard within a plantation, we can begin to understand the complexity of the households that are being represented. For example, in the Bahamas, Wilkie's (2000b) analysis of a single houseyard at Clifton Plantation shows a significantly higher amount of faunal remains recovered when compared with Anderson's (1998) analysis of another houseyard at Clifton. This difference suggests that enslaved people at Clifton were operating as a bigger household, as they were pooling resources that one or two people were processing for the rest to eat. That is, one smaller household may have been doing a significant amount of food processing for several others, and the other households may have been doing different chores, such as watching children or cultivating crops, to work together at another larger level of household. However, Wilkie (2000b:15) also asserts that analysis of the ceramics recovered from all the enslaved African houseyards at Clifton indicates that different households bought their own ceramic vessels. This suggests that smaller households existed within the larger household suggested by the faunal remains. In this case, the concept of coexisting nested households allows insight into the complex social relationships between enslaved Africans without equating household strictly with the bounded space of the houseyard.

A comparison of planter and slave living areas could also provide information about the planter and the slave households on both a small and a large scale. Farnsworth's (1993, 1994, 1996) work at Wade's Green and Promised Land plantations in the Bahamas and Armstrong's (1983, 1985, 1990) work at Drax Hall provide information about differences between planters and slaves, such as consumer choice and ethnicity, through analysis of material remains. Based on an analysis of cost, availability, and preference, these studies provide information about how the planter household and the group slave household were defining themselves on the plantation. For example, Farnsworth's (1994:24) finding that the planter's artifact assemblage at Promised Land resembled a tavern's assemblage based on a high percentage of alcohol storage items and relatively low-cost ceramic assemblages suggests the planter established a "temporary household" at the plantation. However, the slave assemblage at Promised Land includes a high percentage of food consumption and water storage items (Farnsworth 1994:25), providing evidence of daily household tasks. These two assemblages indicate that enslaved people may have been able to organize their households more freely without the planter's permanent presence. It also raises questions about how enslaved people at Promised Land viewed their own household status.

At the macroscale, one plantation representing a single household could be compared with another plantation representing a single household. This unit of analysis might seem unwieldy, but the idea of nested households provides a way to compare smaller groups within the macroscale that can be drawn out to a general comparison of how social relationships are negotiated on different plantations. For example, Heath and Bennett's (2000) work at Poplar Forest in Virginia indicates, through clustering of tobacco pipe fragments, that enslaved people were socializing in a specific area between two houses as well as inside each house. This may indicate that smaller households socialized within their own residences but that a larger household socialized publicly. Interestingly, although neither Wilkie (2000b) nor Anderson (1998) noted clustering of pipe fragments recovered from the slave cabins at Clifton Plantation, Wilkie (2000b:22) recovered at least one decorative pipe that may have been associated with spirituality. This find may reflect a different type of socialization that could have had impacts on household composition. If further comparisons were made between these two assemblages, more information about household organization among enslaved people at each plantation might be discovered. Further comparison between planter and overseer assemblages between the two plantations could provide information about household organization on several other levels. Ultimately, the comparison of these nested households between two different plantations could provide information about how enslaved people negotiated their social relationships in different areas under the same oppressive system.

CONCLUSION

This comparison of nested households is not intended to be a simple solution; indeed, in comparing planter, overseer, and enslaved African living areas on the plantation, the spatial boundaries begin to blur. The houseyard seems a manageable spatial unit of analysis, but when a group of houseyards becomes a unit, boundaries become fuzzy. Also, when group households are being treated as a single unit to be compared against others, it is important to avoid essentializing these groups. The nested household concept provides a framework to use in our attempts to reconcile spatial boundaries with socially fluid concepts. It also points to the idea that there is power inherent in defining the membership of a household and that individuals or groups may have perceived themselves differently from each other or from the way we perceive them. This constant contradiction has the potential to be a valuable concept in archaeology by causing us constantly to shift our perspective from the idea of a discrete spatial unit to the idea of continual fluctuations in the daily negotiations of social boundaries.

ACKNOWLEDGMENTS

I would like to thank Dr. Maria Franklin and Dr. Sam Wilson for their insightful comments on this paper. Also, profuse thanks go to Kerri Barile and Jamie Brandon, who had the patience to organize and edit this volume.

7
Hegemony within the Household

The Perspective from a South Carolina Plantation

Kerri S. Barile

Plantations in the American South were intricate landscapes. They were microcosms of self-sufficiency, designed and altered by the white planter elite to indicate power, status, and ideology. Though the plantations were controlled by the dominant planter class, they were "home" to many other residents, including overseers, indentured servants, and African slaves.

While many scholars have examined hegemonic relationships within the plantation matrix, their works have often concentrated on a single facet of plantation life, such as foodways or architecture, or on one spatial area of the plantation property, such as the slave quarter village or the main house area (see e.g., Heath 1999; McKee 1999; Samford 1996; Vlach 1993). While these types of studies are extremely important to understanding plantation life, the segmentation of these inner-plantation areas and architectural groupings could lead to problematic dissections of the household, as oftentimes the entire plantation functioned as a single, measurable socioeconomic entity within the wider community (Allison 1999a:2). Therefore, depending on one's research questions and the context of a site, the entire plantation and all of its residents could be included in a single household analysis, especially when considering intra-plantation dominance and control.

The historic household was likely defined differently by various inhabitants. An enslaved African American could refer to his or her own individual "home" and its inhabitants as a household or to a particular group of quarters as a household (see Battle, this volume). While white planters might refer to an entire plantation, including the house servants, as a household, they probably did not include the field hands as members of that household, except in an economic sense (Spencer-Wood, personal communication 2002). Since so many variables are involved in a discussion of a plantation and the definition of a household, some authors (e.g., Anderson, this volume; Ashmore and Wilk 1988) have suggested using the *nested household* concept on plantation sites. The concept allows for various levels of the household to be present at one site. I suggest, however, that several households can be grouped into a *household complex*.

A household complex, as I define it, is a group of households who share one or more of the traits of an individual household, such as kin-relations, economic interdependence, or a bounded space/structure. This concept differs from that of a nested household in that the nested concept clearly indicates not only a known progression in the size and hierarchy of each level of household but, more important, an inherent dominance of one household over another. This dominance can be expressed through outright control or larger societal and cultural influence. The household complex idea is fluid, however, and negates the intrinsic dominance implied by a nested household, as it allows for different viewpoints and spatial boundaries of the household for each individual. Within a plantation, for example, grouping all of the various households within the plantation property boundary as a household complex allows for variations in the way we perceive the past and, moreover, alters what can be viewed as a dominant, Anglocentric construction of the household to render all plantation and household inhabitants equally visible. The household complex is defined here, therefore, as all of those people living on one plantation, as well as the structures and landscapes within the plantation boundaries used by the plantation occupants.

The following paper will concentrate on intrahousehold organization (here and throughout this chapter, the term *household* refers to the entire household complex, as I have defined it) and examine how external factors influence changes in the spatial composition of the plantation. As Allison (1999a:2) points out, "studies of the internal dynamics and intra-relationships of a household have been viewed as trivial and insignificant pastimes in the investigations of the patterns of human behavior." With Middleburg Plantation in South Carolina as a backdrop, this paper will examine how outside forces can directly affect the composition of the household. More important, it will illustrate that the study of the internal dynamics of a single household can lead to larger theories on human behavior.

THE PLANTATION AS A HOUSHOLD COMPLEX

Wilk and Rathje (1982:618) stated that "households are the level at which social groups articulate directly with economic and ecological processes." They suggest analyzing the household in terms of "dwelling units," which take into account economic cooperation, co-residence, and kinship to determine the composition of a household rather than kinship alone (Wilk and Rathje 1982: 620–621). Here, though, I will go beyond the individual dwelling unit and focus on the plantation as a whole (the household as household complex).

Within the boundaries of a plantation, the household is defined here as all those living on one parcel of land and involved in the same overall economic enterprise, or what has often been termed a "socioeconomic unit" (see, e.g., Allison 1999a). A plantation household, therefore, includes those living in the Big House (Vlach 1993), as well as all others living in support of the plantation functions. These functions can include, but are not limited to, enslaved and indentured workers and those paid for daily labor, such as overseers, business managers, housekeepers, and agricultural specialists. (For clarity, the term *household* herewith refers to the plantation occupants themselves, whereas the "built environment of the household" involves the structures and landscapes used and altered by the plantation occupants.)

It is recognized that defining the entire plantation as a single household, or household complex, is problematic. Defining the entire plantation as a household differs from the term *community,* however, in that a community is often defined as a group of people who live and work in close proximity to one another, but most often the land they live and work on is not owned by one group or entity. Second, in those few cases where the land is owned by one source, members of the community are usually not employed in agribusiness. It is the plantation as a household complex, therefore, that best describes the situation described here, a parcel of land owned by one person or group that is occupied by many people with various status positions and tasks, primarily employed in agricultural ventures. Moreover, each function and social level of the household/plantation is economically interdependent in one way or another.

At Middleburg Plantation, the household complex included all those living within the main house area, as well as the overseer and the slaves living throughout the property who worked the fields and ran the rice mill. The built environment of the Middleburg household included the main house, kitchen, slave quarters, and all other structures and altered landscapes that were used to produce rice and other agricultural crops. Together, all of the plantation occupants depended upon the work and position of one another to be fed, clothed, and sheltered. Though they interacted daily, the dynamics of interaction among the various household occupants was also radically different than that of other, more "traditional" households, as these intrahousehold relationships were tempered by many layers of control and countercontrol.

Dominance and Resistance within the Household Matrix

Cultures in contact inevitably develop particular social roles and material forms based on both hierarchy and tradition. Moreover, "to accept that power differentials existed in the past or, more explicitly, to accept the presence of inequality and domination in the past means understanding that resistance, as the other half of a dialectical relation of power, did also" (Frazer 1999:5). Here, it must also be remembered that dominance and resistance are not status terms but rather relations among various members of a society. On a plantation, as defined here, the society included all household occupants—owners, paid labor, and unpaid servant.

As expounded upon in his *Prison Writings* (1988), Antonio Gramsci defined hegemony as the concept of intellectual, political, economic, and moral authority/leadership of one group or individual over another. This dominance is often reached through force or coercion. Beyond that, however, Gramsci (1988:211) points out that hegemony is dynamic: "The fact of hegemony presupposes that account be taken of the interests and tendencies of the groups over which hegemony is to be exercized." In other words, power comes in multiple forms and on many levels and, moreover, is always characterized by a careful balance between both the dominant and the resistant.

As defined by Paynter and McGuire (1991:1), domination is "those who use structural asymmetries of resources in exercising power," whereas resistance is "those who develop social and cultural opposition to this exercise." The relations among and between the dominant and resistant are directly tempered by surveillance (Paynter and McGuire 1991:9). It is through surveillance that the dominators repress the subordinates and "any weakness in surveillance and enforcement is likely to be quickly exploited; any ground left undefended is likely to be lost ground" (Scott 1990:195).

Within the plantation, hegemony is often evaluated through the presence or absence of particular material remains, such as colonoware or the ubiquitous blue beads and crystals (e.g., Stine et al. 1996; Thomas 1998). Though Anglo domination is often overt, archaeological explorations of resistance among the plantation workforce has concentrated on covert actions, such as the existence of hidden subterranean pits in slave quarters (see, e.g., Franklin 1997; Kimmel 1993; Samford 1996). Though a few archaeologists have conducted studies on maroon or runaway slave societies (Deagan and Landers 1999), it is most often the historian who examines explicit resistance and its long-term effects on regional populations (e.g., Bracey et al. 1971; Genovese 1979; Jordan 1974). The question is whether overt resistance can be examined archaeologically. And, more important to this study, can these results provide information on dynamics within the household complex?

A BRIEF HISTORY OF MIDDLEBURG AND ITS OCCUPANTS

The Founding of a Town and the Development of a Household

As with many other American cities, Charleston, South Carolina, was founded and flourished under the dualities of religious freedom and economic gain. The peninsula between the Ashley and Cooper rivers (Figure 7.1) was settled in 1670 and named Charles Town to honor King Charles of England (Weir 1983:58).

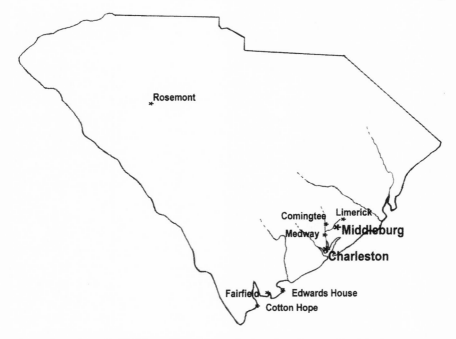

Fig. 7.1. Location of Middleburg Plantation and other sites discussed in this chapter.

The English were sent to this area of warmer climates and extensive waterways with the hope that they could provide the Crown with needed goods, such as wine, olive oil, wax, and spices (Edgar 1998:39). The rivers and creeks helped spread the planters to vast lands with good soil believed to be ideal for their venture (Weir 1983:64–65).

Benjamin Simons, a French Huguenot, received a land grant from the Crown in 1686 for a parcel of land along the east branch of the Cooper River (Simons 1954:74). This land had considerable waterfront acreage and good conditions for the creation of canals, dikes, and water channels for planting. By the spring of 1699, Simons had established a household on the Cooper River property (see Figure 7.1). He named it Middleburg (Salley 1936:142).

The Household Complex Grows and Diversifies

As Simons was settling his plantation, he and his fellow Carolinians quickly realized that their fortunes would not lie with oil, spices, or wine because the climate and soils could not produce the leaves and fruit needed to make them in high quantity or quality. However, another crop soon dominated the low-country—rice. Rice cultivation in the Carolina lowcountry began in 1695 (Gray 1941:278). This area was an ideal growing location because of its river systems and subtropical weather. Since many European settlers did not have any knowledge about rice as an agricultural crop, the planters got advice from Africans brought over as slaves, a group who had been growing it for over 3,000 years.

The Simons family made up only a small percentage of the plantation's historic household population. Slaves from the coastal region of Africa were aware of the need to harness water and use tidal power to flood the rice fields adequately. They also brought the use of hoes and spades to create banks and dikes for proper rice cultivation (Littlefield 1981:97). Though the rough numbers of slaves living at Middleburg are known through census records, no written lists of exact names or jobs have been located in the historical records. Therefore, the enslaved population is unfortunately referred to in the collective rather than as individual participants in Middleburg's history.

Gradual Changes in the Eighteenth Century

Throughout the eighteenth century, the landscape at Middleburg was slowly but regularly altered to provide for adjustments in the economy and varying agricultural needs. Two flanking outbuildings, creating a Palladian Plan, were constructed to the north of the main house some time in the second half of the century (Figure 7.2). The northeast dependency (no longer standing) was an outside kitchen. Oral history indicates that the northwest building was a servants' quarters. Several rows of slave quarters were built east of the main house between 1750 and 1800 as residences for the plantation's enslaved workforce, which averaged between 75 and 100 during most of the century (St. John's, St. Thomas, and St. Dennis Parish Records).

Below-ground Remains of Eighteenth-Century Life. These slave quarters, and the lives of the African Americans living on the plantation, have been the subject of historical inquiry throughout the last 20 years. The University of South Carolina conducted archaeological excavations in the Middleburg main house area from 1986 to 1991 under the direction of Dr. Leland Ferguson (Ferguson 1992). The primary goal of the project was to define the boundaries of the slave village near the main house and locate evidence of its appearance and function.

The artifacts and architectural remains found during the excavations indicate an occupation period between 1770 and 1820 (Adams 1990:93). Among the thousands of artifacts uncovered were kitchen wares, such as slip-decorated and tin-glazed earthenware; architectural remains, such as window glass and nails; and many personal items, such as buttons and kaolin pipe stems. What appeared in abundance, though, were fragments of colonoware, an earthenware currently believed by some archaeologists to have been crafted on southern plantations by slaves (see Ferguson 1996 and Singleton and Bograd 2000 for examples of the colonoware debate).

Colonoware was made using a creolized pottery tradition, drawing on ma-

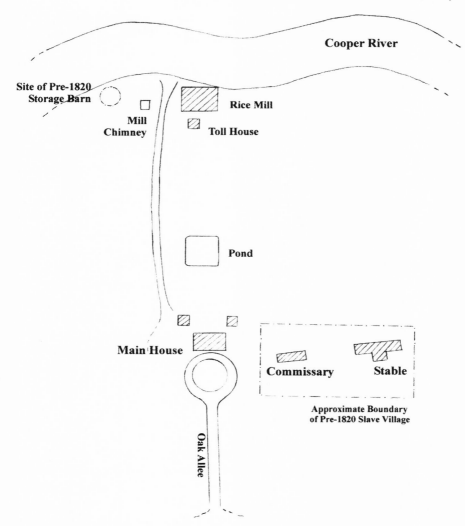

Fig. 7.2. Map of the current and historic cultural resources at Middleburg Plantation.

terials, techniques, and styles from Africa, Europe, and the Native American population (Ferguson 1992:19). In fact, some scholars have viewed colonoware as a form of covert resistance against the Anglo elite (e.g., Ferguson 1992). Nonetheless, most see it as an "intercultural artifact—one that provides opportunities to raise questions and issues about its appropriation and transformative meanings and uses" (Singleton and Bograd 2000:4). The presence of prolific amounts of colonoware at Middleburg raises many questions about both covert and explicit forms of resistance within the plantation household. These questions came to the forefront of inquiry in an investigation of early-nineteenth-century life on the plantation.

Into the Nineteenth Century

On the eve of the nineteenth century, the Middleburg household grew to comprise almost 2,600 acres, and it became one of the most prosperous rice plantations in South Carolina. In 1799, Sarah Lydia Simons, heir to the plantation, married an enterprising young rice planter named Jonathan Lucas (Simons 1954). They continued the Simons tradition of making slow but significant changes to the Middleburg landscape and agricultural operation, including, in 1801, the first toll mill for rice operated in South Carolina (Tricentennial Celebration Committee 1970).

Rapid Changes in the Middleburg Complex

Between 1820 and 1830, Lucas broke with tradition and made several sudden changes to the Middleburg household. Among these modifications were the *allée* of oaks along the main drive, the relocation of the slave quarters, and the enhancement of the formal gardens (Byra 1996). Oral history, backed by archaeological excavations, indicates that the slave quarters were removed sometime around 1820. In their place, Lucas had two large, solid structures built—the Commissary and the stable. The Commissary is believed to have served as an agricultural and rice storage building during the nineteenth century. The current name was derived from the period in the early twentieth century when the structure served as a local store.

The first story of the Commissary is formed of five-to-one common bond load-bearing masonry (Figure 7.3). This brick portion has two small barred windows on each elevation and two large rounded, arched entryways, one on the south and one on the east. The upper one-and-a-half stories are a timber frame construction with board and batten exterior wall coverings, and the steeply pitched gable roof has ball and drop bargeboards. The stable and carriage house structure, destroyed by Hurricane Hugo in 1989, was a one-and-a-half-story, timber frame building resting on brick piers. The exterior walls were board and batten with three large double-hinged doors on the south side for carriage and horse storage.

Following period convention, these two outbuildings were in direct alignment with one another (Vlach 1993:78). What makes them distinctive from the other outbuildings on the plantation is that they were built approximately 30° off the angle of the main house and are elaborately detailed compared to other structures at Middleburg and at buildings on nearby plantations constructed

Fig. 7.3. The southern and eastern elevations of the Commissary.

during the same period. Moreover, they were larger than the main house and built of extra-solid materials.

These two structures were not only solidly constructed, but their location within the larger configuration of the plantation plan is highly unusual. The rice and agricultural storage building was originally located adjacent to the rice mill, along the banks of the Cooper River (see Figure 7.2). It was removed and rebuilt near the main house, a location not only approximately one-third of a mile from the agricultural processing center but also up a moderate topographic slope. The stable building was also moved at this time, from a location southwest of the main house, near the drive, to a site opposite the Commissary. These two structures were built to house valuable goods and equipment, and they were quickly and decisively moved to a location within clear view of the main house.

At the same time that these structures were built, the placement of the slave quarters also changed. Whereas the quarters were once located together in neat rows adjacent to the main house, oral history and limited archaeological testing indicate that the new quarters were divided into several small clusters and placed on the periphery of the plantation boundaries.

Within a few years, the built environment of the household complex was, thus, radically altered. An initial analysis of these changes clearly indicates that this new spatial composition would detract from the flow of the household and thereby make it less productive. It would also strain intrahousehold relationships by subdividing the enslaved population and isolating the Lucas family from most household activities. Why did these changes occur, and how did they affect the household as a social space?

ARCHAEOLOGY AND THE MIDDLEBURG HOUSEHOLD

Though the locations of the aboveground structures and oral histories collected over the years helped to form questions about the household composition, archaeological analysis was needed to determine how and when these changes occurred. In the spring of 1999, archaeologists from the University of South Carolina returned to Middleburg in an attempt to answer some questions about the rapid changes made to the household between 1820 and 1830.

A total of four test units were excavated in the area around the Commissary and Stable—three units were placed adjacent to the Commissary foundation (Units 1999–1 to 1999–3) and one was placed along the stable remains (Unit 1999–4). Unit 1999–1 was placed along the northwest corner of the Commissary to examine its construction methods as well as locate any fence lines or walls constructed in the area to divide the landscape. Similarly, Unit 1999–2 was excavated just outside of the southern entrance to the Commissary (shown in Figure 7.2) to look at how the building was constructed as well as to examine the deconstruction of the slave quarters beneath it. Unit 1999–3 was placed inside the structure to inspect the interior room divisions. Though the Stable was destroyed after Hurricane Hugo, Unit 1999–4 was placed along the Stable foundation to see if any features remain intact from its construction and, more important, to locate artifacts and evidence that could help date the deconstruction of the slave quarters and ensuing construction of the Stable.

Analysis of the artifacts and features from the three Commissary units revealed that it was constructed after 1820. All three units had small whiteware body fragments, among other artifacts, in the builder's trench, giving the Commissary a *terminus post quem* of 1820 (Noel-Hume 1978; South 1977). However, none of the builder's trenches had yellowware or porcellaneous in them, and the layers above the builder's trenches did contain these artifacts, which have a beginning production date of 1830 and 1850, respectively (e.g., Pitman et al. 1987). Thus, the construction date for the Commissary was likely between 1820 and 1830.

Excavation and analysis of the features from the 1999 excavations show that the brick foundation of the Commissary had a 12-inch-thick foundation, terminating approximately 18 inches below modern grade. Two postholes and postmolds, likely from a fence, were found at the same layer as the builder's trench in the corner unit (1999-1). The fact that the postholes were covered by the same fill layer brought in to cover the builder's trench, as well as artifacts found in the postholes themselves, indicate that the fence was constructed at or near the same time as the Commissary, suggesting an immediate desire to divide the landscape.

In Unit 1999-2, located outside the southern entrance to the Commissary, the demolition layer from the slave quarters was directly under the builder's trench level. Most of the artifacts found in this layer were burned in situ, and the brick and mortar found within the matrix were in small, friable fragments with clear evidence of exposure to fire. This find leads to a possible interpretation that the slave quarters in this area were purposefully burned to make way for construction of the Commissary.

The Questions Continue: From Dirt to Documents

The Commissary was built using unusual building technology for this area. The placement of this structure, along with the stable, within the larger plantation landscape is also a puzzle. Since "architecture can never totally dictate the behavior within its spaces" (Allison 1999a:1), the Middleburg study moved to an intensive archival to locate other reasons for the quick and drastic changes to the household matrix. During the archival survey, many documents on the Simons and Lucas families were found relating to plantation business, as expected. The most interesting documents, however, were of a more personal nature and directed the Middleburg inquiry in an unexpected direction. All of these documents dated between 1822 and 1825 and were related to a significant event in Charleston's history—the Denmark Vesey Slave Conspiracy of 1822.

REBELLION IN CHARLESTON

Denmark Vesey was a free black living in Charleston. He was born in the West Indies as a slave but purchased his freedom with the proceeds from winning a lottery (Lofton 1964). In 1821, he began the plans for a revolt of slaves and free blacks in the Charleston district. To aid in the plans, Vesey enlisted six men whom he called "lieutenants"—three were free blacks living in Charleston, two were manservants to planters, and one was the personal servant of Governor Thomas Bennett of South Carolina (Starobin 1971). The revolt was originally set for Sunday, July 14, 1822. Vesey and his lieutenants told the slaves coming to join the insurrection to bring weapons collected from their respective households and to be ready to fight (Starobin 1971:193).

The plot was given away, however, and Vesey and the lieutenants chose to move the date up to June 16 to protect their plans (Vesey Trial Records 1822). In reaction to news of the impending insurrection, the leaders of the City of

Charleston doubled their militia in town and ordered increased security on nearby estates. However, Vesey's plan had completely crumbled when the date was moved up one month. Word did not reach the district plantations; Vesey did not have his backup, and the insurrection failed.

The day after the supposed rebellion, troops went into action, arresting Vesey and his lieutenants, as details and rumors regarding the conspiracy spread. Slaves from outlying plantations were to murder their owners, steal all the horses, weapons, and goods they could get their hands on, and travel to Charleston to join the fight (Starobin 1971:193). Governor Bennett, his wife, and family were to be killed by his manservant and the governor's daughter, Mary Hayes Bennett, was to be saved as the rebels' personal servant and concubine (Lofton 1964:141).

During the ensuing trial, a total of 131 people, 127 of them African-American, were called and questioned regarding the incidents that had occurred. Of this number, 38 were released for lack of evidence; 15 were acquitted; 54 black and 4 white men were sent out of state in permanent exile, seen as too dangerous to remain; and 35 men, including Vesey and his lieutenants, were hanged (*Charleston Courier* 1822:2).

A deep fear was felt among all whites in South Carolina, especially in the Charleston district, where African Americans outnumbered whites seven to one. Federal troops were brought in to protect the city. A set of laws was passed stating: no free blacks who left the state were ever to be allowed to return; the custom of hiring out slaves was to be eliminated; any African-American servant, free or enslaved, who came to the district with a white guardian was to be imprisoned until the guardian completed his or her visit; and any person, white or black, who aided or incited insurrection would be executed (Lofton 1964:197). A new arsenal was built in Charleston "to ensure the safety of life and property" (Powers 1994:33), and a military academy was organized to train the militia that constantly patrolled the city as a result of the conspiracy. This academy became The Citadel.

Vesey and the Middleburg Household

The Vesey conspiracy came close to many of the planting elite in the South Carolina lowcountry, thoroughly alarming the Cooper River plantation owners. The 1820 census indicates that the slave population at Middleburg was 44, though additional slaves likely lived on outlying farms to work the 2,000-acre plantation (St. Thomas and St. Dennis Census Records 1820:111). By 1822, the Lucas family would see this situation as detrimental, as the details of the Vesey conspiracy spread and their involvement became very personal.

Up and down the east branch of the Cooper River, many slaves were called to testify on knowledge of, and participation in, the conspiracy. At Middleburg,

3 of the 44 slaves were brought in and questioned with regard to their involvement in the scheduled revolt (Vesey Trial Papers 1822). Slaves could not be tried without their owners present (Wade 1971:129), so Jonathan Lucas II was also called to court and questioned about the activities of his slaves at Middleburg. All three slaves—Bram, John, and Richard—admitted to knowledge of the events that were to transpire, but all three denied supporting the plan and stated that they were against it (Vesey Trial Record 1822). Among the others called from the Cooper River area were Paris Ball from Comingtee Plantation and Peter Poyas from Windsor Plantation (Ball 1998:265–7). Lucas's three slaves were acquitted; however, Paris Ball was permanently banished from South Carolina because of his involvement, and Peter Poyas, as one of Vesey's lieutenants, was sentenced to death (Vesey Trial Records 1822).

The official Governor's Message Enclosures in the General Assembly papers in July of 1822 reveal another example of the close involvement of the Lucas family in the Vesey trial. *A General Order Citing Regulations for the Conduct of Troops during an Insurrection* (Lucas 1822) details the proper behavior and activity of white troops during an insurrection. The author of this order is Jonathan Lucas III, aide-de-camp of the Charleston district and heir to the Middleburg property.

Though the Simons and Lucas families always employed at least one overseer prior to this event, an overseer was placed directly in charge of the plantation operation and security after 1822. The president of the South Carolina Association, which formed vigilance committees to watch over slave activity after the suspected revolt, was Keating Simons, neighbor and cousin to the Lucas family (January 1977:193). Even though it is not known if Jonathan Lucas II or Lucas III were members of this group, close family ties and watchful neighbors possibly helped guard the plantation.

With the knowledge of their own slaves' involvement in the conspiracy, the Lucas family likely rethought the arrangement of the household. The slaves at Middleburg lived less than 180 feet from the front door of the main house. "Since slaves lived in the same yard with their masters, it was not even possible to lock out the intruder" (Wade 1971:128). Also, as mentioned, the storehouse was located near the river and the stable about .3 miles southwest of the main house. The slaves and free blacks involved in the plot "had noted every store containing arms and had given instructions to all slaves who tended or could get horses as to when and where to bring the animals" (Aptheker 1971:122). This directive provided the need for closer security over valuable goods and the movement of slave quarters away from the main house area, though it also meant that slave activity would be harder to monitor (Stewart-Abernathy, this volume).

Fear and distrust of slaves during this period, especially house servants, were noted in diaries, oral histories, and letters. Nathaniel Ball, a Simons and Lucas relation and fellow planter on the Cooper River, stated that "on the night of the expected uprising the Balls armed themselves with guns in their houses; bonfires were set around the district, and the family stayed awake till dawn, trembling at every noise" (Ball 1998:268). Anna Hayes Johnson, niece of Governor Bennett, wrote of the events in several letters. In these letters, she stated that "we poor devils [young women] were to have been reserved to fill their Harams [*sic*]—horrible—I have a very beautiful cousin who was set apart for the wife or more properly the 'light of the Haram' [*sic*] of one of their Cheifts [*sic*]" (Starobin 1970:6). The cousin mentioned was the daughter of Governor Bennett, Mary Hayes Bennett. She married Jonathan Lucas III of Middleburg in January of 1823 (Hill 1988:7), merging not only two powerful and wealthy families but also two who were greatly affected by the Vesey conspiracy.

FEAR AND THE RAPID RECONFIGURATION OF A HOUSEHOLD COMPLEX

Middleburg and a Developing Theory of Household Change

Pulled together, the archaeological testing and oral history date the construction of the Commissary at 1820 to 1830. It was built with an 18-inch-deep, 12-inch-wide foundation, insuring the stability and permanence of the structure. The small raised windows have 1-inch-thick iron bars allowing natural light and air into the storage area while protecting the goods inside. Soon after construction, an east-west post fence was built from the northwest corner of the Commissary to a point near the main house, thus further dividing the landscape and adding security to this area.

   The slave quarters were moved away from the main house area and divided into several small villages. This change was in direct response to a new law written by citizen groups in a letter to Congress that stated "every care should be taken to prevent their [slaves] association and leagueing [*sic*] together" (Citizens of Charleston 1822). The stable was then brought in closer to the main house to protect the horses and valuables should another insurrection be attempted.

The Theory Tested

Archaeological and historical investigations at a sample of other South Carolina plantations were studied to see if other households were dramatically altered during this time period. Among the plantations showing similar landscape changes during the 1820s were six in the lowcountry, near Middleburg, and one from the Piedmont, showing the extent of the fear of revolt throughout South Carolina (see Figure 7.1 for locations).

Along the east branch of the Cooper River, three neighboring plantations to Middleburg show landscape changes during the period in question. At Medway Plantation, a series of changes that took place between 1822 and 1825 included an oak-lined drive and the movement of several plantation outbuildings to within the main house area (Stoney 1938:36). At Comingtee Plantation, a new rice barn was built in the 1820s that was located closer to the main house than its predecessor by several hundred feet. This new barn was larger and had thick brick walls (Bull 1979:27). Comingtee Plantation was the home of Paris Ball, one of the slaves banished from South Carolina because of his knowledge of, and involvement in, the Vesey conspiracy.

Limerick Plantation, located just north of Middleburg, also exhibited rapid changes in the household configuration at this time. Through archaeological and architectural investigation (e.g., Babson 1988; Lees 1980), it was discovered that all of Limerick's enslaved workers lived on what was known as Tanner Road. Between the period of 1820 and 1830, the Tanner Road settlement was abandoned, and the slave community was split into several small villages placed on the periphery of the plantation. A fear of revolt was expressed by the plantation owner, Dr. Frederick Poyas, who stated that the slaves would riot "without anyone to control them" (Babson 1988:68).

The Sea Islands near Charleston were home to numerous antebellum plantations that grew rice, cotton, and indigo. At the Edwards House, a cotton plantation on Spring Island, architectural historian Colin Brooker noted that two large outbuildings were constructed close to the main house between 1820 and 1830. Both structures lacked chimneys or hearths and had little fenestration. According to Brooker (1990:143), they were "suitable for little more than storage, their proximity to the Main House ensuring security." Archaeologists found that during this same time period, the slave quarters were removed from their previous position within the main house area to a contained yet safe distance from the house (Trinkley 1990a:148).

Fairfield Plantation (also called Stoney's Plantation) on Hilton Head Island also witnessed the removal of the slave quarters from the main house area. Between 1820 and 1830, the quarters were removed from the formal Palladian plan of outbuildings surrounding the main house to another location several hundred feet away. There was an "enclosure aspect of this modification" (Trinkley 1988:67), as the slave quarters were not only removed in space, but a series of trenches and mounds were constructed between the slave villages and the main house area (where the storage buildings and stables were located) in an attempt to segregate valuable goods from the "unstable" slave population.

Mirroring the situation at Middleburg, Cotton Hope Plantation (also known as Skull Creek Plantation) on Hilton Head Island went through several changes in household layout. In the late eighteenth century, a row of slave quarters was built near the waterfront, with the cabin of the overseer directly adjacent to the quarters. The overseer often watched over the plantation when the owner, Thomas Henry Barksdale, was away on business (Trinkley 1990b:24). Sometime between 1820 and 1830, the slave quarters were removed from this location, and two large storage barns were placed next to the overseer's cabin. These new storehouses were placed at odd angles to every other structure on the plantation, as seen at Middleburg. This change indicates an immediate need for safety and security that arose between 1820 and 1830, as the storage barns were rebuilt to ensure they were guarded, and slave quarters were removed from their single group of rows and divided into smaller villages.

The sudden need for security between 1820 and 1830 was not limited to the area directly surrounding Charleston, the seat of the Vesey Rebellion. Landscape change can also be seen in the Piedmont. For example, at Rosemont Plantation in Laurens County, South Carolina, "the owners mirror social action and economic condition in their plantation layout" (Trinkley et al. 1992:31). As seen at Middleburg, between 1820 and 1830, the storehouse and barn were moved "within sight of the house," and the slave quarters were placed "in a number of scattered locations across the plantation, rather than in one central row or settlement" (Trinkley et al. 1992:34), all in an attempt to conquer fear and retain security.

A RETURN TO HEGEMONY AND THE HOUSEHOLD

It now seems clear that several South Carolina plantations underwent major alterations within the household complex between 1820 and 1830. In all the examples, the change was drastic and sudden. A significant event took place to influence planters all over the state to change their plantations' spatial patterns and architectural structures in exactly the same way. That incident is believed to be the Denmark Vesey Slave Conspiracy of 1822, after which the Charleston District and the state of South Carolina "never again relaxed the outward forms of vigilance" (Channing 1970:45).

What do these changes reveal about archaeology and "studies of the internal dynamics and intrarelationships of a household" (Allison 1999a:2)? They show that outside forces can directly affect the internal composition of the household, as was expected. More important, they indicate that the study of the internal dynamics of a single household can develop larger theories on human behavior, which can then be applied to a host of households. For example, the white owners at Middleburg radically altered the spatial composition of the built environment of the household complex despite the fact that these changes would end up costing them a great deal of money and time. The storage building was placed in a location where all goods and equipment would have to be carted up a hill and brought across over one-third of a mile. They feared an uprising within the household and, because of their dominant position, were able to forgo convenience for security. After all, while this change could cost them profit, they were not the ones to labor in the fields and bring the goods up to the new, safe structures.

This chapter also raises additional questions on the study of plantation hegemony. To use Scott's (1990) dialectic, the changing of landscapes appears to be a *public* form of reassertion of dominance over the resisting slaves. How did slave revolts modify the *private* relationship between planters and the slaves? Archaeologists have noted a severe decline of traditional goods found on slave quarter sites around 1820 to 1840, such as the disappearance of colonoware (Ferguson 1992:107). Moreover, before this time, African Americans were often viewed as mere chattel by their masters. A revolt such as Vesey's, rumored to include over 10,000 people, showed the biased and Anglocentric planters that slaves and free blacks alike were actually capable of rational thought and calculated risks. The planters were forced, therefore, to look at their workforce in a whole other light, which greatly altered the already tumultuous planter/slave relationship. How can this information help us examine other aspects of intra-household dynamics at this time? And how does it alter our current interpretation of antebellum landscapes?

By examining the plantation as a household complex composed of numerous individual households and as a single, measurable socioeconomic entity within the wider community, this paper closely inspected intraplantation dominance and control. Moreover, the reaction of the white planting elite to the suspected 1822 revolt showed a patterned behavior among one facet of the plantation household, as the dominant group quickly realized that the enslaved workforce was capable of logical thought and outright resistance. The plantation landscape was, therefore, even more intricate than anyone could have thought.

ACKNOWLEDGMENTS

Foremost, this piece would not have been possible without the continued support and guidance from Maria Franklin, Leland Ferguson, and Doug Sanford. Fieldwork was generously supported through a grant-in-aid from the Archaeological Society of South Carolina, and the Max Hill family of Charleston graciously welcomed me onto their beautiful property to conduct the excavations and architectural analysis of the Commissary. Thank you, also, to Skip Stewart-Abernathy, Whitney Battle, and Sean Maroney, who read preliminary drafts of this paper and provided many helpful and insightful comments.

8

A Historic Pay-for-Housework Community Household

The Cambridge Cooperative Housekeeping Society

Suzanne Spencer-Wood

INTRODUCTION: ARE COMMUNITY COOPERATIVES HOUSEHOLDS?

The Cambridge Cooperative Housekeeping Society (CCHS) was the first pay-for-housework movement. It was also the earliest cooperative housekeeping enterprise identified in the United States to date. Housekeeping cooperatives were one of the nineteenth-century women's reform movements that I call "domestic reform." Domestic reformers, who were predominantly middle-class women, transformed the dominant gender ideology by combining the domestic and public spheres in a number of ways. A feminist inclusive theoretical approach permits the consideration of sites as both domestic and public rather than exclusively one or the other (Spencer-Wood 1999a:166, 170).

In cooperatives women aimed to raise their status by transforming household chores into public businesses and female professions of equivalent status to male professions. Reformers created new women's public institutions and professions to make women economically independent because they thought women's economic dependency on men was the cause of their inequality. The professionalization of women's household chores was symbolized and implemented with special, often scientific, equipment, built environments, and training by professional female teachers in classes, schools, and colleges (Spencer-Wood 1991b, 1994).

Reform-minded women founded two types of public cooperative housekeeping enterprises: community cooperatives and low-cost or charitable cooperatives to assist working women with childcare and housework. In cooperatives some chores repetitively performed in each household were replaced with socialized performance of these chores by wage labor in public institutions or businesses. A few community cooperatives were voluntarily organized and operated by working-class women and their children to assist each other with the chores involved in providing a hot dinner for their families. In most community cooperatives, such as the CCHS and dining clubs, middle-class housewives cooperatively organized themselves and their servants or other wage laborers to perform some household chores more efficiently. The middle-class housewives usually volunteered and occasionally were paid to supervise wage laborers (Spencer-Wood 1991b:259–260).

Are cooperatives a type of household? They do not meet the co-residence requirement in some definitions of the household (e.g., Hendon 1996:47; Wilk and Netting 1984), but they do fit other definitions that focus on how the household functions as a social institution for performing certain chores and activities. Wilk and Rathje (1982) classify four categories of household chores and activities: production, distribution among households, reproduction, and intergenerational transmission of property. Yanagisako (1979) argues further that primary household functions involve food production and consumption and social reproduction of labor. A number of archaeologists consider consumption to be a primary function of households (e.g., Spencer-Wood 1984:90; 1987a; 1987c:7–8; Wilk and Netting 1984).

Cooperatives can also be analyzed from postmodern feminist perspectives concerned with household composition, life cycle, and power dynamics among household members involved in performing chores (Hendon 1996:48, Tringham 1991:101). Cooperatives fit Marxist-feminist definitions of households as workplaces for housewives' unpaid labor, which is essential to reproduce labor biologically and socially (Donovan 2001).

Cooperatives fit functional definitions of households at the community level in the sense that cooperative workers performed some chores for a number of individual households. For community cooperatives, as well as their middle-class urban household members, production must be broadly defined as production of use-value goods for household consumption, exemplified by the value added by domestic labor to transform raw foodstuffs into meals. Cooperatives that produced meals, clean laundry, or child care also provided household functions necessary for the social reproduction of labor. Housekeeping cooperatives further provided the function of distributing cooperatively produced use-value goods such as meals or clean laundry to households who were members of the community cooperative household.

Netting (1993) has proposed that the static definitions of the noun *household* be transformed into the verb *householding* to express a more dynamic view encompassing process and change. The term *cooperative housekeeping* used by historic reform women reflects their view of cooperatives as involving the process of performing household chores. Cooperatives also materially embodied changes in the way household workers organized and performed chores. Individual housekeeping rituals were replaced with a cooperative organization of workers to perform household chores more efficiently for a community of individual households.

Feminists problematize and unpack ahistorical universal definitions of *the* household to look at diversity and flexibility in the performance of household chores. Feminist standpoint theory leads one to ask, from whose viewpoints were cooperatives a type of household? This question is inextricably interrelated with the composition of housekeeping cooperatives. Two types of cooperatives functioned as community household workplaces for all members: working-class cooperatives of housewives and their children and middle-class cooperatives in which housewives supervised their servants. In both these cases cooperative workers were all members of individual households participating in the cooperative. However, power differentiated middle-class housewives, who had hierarchical authority over their working-class paid servants, whether white or African American.

When a cooperative was composed of housewives and wage laborers who were not their servants, then it functioned as a community household only for the housewives and was a workplace only for the wage laborers. Wage laborers in cooperatives were not usually performing their own housework because they could not afford to pay for someone else to do it. Domestic day laborers in cooperatives and individual households did not suffer from the social stigmatization of domestic servants who were always on call to serve their masters. Day laborers were also free from the control of servants' lives by masters who did not allow servants to marry and sometimes sexually harassed or seduced/raped female servants.

In some cases, cooperative housekeeping enterprises were organized by adjacent households as neighborhood household cooperatives. In other cases, such as the CCHS, cooperatives were formed by individual member households who were not all in the same neighborhood but who formed a community of shared values, class, ethnicity, race, or other social dimensions. The women and men who organized the CCHS were all middle-class and white. However, the cooperative workers were lower-class and may have been of a different ethnicity or race from the cooperative organizers. Applying Anderson's framework of nested households (this volume), the individual households were members of a higher-level household, whether a local neighborhood cooperative or the geographically larger-scale community cooperative.

The composition of housekeeping cooperatives also changed during the lifetime of the cooperative, as different individual households became members or dropped out of cooperatives through its life cycle, from its founding until it was dissolved. The workers also changed during a cooperative's lifetime, possibly changing its ethnic or racial composition. The CCHS exemplifies how a cooperative household's composition and gender power dynamics could lead to the loss of members and the demise of the cooperative.

Feminist theory brings to household definitions the analysis of complexly interrelated gender, class, racial, and ethnic power dynamics involved in differing household compositions (Hendon 1996:48; Spencer-Wood 1995:129; 1996: 411–412, 423). In founding cooperatives, housewives were resisting the male-dominated individual household to create a female-controlled space for the performance of household chores using the female associated power of cooperation (see conclusion). Working-class women's cooperatives would operate out of the household kitchen of each cooperative member on a rotating basis, creating a female-dominated and -controlled space within each male-dominated household. In middle-class and elite individual households, male hierarchical domination led to the performance of household chores such as laundry and cooking in marginal spaces such as dark, damp basements. In cooperatives, middle-class housewives created more efficient and healthier built environments for performing household chores by rationally arranging equipment for large-scale laundry or cooking in large, airy, first-floor rooms with many windows and good ventilation (Mitararchi 1978; Peirce 1868:691).

Cooperatives were the material embodiments of changes the reformers created in gender and class power dynamics involved in the performance of household chores. From the viewpoint of housewives, they gained some freedom from the demands of constantly supervising servants and, in many cases, used their newfound free time to participate in domestic reform organizations. From the viewpoint of domestic servants, cooperative environments were usually more pleasant than their workspaces in individual households. Cooperative labor was also considered more pleasant because, as the saying goes, "many hands make light work." In addition, cooperatives often had more up-to-date equipment than individual households, equipment that performed more of the work. Working in cooperatives instead of individual households also freed servants from membership in the households of their employer with its risks of sexual assault. Cooperatives transformed servants into higher-status wage laborers and permitted them to marry and create their own separate households.

Hendon (1996) pointed out that households cannot be separated from the larger economic structure of society. A major trend has been the increasing performance of household functions by larger-scale public units outside the home. For instance, housekeeping cooperatives, cooperative hotels, and boarding-houses are similar in combining businesses with public households for production of use-value goods, distribution, social reproduction of labor, and consumption (Spencer-Wood 1991a:238). Reform women argued that cooperatives transformed private housekeeping into public businesses. In the municipal housekeeping movement, reform women further argued that towns and cities were community households because municipalities supplied individual households with services necessary for the social reproduction of labor, including water, and the cleaning chores of household garbage removal, sewage systems, and street cleaning (Spencer-Wood 1994:180).

FOUNDING THE CAMBRIDGE COOPERATIVE HOUSEKEEPING SOCIETY

Melusina Fay Peirce was a renowned social reformer in her day who was best known for originating the theory of cooperative housekeeping and attempting to put it into practical operation in the CCHS in 1869–1871 (Johnson and Brown 1904). Melusina and many of the society's other members were Harvard faculty wives. The society was governed by an all-male Council of Gentlemen composed of members' husbands. In the remainder of this chapter, I examine how household gendered power-relations, especially between husbands and wives, affected the operation of the CCHS.

In an 1864 article in *The World,* Melusina first imagined a housekeeping cooperative of fashionable ladies who voluntarily supervised lower-class women in producing and distributing food to families who would pay for the service. Her ideas were iconoclastic and revolutionary because in the dominant gender ideology it was not considered respectable for ladies to work in public. Her writings show the influence of her great-aunt Caroline Howard Gilman's book *Recollections of a Housekeeper* (1834), which advocated the professionalization of housekeeping services, including cooking establishments to provide families with prepared food.

Following her article in *The World,* Melusina wrote a groundbreaking series of articles in the *Atlantic Monthly,* from November 1868 to March 1869, in which she developed her seminal theory of cooperative housekeeping within the context of a broader philosophical critique of women's loss of status, power, and value as they transformed from producers on farms to increasingly "parasitic" ladies whose roles were limited to consumption and managing household servants. She preceded Marxist feminists in viewing unpaid domestic labor as the source of women's economic and intellectual oppression.

Melusina was also feminist in arguing from her own experience that women's intellectual talents suffer a "costly and unnatural sacrifice" to "the dusty drudgery of house ordering" as she put it (Peirce 1884:181). In her own experience the daily demands of housekeeping, even without children, interfered with her attempts in the 1860s to study and write about the true causes of African slavery (Peirce 1864). She argued that women's higher talents were going to waste because of the demands of their household duties.

Melusina advocated that women regain their earlier economic independence and power as producers by organizing into a commercial housekeeping cooperative in which middle-class housewives would be paid a decent wage for directing and supervising housework cooperatively. She further advocated a combined producer/consumer cooperative, in which women would not only cooperatively produce clean laundry and food but also would exercise their combined power as consumers by buying as a group to reduce prices. She pointed out that housewives could make a profit by pooling their housekeeping allowance to purchase supplies in bulk and sell them at retail in a cooperative store that would provide top quality goods at cheaper prices than other retailers. Zina suggested that women were better suited than men for the developing retail industry because of women's supposedly innate characteristics, including conscientiousness, accuracy, efficiency, tact, taste, and prudence.

A few months after her last article was published in the *Atlantic Monthly*, Melusina put her detailed plans into action in organizing the Cambridge Cooperative Housekeeping Society. The members listed in its 1869 prospectus included 12 wives of Harvard professors, including Zina (CCHS 1869). On July 2, Melusina's husband, Charles S. Peirce, wrote a letter of introduction for her to Harvard's president, Charles W. Eliot, asking him to provide Harvard University buildings for the CCHS. However, Eliot was either unwilling or unable to do so, for the group had no formal tie to Harvard despite the support of a number of faculty on its organizing committee (Eliot Papers). Zina was not discouraged by President Eliot's refusal to provide a university building and proceeded with her plans to organize the CCHS.

A few days later, on July 10, 1869, another article by Melusina in *The World* (Peirce 1869b) explained the reasons why ladies should join the CCHS. She first gave three practical reasons for a housekeeping cooperative: the cost of food had practically doubled; the cost of servants was increasing while the quality of their work was decreasing; and servants were disrupting family life by leaving their jobs after very short periods of employment. Second, she repeated her theoretical arguments for cooperation from her *Atlantic Monthly* articles. She argued that for women to become economically and emotionally independent from men, they needed to apply two capitalistic principles to cooperation: the raising of capital for a cooperative enterprise and the organization and division of labor, in which women would perform specialized tasks instead of the many different tasks that generalized housekeeping demanded. Zina used the need for specialization to justify her elitist contention that workers in cooperatives had to be supervised by middle-class housewives, duplicating power relations in domestic service rather than empowering working women to supervise their own work cooperatively.

In the same issue of *The World*, an editorial took a male viewpoint in praising Melusina's ideas because cooperative housekeeping would benefit men through more pleasant homes without kitchens and laundries. However, the editorial made the patriarchal suggestion that her plans could be most profitably realized by putting experienced businessmen in charge of the cooperative. Creating cooperatives as male hierarchically organized businesses would have defeated the nonhierarchical female cooperative housekeeping plans that had already led to Zina's reputation for expertise in cooperation. As her mother-in-law, Sarah Peirce, wrote to her son, Benjamin, in Wisconsin (Peirce 1869), "Bertie tells me Zina is considered a great wonder up at Marquette and indeed she has succeeded in making herself quite famous."

The first meeting of the CCHS was held on May 6, 1869, at the home of Charles S. Peirce's parents, Harvard professor and Mrs. Benjamin Peirce, both of whom were members, as well as Zina and her husband, Charles. The other members attending were Mary Peabody Mann, the widow of Professor Horace Mann, Professor and Mrs. Nathaniel S. Shaler, Mr. and Mrs. H. O. Apthorp, Professor Francis J. Child, Professor George M. Lane, William Dean Howells, and the Reverend and Mrs. Joseph H. Allen. Benjamin Peirce chaired this meeting, and a man chaired all subsequent mixed-gender meetings.

Melusina was elected to a committee of three to devise the steps for getting subscriptions to the society (Atkinson 1983:54). After two more organizational meetings and the issuing of a public announcement, a public meeting was held in the "room back of the [Cambridge] Post Office," attended by 75 to 100 women (Hayden 1981:80). It was decided to turn the organization of the CCHS over to the women, who would continue to hold regular mass meetings. When the women met separately, Melusina chaired the meeting (Atkinson 1983:54).

Melusina decided that the CCHS would be overseen by a Council of Gentlemen made up of the husbands of members, since the women had to have the permission of their husbands to participate in the society anyway, because, as she put it, "man is the head of woman." Melusina felt that the Council of Gentlemen could be manipulated into ratifying whatever the women voted for (Peirce 1869b).

In meetings from June to December 1869, a number of issues were decided, including the cost and method of selling subscriptions, the issuing of a prospectus, and the question of incorporation (Atkinson 1983:54–55). The prospectus stated that the CCHS would follow the practices of the famous cooperative store established in England by the workingmen's organization, the Rochdale Equitable Pioneers. These practices included conducting business on a cash basis, selling to members at current retail prices, paying interest on shares, and dividing profits among members in proportion to the amount of their purchases (CCHS 1869:1).

The most important ongoing issues for the CCHS were the framing of a constitution and the location and purchase of a building, or a lot where a building could be built. Mixed-gender committees were formed to deal with these problems, with Zina on the constitution committee. By January 1870, seven women had been elected as a Board of Managers, with Zina as treasurer (Atkinson 1983:55; Peirce 1872:8). The constitution was approved after a great deal of discussion and revision at the urging of the men. Subscription costs were decided on: $50 for the laundry, $100 for the kitchen, and $25 for the storeroom (CCHS 1869:1).

In the prospectus, the list of subscribing members of the CCHS totaled 35, including two unmarried men living in boardinghouses. In nineteenth-century androcentric tradition the married members were listed by their husband's names, such as Mrs. John B. Perry. Beyond mere convention, the use of their husbands' names expressed the fact that married women were considered civilly dead and without legal rights, being publicly represented by their husbands (Donovan 2001:22, 33; Millett 1970:67–69). The membership included two single women and three widows who were listed under their own names in the 1870 Cambridge Directory. Melusina had argued in her *Atlantic Monthly* series that single women who worked in a housekeeping cooperative would be doing something much more meaningful than the feminine ideal of wasting all their time just acting as social butterflies (Peirce 1869a:37–39).

At least 12 Harvard professors were members of the Council of Gentlemen that oversaw the CCHS, although only their wives were listed as members. In addition, according to the prospectus, Professor Blot had promised to superintend the kitchen himself or procure a chef for the society. Besides the five members' husbands on the organizing committee who were Harvard professors, other husbands of members who were also Harvard professors included James C. Fisk, dean of students; Mr. Parkman, professor of theology; Oliver Stearns, dean of the Divinity School; Professor Joseph Winlock, director of the Harvard College Observatory; Alexander Agassiz, professor of zoology and geology; Assistant Professor John B. Perry, curator of the Zoological Museum; E. W. Gurney, professor of Latin; and Lucien Carr, professor of archaeology (CCHS 1869; City of Cambridge Directory 1870). Although these men were not on the membership list, they held hidden controlling power over the CCHS through the Council of Gentlemen.

OPERATION OF THE CAMBRIDGE COOPERATIVE HOUSEKEEPING SOCIETY

After the CCHS considered various possible sites for its cooperative, the Meachum House on Bow Street was rented on March 7, 1870 (Peirce 1872:6). It is probably more than coincidence that this location was closest to Melusina's house (as well as the Shalys and Professor Love), while most of the members lived on the other side of Harvard Square, requiring a walk of between 10 and 30 minutes (Cambridge Directory 1870; Hopkins 1873). During the following month, the house was fitted up with large-scale equipment and ordinary domestic furnishings for the laundry and the kitchen, the latter with its subdivisions of storeroom and bakery.

Melusina's brief description of the outfitting of the co-op does not seem to conform completely to her utopian design of a housekeeping cooperative in her *Atlantic Monthly* series. No mention in the fitting-up is made of Zina's designs for a sewing workroom, a fitting room, a workers' lounge and dressing room on both the first and second floors, and third-floor spaces for the workers —a gymnasium, a reading room, and a dining room with dumbwaiter, all with movable walls so the space could be opened up to create a ballroom for monthly dances for workers arranged by the middle-class housewife/cooperators who oversaw their work (Peirce 1872:6) (Figure 8.1). These spaces were probably omitted because of financial constraints of the undercapitalized enterprise.

The "First Quarterly Meeting" was held at the Bow Street house on April 20, 1870. Mrs. G. W. C. Noble was elected president, Mrs. E. M. Richardson to run the laundry, and Mrs. Horace Mann to run the bakery. It was probably not a coincidence that both were widows whose work at the cooperative would not have disrupted their domestic duties. Melusina expected that she would run the cooperative store.

The prospectus of the CCHS (1869:2) stated that the middle-class housekeeper/members elected to direct the business of the society would at first be paid salaries at the going rate for women's labor. As soon as the association became a financial success, these salaries, as well as the wages of the workwomen, were to be raised to the going rates for men's labor for similar services. At this meeting it was decided to allot a salary of $100/month for the treasurer. Melusina later stated that this was a mistake, because even though she refused this salary, it led other members to expect her to do most of the work and discouraged them from volunteering to work the three hours a week originally proposed by Zina in her articles.

The laundry was opened first, on April 23, because the lady members voted they needed it most. Workers were paid higher wages than at other laundries, and gradually the lazy, shiftless workers who required constant supervision were replaced with reliable and skillful workers. Melusina reported that

(laundry work is so hard that it seemed cruel to pay less than eighty cents or a dollar a day), the rooms were pleasant, the employment was constant, and the women loved to work there. It seemed to your Treasurer, could other ladies have only realized it, that here was the true relation between

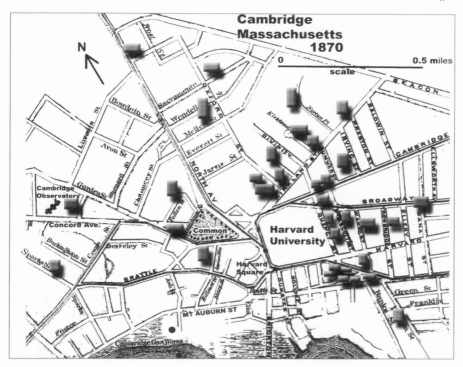

Fig. 8.1. 1870 Cambridge, Massachusetts, directory map, modified with floating rectangles showing approximate locations of the CCHS cooperative and member households. Only approximate addresses were available for many households and for the cooperative. The building is located in the densest cluster of member households just south of Harvard University. Melusina and Charles Peirce's house was the southeasternmost house in this cluster, at the intersection of Arrow Street and North Avenue (now Massachusetts Avenue). A couple of member households were outside Cambridge and could not be included on this map. Names and addresses were not available for employees of the CCHS.

the well-off woman and the poor one,—that of sympathizing employer to honest laborer rather than that of charity-giver to semi-pauper, as in our Humane Societies; while every week more encomiums of the good work that was sent home, and of the "comfort" of such work at the moderate prices asked, came in to cheer your Treasurer's heart." (1872:7–8).

On July 1, 1870, Melusina took charge of the laundry after three previous paid superintendents had produced average losses of $15.12 per week. This resulted from the fact that the washing sent to the laundry was one-quarter the size for which machinery had been installed. The rent for the large space and the cost of fuel for the large stoves was more than the small wash could cover at the low prices set by the CCHS. Melusina decreased the laundry's expenses by running it as the superintendent without pay, and it would have made a profit except that the amount of laundry further decreased in the summer, resulting in a smaller weekly loss of nearly $8. She concluded that the prices estimated in papers on laundry cooperatives and adopted by the CCHS were too low. However, the prices were not raised. Participating cooperative members profited, one saving the price of her $50 share in 16 weeks (Peirce 1872:5–6).

Following a vote of the society, the cooperative store was opened July 2, 1870. Melusina had expected to manage the store but was only able to do the initial buying because she had volunteered her time to manage the laundry. Only 10–12 subscribers patronized the store and the laundry, resulting in sales that were one-third the size of expenses. As a result, the store could not be restocked, and orders were filled by buying at full retail cost from local grocers, whose goods sometimes elicited complaints because of unsatisfactory quality (Peirce 1872:6–7; 1884:79).

The bakery was started soon after the laundry but "was abruptly closed because there was no one to take sole charge of it; and a large baking, which, with a horse and cart, could have been sold off fresh, grew stale on our hands, and was almost a total loss" (Peirce 1872:7). The planned horse, cart, and delivery man could not be afforded because $900 of expected capital was never paid in by members who defaulted on their pledges.

FAILURE OF THE CCHS AND MALE DOMINANCE IN HOUSEHOLD GENDER RELATIONS

Melusina reported three reasons for failure in the final report of the CCHS of 1872 and supplied further details on the primary reason in her 1884 book, *Cooperative Housekeeping: How Not to Do It and How to Do It, a Study in Sociology*. The most fundamental cause of failure was the gendered power relationships between housewife members of the CCHS and their husbands. In 1884, Zina stated that "a few men sustained the attempt most loyally, but most of the husbands laughed good-naturedly at the whole thing, prophesied its failure and put their wives out of heart and out of conceit with it from the beginning" (Peirce 1884:109).

Melusina stated she believed that "there *is* a 'lion in the path' [to cooperative housekeeping], and a very real one—HUSBAND-POWER which is very apt to shut down like an invisible bell-glass over every woman as soon as she is married and say to her, 'My dear, thus far shalt thou go and no farther' " (Peirce 1884:106–107). She detailed specific examples of dominating behaviors by husbands who forbade or discouraged their wives from participating in the CCHS.

She described the reaction to the CCHS by a distinguished Cambridge abolitionist: "'What!' exclaimed this apostle of freedom for negroes, '*my* wife "cooperate" to make other men comfortable? No indeed!'—Now was not that the
crack of the slave-driver's whip, though the master this time was not a southern
planter, nor the slave a colored brother?" (Peirce 1884:108). This statement demonstrates Zina's awareness of the development of the suffrage movement out of an
analogy between African-American slavery and white women's lack of rights.

The husbands of a number of members of the CCHS exhibited other dominating behaviors that made it difficult for the members of the society to meet.
Melusina reports:

> After the Association had been at work for a few weeks, the president had
> to resign because the lady directors called at her house for conference
> oftener than suited her husband, and once kept him waiting for a button
> to be sewed on. Another husband would not let his wife be president be-
> cause he said if the Association failed it might "injure his position." A
> third allowed his wife to join the undertaking and pay her subscription
> on condition that she should never go to any of the meetings. One young
> man convinced his widowed mother that everything was being mis-
> managed, and made her a continual "thorn in the side" of the directors
> of the Association from the beginning to the end of its existence. (Peirce
> 1884:107–109)

The two widowed members of the society from the outset were Mrs. E. M.
Richardson and Mrs. Horace Mann (CCHS 1869). Since Mrs. Mann was a dedicated reformer, it seems most likely that Mrs. Richardson was the widow referred to by Melusina.

Hayden (1981) has suggested that some husbands, including Charles Peirce,
Dean Howells (editor of the *Atlantic Monthly*), James Fisk, and John Perry may
have organized a club in 1870 that discussed not only philosophy but also the
ridicule and sabotage they perpetrated against the CCHS. This exclusively male
club met one Tuesday a month at a member's house for dinner prepared by his
wife and servants. Hayden challenges the assumption of male historians that
this club, called The Club or The Metaphysical Club by some members, was
purely intellectual (Cady 1956:145–146; Hayden 1981:81).

Husbands of members also acted to create the failure of the CCHS by using
their positions of dominance on the Council of Gentlemen. Melusina had
made the mistake of giving controlling power over the organization to the
council in recognition of the fact that their permission was required for the
participation of their wives. The council changed the constitution originally
voted in by the ladies, replacing four directresses to manage each department

and report to a thirteen-member Executive Committee with a board of seven managers and Melusina alone as "the active and responsible agent for the whole, as in a manufacturing company." "Nothing but ample funds to pay capable subordinates could enable even a thorough business man, who had no domestic cares at home, to do it. But had each department had its own directresses, the thought, the labor, and the responsibility would have been so shared that it would not have fallen too heavily upon any, and the decisions arrived at in a number of cases would have been wiser" (Peirce 1872:8–9). The Council of Gentlemen set up the CCHS for failure by unreasonably placing sole responsibility for all supervisory work on Melusina's head. This organizational change was no doubt related to the husbands' desires that their wives not be distracted from meeting family needs at home. They exerted their culturally sanctioned dominating power to monopolize their wives' labor for the sole benefit of each individual household.

The ladies on the Board of Managers began to avoid the house rented by the CCHS because of the opposition of their husbands and the related lack of patronage by members, who stuck with their previous, more expensive suppliers because they did not want to be associated with failure. By October 1, 1870, Melusina, "unable any longer to bear unassisted the physical fatigue of the roles of head laundress and superintendent in one,—and convinced of the hopelessness of making the Laundry pay expenses unless the ladies themselves would superintend it, she advised the closing of that department and, resigning her office called a general meeting of the Society to appoint a successor. Two members and two managers attended this meeting" (Peirce 1872:8). The vast majority of members had been discouraged from continuing to support the efforts of Melusina to maintain the CCHS by herself.

In the fall of 1870, Charles Peirce wrote to Zina "so continually from Europe to come over and join him [on the American Eclipse Expedition to the Mediterranean], that at last she felt forced to go and leave the Association to get on without her as best it might!" (Peirce 1884:109). She left Cambridge on October 8 and returned in April 1871. She found the laundry already closed because it had lost money under a number of paid supervisors, as the ladies would not each voluntarily supervise it one day a week (Peirce 1884:80–81).

The laundry closed on March 7 and the store on April 1, 1871, "when the Society was dissolved by a two-thirds vote of its members, ratified by a unanimous vote of the Council of Gentlemen" (Peirce 1872:6, 8). Melusina criticized the husband of one inactive member who attended the final meeting "determined that the attempt should end then and there." Other husbands said they wanted to "prevent misconception on the subject of feasibility of cooperation in this community" (Peirce 1884:110). The Council of Gentlemen exerted their culturally sanctioned dominating power to control their wives and the community cooperative. The fact that Zina recorded voices only of men in favor of dissolving the CCHS suggests that the women members may have been intimidated by their husbands into silently voting to dissolve the CCHS.

In the final report, Melusina noted two other reasons for the failure of the CCHS. One was the ladies' vote to begin with the laundry because it was most needed and therefore more likely to succeed, despite Melusina's expectations that it would be more trouble and less profitable than any other department. Previous cooperatives by workmen's associations started with a store, the easiest and most profitable cooperative.

Melusina self-critically reported her own mistake—the second reason—in expecting a cooperative society to pay high rent and salaries at the beginning when English cooperative societies initially paid low rent or none at all and their members volunteered as supervisors and clerks. The lack of voluntary service by CCHS members cost the society over $500. Zina concluded that although the CCHS was undercapitalized, it failed for lack of cooperation among the members, which could have made up for the low funding (Peirce 1872:9).

In addition, Melusina pointed out that men would rather pay more for food and domestic services than allow their wives to be preoccupied by a "Society" that Melusina now estimated

> would take six capable housekeepers six months of hard and anxious work—of work such as men bestow upon their enterprises—to organize properly such an undertaking as we attempted, and during those six months their families might suffer something as families do in moving; that is, there could hardly fail to be home dislocation and discomfort. That afterward things would be immensely *more* comfortable and economical than before, your Treasurer believes as firmly as ever. But even could the six capable housekeepers be found who would undertake it, where in one town are there six families who would *allow* their mistresses thus to make them secondary for six months? Women not being free agents, therefore, it is not probable that we shall soon see a successful experiment in "Cooperative Housekeeping." (Peirce 1872:10)

Zina euphemistically used the word "families" when she elsewhere explicitly detailed the domination of women by their husbands as the primary cause of the demise of the CCHS.

HISTORICAL ARCHAEOLOGY OF THE CULTURAL LANDSCAPE

The CCHS was mapped as a community household, showing geographical relationships between member households and the cooperatives on the urban landscape of Cambridge. In completing the mapping of sites begun earlier (Spencer-Wood 1987b:14), this research provides new insights into the failure of the cooperative. Distances between the houses of members and the cooperative laundry, store, and bakery gave spatio-material meaning to the performance and practices involved in the dominant Victorian gender ideology.

House sites of CCHS members were mapped as accurately as possible from addresses in Cambridge directories from 1863 to 1870, a map in the 1870 directory, and houses mapped and labeled by owner in the 1873 Atlas of Cambridge. In many cases, the addresses in the Cambridge directories did not specify street numbers, but just the intersection of two streets where the house was located. Addresses for the cooperative enterprises were provided only in general in the reports of the CCHS (see Figure 8.1).

Examination of the map provides significant insight into the material reality of the CCHS and may contribute new information concerning the reasons for its failure. It is especially interesting to note that most members' houses were within a 15–20-minute walk of the cooperatives, yet the bread went stale on the shelves of the bakery for lack of a delivery truck and delivery man. This reality indicates that the normative expectation was that women would fulfill the dominant gender ideology by remaining within their domestic sphere of the home while men delivered goods over men's public landscape to the individual islands of women's domestic built environments. The spatial evidence suggests the strength of the sanctions against "respectable" middle-class women leaving their houses during the day and walking alone in public. It also suggests that the middle-class household managers were unwilling to send their servants, who were also female in most cases, out in the public landscape on their own. Perhaps the problem was the lack of an escort, which feminist historians have found recorded as a necessity for "respectable" women in the public landscape (e.g., Ryan 1990:16, 68, 83). Or perhaps wives were simply discouraged by domineering husbands from using the cooperatives, as noted by Melusina Fay Peirce (1884). However, some housewives did patronize the store and laundry, so some must have been willing to send their servants out or to travel themselves to the cooperatives, while others were not able or willing to do so.

The location of the cooperatives may have also discouraged their use by many members. The cooperatives were not centrally located within the membership but rather at one end of their geographical distribution on the landscape. This meant that at least 10 members—almost one-third of the total membership—lived too far away to walk comfortably to the cooperatives. This number sheds new light on the importance of a delivery wagon and delivery man not only for the bakery but for the cooperative store and the cooperative laundry. In the case of the laundry and possibly the store, a vehicle would have been needed to transport any quantity of goods bought at the store and any quantity of laundry to and from that cooperative.

Examination of the map further revealed that the laundry was closest to the residences of the Shalers, Gordon McKay, and Mr. and Mrs. Charles Peirce. Melusina may have wanted to establish the cooperatives close to her house because she founded them and was doing most of the work running the co-operatives. However, other members may have seen this as self-serving on Melusina's part because the cooperatives were located at substantially greater distances from the houses of most other members. The plan to pay Melusina for her time may have also seemed unfair to other women, who were asked to volunteer, and may explain why she refused payment. The lack of pickup or delivery service for the laundry may have discouraged participation for the same reasons as Melusina thought it did at the bakery.

This field site survey further revealed that the Cambridge Cooperative So-ciety buildings housing the cooperatives have probably been destroyed, as well as most of the houses of the cooperative's members. This result was expected based on the few domestic reform sites found to be preserved in Boston (Spencer-Wood 1996: Appendixes A, B). For many sites, the less specific addresses involv-ing only street intersections provided in Cambridge directories made it difficult to assess whether a house had survived or not, unless the houses on all four corners of an intersection had been either preserved or destroyed and replaced by later buildings. The buildings were dated architecturally to assess whether they could date from the 1869–1872 period of the Cambridge Cooperative House-keeping Society. Further, when available, the building outline on a historic map was compared to the outline of any surviving building on the site. This process permitted a more conclusive assessment of the survival of houses and build-ings connected to the CCHS.

Archaeologically, it would probably be impossible to distinguish the houses of members of the CCHS from those of other middle-class families, as the CCHS did not involve any long-term change in the lives of its members that can be expected to leave archaeological remains. It is also unlikely that archaeo-logical evidence at the sites of the cooperatives would permit their identifica-tion. The large-scale laundry stoves and other equipment from the laundry, bakery, and store were carefully inventoried in the final report of the CCHS, indicating that they were not discarded in the cooperative site yards. Other than the large stoves for heating the laundry water, the descriptions of equip-ment for the laundry, the bakery kitchen, and the store cannot be distinguished from ordinary household equipment.

The primary new insights gained from this research about the CCHS re-sulted from the landscape archaeology of the geographical distribution of sites.

It was essential to identify and map cooperative sites from documentary data because they are unlikely to be identifiable from excavated data alone. Documentary and landscape archaeological data have been used conjunctively to gain greater insights into the past than either source of data could provide alone.

CONCLUSION

Historical archaeological research has been conducted to gain greater insight into the reasons for the failure of the Cambridge Cooperative Society than could be gained from documents alone. Landscape archaeology concerning the geographical distribution of sites connected to the CCHS revealed how distances from member households to the community cooperatives may, in some cases, have created a barrier to using the cooperatives because they did not provide delivery of goods. It may also be the case that some middle-class housewives and their servants felt they would not be "respectable" in the dominant gender ideology if they transgressed on men's public landscape without a male escort to shop at the cooperatives. The arrangement of sites on the landscape also expressed women's power relations in the CCHS, in the sense that the cooperatives were located closer to the residence of Melusina and Charles Peirce, the woman who founded the organization and ran the cooperatives, than to most other members of the cooperative.

Significant conclusions from this research include feminist critiques of, and additions needed to, the definition of household. In contrast to the stereotypic identification of the household as exclusively domestic, the definition needs to recognize that the household combines the private domestic sphere with the public sphere of work in the performance of household chores. Consumer goods were produced by housework as much as by production in public businesses. The household is a workplace for housewives, servants, slaves, children, husbands, and in some cases extended family, who provided unpaid labor to perform household chores. Further, for paid servants the household fit the male/public definition of a workplace. In middle- and upper-class households with servants, children and husbands might not perform household chores.

Cooperatives were the beginning of a major cultural trend of transforming household chores into public household businesses. Melusina's attempt to perform household chores on a business basis in the CCHS was an early feminist recognition that the household is a workplace where housewives perform unpaid labor that should be recognized and paid as wage labor. Zina voiced the idea that women should perform household chores in the same way as men's businesses, including paying housewives to supervise wage laborers performing the chores. Zina's pay-for-housework argument precedes the Beecher sisters' aim "to elevate both the honor and the remuneration" of housework, voiced in *The American Woman's Home,* which became the most popular domestic manual in the second half of the nineteenth century (Beecher and Stowe 1869 [1985]:13).

Perhaps the greatest insight gained from this research concerns the fundamental importance of gendered power dynamics to understand how households functioned. The definition of household needs to include gender power dynamics, as well as power dynamics owing to age, class, and race or ethnicity of household members, including servants or slaves. Power dynamics in household relationships affect where and how household chores are performed and by whom. Households function differently in the ways they organize to perform chores depending on the power dynamics between household members. Further, the case of the CCHS shows how household composition affects power dynamics among household members.

The case of the CCHS demonstrates relationships between different types of power used by women and men to organize the performance of household chores. Melusina's attempt to create a community household controlled by women failed because men dominated their wives and controlled how household chores were performed, both in their individual households and in the community household of the CCHS. Documentary data revealed that the failure of the CCHS was, in large part, because of husbands' culturally and legally sanctioned hierarchical dominating powers-over their wives (see commentary by Spencer-Wood, this volume). Many men actively discouraged or forbade their wives from participating in the CCHS. The dominating power of husbands extended to their control over where and how their wives could perform household chores as well as how they spent their time.

In the nineteenth century, wives legally belonged to their husbands as chattel, although married women had gained the right to own property in the 1850s (Millett 1970:66, 99–101). Many husbands used their legal rights as the dominant group to order their wives not to cooperate with other women in performing housework communally and instead to continue performing their household chores in their own households, isolated from other women. Men's use of their dominating powers over their wives shows how revolutionary were the arguments by domestic reformers concerning women's control of the domestic sphere (Spencer-Wood 1991b:250).

The freely voiced disapproval of the CCHS by a number of husbands was recorded by Zina, who did not record any voices of the female members, probably because they had been muted by their dominating husbands. The legal status of wives was similar to that of slaves, and men had the power to keep them separated in individual households and prevent them from organizing for household chores or for political causes such as suffrage or freedom.

Although Melusina intended the CCHS to be a community household business controlled by women, she made the mistake of creating a supervisory Council of Gentlemen, through which men exerted their dominating powers over the women's cooperative organization. Zina thought she could manipulate the men but lost in negotiations to retain control over the CCHS. The men quickly transformed it into a hierarchical organization, following the model of men's businesses. The male-associated model of power only as power over others led the men to create a hierarchical organization that discouraged the egalitarian cooperation by CCHS members envisioned by Melusina Fay Peirce.

Men's imposition of a hierarchical organization stemmed from their experience with the male-associated competitive values of capitalistic business. They may have felt these values were appropriate for the CCHS because of Melusina's argument that through public cooperatives, housework could be conducted in similar ways to men's businesses. However, she didn't have the authoritian power or capital to hire management subordinates required for the three cooperatives to operate as hierarchical business organizations.

Melusina Fay Peirce envisioned the CCHS as a women's organization that would have operated through female-associated communitarian values and what I call cooperative "powers with" the women members (see paragraph following and Spencer-Wood, this volume). Communitarian cooperative values and powers that were associated with Protestantism came to be associated with women as men increasingly left their churches because of capitalism's conflicting competitive values and valorizing of profit and money-lending, which were considered sins in the Bible. Women came to be considered innately more pious and moral than men because women were removed from capitalism in their domestic sphere and were considered closer to nature and, therefore, to God.

Women came to be associated with higher morality and communitarian "powers-with" people, such as cooperation, persuasion, "moral suasion," inspiration, empowerment, negotiation, and collective action (see Spencer-Wood commentary, this volume). These were the kinds of powers used by reform women to establish successful cooperative housekeeping institutions at the turn of the century. The prospectus of the CCHS specified cooperative power-sharing among a large number of housewife members who were expected to volunteer their time in exerting hierarchical supervisory powers-over wage laborers working in the cooperative laundry, bakery, and store.

After the failure of the CCHS, Melusina continued to write in an increasingly feminist voice, progressing from her muted 1872 report on reasons for failure of the CCHS when she was still with her husband to her 1884 book after she left Charles Peirce; it more explicitly critiques the dominating power used by husbands to prevent their wives from participating in the CCHS.

Melusina Fay Peirce became a well-known reformer for her theory of cooperative housekeeping and her designs for kitchenless and laundryless houses in neighborhoods with central cooperatives for cooking, laundry, and sewing (Malone 1934; Johnson and Brown 1904). She correctly claimed that she had earlier published many of the utopian ideas on domestic industry expressed by Edward Bellamy and by Charlotte Perkins Gilman (Peirce 1918:14–15). A number of later notable domestic reformers noted Melusina's work, including Mary Livermore, Ellen Swallows Richards, Mary Hinman Abel, Helen Campbell, Lucy Salmon, and Arthur Calhoun (Hayden 1981:87–88).

As a result of writings by Melusina Fay Peirce and other reformers, by the early twentieth century dining cooperatives and cooked food delivery services became the most widely successful neighborhood and community cooperatives in the United States. Many middle-class men from small towns to large cities supported their wives in cooperatively organizing servants or workers to provide the customary large Victorian meals that took so much energy for wives and servants to prepare in individual households (Hayden 1981:206–227). Cooperatives performed some household chores at the scale of the neighborhood or the geographically larger-scale community.

Housekeeping cooperatives demonstrate the utility of the concept of nested households because cooperatives included a number of individual member households and operated at a number of levels, from public institutions to neighborhoods, communities, and towns. Cooperatives shifted the location for performance of household chores from dispersed individual household sites to one centralized building. Cooperative housekeeping led further to the reform women's municipal housekeeping movement, in which towns and cities were viewed as households (see Spencer-Wood commentary, this volume).

More comprehensive cooperatives further merged the household with the community. In the United States, England, and Russia, some neighborhoods of kitchenless houses were built with centralized cooking and dining facilities. In America, neighborhoods with cooperative facilities ranged from a group of ordinary-looking middle-class houses, to cooperative hotels for single working women or middle- to upper-class families, cooperative boarding homes for working women such as the YWCA, and ordinary-looking working-class apartment houses with centralized housekeeping facilities. In Russia, cooperative apartment houses were designed in the form of eighteenth-century English reform designs of prisons, with linear wings of kitchenless apartments branching off from a central hub with cooperative cooking and daycare facilities. In England, the design of cooperative neighborhoods took the form of university quadrangles (Hayden 1981:228–265; Spencer-Wood 1999a:176–177, 179–180). Israeli kibbutzim had separate cooperative buildings for child care and for cooking and eating. These experiments indicate how cooperative changes in the material organization of housework entailed restructuring both the architecture and landscape of households and the neighborhood. If enough neighborhoods were restructured, cooperative housekeeping would transform the landscape and architecture of towns, cities, and entire cultures.

ACKNOWLEDGMENTS

This chapter could not have been written without the assistance of librarians and archivists at the Harvard University Archives, Houghton Library, and Widener Depository Library at Harvard. My thanks for helpful comments to the reviewers of this volume, and especially to the editors, Kerri Barile and Jamie Brandon.

9
Fictive Kin in the Mountains

The Paternalistic Metaphor and Households in a California Logging Camp

Efstathios I. Pappas

INTRODUCTION

The study of industrial labor and work camps is a topic of increasing attention in historical archaeology. The focus of these studies has usually been the interplay between company and social dynamics in a camp setting. The major areas of interest remain gender, ethnicity, and class, as they manifested themselves in the lives of workers. Of this triad of issues relating to industrial labor forces, gender has often received the least attention, with most activity given to female-focused studies or to methodological concerns for distinguishing single-gendered households (Hardesty 1988, 1994, 2002). Ethnicity and the interaction between different ethnic groups within the context of work, on the other hand, have been well studied and are the subject of a lively, ongoing discourse in historical archaeology (Silliman 2000; Veltre and McCartney 2002).

However, the concept of class in the industrial workplace is perhaps the most unique aspect of these three issues in terms of industrial labor communities. Capitalism and the use of resources to gain wealth spawned the dynamic class system of the nineteenth and twentieth centuries. However, recent scholarship has often ignored Weber's interplay between socioeconomic class and socially ascribed status (Gerth and Mills 1946). Status can be manipulated based upon performance and manipulation of class-based symbols (Mullins 1999b). Thus, both class and status are subject to change and negotiation, and they are the result of social dialogue, not simply societal imposition of social standing.

One of the most often used perspectives for understanding class is the Marxist viewpoint. This framework allows for an increased understanding of the subtle interactions between on-site power interactions, ideologies, and the changing nature of industrial labor from craft production to less-skilled operator production (Braverman 1998; Gutman 1976b). This perspective focuses on the nature of conflict between competing ideologies, although it can also be used to understand more mutual social negotiation and has been most recently applied to western labor camps by McGuire and Reckner (2002), Van Bueren (2002), and Maniery (2002). Yet it must be noted that a Marxist paradigm alone cannot explain the "ethnogenesis" of small-scale industrial societies (Hardesty 2002).

Archaeological interpretations that stress community are a fundamental component of such discourse. Unfortunately, community usually has been inferred in archaeology, which often uncritically assumed that cohabitation alone creates a community. In order to address industrial communities adequately, an open model of community creation based on personal interaction is required. Instead of relying on sociospatial definitions, it is more helpful to define community using Watanabe's (1992) concept requiring only people, a place, and a premise for the creation and maintenance of a community. Thus, community is based on human interaction involving co-presence, which in turn forms a unity of experience. This interactionist focus allows communities to be viewed as dynamic entities where identity and society are always changing and re-creating themselves. This community focus serves to temper the dialectic nature of Marxist theory and allows for more subtle interpretations regarding industrial communities.

It is also important that a sense of community and shared experience can form in the absence of co-presence or daily interaction (Douglass 1998). Although small-scale communities such as labor camps depend on interactional models of community, large-scale concepts that involve a shared sense of community, such as globalization, industrial worker ideology, and unionization, demand a more flexible definition. In these cases, a sense of community is formed less by direct interaction and depends to a larger extent on unity of experience among sometimes isolated groups of individuals. This understanding of the nature of industrial communities provides an important tool for the comparison of different camps in order to uncover the nature of competing industrial ideologies and value systems.

However, the paternalistic order present in many work camps goes beyond expressions of community, class-based analysis, and studies of ethnicity and gender. In particular, the presence of paternalistic managerial strategies, or the creation of prestige and status distinctions based on metaphorical family hierarchy, suggests deeper symbolic and ideological systems than gender, ethnic, or class-based analyses alone can detect. These approaches to social control in industrial settings were actively created and disseminated during the late nineteenth and early twentieth centuries and differ markedly from other strategies employed in organizations such as the military (Allen 1966; Garner 1992). The fact that the entire paternalistic system was a fabrication based on the needs and limitations of an industrial order signals the opportunity to study the negotiation between industrial ideology and worker identity to create a unique form of industrial community.

Company paternalism created a network of fictitious kin relationships that were expressed in terms of residence patterns, social status, and corporate morality. As the twentieth century progressed, the physical layout of work camps became increasingly structured in order to promote corporate control of the lives of workers (Foster et al. 1988). The creation of domestic space and households for male workers, taken in conjunction with an enforced social childhood, indicates that more was at work than mere class, ethnic, or gendered social manipulation. In order to understand the social dynamics within this industrial community, it is possible to study the effects of company paternalism by invoking a "house" perspective. The creation of metaphorical kin-like relationships between managers and workers within the camp environment established a social group bound in a manner similar to Claude Lévi-Strauss's (1982, 1987) concept of house societies.

The use of "house" as an analytical category admits that the social dynamics present among people living in a self-defined domestic space and reproduced by real or fictive kinship ties is a deeper social phenomenon than units of analysis such as domestic space or family. Therefore, in this context, houses are defined as "corporate bodies, sometimes quite large, organized by their shared residence, subsistence, means of production, origin, ritual actions, or metaphysical essence, all of which entail a commitment to a corpus of house property, which in turn can be said to materialize the social group" (Gillespie 2000:1). In terms of industrial camp environments, the paternalistic metaphor was applied as new members of the community were assigned their places in the camp. Those who came as single laborers were often placed in a largely authoritarian central dwelling area consisting of direct and symbolic managerial oversight. Single male workers were assigned to this area, or "house," where managers oversaw their behavior at all times and enforced corporate ideology through a hierarchical relationship similar to that in a nuclear family. The continuity of this house was assured by a mythology of woods management being drawn from those who had begun their careers in the same manner as low-status laborers. Thus, the paternal heads of household were naturalized through social and physical means as being different in power and prestige but not in quality. Those who sought to leave the central house were encouraged to begin their own houses by integrating their family life into the camp, creating a system of nested households within the camp community (see Anderson, this volume). Although Lévi-Strauss's house concept was intended for "primitive" societies, the presence of different households created for and in response to company paternalism provides an analogous social landscape to his "house societies." In terms of the paternalistic metaphor, social ties and obligations were created in the image of kinship to provide a functional and meaningful working and social experience within industrial capitalism.

In order to uncover the rich mosaic of social interaction in an industrial setting, it is crucial to understand the interactions between the physical and social landscapes and systems of meaning. Company paternalism creates a larger and deeper spectrum of personal interactions at the camp level, which ultimately serves to "differentiate social groups, especially in terms of hierarchical differences" (Gillespie 2000:3). This results in a negotiation of rank that is manifested in the architectural, spatial, managerial, and social layout of the camp. The ascription of rank and status through the use of constructed households goes beyond standard conceptions of class and thus puts the physical landscape into a causal relationship with the social landscape of the camp. The power of the paternalistic metaphor will be shown to create such a social body in an industrial work camp environment.

In order to demonstrate this type of camp environment, this study will analyze a logging camp in the Sierra Nevada Mountains of California. In 1955, the Pickering Lumber Corporation of Standard, California, opened Soap Creek Pass, which was to be its last and largest railroad logging camp. The camp was a hybrid intended to combine the efficiency of truck logging with the dependability of railroad transportation. Built to house over 250 people, it was intended to be a mainstay of operations for twenty to thirty years and thus was built to high standards of comfort and permanence (Momyer 1990). In addition to employing a traditional means of industrial production, the Pickering Lumber Corporation also utilized a paternalistic managerial strategy, an approach already being replaced by the majority of the timber industry with less invasive methods of control. Built with high hopes and optimism, the railroad and camp were abandoned after only a decade, as they were unable to compete with the advances in truck logging and decentralized woods management.

Soap Creek Pass reflects an important turning point in industrial social history. It was an amalgamation of old and new approaches in technology, managerial strategies, and social dynamics. The company paternalism at Soap Creek Pass created the company as a surrogate parent for its employees, acting alternately as disciplinarian and as patron to control social behavior. This paternalistic arrangement became a complex dialogue to establish and maintain the industrial order. This dialogue involved all aspects of camp life, including the physical layout of the camp, the creation of social houses based on fictive kin networks, and an enforced childlike status used to control the single labor force. At the same time, this family metaphor itself was naturalized by the company's active recruitment of families to live on site to serve as models for single workmen and to justify their childlike status. In this manner, the company acted as an authoritarian figure for single employees yet assumed the role of patron in the case of families. Thus, the creation of a system of nested households within the camp created and maintained effective control over the company's labor force and served to naturalize the imposed order.

THE SITE

Although the distribution of dwellings changed slightly over time, five primary habitation areas seem to have been present during most of the active life of the camp. Allotment of these housing units was based primarily on marital status, but occupational prestige was also a factor in the case of more elaborate dwellings. Perhaps the best illustration of the physical arrangement of these habitation areas can be found in the 1957 Fred S. James and Co. Engineering Dept. map (Figure 9.1). From this resource, all the major buildings used during logging activities at Soap Creek Pass are shown as the camp was laid out for the first two years of its existence. Some change to the camp layout did occur over its working life span, the most obvious example being the family cabins in the southwest dwelling area, which disappeared entirely by 1968. However, the camp remained remarkably stable in terms of general spatial distribution.

At the most basic level, single men or those working in camp without their families lived in the dense central dwelling area that consisted of 38 small three-man cabins in the heart of the camp, while families lived in larger dwellings placed in small clusters surrounding the central area. In this way, Soap Creek Pass differed from most other logging camps, since normally families were not brought into the woods environment.

These cabins were generally the oldest buildings in the camp, and half had been used in at least one previous camp (Figure 9.2). The interior arrangement of these cabins was quite standard, the only amenities being three metal bunks, two light sockets, and a 24-inch boxwood stove. During the examination of the six surviving structures, no major evidence was found indicating any attempt to demonstrate individuality or personal expression. Although highly altered by later activity, traces of original paint indicated a uniform paint scheme, which was a solid white exterior with a grey interior. The only obvious evidence of customization present were thumb-tack holes on the interior wooden walls, likely for hanging posters or other decorative paper items. This lack of customization seems in keeping with the transient nature of the single laborers at camp. In the early years, there was a great amount of employee turnover in low-status labor positions.

In addition to the single laborer's cabins, Soap Creek Pass included a number of enclaves of cabins for workers who brought their families into the woods.

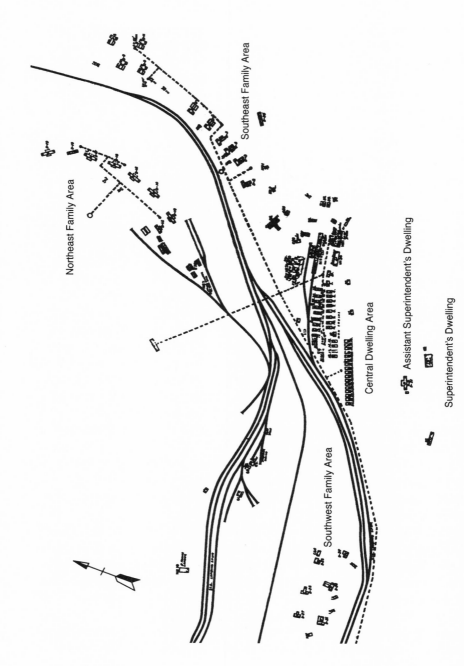

Northeast Family Area

Southeast Family Area

Central Dwelling Area

Southwest Family Area

Assistant Superintendent's Dwelling

Superintendent's Dwelling

Fig. 9.1. Map of Soap Creek Pass, 1957 (base map from Fred S. James Engineering Department).

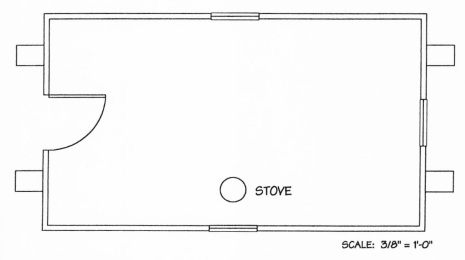

SCALE: 3/8" = 1'-O"

Fig. 9.2. Plan drawing of three-man cabin at Soap Creek Pass.

All family dwellings exhibited certain attributes that clearly linked them as being variations of a standard plan. The first and most common family cabin was
the T-shaped variety (Figure 9.3). Their construction was originally identical, two 10-×-24-foot cabins built on skids and joined on site. These cabins
were well wired for electricity, having ten double electrical outlets, four light
switches, and lights inside and out. Although primitive, bathrooms were located on the rear screened porch and consisted of a toilet and shower only.

In the case of the five surviving T-shaped family dwellings, a great deal of
alteration and personalization was observed. Each surviving cabin exhibited
structural elaboration based on the preferences of the inhabitants. Within these
surviving dwellings there was a great deal of variation in interior paint schemes,
construction of flower beds surrounding the buildings, and structural embellishments such as yard fences, decks, and screened porches.

The other style of family dwelling in place at the camp was the cruciform
variety. These were located north and across the railroad tracks from the T-
shaped dwellings. Although none of these structures survives today, the assistant superintendent's dwelling was also an example of this type of structure.
It followed much in the same line as the T-form family dwellings (Figure 9.4).
A certain amount of elaboration was present in this structure, but for the most
part it did not depart radically from the other family cabins preserved on the
site. In front, entrance to the building was through a screened porch similar to
several examples of the T-shaped and cruciform family cabins. This structure
exhibited evidence of individual choice for the interior paint scheme, although
using the same palate of colors as those found in the family cabins. To the back

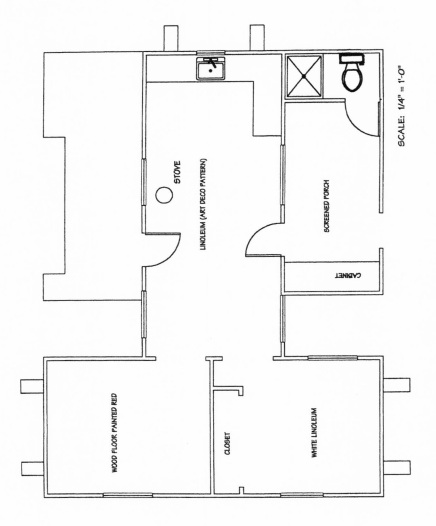

STOVE

LINOLEUM (ART DECO PATTERN)

SCREENED PORCH

CABINET

WOOD FLOOR PAINTED RED

CLOSET

WHITE LINOLEUM

SCALE: 1/4" = 1'-O"

Fig. 9.3. Plan drawing of a "T" family dwelling at Soap Creek Pass.

of the building was a 20-×-8-foot addition that contained the bathroom, which consisted of a toilet and shower, and a fourth room. The backyard area was enclosed with a large expanse of fence made from reused railroad ties and wire fencing material.

Although examination of the assistant superintendent's dwelling was helpful in order to understand the cruciform family cabins that no longer existed on site, unfortunately it cannot be used as a direct analogue. Since the assistant superintendent, Fred Houk, and his family used this dwelling, this structure probably contained higher-status improvements than the dwellings for ordinary workers. Unfortunately, this cannot be proven by comparison since none of the other cruciform structures survive. In addition, none of the informants questioned regarding the site could remember details for the dwellings in the northeast family area that were exact enough to allow for deeper analysis. However, certain differences can be noted from the remains of the other buildings as well as from the documentation of the 1968 appraisement.

By the end of operations, all the other cruciform family dwellings were equipped with screened porches both front and back (General Appraisement Company 1968). Thus it is clear that although the assistant superintendent did not warrant the extra expense of a home similar to the superintendent's home, he and his family were considered different and possessed a status elevated enough to deserve further indoor living space as well as indoor bathroom facilities. In addition, this building came complete with a fenced backyard as well as a small driveway with easy access to the road out of camp. All other cruciform family dwellings had very limited space for vehicular parking and were somewhat isolated from the road.

Finally, the superintendent's dwelling perhaps best illustrates the differences between the dwellings of standard labor and woods management (Figure 9.5). It was the largest covered private space constructed at the camp, consisting of 840 interior square feet, with an extra 264 square feet in porches. However, this structure showed less in the way of elaboration than did some of the family cabins described earlier. At one time, the structure had flower boxes on the front windows and the remains of a small fence at the entrance to the precinct. The structure featured the same palate of colors on the interior, although, as with all other cabins, the use of the palate was at the discretion of the inhabitants.

COMPANY PATERNALISM

As was the case in many industries where company and personal life had to coexist, the Pickering Lumber Corporation assumed a paternalistic management style for dealing with its many employees. These paternalistic attitudes

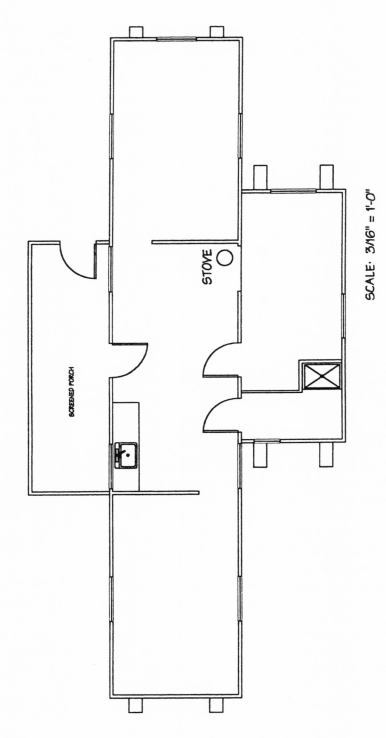

SCALE: 3/16" = 1'-0"

STOVE

SCREENED PORCH

Fig. 9.4. Plan drawing of assistant superintendent's dwelling at Soap Creek Pass.

extended into all aspects of life, with the company imposing a moral order on the job as well as in the homes of its workers. By the 1950s this managerial technique had all but disappeared in the mainstream lumber industry, thus demonstrating Pickering's conservative approach to corporate change (Allen 1966). However, it is clear that this style of management was effective in its own way and provided for orderly daily operations in the woods. By consulting the informants for this study, it is evident that the efforts of the corporation to take care of its labor were well appreciated.

In many ways, the company intruded into the private lives of its workers, insisting on moral standards and establishing an authoritarian regime analogous to intrafamily relationships. General paternalistic institutions included establishment of company trading posts. At these stores, anything from groceries to caulked boots could be bought at prices comparable to those available at stores in town (Houk 2000). Pickering provided these company stores to ease the stresses of living in an isolated logging camp. For those families who lived on site, anything that was required that was not in stock at the store could be ordered with delivery in approximately one day (Houk 2000). The enterprise was certainly not profitable for the company, and much money was expended in labor and transportation of goods to the camps.

In addition to the establishment of company stores, the company also provided company money as a further service to its employees. This money was called "Pickering Picks," a name standing for the company logo, which included a pick and ring. Scrip was given to workers in need of a cash advance, and the amount given was subtracted from the worker's next paycheck (Dambacher 1989). This practice demonstrates that the company did attempt to provide for its employees, yet at the same time it did not trust them with a true cash advance. The company made sure its employees spent this borrowed money on the wholesome goods provided at the company store and not on vice-related items such as alcohol, which was viewed as a major evil by the company (Pland 2000). Thus, the company did its best to provide a model of ideal life and proper living through the goods sold at the store, while at the same time preventing goods viewed as disruptive from being introduced into the woods work environment.

In the case of unmarried workers who lived in the central dwelling area, the authoritarian role of the company was particularly strong. This area was an engineered household, which was created based on metaphorical kinship between single laborers and the woods management. First, the three-man cabins were concentrated in one area located just down the hill from the homes of both the superintendent and his assistant, allowing management to keep a close watch on all events happening, as in Foucault's Panopticon (Foucault 1979). This proximity indicates management's desire for a presence in the lives of

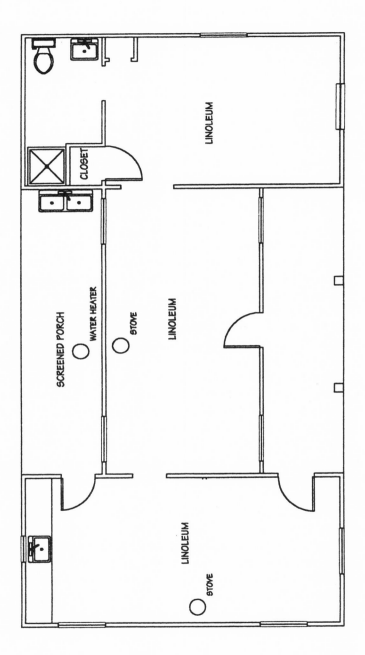

SCALE: 1/4" = 1'-0"

Fig. 9.5. Plan drawing of superintendent's dwelling at Soap Creek Pass.

these workers, even during personal time, in order to remind them of their moral obligations to the standards and rules of the company.

This insistence on management's supervision of the single workers was extreme. The company viewed them like children, needing constant attention and guidance. For example, in order to keep the camp tidy and conditions hygienic in the central dwelling area, it was the job of the "bull cook" to change the sheets on every bed and sweep out every cabin each week in the single men's dwellings. For this service 50 cents was deducted from a laborer's daily earnings (Fouts 1990). Although this was of great benefit to the cleanliness of the camp and was seen as a positive service by my informants, it also demonstrated the company's belief that the single employees would not keep a high standard of hygiene and order. As a result of this view, they were punished by having a portion of their paycheck garnished each day.

This "child" status of single laborers seems to have been pervasive and was common in many other aspects of camp life such as dining practices. According to Dick Pland, all single workers dined in the mess hall located in the central dwelling area. Eating arrangements were family style, with approximately eight to ten people sitting at a table. However, the superintendent, side rods (crew foremen) and other important people all sat at what was called the "blue table," which was located closest to the kitchen, and they were served first. This position seems to have served multiple functions, since the prestige of higher positions warranted more prompt refills of food. It also was a paternalistic symbol of authority. The presence of camp leaders at this table was not an accident, and as in the case of Fred Houk, many of these leaders had families with whom they just as easily could have dined. Instead, the desire for the paternalistic heads of the household to dine with their workers served as more than a community building mechanism and strengthened the family metaphor.

Also part of the daily dining ritual was the imposition of social decorum. Strengthening the creation of a paternalistic household, table manners were quite refined, something that was encouraged with negative reinforcement if necessary (Pland 2000). Several informants related accounts of new workers rudely reaching for platters or taking more than a fair serving who were reprimanded severely by management. Thus, even eating accommodations were used by the company as a moralistic statement on proper behavior.

Thus, the "child" status of single workers seemed to be communicated in a variety of ways, indicating that the company viewed single men as potentially quarrelsome, unclean, lazy, and in need of guidance. In order to counteract these undesirable traits, the company created a large "house" of single workmen by using the paternalistic metaphor that allowed greater managerial oversight and control.

However, company policy toward married labor and their families was almost the opposite. In fact, it seems as if the company did much to encourage individual family life in both the physical distribution of camp and in the freedoms allowed to a married worker. The family cabins were not only larger but also reflected the ideal of a home, with domestic space, increased privacy, room for personal expression, and freedom from company "familial heads" after the workday ended. These cabins were in areas removed from the controlling eye of the woods management, focused into small clusters and almost forming small communities unto themselves. Family cabins were arranged so that they formed four separate family living areas. The symbolic separation of family life from the central dwelling area was further enforced by the fact that families were allowed to personalize their homes in almost any way, inside or out, as long as it did not alter the basic integrity of the structure (Pland 2000).

It is clear that the power structure found at Soap Creek Pass involved much greater managerial power than could be found in other industries. The rule was strict and judgment swift, but the disciplinary actions taken were not intended as punishment for the sake of retribution. The strict rule in camp was a means of teaching proper behavior while at the same time removing dissident elements that might sour the moral dynamic in the woods. Thus, examples were made of those who misbehaved in order to reaffirm the righteousness of those who did not break the rules. Everyone interviewed had a low opinion of those who were lazy, rude, or difficult at the camp. It was particularly provocative that nobody saw any particular dismissal as overly harsh, with one informant even saying that all those fired on the job usually deserved removal earlier (Pland 2000).

In this way, the family-like management strategy seemed to be quite effective. The company used the power and authority of management to teach a moral code beneficial to the work of the camp, and anyone who interfered with this order was promptly dismissed. At the same time, the corporation attempted to care for its workers by providing services that were intended to ease the rigors of living in a company camp.

PHYSICAL MANIFESTATIONS OF PATERNALISM

Thus, based on the information presented, it is clear that the Pickering Corporation acted as more than employer and fulfilled the roles of patron, moral guide, and disciplinarian for its employees. However, paternalism was very traumatic at times for employees, and it required a great deal of maintenance on the part of the company to prevent labor unrest. In order to naturalize this paternalistic relationship, the company used the physical landscape of the camp to further the established social order. The camp itself was constructed and maintained in a manner that made paternalism appear as a natural part of camp life instead of an imposed management strategy used by the corporation.

In the case of the single labor pool, the childlike role into which the men were forced was rooted not only in the relations with the woods management but also in the very layout of the central dwelling area. As noted, the social dynamic of this area was that of a single household, consisting of a family of single laborers and their metaphorical family heads. In terms of the layout of the camp, deliberate engineering of the landscape occurred to legitimize this relationship. The level of concentration exhibited in the central dwelling area was difficult to achieve owing to the hilly nature of that part of camp. The lack of flat ground on which to place structures had to be overcome by terracing the hillside in order to achieve the neat rows of three-man cabins. In 1954, Garnet Dambacher (1989) worked on the crew grading the terraces for cabins, and he said it took several weeks to prepare the entire area for structures. Such construction would be necessary if the entire site exhibited such undulating terrain; however, more than enough flat ground existed in the area where the southwest family area was constructed. This area would have allowed for cheaper construction, less grading, and a much larger area for construction. The placement of the central dwelling area seems to have been a direct attempt on the part of the corporation to establish the authority of the woods management in the physical landscape of the camp. The central dwelling area was located literally under the eyes of the woods management, with the dwellings of both the superintendent and his assistant placed on the hillside above the three-man cabins.

The construction found in the central dwelling area also reaffirmed the parent/child relationship. All three-man cabins were built on skids in a style that had been used by the company since the 1920s. For those cabins built prior to the creation of Soap Creek Pass, this technique was an issue of convenience and economics, since these structures had to be easily transported. The skids allowed the buildings to be dragged into position using a donkey engine, or a caterpillar tractor after 1930 when the company eliminated donkey logging (Hungry Wolf 1978).

However, almost half of the three-man cabins were built specifically for Soap Creek Pass, using the same basic plan as the earlier examples with a few simple modifications. These changes were made to the standard design in order to expedite construction, since these structures were not intended to be moved after placement at Soap Creek Pass (Momyer 1990). However, a great amount of money and time was spent in order to build them to withstand multiple moves to which they would never be subjected. The amount of lumber used in the massive 1-×-1-foot skids alone under each of these structures would have been a large misuse of resources. A rough estimate of the lumber used amounts to over 32,256 board feet. Much money and time could have been saved if these structures had been built using standard prefabrication techniques and permanent pile foundations. Furthermore, it is clear that the corporation was familiar with this cheaper, less robust construction than the traditional skid shed design. In the case of the first aid building, railroad crew cabins, timekeeper's office, mess hall (in later years), bathhouse, bunkhouse #35, cat shop, and welding shop, the company built using permanent pile foundations. Similar three-man cabins built for use at Camp Curry, a small camp nearer the felling activity for truckers, were clearly constructed on pile foundations. Thus, the management was quite familiar with the economy of building cheaper permanent structures.

In light of this finding, it is interesting that the superintendent's dwelling was built in place. Although this building accounts for an overall footprint of 24 × 46 feet, it could have been constructed in a similar manner to the family dwellings, where separate sections were skidded into place and joined on site. There seems to be little reason for the use of this type of construction other than the symbolic value of a permanent structure in order to naturalize the paternalistic role of the woods boss. Even the assistant superintendent did not warrant a permanent dwelling and had to make do with an elaborated version of a family cabin. The superintendent's dwelling can be seen as a physical manifestation of power and prestige. It not only directly overlooked the single labor housing, but it also was rooted in the ground with an air of permanency, as opposed to the temporary skid shacks of the workers.

The superintendent's dwelling clearly demonstrates that much time and resources were expended in order to create this naturalization of authority. Indeed, even the lasting qualities of the pile foundation were perceived to be inadequate for the authority vested in the structure. According to period photographs, the foundation was covered with trim boards to present an even greater air of strength and permanence. Also important is the fact that unlike every other structure, where roofed porches were screened, the front porch of the superintendent's dwelling has no screen or framing to serve as a barrier from the outside world. It is clear this structure was intended to demonstrate a difference in kind. The symbolic and true head of the camp belonged in the woods, whereas everyone else was just a temporary occupant.

However, it is interesting that this building does not depart radically from the basic building techniques and spatial relationships found in standard family cabins. The ornamentation and elaboration found in the structure seem to have been merely a step further than what was found in the rest of camp. Simple ornamentation such as the beveled corners of the front porch indicates a higher status when compared to the utilitarian construction of every other structure found in camp. However, these embellishments were still built using the same materials and techniques found elsewhere. Clearly, the structure was intended to naturalize the power of its inhabitant yet at the same time demonstrate that the ideals manifested in the position, structure, and person were obtainable by anyone. In this way, the superintendent's dwelling did not imply a difference in the quality of the inhabitant. The quality of the components and the construction were all similar to those found in the family cabins, creating a unity of experience with those who incorporated their domestic lives with the company. The physical structure of the superintendent's dwelling served as a lesson regarding the similarities between the labor pool and the management, thus avoiding worker dissatisfaction resulting from differential access to comfort. While the structure did much to highlight the differences in power between the occupant and others, it also communicated a more democratic message of similarity of conditions

However, it is important to realize that this democratization of living conditions was experienced only by those men living in family cabins. For single men, there was no hope of improving their accommodations and living in a manner similar to their leaders. The only way to improve one's living condition at camp was to be married and be granted a family cabin to live in for the logging season. The family metaphor used in company paternalism became so strong that it extended even into true family life itself. The company acted as a moralizing institution that taught a moral order in which commitment to a family was encouraged just as much as commitment to the corporation. By becoming the head of one's own house, an employee became the superintendent of a house unit analogous to the central dwelling area. This action not only served to relieve the hardships of separation from family but also further naturalized the managerial structure in the camp.

In order to further this perceived autonomy, the company allowed for personal expression within these family houses. It must have realized the benefits of this allowance as a relief valve for the frustrations present in the industrial landscape. The fact that resident families were allowed to personalize these structures and create a feeling of ownership was in marked contrast to the drab militaristic order that seems to have typified the central dwelling area. Both Houk (2000) and Pland (2000) revealed that the company was very permissive regarding alterations to the family cabins as long the inhabitants did not change the basic structure of the building or create a nuisance to others.

In the case of interior color, the company allowed the resident to select those colors from a preselected palate that best suited their esthetics and identity. The management also allowed families to create fences and landscapes that further separated family life and personal space from the company and camp. Examples can be found in the surviving family cabins, as well as at the assistant superintendent's dwelling. This was a reward system that encouraged workers to incorporate their family life with the life of the camp, thus reinforcing the value of family and cooperation in the company/employee relationship.

CONCLUSION

The interplay between company paternalism and employees was a complex dialogue that involved everything from the physical layout of the camp to the creation of different households in order to naturalize and preserve the industrial order. The company assumed the role of head of family; its employees were its responsibility, to teach and guide in all aspects of life at camp. This included a company morality of hard work, honesty, and cleanliness that was at times enforced quite harshly.

In order to establish power networks with true authority, the company employed the paternalistic metaphor to create a nested system of households with fictive kinship ties at its core. This metaphor was naturalized by the creation of a social and physical landscape similar to Lévi-Strauss's house societies. At the same time, the company justified this family metaphor by encouraging true families to live on site, thus further reinforcing a childlike status on single workers. In order to attract families to the camp, the company also relaxed its strict rule and allowed individual expression, a certain amount of autonomy, and a "fiefdom" that served as a metaphor for the central dwelling area, thus further naturalizing the power of the management. Finally, it seems that management assumed the role of strict authoritarian when dealing with single employees yet became the benevolent patron in the case of families. Thus, company paternalism spawned a unique form of community, created to suit the needs of an industrial order yet executed with a spirit of preindustrial social relationships.

ACKNOWLEDGMENTS

Special thanks to Professor Donald Hardesty, Kate Kostlan, Professor Patrick Martin, Professor John Pappas, Paula Pappas, and Professor Laurie Wilkie for help, guidance, and support throughout this project. I would also like to thank those who lived at Soap Creek Pass and shared their experiences. This is just a part of their story.

Part III
A Sense of Being

10

The Ethnohistory and Archaeology of Nuevo Santander Rancho *Households*

Mary Jo Galindo

INTRODUCTION

Historical archaeology in South Texas and northeastern Mexico began with the limited excavations and surveys conducted before Falcon Dam and Reservoir were constructed in 1953 (see Bonine, this volume). In February 1949, Jack Krieger from the University of Texas at Austin surveyed the new spillway area for the National Parks Service (Krieger and Hughes 1950). The next year, the River Basins Survey of the Smithsonian Institution conducted emergency excavations at three sites, including two historic sites, in what became the first major archaeological investigation in the area (Hartle and Stephenson 1951). Fortunately, the artifacts from these excavations were recently analyzed (Bonine 2001), and this analysis can be added to investigations at Cabaseño Ranch in Zapata County, Texas (Perttula et al. 1999) and research of a more ethnographic nature focusing on Mier, Tamaulipas, Mexico (Galindo 1999). In this chapter, I explore the concept of rancho households based on a combination of census and demographic data, along with the limited archaeology accomplished to date in the area.

Until recent decades (Alonzo 1998; Chipman 1992; Jackson 1986; Montejano 1987), Texas historians and scholars have either ignored (Tjarks 1974) or minimized the contributions of Spanish colonial ranching families. The lack of rigorous scholarly attention to their contributions has compelled local historians and avocational genealogists to fill the void (Gonzalez 1998; Graham 1994; Guerra 1953; Myers 1969). Although Spanish and later Mexican bureaucracies created a wealth of information about these early colonists, they also left unanswered many questions about their daily lives. Archaeology is best suited to recover the material culture that can illuminate the colonists' daily practices and provide the context needed to interpret these activities.

Historical archaeology in South Texas and northeastern Mexico is a nascent field, one well positioned to incorporate recent theoretical debates regarding household archaeology (Ashmore and Wilk 1988; Hendon 1996; Netting and Wilk 1984; Yanagisako 1979). An important trend in historical archaeology is toward a multidisciplinary approach, rooted in anthropology and history, that focuses on illuminating the daily lives of ordinary people—subjects traditionally ignored in academia (Orser and Fagan 1994).

Here I summarize the various archaeological concepts of households and household production with the goal of thoroughly understanding the morphology and functions of Spanish colonial rancho settlements. This study is also an exercise in developing research methods and designs, including both archival and excavation strategies. I first summarize the archaeological conceptions of the household and then present three brief reconstructions of ranchos, as recorded in census data for Mier, Tamaulipas, Mexico. After comparing the two characterizations, I offer a definition for rancho households based on the two sets of data, while considering the implications of this definition for future archaeological excavations.

ARCHAEOLOGICAL CONCEPTIONS OF HOUSEHOLDS

Archaeology at the household level is not unique to historical archaeology, but it is in this area that distinct households are identifiable, both on the ground and through documentary evidence. This concept is relatively new, with the main theoretical foundations laid out fewer than 20 years ago. But there is a strong bias from a functional, structural, and cultural perspective that shapes the definition of household. This perspective is counterbalanced by a regard for the activities of its members (Ashmore and Wilk 1988; Netting and Wilk 1984) and the corresponding symbolic dimensions of households (Hendon 1996; Yanagisako 1979).

The following is a summation of the various theoretical sources that have influenced my approach to an ethnohistorical account of the Spanish colonial settlement of Mier. It is guided in general by Mary C. Beaudry's (1989a) call for a contextual and interpretive approach to household analysis, with attention to the variation of households. She wants detailed, interpretive studies of individual home sites that account for site formation processes and that focus on the contextual relationships among artifacts and soil strata. In other words, she advocates conducting highly detailed, multidisciplinary case studies of individual sites and their histories. Specifically, she calls for the "combination of different forms of contextual analysis—cultural and historical context derived from documentary evidence and environmental context derived from ecological data" (1989a:89). Together, these analyses provide historical archaeologists with a "powerful interpretive device that allows for greater . . . understanding [of] how cultural behavior at the level of the household has influenced the formation of the archaeological record" (1989a:89).

The theoretical framework upon which I base my working definition of "household" incorporates primarily the ideas of Robert Netting and Richard Wilk (1984), who established the distinction between the morphological ways of describing households in terms of kinship and residence patterns from the structural and behavioral aspects of the household. They sought to change the questions that archaeologists ask about households from those grounded in structure to those grounded in activity. They advocated "relating both the morphology and the functions of the household groups to each other and to wider social, economic, and cultural realms" (1984:4).

DEFINING HOUSEHOLDS

Netting and Wilk (1984:7) define five categories of household activity: production, distribution, transmission, reproduction, and co-residence. The intensity of production is seen to affect the size of households. Simultaneous labor requirements of major productive tasks and the existence of diverse tasks within a yearly cycle contribute to a tendency for larger household groups.

Distribution involves transactions between households. Larger groups may pool their resources to compensate for sources of income that are diverse, seasonal, variable, or unpredictable (Netting and Wilk 1984:9). Transmission refers to the intergenerational transmission of property within households. "In general, socioeconomic stratification appears to be directly reflected in average household size. Wealth and prestige attract and hold the members of larger households while the poor can usually sustain only smaller groups of co-residents" (Netting 1982, as cited in Netting and Wilk 1984:13). Co-residence, according to Wilk and Netting's definition, refers to household members sharing living space, the physical confines and availability of which condition the size and composition of households.

Wendy Ashmore and Robert Wilk (1988) add consumption to the list of household functions and refine the terms used to describe aspects of households, such as *co-residence groups* and *dwelling*. A co-residence group is a group of people who regularly share living quarters without necessarily sharing household activities (what Laslett [1972] defined as "housefull"). A dwelling is the physical structure within which residential activities take place. Households can be dispersed among a number of dwellings (Horne 1982, as cited in Ashmore and Wilk 1988:6).

Ashmore and Wilk consider household archaeology as an extension of settlement archaeology. Settlement patterns are seen to consist of a hierarchical set of patterns at different scales usually involving three tiers: single structures, site layouts, and intersite distribution (Ashmore and Wilk 1988:7).

S. J. Yanagisako (1979) explores the contested meaning of "domestic," which she presents as having at its core two sets of functional activities: those pertaining to food production and consumption and those pertaining to social reproduction, including child-bearing and child-rearing. She proposes that there are three types of variables that underlie variations in domestic organization. She postulates that as domestic groups move through their developmental cycles, one can expect not only changes in the demographic structure but also an impact on the economy of the household as its size and the composition of the eligible producers within the domestic group change. The third variable is stratification, which is evident in fluctuations in size and wealth, social mobility, and the kin ties that bind together households in different strata (Yanagisako 1979:193).

Yanagisako advocates the study of kinship as a symbolic system in which "meanings attributed to the relationships and actions of kinsmen are drawn from a range of cultural domains, including religion, nationality, ethnicity, gender, and folk concepts of the person" (1979:193). This symbolic system approach helps to make sense of the range of diversity present in family and kinship organizations within one society. It also aids in the study of inequality within domestic organization, specifically with respect to the political and economic processes of societies (1979:196).

Julia A. Hendon expands on the symbolic dimension of households by applying Bourdieu's sense of practice to the term. Thus, she arrives at her definition of household by considering what people do as members of a domestic group and the meanings assigned to their actions. She uses *household* and *domestic group* interchangeably to refer to the task-oriented, co-resident, and symbolically meaningful social group that forms "the next bigger thing on the social map after the individual" (1996:47). Hendon emphasizes the conflict inherent in a domestic group that consists of social actors differentiated by age, gender, role, and power whose agendas and interests do not always coincide. "The household is, in effect, politicized in that its internal relations are inextricable from the larger economic and political structure of society" (1996:46). She also addresses the implications of craft specialization at the household level by pointing out that "incorporating specialized production into the household's definition of its appropriate and necessary tasks must result in reallocations of time and responsibility for specialists and other household members alike" (1996:52). "It may also change the balance of power among household members and how certain tasks are valued" (1996:52).

LOS RANCHOS DE MIER

Mier was established in 1753 at the confluence of the Río Grande and the Río Alamo by Capitán José Florencio Chapa and 38 families from Cerralvo, who joined 19 families already living on ranchos in the area (Graham 1994; Sánchez 1994). The settlement was part of José de Escandón's colonization plan for the Province of Nuevo Santander (Alonzo 1998). Escandón, Conde de Sierra Gorda, received a viceregal commission in 1746 to conquer and settle the area that lay east of the Sierra Madre Oriental and stretched from the Panuco River in Mexico to La Bahía del Espíritu Santo on the present-day Texas Gulf coast (Myers 1969) (Figure 10.1).

Mier grew out of the rancho headquarters of José Felix de Almóndoz that was formed in 1734 by 166 people in 19 families (Casteñeda 1976; Graham 1994). It was originally called El Paso del Cántaro, located eight leagues northwest of Camargo. When Camargo was established in 1749, these 19 families were forced to enroll as settlers of that community or be driven off their land (Casteñeda 1976). These same families would form the core of the population of Mier in 1753, when the town was renamed and organized as part of Nuevo Santander (Guerra 1953). The site of an easy ford on the Río Alamo, Mier is located among high-quality limestone deposits that were exploited by colonists for construction material (Scott 1937). It was primarily a ranching community but also enjoyed good commerce with Nuevo León, where many settlers had their origins and maintained connections (Scott 1937).

The colony of Nuevo Santander had no presidios and few missions; therefore, the private rancho became the primary method of settlement for the first 100 years (Graham 1994; Myers 1969). Indeed, "the ranch outlasted the mission and the presidio and became the only great Spanish institution to survive nearly intact into the modern age" (Myers 1969:56). Nuevo Santander was the last province to be established in the present-day Texas-Mexico borderlands. Many of its settlers came from ranching areas in the provinces of Querétero, Nuevo León, and Coahuila and brought with them their brand of ranching culture (Graham 1994).

Mier's livestock tradition was not unique—other contemporary settlements in the area also grew out of rancho headquarters, including Laredo, Guerrero, and Matamoros. The later communities of Zapata, Roma/Los Sáenz, Garceño, and Río Grande City also originated as rancho headquarters on early land grants (Graham 1994).

According to a census conducted in 1757 by Don José Tienda de Cuervo, Mier had 274 inhabitants and a total of 44,015 livestock, including horses, cattle, burros, mules, sheep, and goats (Myers 1969). The entire colony, according to

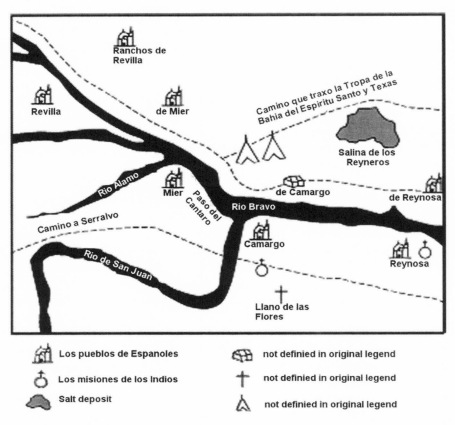

Legend:

Los pueblos de Espanoles

Los misiones de los Indios

Salt deposit

not definied in original legend

not definied in original legend

not definied in original legend

Fig. 10.1. Map of Nuevo Santander in the late eighteenth century illustrating the ranchos of Mier and other communities on the north bank of the Rio Grande. (Detail redrawn from a 1792 map of Nuevo Santander in *Monumentos para la historia de Coahuila y Seno Mexicano,* Archivo General de la Nación, Cat. 221, Historia, Vol. 29, f. 190.)

the same census, had 80,000 *ganado major* (horses, mules, and cattle), and more than 333,000 *ganado menor* (sheep and goats). Thus, the number of animals per capita in Mier in 1757 was 161, and the colonists of Mier controlled approximately 11 percent of the total livestock of Nuevo Santander at that time.

After the land grants were awarded in 1767, during the General Visit of the Royal Commission of the Colonies of Nuevo Santander, the new owners were required to take possession, construct homes on the ranch, mark the boundaries of their property, and stock the land with animals in order to validate their land claims (Graham 1994). Thus, many families who had lived for years in the towns of Camargo, Revilla, Reynosa, and Mier now relocated to ranchos (Graham 1994). The women and children from those families who could afford it remained in town for amenities such as schools, churches, and protection from Indian raids that the towns provided, while the men of these families spent certain seasons on the rancho. The men of the wealthiest families were able to remain in town and, instead, sent workers to the rancho to care for the animals (González 1998; Graham 1994).

Land grants in Camargo, Revilla, Reynosa, and Mier were awarded in 1767 on both sides of the Rio Grande. At this time, the river was not a divider of nations; rather, it existed as a clearly defined geographic entity that served to unite people (George 1975; Graham 1994). The ranchers who claimed land and maintained herds on both banks best exemplify this fact (Graham 1994). An anonymous illustration from 1792 of Nuevo Santander (see Figure 10.1) depicts ranchos associated with Revilla and Mier on the north bank of the Rio Grande in present-day Zapata and Starr counties.

ARCHAEOLOGICAL APPLICATIONS
OF HOUSEHOLD THEORY

The theoretical framework of the household can facilitate our understanding of the organization and production systems of rancho households, thereby illuminating the motivations and survival strategies employed by eighteenth-century colonists. Knowledge of this sort can be used to guide future archaeological excavations. For example, census data revealed that multiple households, as defined earlier, resided on each rancho (Galindo 1999), so survey and excavations must consider the number and arrangement of structures across the landscape that constitute a single rancho. The number and type of animals each family possessed (also accessible through census data) can help plan the appropriate scope of archaeological investigations, specifically, how activity areas were located and in what combinations they are likely to be found. Ethnographic data reveal that socioeconomic factors influenced residence patterns, such that one household may have maintained both a dwelling in town and one on the rancho.

A SAMPLING OF ANCIENT RANCHOS
AS RECORDED IN THE CENSUS OF 1817

Methodology

The following reconstructions are based on information contained in a portion of a census from approximately 1817. I cross-referenced these data with information from the baptism, marriage, and death records of Mier, Tamaulipas, Mexico, as published by the Spanish American Genealogical Society. The approximate date of the census was determined after comparing the baptism records of 15 residents of El Rancho San Lorenzo de las Minas with their ages as recorded on the census (Galindo 1999). This partial census comes from an individual's private collection and was analyzed with permission. It is reprinted in its entirety in the author's master's report (Galindo 1999).

The census documents the residents and livestock on eight ranchos: Santo Tomas de Sabinitas, Santa Teresa de Guardado, San Gregorio del Saleno, San Pedro de las Flores, Santa Barbara de Morteritos, San José de la Rinconada, Jesús de Buenavista, and San Lorenzo de las Minas. A total of 411 residents in 76 families lived on these 8 ranchos. An average of about 10 families lived on each rancho, with the average-sized family containing about 6 members.

Descriptions of Three Spanish Colonial Ranchos

In the following description of three of the eight ranchos recorded in the 1817 census, an effort was made to trace the genealogy of the residents of the ranchos to expose settlement patterns. The descriptions include information about the top livestock owners for each rancho. The three ranchos are presented according to the number of livestock the residents owned, beginning with the one with the fewest animals, El Rancho San Pedro de las Flores.

For this first rancho, I was able to trace each family back to two Sáenz families. The same is true for El Rancho San Lorenzo de las Minas, where all residents are a part of the Ramón Guerra and Rosalia Hinojosa family. At El Rancho Santo Tomas de Sabinitas, however, a lack of archival information made it impossible to determine if or how 6 of the 17 families are related to the Manuel Angel Hinojosa and Juana Sanchez family. All six families are Hinojosas, which makes it likely that they are blood relatives.

El Rancho San Pedro de las Flores. According to the 1817 census, this rancho had 45 residents in 9 families, who owned 54 animals. All nine of these families have been traced through marriage, baptism, and death records of Mier to the two *poblador* families of Juan Francisco Sáenz and Teresa Peña and of Miguel Sáenz and Gertrudis Hinojosa (Figures 10.2, 10.3). The exact relationship between Juan Francisco and Miguel Sáenz could not be determined from the Mier records. Juan Francisco received Mier Porción 7 and Miguel was awarded Porción 73 in 1767 (Figure 10.4). Rancho residents include the children and grandchildren of these pobladores.

In terms of livestock, San Pedro de las Flores ranked seventh out of the eight ranchos in the partial census (Table 10.1). The largest livestock owner was Juan Francisco and Teresa Peña's son, Francisco Sáenz, who owned 27 cows, horses, and mules. The next largest owner is the husband of Miguel's great-granddaughter, Emenegildo Guerra, who had 16 cows, horses, and mules. The average family size was five, with a range from three to nine. More than one-

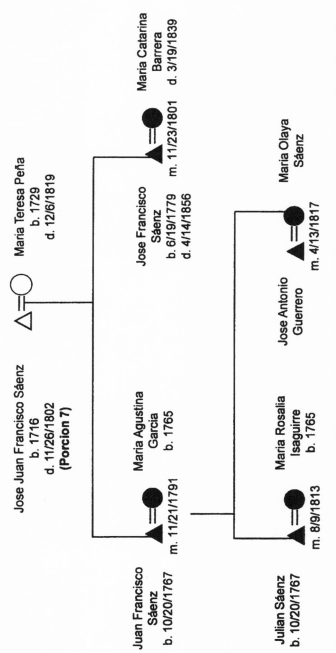

Fig. 10.2. Part of the Juan Francisco Sáenz and Teresa Peña family, with residents of El Rancho San Pedro de las Flores indicated by solid symbols (based on information in SAGA publications 1989).

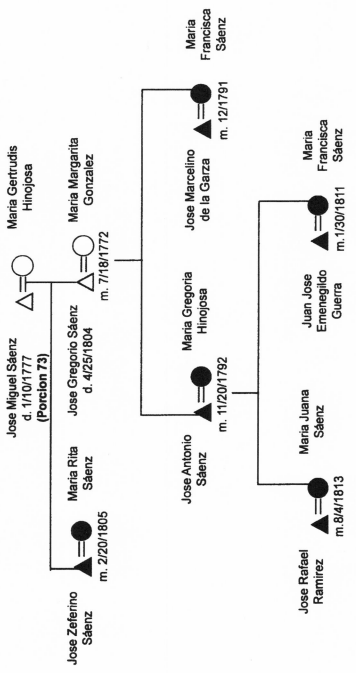

Fig. 10.3. Part of the Miguel Sáenz and Gertrudis Hinojosa family, with residents of El Rancho San Pedro de las Flores indicated by solid symbols (based on information in SAGA publications 1989).

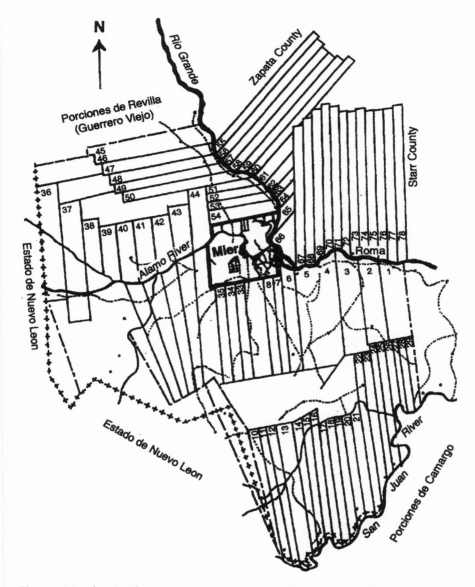

Fig. 10.4. Map showing the porciones awarded in 1767 to the pobladores of Mier, Tamaulipas, Mexico (Galindo 1999). Juan Francisco Sáenz received Porción 73, Miguel Sáenz received Porción 7, Manuel Hinojosa received Porcion 4, his son Manuel Angel Hinojosa received Porción 5, and Ramon Guerra received Porción 6 (*Auto de la general visita, 1767*, the Acts of the Visit of the Royal Commissioners, as cited in Scott 1937).

half of the residents are under age twenty. Another third are between the ages of twenty and thirty-nine.

El Rancho de Santo Tomas de Sabinitas. According to the 1817 census, this rancho had 80 residents in 17 families, who owned 319 animals. Eleven of these families have been traced through marriage, baptism, and death records of Mier to the Manuel Angel Hinojosa and Juana Sanchez family (Figure 10.5). Manuel Angel was awarded Mier Porción 5 in 1767 (see Figure 10.4). The extended families of two of their daughters and two of their sons resided together on this ranch.

In terms of livestock, Santo Tomas de Sabinitas ranked fourth out of the eight ranchos in the census (see Table 10.1). The eldest son of Manuel and Juana, Santiago Hinojosa, is the largest livestock owner with 256 animals, including 200 sheep and 50 goats. No one else on the rancho owned sheep or goats. Santiago's younger brother, Marcelino Hinojosa, owned 17 cows, horses, and mules. Of the two daughters of Manuel and Juana who lived on the ranch, Anastacia's husband also owned 17 cows, horses, and mules and Gertrudis' husband owned 5 cows and horses. The average family size was 4.7 people, with a range from two to nine. Half of the residents were under age twenty. Twenty-five percent were between the ages of twenty and twenty-nine.

El Rancho San Lorenzo de las Minas. According to the 1817 census, this rancho had 63 residents in 11 families, who owned 1,824 animals. All of these families have been traced through marriage, baptism, and death records of Mier to the Ramón Guerra and Rosalia Hinojosa family (Figure 10.6). Ramón was awarded Mier Porción 6 in 1767 (see Figure 10.4). Rosalia's father, Manuel Hinojosa, was awarded Porción 4 and her brother received Porción 5.

Three sons and three daughters of Ramón and Rosalia, along with their families, resided on the ranch. After the death of their son, Vicente Guerra, their daughter-in-law, María Josefa Ramirez, continued to reside on the ranch, even after she remarried. Her second husband, Ramón Barrera, was the largest livestock owner, with 1,144 animals, including 800 sheep and 300 goats. In terms of livestock, San Lorenzo de las Minas ranked second among the eight ranchos in the census (Table 10.1). Alejandro Guerra, the eldest son of Ramón and Rosalia, was the second-largest livestock owner, with 451 animals, including 400 sheep and 36 goats. The average family size was 5.7, with a range from two to ten. More than one-half of the residents were under age twenty. Another 25 percent are between ages twenty and thirty-nine.

Summary and Analysis of Census Data

The census data for Mier ranchos reveal a settlement pattern of multiple closely related households residing together on one rancho (Galindo 1999). Livestock was concentrated in the hands of a few male members, although not

Table 10.1 Amount of livestock owned per ranch according to the 1817 census data for Mier, Tamaulipas, Mexico.

Ranch Name	Sheep	Goats	Cattle	Mares	Horses		Mules		Total Animals per Rancho
					Tamed	Colts	Tamed	Colts	
Santa Teresa de Guardado	2037	769	16	34	16	3	6	0	2881
San Lorenzo de las Minas	1400	336	34	22	16	1	14	1	1824
Jesus de Buenavista	900	300	30	29	14	10	14	9	1306
Santo Tomas de Sabinitas	200	50	22	10	16	0	20	1	319
San Jose de la Rinconada	0	0	54	14	6	0	7	0	81
San Gregorio del Saleno	0	0	29	23	9	0	15	0	76
San Pedro de las Flores	0	0	13	18	11	1	11	0	54
Santa Barbara de Morteritos	0	0	8	0	0	0	0	0	8
Total	4537	1455	206	150	88	15	87	11	

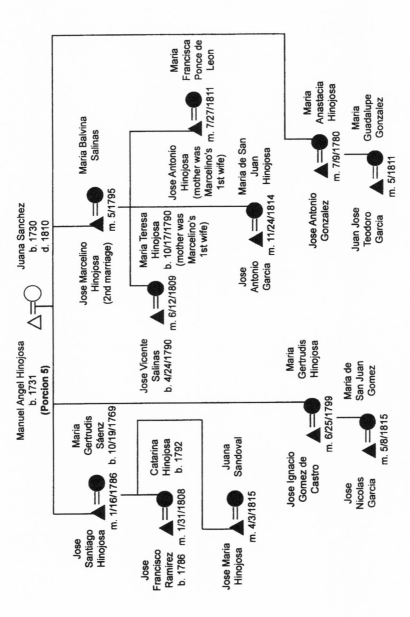

Fig. 10.5. Part of the Manuel Angel Hinojosa and Juana Sanchez family, with residents of El Rancho Santo Tomas de Sabinitas indicated by solid symbols (based on information in SAGA publications 1989).

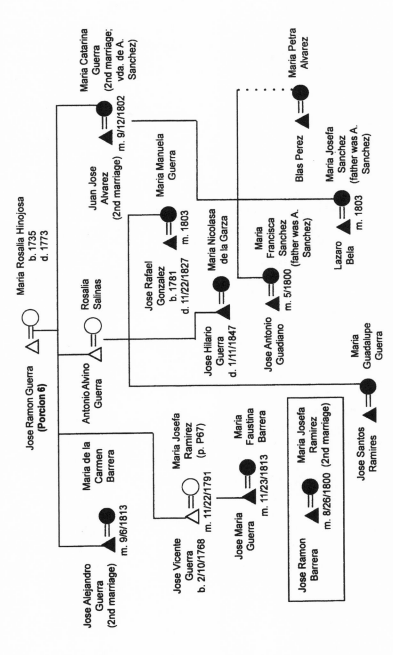

Fig. 10.6. Part of the Ramón Guerra and Rosalia Hinojosa family, with residents of El Rancho San Lorenzo de los Mines indicated by solid symbols (based on information in SAGA publications 1989).

always the eldest males of the lineage. Male in-laws often had significant live-stock holdings. The distribution of livestock among males within a rancho sheds light on inheritance patterns and marriage strategies. Distinct animal husbandry strategies are evident in the census, with some ranchers choosing to raise more sheep and goats than cattle or horses. Others raise cows and horses to the exclusion of sheep and goats.

The distribution patterns of livestock ownership could also mirror the dis-tribution pattern of people on the ranchos. For example, households with larger herds might live farther apart from each other than those with smaller herds because of pasture requirements. It is also possible, given the likelihood of attack on the frontier, that households were located in relatively close prox-imity for mutual protection.

Thus emerges a settlement pattern of multiple extended families residing together on one rancho and constituting, at a certain scale, a household in terms of production, distribution, transmission, reproduction, co-residence, and consumption. The exact arrangements of structures across the landscape re-main unattainable if one relies solely on this definition; however, the settle-ment patterns of other rancho communities can be used to anticipate the size, number, and placement of structures.

DISTRIBUTION OF PROPERTY

The distribution of livestock among male relatives within a rancho gives some insight into inheritance patterns and marriage strategies. This pattern of live-stock distribution may also hold clues to the distribution pattern of people on the physical landscape of the rancho. For example, pasture requirements may have distanced large livestock owners from one another despite the risks. The necessity of living in close proximity for security, however, may have caused the settlers to rely on alternative methods. The management of the herds may have been accomplished by mobile teams of horse-mounted *vaqueros* working at great distances from their primary dwellings.

Livestock is exclusively male-owned except for two instances of property owned by women, both of whom are listed as widows and heads of families. The census data also contain evidence of distinct animal husbandry strategies, with some ranchers choosing to raise more sheep and goats than cattle or horses. Others raise cows and horses to the exclusion of sheep and goats. These strategies reveal a specialization of production at the household level that im-plies mutual cooperation among rancho residents. There was probably a high degree of self-sufficiency in terms of crop and livestock production of the ranchos. Coupled with cooperative practices among neighbors, it no doubt worked to ensure the survival of all rancho residents and neighbors.

DEFINITION OF HOUSEHOLD FOR
SPANISH COLONIAL RANCHOS

I offer the following definition of the household customized for Spanish colonial ranchos. Informed by the noted theoretical approaches and based on the census data, I define the rancho household as comprising members of an extended kin network, residing in multiple structures, arranged strategically along the landscape. Their land would have belonged jointly to the kin network or lineage, while each unit of the network would have exerted control over their respective livestock and pastures. The overall economic strategy would have favored the rancho as a whole over individual kin units. Thus, Spanish colonial ranchos were characterized by a high degree of mutual cooperation and organization based primarily on kin relationships, although there was room for fictive kin and laborers on the ranchos.

This is a working definition and no doubt will be modified as future excavations and research proceed. It may prove cumbersome to define a rancho as composed of 10–15 households as well as impossible to locate archaeologically. This definition will have to evolve to account for the instance when one family or lineage maintained two separate residences, one in town and one on the rancho. Future documentary research may reveal more about the economic workings of the ranchos, specifically, whether they were economically unified or if individuals transacted independently of other rancho members. The complementary distribution of livestock (different kin units specializing in certain animals) suggests that economic activity was more on the level of ranchos rather than on the level of an individual kin unit.

IMPLICATIONS FOR FUTURE ARCHAEOLOGICAL
AND ETHNOGRAPHIC RESEARCH

The definition of Spanish colonial rancho households as extended kin networks residing in multiple structures arranged strategically along the landscape can help guide archaeological and ethnographic research in a variety of ways. When surveying a rancho site, it will be necessary to test a sufficiently large area around known structures to find other structures and activity areas. Ideally, one would survey the entire area of the original land grant to locate contemporary rancho sites, but examples of intact porciones are rare except for a few examples in Tamaulipas. The scope of surveying, testing, and excavating should correlate with the expected size of the rancho layout based on documentary sources. Archival research and ethnographic interviews may help answer questions about the unified nature of economic strategy among rancho households. These types of research could also identify households with residences in both the town and on the rancho.

Defining rancho households runs the risk of focusing on an inappropriately small scale, but connections between rancho residences and the wider community should not be ignored. Indeed, it is because of their connections to the rest of society that a greater understanding of Spanish colonial ranchos and their role in Texas history is necessary and long overdue.

ACKNOWLEDGMENTS

I would like to thank Profra. María de Lourdes Balderas who, in her capacity as archivist for the City of Mier, Tamaulipas, helped me locate the partial census upon which this article is based. Equally, I owe a debt to the Spanish American Genealogical Society (SAGA) of Corpus Christi, Texas, whose publications of the baptismal, marriage, and death records for Mier facilitated this study of rancho households.

11

Reconstructing Domesticity and Segregating Households

The Intersections of Gender and Race in the Postbellum South

Jamie C. Brandon

In the coda to a remarkable work on race, feminism, and abolition, Karen Sánchez-Eppler (1993:133) turns to an object of domestic material culture to make her point: the object, a "topsy-turvy doll," was quite popular in nineteenth-century America. It is effectively two dolls in one—one end an elegant, white "missy" and the other a manifestation of the well-used stereotype of the "wild-eyed pickaninny." The skirt on this doll covered the head of one manifestation when the other was in view, making it a horrific metaphor for racialization in America; the two are inextricably attached and cannot exist without the other, while simultaneously they are unarguably in two different worlds as they cannot be seen together (this is perhaps a precursor to the "separate but equal" policies that would become a defining aspect of the modern South).

As a doll, this piece of material culture implicates childhood and the home as important loci for learning about race and imposing racialized hierarchies and sterotypes. Although it should come as no surprise to those familiar with personal race narratives about childhood that have been used in a variety of academic settings (e.g., Flores 1998; hooks 1990:41–49; McLaurin 1987; Roediger 1991:3–5; Walton 1996), it is interesting that archaeologists continue to examine households primarily as the terrain of gender construction and sexual power. I cannot argue that this line of inquiry has been, and will continue to be, an important mode of analysis within historical archaeology (see e.g., Gilchrist 1999; Spencer-Wood 1994, 1996). I can propose, however, that we take heed of the countless racial theorists who have placed childhood and the household as an important nexus in the racial/gender project—a nexus of resistance and criticism as well as hegemony. In addition, I posit historical archaeology as a well-suited discipline to examine the historical interconnectedness of race and gender, especially when examining the radical yet, at times, subtle changes that took place within the rubrics of race and gender following the trauma that was the American Civil War and into the dawning of modern America.

In this chapter I set out to accomplish three things: to explore the historical support for the entanglement of gender, race, and modernity; to examine the way that households (their function and definition) transformed in the American South in response to changes in the aforementioned entanglement following the Civil War; and to propose ways for historical archaeologists to look for material manifestations of this entanglement and their changes. This work cannot, of course, fully satisfy all the questions surrounding race, gender, and class at a given moment in time at a given site. Rather, it is a preliminary attempt to bring to archaeology the call for "empirically detailed, hands-on historical studies . . . that 'front-stage' one or two phenomena but always allow the others room in the script" (Di Leonardo 1998:22).

HOUSEHOLDS, MODERNITY, URBANIZATION, RACE, AND GENDER

It has been said that "none of the various names attached to the American Civil War adequately convey the scale of disruption unleashed by the conflict" (Brundage 2000:81). The event momentarily destroyed the illusion of American unity even as it forged a greater sense of national identity. In many ways, time took on an apocalyptic cast for both white and black southerners. Most important, I think it can be seen as the beginning of the South's full articulation with modernity (as theorized by Giddens 1990; Harvey 1990:10–38; Jameson 1991:53–66; Soja 1989:10–42), as the war "propagated an economic and social agenda that functioned to catapult the United States into an emerging capitalist economy" (Flores 2002:32). Although many historical narratives do stress the continuity of the antebellum and postbellum South, closer examinations reveal that these narratives are historically grounded in a reactionary way—as a "strategy of containment" meant to naturalize the discourses on social hierarchy (Jameson 1981:10).

Some scholars have referred to the "tradition-bound South locked in a death struggle with the forces of modernization" (Cobb 1999:185). This view, I believe, plays into these strategies of containment by depicting an "unchanged" postbellum South embattled with a new social milieu (characterized by an urbanized, industrialized, rational society in which minorities would be treated "undeservingly" as equals) forced upon it from an outside "other" (most likely the northern states). Postbellum attitudes toward urbanization and modernization were much more ambivalent than this view allows, and, more important, there were major differences in social order within the antebellum/postbellum continuum, whose sharp relief has been smoothed over by discourses stressing the continuities between the old and the new South. These changes, however, were structurally superficial, as they indicated not a decline in white patriarchal control but its transformation into another framework. Moreover, the war itself is a convenient, but somewhat misleading, marker for these shifts. Significant changes had been occurring within the social structures of the South *prior* to the Civil War, rendering the war itself an "attempt to slow down the pace of change and manage the changes that had already taken place, rather than an effort to prevent change from occurring at all. To the horror of those who led the South out of the Union, the outbreak of the war in 1861 accelerated the pace of change, unleashing a flood of unanticipated consequences, not the least of which was emancipation" (Bardaglio 1995:xv).

Attempts at industrialization in the South, southern urbanization (see Cobb 1984 and Davidson, this volume), and a general reorganization of social relations in the South following the physical and psychological destruction that accompanied the war *did* require a new set of social codes in order to stabilize the changing constructions of race, gender, and class. Along racial lines these codes were overtly provided by the 1896 *Plessy v. Ferguson* decision, the systematic disfranchisement of black voters throughout the South between 1895 and 1909 (Du Bois 1940:55), and the enactment of Jim Crow laws wherein "whites tried to order the world to prevent African Americans from rising" (Gilmore 1996:15).

Meanwhile, on another legal front, statutory approaches to family and household in the South underwent a shift from outright white patriarchal dominance to a more subtle subordination of women and minorities within the modern paternal state. In the antebellum South, the legal canon shored up white patriarchal dominance in a subtle way—by its reluctance to intervene in household matters involving women and slaves (Bardaglio 1995:34). The doctrine of coverture and various "slave as property" rulings declared these subjects to be "household matters" and clearly within the purview of the husband/master/father—a point that lends some credence to archaeological approaches that treat entire plantations as functioning households for certain analytical purposes (e.g., Barile and Anderson, this volume). Following Reconstruction, a new, decidedly modern set of legal doctrines slowly pierced the veil of the antebellum household. These doctrines saw both women and children (regardless of race) as individuals and placed the paternal state in the position to arbitrate justice on their behalf (Bardaglio 1995:85). This "rational" law, of course, was no less racist or sexist, as critical race theorists attest (e.g., Gotanda 1995; Haney Lopez 1996; Harris 1995).

Further complicating our understanding of period households is the process of southern urbanization. Simultaneous with the end of Reconstruction (1877–1910), the South moved to town and did so across class and race lines (Hale 1998:123). Urbanization is often articulated with modernity in a way that emphasizes the commercial character of cities and a rearrangement of landscape spaces, stressing naturalized, hierarchical social relations (Lefebvre 1971; Soja 1989), and the American South is no exception.

It is easy to see how it becomes increasingly difficult to untangle the various strands of structural change in an era where virtually every aspect of the household is changing—and for African Americans in the postbellum South, this is certainly the case: emancipation, the move to town, a shift to a wage economy (often with female breadwinners), and the experience of modern segregation all happened in quick succession. Here, the formation of the so-called black middle-class is crucial. African Americans led a "deliberately conspicuous life" where in "towns and cities class showed the most" (Gilmore 1996:12, 15). The formation of a black middle-class itself can be seen as an act of both accommodation and resistance to the larger, class-based society (see discussion of the rise of black lawyers in Gilmore 1996:21 or black undertakers in Dallas in Davidson 1999:100–130). Moreover, it seems to have opened up a variety of political avenues for black women who began reform campaigns that paralleled their white counterparts (Spencer-Wood 1994:188).

More radically, the conceptualization of whiteness itself (that which blackness gets defined against) has been linked to this transition to modernity (e.g., Flores 2002; Ignatiev 1995; Jacobson 1998; Roediger 1991). Having lived through this postbellum transition, W. E. B. Du Bois (1920:17) made the bold statement that "the discovery of personal whiteness among the world's peoples is a very modern thing—a nineteenth and twentieth century matter, indeed."

It is within this shifting, unevenly experienced modernity that generative changes began occurring within southern households—both black and white. As Spencer-Wood (1994:181) has suggested, we need to be vigilant against universalizing stereotypes of gender construction in the archaeological record. Likewise, I purport that there was a great deal of variability within the postbellum attitude. I offer the following sections as a baseline demonstrating the decidedly southern variations of modern gender constructions and their racial linkages, something archaeologists should keep in mind when excavating late-nineteenth- and early-twentieth-century southern households.

FEMINISM, RACISM, DOMESTICITY, AND HISTORIC PRESERVATION: WHITE WOMEN AND THE MODERN SOUTH

Historical archaeologists working in the mid- to late nineteenth century have explored the relationships among feminism, various reform movements, and domesticity—especially as it relates to white middle-class women in the northern portion of the country (e.g., Scott 1994; Spencer-Wood 1991b, 1994, 1996, 1999a). These studies have begun to reflect in an important way how minority and lower-class women articulated and interacted with these ideological movements (Spencer-Wood 1994). However, the degree to which racialization, feminism, and regional identity are interconnected has not been fully explored in archaeological literature. One does not need go too far to discover the way nineteenth-century feminists used racialized metaphors to express their case. For example, in the 1850s, Elizabeth Cady Stanton would state unflinchingly, "A woman has no name . . . just as she changes masters; like the Southern slave, she takes the name of her owner" (quoted in Sánchez-Eppler 1993:19). Her quote is only one of many that draw on established abolitionist indignation to make a case for women's rights—and, in the process, attempt to place northern men in the uncomfortable position of southern slave-holder. We find, however, a quite different strategy being employed by those advancing women's roles in the South. Interestingly, I believe this strategy is deeply connected to the different ways in which southern households and southern history are constructed.

While in the North middle-class identity was structured in opposition to the decadent, slave-dependent antebellum plantation household (which was placed in discursive opposition to the rational, modern "domestic sphere"), the southern white middle class during Reconstruction sought to draw as many linkages to antebellum plantation life as possible (Hale 1998:88–93). It should come as no surprise that "part of the white south froze looking back over its shoulder at a mythical antebellum romance" (Gilmore 1996:13), but it is also clear that "myths and cultural memories more generally, are not stratospheric tales but deeply grounded narratives through which communities express their heartfelt convictions" (Flores 2002:xv), and these "heartfelt convictions" had a lot to do with racial hierarchy and the home.

Conflation of the new, white, middle-class southern home and old plantation household helped "ground the white southern middle-class' new racial order" (Hale 1998:87), even as it embraced a modern construction of domesticity (Bardaglio 1995; Spencer-Wood 1999a). In fact, the "white middle-class home was a more domestic, female-centered space than the antebellum plantation," which allowed for little separation between public (economic) and private (domestic) spheres (Hale 1998:94). It seems clear that antebellum southerners did not envision families or households as exclusively feminine terrain (Fox-Genovese 1988:195) but held on to a patriarchal model of household that was characteristic of the southern version of Victorian gender ideologies (Bardaglio 1995:82–84).

Following Reconstruction, even as codified segregation set in, the white southern household continued to be a locus of racial mixing due to the number of African Americans employed as domestics and laundresses (Davidson, this volume; Hale 1998:96). Thus, the "white home served as a major site for the preservation of racial identity" through the presence of black house workers (Hale 1998:88). This fact not only made the household the primary space where white children learned about race but also gave rise to the racialized woman-hood that was the "cult" of the black mammy (Hale 1998:98–114; Roberts 1994) while simultaneously freeing middle-class and elite white women to take a greater role in the public sphere. Through this trope the black women served as a real and symbolic labor connection to the antebellum South, rendering it seemingly impossible to imagine a white southern home without "surround-ing it with images of blackness" (Hale 1998:115). Interestingly, at the very mo-ment that southern women embraced the construction of a separate domestic sphere, they expanded their role into the so-called public sphere via reform and historical movements. Some, like the temperance movement, they held in com-mon with nonwhite and nonsouthern women (Gilmore 1996:45–59; Spencer-Wood 1991b, 1994), and others were purely white and southern.

By now it should be passé to make the "radical" claim that postbellum nos-talgia for the antebellum South and the era of the Civil War is, in fact, based more on contemporary social relations than any real want to understand and contextualize the past (see Levinson 1998; Loewen 1999). Far less analyzed within this debate about cultural memory is the way in which women, particu-larly middle-class and elite white women, utilized regional historic preserva-tion to transform their roles in society and move "beyond the pale of southern ladyhood" (Gilmore 1996:47).

White southern women working in the public sphere to preserve the tradi-tional South were a contradictory force in the face of notions of a gendered white feminine purity and passivity (for example, as depicted in Thomas Dixon's infamous 1905 novel, *The Clansmen*). Nonetheless, we see over and over again southern women taking an active, if not primary, role in the development and growth of the post-Reconstruction nostalgia for the Old South. They were that "noble band of women to whose untiring efforts we are chiefly indebted for our Confederate monument[s]" (Marshall quoted in Bishir 2000). Figures such as Oliva Raney, Belle Kearney, Mildred Rutherford, Susan Pringle Frost, Nell McColl Pringle, Clara Driscoll, and countless collective women's clubs served as the primary shapers of public memory invoking tropes of the Lost Cause and the Chivalric South while transforming the symbolic landscape of the postbellum South through the erection of countless Confederate monu-ments (Bishir 2000; Flores 2002:61–92; Hale 1998:107–111; Loewen 1999; Yuhl 2000) and, more subtly, through the restoration of the historic properties under their control.

It is within the realm of historic preservation, interestingly, that once again the domestic household becomes entangled with race, gender, cultural memory, and modernity. After all it was the *homes* of historic importance that were most often the rallying point for early historic preservation societies. Prime ex-amples are the Mount Vernon Ladies' Association, the Ladies' Hermitage Association, and Charleston's Society for the Preservation of Old Dwellings (Battle, this volume; Shackel 2001b:10; Yuhl 2000), but there are many others. These pioneering organizations influenced not only what types of spaces and sites were preserved but also the decoration and representation of these historic homes, filling them with material culture and interpretations infused with their decidedly feminine understanding of history (e.g., Yuhl 2000).

The postbellum, post-Reconstruction historic preservation phenomenon not only aided white women in claiming a larger part of the public sphere and adding a decidedly domestic cast to historical interpretation; it also (unfortunately) helped install a portion of the framework of modern racism through the celebration of the antebellum South as idyllic. Slaves were depicted as subservient, even nonhuman, beings who benefited from their association with the great men whose houses they served.

In a more overtly political vein, southern white women took a variety of public political stances during the period. For example, Mildred Rutherford, the first historian general of the United Daughters of the Confederacy and a staunch antisuffragist, often denounced both the "New Negro" and the "New Woman" and called the organization of the Ku Klux Klan "a necessity" (Hale 1998:107; Sebesta 2002). More common was the tendency of many other white southern feminists, such as prominent Mississippi suffragist Belle Kearney, to shift her general stance for women's rights to frame the debate in racial terms, arguing that granting white women the right to vote would, in effect, cancel out African-American suffrage: "the South is slow to grasp the great fact that the enfranchisement of women would settle the race question in politics . . . surely will the South be compelled to look to its Anglo-Saxon women as the medium through which to retain the supremacy of the white race over the African" (Kearney 1903).

Thus, whatever the ideological stance of the individual, it becomes impossible to separate southern women's quest for empowerment and equality from racial discourse in the late nineteenth and early twentieth century. This gender/race rubric is in turn decidedly *domestic* in character, as white feminist discourse commonly centered on the dominant Victorian ideology of "separate spheres" wherein women's role was *in the household*. White southern feminists did transform this ideology to embrace power over all things "outside" the economic sphere, including such things as fine arts and historic preservation. Like their northern counterparts, white southern women had to reposition their enlightenment-based arguments for equality to arguments that seemed more in accordance with andocentric dominate ideology (Spencer-Wood 1996:415)—for instance, the proposition that women *did* belong to separate spheres but that those spheres were equal. In other parts of the United States, these strategies led to a decidedly class-based discourse, but in the South they led directly to a deployment of race and the South's obsession with the dangers of free African Americans.

THE TERRAIN OF BLACK FEMINISM IN RECONSTRUCTION AND IN THE MODERN SOUTH

Social theorist bell hooks (1990) has postulated the black American household (or "homeplace" in her terminology) as an important site of resistance, a site within which cultural criticism and politics are taught and practiced. The way that these resistive strategies attempt to confront or circumvent white structurally racist strategies of containment is documented in both historical and archaeological works (e.g., Gilmore 1996; Mullins 1999a, 1999c, 2001).

I have postulated that the end of the American Civil War represents a convenient, if perhaps misleading, moment that marks the American South's full articulation with modernity and its full-blown capitalist engine. This point is doubly true of the recently emancipated population of southern African Americans. Although the enslaved were familiar with monetary exchange even when in bondage (Hudson 1994), nothing could quite prepare them for their new status as "free" wage labor and consumer in an unapologetically racist marketplace.

For many who entered the blossoming farm tenancy system in the rural areas of the South, much remained familiar, although transformed; little money exchanged hands as tenancy was part and parcel of a credit system designed to keep tenants in debt to their landlords (Flynn 1983; Orser 1988; Whayne 1996). But for the many others who fled, the increasingly urban southern cities represented a land of promise where African Americans may not have been able to amass great fortunes but could become "financially successful in a modest fashion" (Drake and Cayton 1945:49).

Among the mass of African Americans in the postbellum period, the household is truly a shifting and fluid entity. Households in both urban and rural areas could be stable or quite erratic (see Davidson, this volume; Wilkie 2000a: 73–79). Moreover, many African-American women found themselves the sole breadwinners, a fact attested to by the growing number of archaeological investigations focusing on households headed by black women (see, e.g., Patten 1997; Wilkie 2000a). Of course, these women entering the cash economy meant consumption and inevitably the growth of class differentiation, especially in the urban areas of the African-American South.

Following Reconstruction, a growing number of African Americans were beginning to articulate the "mass prophesy that material affluence harbored inevitable social empowerment" (Mullins 1999a:1), a theory canonized in the national-level discourse of the period, for example in the writings of Booker T. Washington (1907), and documented in a variety of localized contexts, such as Durham (Du Bois 1995:253), Annapolis (Mullins 1999a:1), Chicago (Drake and Cayton 1945:51), Dallas (Brandon 2000), New Bern, North Carolina (Gilmore 1996), and the Arkansas lowland delta (Gordon 1995). As the black middle classes began to form across the nation (a process that happened unevenly across time and space), attempts to equate participation in the capitalist economy with social equality went hand in hand with the attempt to define oneself through that consumption. This consumption/identity process was, of course, occurring across race, class, and gender lines as the country's growing "culture industry" began to gear up following the Civil War (Horkheimer and Adorno 1944:154–155). For instance, the importance given the common household knick-knack as symbolic capital (and proof of one's humanity) among free African Americans is evident in Mullins's analytic work (1999a:155–184; 2001), as well as being alluded to in literary treatments (e.g., Agee and Evans 1939:162–165; Ellison 1947:272–273; Steinbeck 1939:139–140).

Of course, in the post-Reconstruction period consumerism is a double-edged sword, as the racist underpinnings of consumer space and the racialization of products made almost every transaction a confrontation with one's racial identity. Mullins (1999a:3–4), like bell hooks (1990:3–5), proposes a critical awareness in African-Americans' consumption, but it is an awareness that does not preclude their desire to consume (cf. Horkheimer and Adorno 1944:167). They did, however, "probe the relationship between consumer space's racist underpinnings and the economic, labor and political implications" of their consumption (Mullins 1999a:3).

This is the same participation in consumption that may have been a factor in anxiety-driven white racism. Period diatribes on the subject of African-American consumption tend simultaneously to trivialize it and fear it, concentrating often on these small, mundane objects mentioned earlier (Mullins 1999a:162–170; 2001). Not only has Mullins pointed out that "relatively mundane objects inspired apprehension because they posed the specter of a society in which material culture would not clearly mark subjectivity" (1999a:156), he likewise figures consumption as one of the terrains where social struggle can take place with profound implications for citizenship and racial subjectivity. The opening of this terrain elicited dramatic responses from threatened whites anxious about their own position: many racial "riots" seem directed at African-American property holders (Gilmore 1996:81–103) or at those who were perceived to threaten white access to jobs and, thus, to consumption (Foley 1997; Roediger 1991; Whayne 1996). Moreover, a plethora of African-American theorists of the period from the 1890s to the 1940s agreed that economically successful blacks, and the fear they evoked in white America, was *one* of the factors leading to the institution of Jim Crow–era segregation (Du Bois 1940; 1995:174–192; Drake and Cayton 1945:51; and many others).

Among the new black middle-class women, the household would take an important, if at times covert, position. The agency of African-American women in southern history is obscured owing to power relations embedded in the production of the historical record. When they do appear, the narrative usually depicts them as stalwart, self-sacrificing, community-based activists whose work inevitably links forward into the civil rights movement (Gilmore 1996:93). But for many southern black women, "politics began at home, blending the public and the private" (Gilmore 1996:101), and the home was "the one site where one could freely confront the issue of humanization, where one could resist" (hooks 1990:42). Here we see the complementary opposite of the role of the household among white children: the African-American home could be the only open venue in which young black children could learn both the rules of a racist society and establish a critical stance toward it (hooks 1990:47; see also Du Bois 1940:8–24). Black women "first forged their ideas of gender and race equity within their families and homes," then their "public sphere" encounters through education, consumerism, and volunteerism tested and refined those ideas (Gilmore 1996:32).

Further complicating the issue, however, is the erasure of the African-American household in the postbellum South. It takes place both geographically and ideologically, first by spatially segregating households into white and black categories and then by effectively denying a private sphere to black women who must be available at all times to serve the white community as domestics and laundresses.

Conversely, while white southern Victorian attitudes toward womanhood devalued outspokenness among women, some have postulated that southern African Americans held different ideals that expected women to be active in the public sphere (Gilmore 1996:43). It is true that black women had overtly "empowered themselves by organizing into separate parallel institutions" to white reform organizations (Spencer-Wood 1994:188), but this parallel structure was the direct result of the failure of black auxiliary arms associated with white women's groups such as the Women's Christian Temperance Union. These black auxiliaries failed across the South because, as mentioned, the politics of white and black southern women often diverged when it came to addressing the race issue directly (Gilmore 1996:45–50).

Finally, as consumerism, volunteerism, and education worked to transform the black middle-class household in a positive, emancipatory way, it also brought about social division. Middle-class African-American families often adopted not only Victorian bric-a-brac but also the prescriptive "Christian principles" bolstered by white reform movements. Thus, as reform "joined black women's religious and class values to their activism even as it provided a safe forum for agitation" (Gilmore 1996:49), it also carried extensive class baggage with its empowering message. Moreover, as certain African-American households embraced bourgeois individualism, cooperative ideology (i.e., ideas about "the race") weakened in one sense but grew in another.

While some working-class blacks would resent the growing material and cultural differences between them and their middle-class peers, white ideology privileged race above all else and attempted to blind itself to the substantial differences between black laundresses and black doctors. Thus middle-class African Americans became increasingly conscious of lower-class actions and demeanors. This awareness created a striking difference between black and white reform movements in the South: black women had to worry about issues such as alcohol not only in a domestic setting but also for the entire race (Gilmore 1996:49)

RACE, GENDER, MODERNITY, AND THE ARCHAEOLOGY OF HOUSEHOLDS

This exploration of some of the ways in which gender and race are entangled with households and modernity from the mid-nineteenth to the early twentieth century serves to call attention to the complexity and interrelatedness of any categorical analysis (i.e., race, class, gender, etc.). I have only scratched the surface of the complexity, but I have attempted to focus on aspects which we archaeologists have not treated extensively in our investigations.

To be sure, historical archaeology has improved approaches to both gender (e.g., Gilchrist 1999; Spencer-Wood 1994, 1996, 1999a) and race (e.g., papers in Franklin and Fesler 1999; Orser 2001; Singleton 1999b; Wilkie 2000a) greatly over the past decade or so. What we are failing to do, however, is examine the intersection of two or more of these phenomena (cf. Franklin 2001a). I believe that household-level archaeology at sites in the antebellum/postbellum continuum may provide us with an opportunity to explore the intersections of race and gender.

First, it is crucial to recognize that the household is not only a locus for gendered power struggles but is also where children learn about race and resistance to racism. It can shed light on the interpretive complexities of artifacts such as the black painted porcelain doll recovered from Old Washington (Stewart-Abernathy, this volume) or the children's toys recovered from the freedman's cabin during my own work at the mid-nineteenth-century sawmill community known as Van Winkle's Mill (Brandon and Davidson 2002; Brandon et al. 2000a).

These children's toys recovered from archaeological contexts return us to the doll with which I opened this chapter. Very few pieces of material culture encapsulate so well a rubric of ideologies as does the "topsy-turvy" doll, but all material culture reflects identity in multifaceted, and often contradictory, ways. Children's toys are especially evocative as they are tied into the household, "the realm within which identities are initially constructed and reinforced" (Wilkie 2000a:134). Thus, households are the crucible for gender and race ideologies as well as many other identities. As material culture is the basic framework from which archaeologists interpret the past, I will begin here to outline methodological ways in which we might address the complicated entanglements outlined here through household archaeology.

Archaeologists should turn to building an understanding of *local* representations of race and gender across the antebellum/postbellum continuum. There are many recent examples of critical historical work that have fruitfully examined racial and class identities from a local perspective, especially when compared to and contrasted against the overarching national-level (or global) discourse on racial formations or class consciousness (e.g., Foley 1995; Foley 1997; Gilmore 1996; Gordon 1998; Gyory 1998; Hall 2000; Hartigan 1999; Limón 1998; Mitchell 1996).

These works have either laid bare articulations not visible on the national level—such as the examination of the non-overt, yet concretely political, role of middle-class African-American women during and after Reconstruction in North Carolina (Gilmore 1996)—or challenged the national-level understandings of the underpinnings of race and class, such as the refutation of working-class racism as the prime mover for the adoption of the Chinese Exclusion Act of 1882 (Gyory 1988; *contra* Roediger 1994; Saxton 1971; and many others).

In addition, an increasing number of researchers have pointed to the local terrain as the one on which "provisional," "fluid," and "situational" identities such as race are best discerned from their more reified abstractions commonly used when discussing the larger "collective" experience (Franklin 2001b:89; Gordon and Anderson 1999:91–118, 293–294; Hartigan 1999:13–16). This move to the local analytical register also serves to underscore the important role of *place* in the construction of identity.

Discussion of place in historical archaeology inevitably leads to a discussion of the now well-explored subject of landscapes. It should be no great revelation that cultural landscapes—series of places through which people's lives are threaded—help people "give account of their own identity" (Knapp and Ashmore 1999:10) and are "arena[s] in which and through which memory, identity, social order and transformation are constructed, played out, re-invented and changed" (Thomas 2001:173). But most landscape analyses, including my own at Van Winkle's Mill (Brandon and Davidson 2002; Brandon et al. 2000b), have stressed a relatively coarse scale that privileges racial analysis at the expense of gender. It has been pointed out that "women and children often disappear from the past" in large-scale analyses where "cultures are often defined according to male-controlled social, political and economic structures" (Spencer-Wood 1999a:163). Households and women are, in fact, often analytically subsumed under larger social formations; we have done so with class and race at Van Winkle's Mill.

To get at the intersection of race and gender, we are going to have to change the scale, but perhaps not the character, of our analysis. That is to say, most landscape analysis has focused on the larger-scale phenomena—the relationships of buildings to one another, for instance. As nineteenth-century gender constructions do not appear, in most cases, to have been expressed on this level (that is, spatial distribution of buildings does not often cleave along gender lines), we need to change the scale of our analysis to attempt to read the gender-related texts expressed in the use of space (Moore 1996:80–97). The next scale of analysis, the household level, has the potential to reveal much about the lives of the women *and men*—we hope that it will enable us to get at daily practices and how they followed and changed the structures of the community(ies). Taken together with the more traditional landscape analyses that categorically examine race (e.g., Barile, this volume), we may be able to get beyond simply addressing the "fecundity" of enslaved and later freed African-American populations (cf. Delle 2000). Emphasizing the "lived experience" aspect of space while placing the landscape analysis in dialogue with the local race/gender context will result in a much more nuanced understanding of our sites as *places*—although a place that may be contested or fragmented (Adams et al. 2001:xxi).

ACKNOWLEDGMENTS

I would like to thank Maria Franklin, James Davidson, Richard Flores, and John Hartigan for their input and support. In addition, thanks are due to Kerri Barile for her patience. All errors made within are my own.

12

Working-Class Households as Sites of Social Change

Margaret C. Wood

INTRODUCTION

Men and women who lived in the southern Colorado coal town of Berwind in the early twentieth century may have spent a warm summer evening in their yard washing clothes, peeling potatoes, sharing a drink with neighbors, or just spending time with family. As dusk gathered over the rolling hills, playing children may have dashed across the sloping landscape as their mothers washed dinner dishes and their fathers read the newspaper or headed down the dusty road to the saloon. It was in places like this that the domestic side of industrial life played out, away from the cramped recesses of the coal mines. Homes and the activities that occurred in them, however, were not separate from other aspects of industrial life; they were simply another aspect of it.

Archaeologists, historians, and social scientists have long recognized the interconnections between households and larger political and economic processes. They have emphasized that household relations are not isolated from society as a whole but rather have broader political and economic significance because they are an integral part of relationships and processes that make up the "public domain" (e.g., Conkey and Gero 1991:16; Ehrenreich and English 1978; Gutman 1976b; Hendon 1996:47; Kaplan 1982; Shackel 1996; Wall 1994).

Historical archaeologists have begun to recognize the creative and insurgent potential of domestic relations and domestic activities (Bassett 1994:55–80; Beaudry et al. 1991; Deagan 1983:263–271; Shackel 1996; Wall 1994). Women's labor in the home, however, has received only sparse attention from scholars (for an exception, see Wall 1994). Housework is generally seen as an unchanging, nondynamic set of tasks conducted in the isolation of the domestic realm (Schwartz-Cowan 1983). Domesticity in this view is a quaint cultural development, a sideline to other changes in society.

In this chapter I combine the concerns of labor, culture, and gender to explore the ways in which women participated in the struggle for social change through their work in their households. The men and women who lived in the coal mining community of Berwind endeavored throughout the early twentieth century to achieve workers' rights and social justice. The region was rocked by a series of violent strikes that culminated in a bloody event in 1914 known as the Ludlow Massacre. During this grizzly affair, the Colorado National Guard killed 2 women and 11 children, the wives and children of striking miners (Beshoar 1942; Long 1996; McGovern and Gutridge 1972; Papanikolas 1982).

The bulk of research pertaining to labor struggles in general, and this strike in particular, has emphasized the institutional causes and effects of labor action, stressing the role of male workers, union organizers, and owners who negotiated labor's demands in the public arena (Gitelman 1988; McGovern and Guttridge 1972; Papanikolas 1982). Researchers have tended to emphasize the commonalities of the work experiences as the source of social consciousness that united the ethnically diverse mining community. When issues of home life are considered, labor historians generally go only as far as to link workers' willingness to participate in strikes to the biting oppression and poverty that mining families experienced in the coal camps. The effective action of women and men in labor struggles cannot be fully understood, however, when viewed only as reactionary. Rather, it is important to examine the ways in which working-class people organized themselves in their daily lives and how that organization was instrumental in the formation of effective class action.

Women in the coal camps did not work for wages outside the home. They were wives, sisters, daughters, and mothers whose job it was to care for the mineworkers—their husbands, fathers, sons, brothers, and boarders. Conceptually separated from the world of production, working-class immigrant housewives typically recede into the backwaters of history. By placing women at the center of community struggle and collective action, however, our attention is redirected to the importance of daily life in working-class efforts to resist capitalist oppression.

Women's domestic labor—or housework—is used as a point of departure to explore how women created and participated in social relations that facilitated collective action. By examining the remains of household refuse, as well as the landscapes in which mining families worked and lived, I began to piece together the kinds of labor in which housewives were engaged and to flesh out the social relations built around that work. Patterns related to the use and disposal of material culture at Berwind reveal information about how relations between men, women, ethnic groups, and households were created and re-created through the productive activities of women and their consumption choices. Ultimately, relationships that emerged from the household shaped social life, community life, and the nature of social protest.

CONCEPTS OF THE DOMESTIC:
THE MIDDLE-CLASS NORM

Historical archaeologists seldom see domestic contexts as sites of social change, owing in part to commonly held stereotypes of families, gender relations, households, and women's work. Both past and present class relations profoundly shape these idealized images.

Historians tend to characterize the nature of housework based on middle-class experience. According to them, the work of middle-class women changed significantly in the late nineteenth and early twentieth century. Families became increasingly privatized as servants, boarders, and extended family members moved away from the nuclear family household (Hareven and Modell 1973). Women began to purchase more mass-produced products and labor-saving devices (Schwartz-Cowan 1983, 1992). As women became increasingly defined as consumers and household managers, the home was constructed as a site of consumption and leisure (Ehrenreich and English 1978; Hartmann 1974; Mintz and Kellogg 1988; Schwartz-Cowan 1983; Strasser 1982). The tendency for all productive labor to move outside the home, a trend that had begun in the mid-nineteenth century, continued and was solidified during this period.

The changes outlined for middle-class homes did not sit comfortably with the picture of home life at Berwind that was emerging from the archaeological material and historical data. It was clear that the women of Berwind and the middle-class women who were the subjects of so much historical inquiry had very different domestic lives. The experiences of working-class housewives seem to have fallen through the cracks of history.

Historians have attempted to piece together details of domestic life based on prescriptive literature, cookbooks, and magazines, literature designed for the middle class with the purpose of perpetuating middle-class values (Scott 1997; Wall 2000). By relying on these sources, they have set up middle-class domesticity as the benchmark for comparison. The actual complexity of domestic life over time and space has been collapsed into a simple, monolithic representation that is strongly influenced by middle-class values, both past and present (Coontz 1992). Although most researchers acknowledged the differences that class and ethnicity can make in family and household relations, only a few have found ways to explore forms of domesticity that are distinct from the middle-class norm (O'Neill 1993; Schofield 1983; Stansell 1995).

The powerful impact of the middle-class norm in historical archaeology has limited the ways in which we envision homes, families, and women's work. Following the publication of Diana diZerega Wall's (1991) influential research on middle-class Victorian domesticity, a number of studies appeared that sought to explore the extent to which women in various contexts adhered to middle-class ideals of domesticity and gentility (Fitts 1999; Hardesty 1994; Praetzellis and Praetzellis 1992a, 2000). Middle-class Victorian womanhood and its associated behaviors have become the yardstick by which all forms of domesticity are measured. People who did not utilize material culture in ways that were consistent with middle-class patterns are assumed to have resisted middle-class hegemony. Alternatively, when working-class people used material culture in ways that mirrored middle-class behaviors, it is assumed that they aspired to middle-class status (Beaudry et al. 1991). As a result, all questions about domesticity lead back to the middle class.

Certainly the decades from 1890 to 1920 were a period during which the middle class ballooned in terms of size and power, but domesticity, as the middle class defined it, was not an option for most people. The middle-class ideal of the housewife was contradicted by the reality of the millions of working-class women who labored in factories and fields across the nation. In fact, deviation from the domestic ideal was essential to the maintenance of middle-class life. For every nineteenth-century family that sheltered the wife and child within the home, there was an Irish woman scrubbing floors in that middle-class house, a Welsh boy mining coal to keep the home warm, and a black woman doing the family's laundry (Coontz 1992:11). The lifestyles and domestic ideals of middle-class women were based on the oppression of other women, men, and children and reflected only a partial reality. The middle-class domestic ideal was really a symbol of the economic prosperity enjoyed by the emerging middle class.

Domesticity is not a simple, benign, or straightforward arrangement. Rather, it is contested terrain where specific class and gendered interests are played out. The prescribed role of the housewife was rooted in the social conditions of the middle classes, and as hegemonic ideologies "domesticity" and proper gender relations established the roles of housewife and mother as universal roles of womanhood. All women were expected to conform to gendered expectations that were considered to be their natural vocation. Seen in this way, domesticity can be viewed as a relation of power and the household as a site of the practice of power. The assertion that middle-class domesticity was the norm, or was the most desirable organization of family life, had been a claim to power by the ascendant middle class in the past. Archaeologists who today reify this middle-class standard are implicitly repeating middle-class claims to all-encompassing social power in both past and present.

Feminist archaeologists have produced a great deal of criticism relating to researchers' tendency to project gender roles and an assumed gendered division of labor into the distant past (e.g., Conkey and Gero 1991; Nixon 1994). For prehistoric archaeologists, the central challenge has been to develop a critical awareness of present-day, taken-for-granted notions about gender relations that are shaped by our contemporary social worlds (e.g., Leacock 1983:263). For historical archaeologists, it has been somewhat more difficult to surmount these ideological barriers. Because we study the fairly recent past, it is assumed that gender relations and household relations among the people we study were similar to familiar gender relations that we see in the world today. As mostly middle-class practitioners, our historical notions about households are very much influenced by the gravity of our own class-based authority. For historical archaeologists, then, the central challenge may be to develop a critical awareness of our class-based assumptions about households and gender relations.

Archaeology has the potential to be a powerful tool for examining alternative forms of domesticity and household relations. Documentary information has played an important role in unraveling the intricacies of middle-class family life (Scott 1997). Archaeological analysis has been effectively combined with these sources to produce a complex picture of middle-class households and domestic life. It may be necessary, however, for archaeological material to play a more primary role in the examination of domesticity among working-class and ethnically diverse households, for whom the same type of written material does not exist. If part of the goal of historical archaeology is to explore the pasts of the "inarticulate," then an examination of domesticity among working-class and ethnic households would allow archaeologists to fill some of the gaps in our historical understanding of the complexity and variety of household arrangements. Clearly, these "other" kinds of households exist within the relations of capitalist production and need to be understood within the context of social, economic and political power. The practice of social power both on the level of class relations and on the level of household relations should remain central to this endeavor.

At Berwind, household relations and domestic labor did not in any simple way conform to or resist middle-class patterns. I will argue in the rest of this chapter that the men, women, and children who lived in these households created for themselves their own forms of domesticity, which served their class-based needs.

Working-Class Households at Berwind: Class, Ethnicity, Domesticity, and Collective Action

The remains of the town of Berwind lie on either side of a twisting dirt road that cuts through a canyon approximately 4 kilometers from the site of the Ludlow Massacre (Figure 12.1). The ruins of houses and industrial equipment lie in silent, neat rows that extend nearly 2 km up the canyon. It is difficult to imagine that this quiet and empty place was home to more than 800 people only 80 years ago. Berwind was founded in 1888. The population remained small and scattered until 1892, when the town and surrounding coal veins were purchased by the Colorado Fuel and Iron Company (C.F.&I.) (Camp & Plant Magazine 1902). Purchase of the Berwind mine and several other properties in southern Colorado made C.F.&I. one of the hundred largest firms in the United States. By 1910, it employed over 6,000 coal miners in southern Colorado. It controlled the county government through election fraud, dominated the region's other coal firms, and enjoyed a large influence in state government (Long 1991). John D. Rockefeller, who owned a controlling interest in the company, was himself worth over $1 billion in 1910.

While Rockefeller and C.F.&I. reaped enormous profits, the coal miners and their families lived in conditions of poverty and oppression (Long 1991; Margolis 1985; McGovern and Guttridge 1972; Papanikolas 1982). Men worked 10–16 hours a day and sent their sons into the mines when they were as young as ten years old. They were sometimes paid in scrip, a form of currency redeemable only at the company store. A miner's wages depended not on the number of hours he worked but on the tons of coal he excavated. Company scales that measured a worker's output were often rigged, resulting in underpayment. They also were not compensated for the time-consuming labor related to maintaining their work site, such as timbering the roofs and walls of the shaft. This policy exacerbated the already dangerous working conditions in the mine. A man working for the C.F.&I. in 1911 had a one in three hundred chance that he would die at work (SIM 1911). Mining families lived in company-owned housing from which they could be evicted on as little as three days' notice. Armed company guards patrolled the communities, and access into and out of the camp was tightly controlled.

Many immigrant families moved to the United States to find a free and democratic society, but it did not exist in the coal camps of southern Colorado. Mining communities housed a working-class population of astounding ethnic diversity. In 1910, there were 26 nationalities represented among the mining families who lived in Berwind (U.S. Census 1910). The ethnic composition of the community fluctuated over time, but in the years leading up to the strike it was dominated by people from Italy, Eastern Europe, and the United States. The remainder of the population was from the United Kingdom, Greece, Germany, Mexico, and Japan (Figure 12.2).

Ethnicity and the Use of Space

For researchers studying working-class families, households, and neighborhoods, ethnicity is often viewed as a source of strength that enables immigrant workers to negotiate their lives and the industrial workplace (Hareven 1982; Yans-McLaughlin 1971). For those studying class conflict, however, ethnicity is often construed as a force that limits the possibility of organizing workers

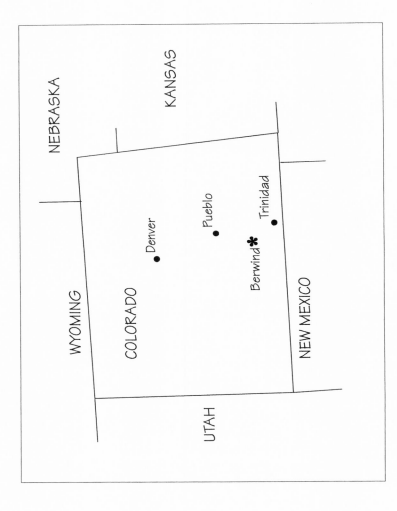

Fig. 12.1. Map of Colorado showing location of Berwind.

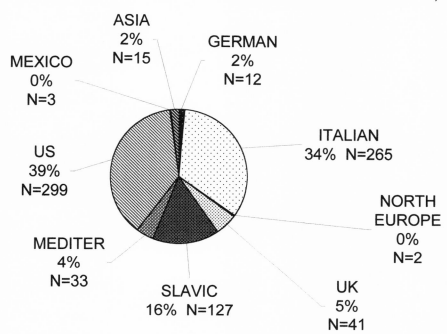

Fig. 12.2. Pie chart showing national origin of residents of Berwind.

who lived in multiethnic communities (Cohen 1990). In a recent study of coal-mining towns in the early twentieth century in nearby Huerfano County, Colorado, Denise Pan (1994) argues that workers before and after the 1913–1914 strike were able to *overcome* their ethnic differences to organize as a class. Within this scenario, if ethnicity provides a dominant set of relations, then collective action along class lines is difficult or even impossible. If, on the other hand, workers unite as a class, it is assumed that ethnic differences fade into the background. Workers presumably chose allegiance to *either* ethnic relations *or* class relations. Among workers struggling to unionize, it is generally assumed that ethnicity divides and class unites.

In southern Colorado, it appears that something very different from this proposed model was going on. Miners here utilized ethnic relationships to build class solidarity. Some of the United Mine Workers of America's best organizers were members of the major ethnic groups working in the coal camps (Long 1991:265; McGovern and Guttridge 1972; Papanikolas 1982). These organizers recognized that ethnicity was an important part of workers' everyday lives. During the strike, the miners walked off the job as distinct ethnic blocks, not as a homogeneous working class (Figure 12.3). The question remains though, how did workers build ties among these ethnic groups in order that they act as a class?

The Colorado Fuel and Iron Company also recognized the power of ethnic groups. One union representative contended that "the coal companies . . . place an Italian working alongside of a Greek, a Croatian working alongside of an Austrian, and so on down the line of 22 or 23 different nationalities. The purpose is that no two of them shall get together and discuss their grievances" (Committee on Industrial Relations [CIR], McLellan Testimony: 6531).

Archaeological and historical evidence indicates that the company was utilizing this strategy not only in the workplace but also in the neighborhoods where workers lived. In the coal camp of Berwind, excavations were conducted in one neighborhood dating to the period before the 1913–1914 strike, where ten domestic structures occupied a broad flat area between 1902 and 1915. The slope of the canyon, which distinguished this residential area from others in the town, defined the neighborhood.

By matching the house numbers recorded on a historic map of the community with census enumeration lists, it is possible to determine the composition of the households and the national origins of the residents. Although ethnicity and national origin are not one and the same, for the purposes of this analysis a shared place of origin is used as an indication of at least some level of shared heritage. Using the head of household to identify the origin of each house, we can see how groups were distributed on the landscape.

Despite the fact that over half the neighborhood population was Italian, no household in this neighborhood shared the same origin with both of its neighbors, and only a few shared the same place of origin of one neighbor. This left 68 percent of all households surrounded by households with a different place of origin. In the duplex structures the different halves of the building are, in all cases, occupied by people from different regions of the world, creating a checkerboard effect. A chi-square test of the distribution of households indicates that it is not likely that people would randomly arrange themselves on the landscape in such a way. If people were forming ethnic neighborhoods, it would be more likely for them to share their national origin with two of their neighbors. If national origin had no relationship with where people were living, we would expect to see values that more closely approximated a random distribution. What we see, however, is a tendency for people to live near others who did *not* share their national origin. Thirteen of the nineteen households in this area did not share a common ethnic heritage with any of their closest neighbors, and only six households shared an ethnic link with one neighbor. A chi-square test shows that the pattern in this area is not random and that people of shared national origin tended to live apart more often than statistically expected. Although the sample size of this neighborhood is small, a simi-

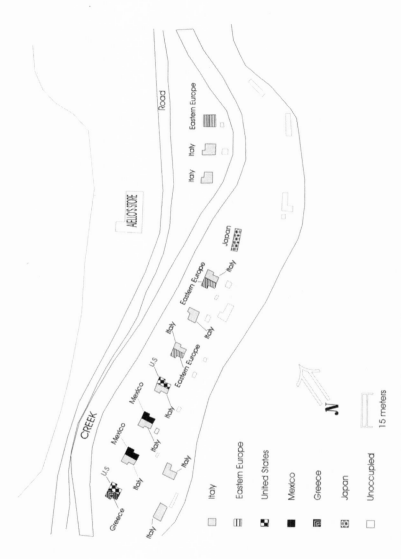

Fig. 12.3. Map showing households in pre-strike locus.

lar examination of the community as a whole revealed a similar result. Clearly, C.F.&I. had specific policies aimed at blocking association of ethnic workers in these neighborhoods.

Despite these barriers workers clearly participated in the strike based on ethnic affiliations. While the company appears to have been attempting to divide workers on the landscape, residential patterns within households suggest how women's domestic labor may have been instrumental in bringing workers together. By opening up their homes to boarders who shared their ethnicity/national origin, women provided the basic framework on which many ethnic relations were built.

In a mining family, a wife was responsible for cooking, cleaning, and laundry for her family, maintaining her household, and providing domestic services for boarders. A study by the Women's Bureau of the Department of Labor (U.S. Department of Labor 1925) concluded that, in coal mining communities, many women were a direct economic factor in the support of their families, serving in the capacity of actual breadwinners in addition to the role of homemakers. The bureau reached this conclusion despite the fact that in the bituminous regions of the country, including Colorado, employment opportunities for women outside the home were virtually nonexistent. Coal camps in the West were commonly located in isolated, rural areas where jobs for women were scarce. In the context of the extractive coal mining industry, women in the coal camps developed their own form of service industry by taking in boarders.

These activities, however, were not constant. Women intensified their work by taking in boarders in the years between 1900 and 1910 (Figure 12.4). In 1900, only 14 percent of households at Berwind took in boarders. Ten years later, this pattern had changed drastically, and the number of households taking in boarders increased to 45 percent. Women who took in boarders tended to take three or four single men into their homes, and many women took in even more. Angelina Ravenelli, for example, was a twenty-seven-year-old immigrant from Italy. She and her twenty-four-year-old sister, Rosa Fedrizzi, cared for a household of 18 people, including both of their husbands, two children, and twelve boarders (U.S. Census 1910).

Given the fact that the coal company took steps to discourage interaction between people of shared ethnicity in neighborhoods through residence assignment policies, ethnic relations and interactions within the household took on increasing significance. In this neighborhood households were large, averaging seven persons per household. Over one-half of the members of many households were boarders. Of the 44 boarders living in this neighborhood, 81 percent shared the same ethnicity as the wife of the household (U.S. Census 1910). Both the women and the men they took in contributed to the tendency for ethnic groups to cluster within households. Shared language and cul-

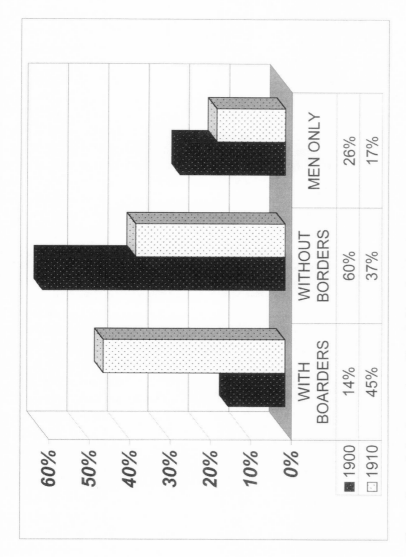

	WITH BOARDERS	WITHOUT BORDERS	MEN ONLY
1900	14%	60%	26%
1910	45%	37%	17%

Fig. 12.4. Bar graph showing number of households with and without boarders.

ture were important factors that determined who a woman would take in as a boarder and where a man would choose to live.

All of this indicates that in the midst of corporate policy that was intent on dividing ethnic workers by disbursing them broadly across the landscape, workers were able to maintain social relations based on ethnic identity within households. In the physical and social spaces in homes, interactions between men and women, boarders and families, children and adults fostered relationships that were strongly influenced by their ethnic identities. Women's work provided the basis for these activities. Unlike middle-class families, who could easily see the interests of the privatized family in contrast to the interests of outsiders, working-class families, their social interactions, and their household economies were profoundly integrated with the interests of people who fell outside the family unit. Through these links, families were articulated with broader interest groups within their households and the community.

Tin Cans and Women's Work

Approximately 300 meters from the nearest house in this neighborhood, on a low hill, was a large communal midden associated with the households in the area. Seven contiguous 1-×-1-meter test units were excavated to uncover this feature, which included a wealth and variety of material culture, including bottles, cans, bones, and even newspaper fragments and leather shoes. Four of the units had significant disturbance from recent bottle-hunting activities. For the purpose of this analysis only material culture excavated from units with intact strata was considered. Using glass bottles as a chronological marker, the mean date of this feature was determined to be 1908. The stratigraphy exhibited two distinct chronological levels; the lowest level dates after 1904, the upper after 1907 (Figure 12.5).

When we compare the assemblages from these two levels, a pattern becomes apparent. In the lower level the number of tin can vessels is relatively low. In the upper level, which dates to a period after 1907, there is a sharp increase in the number of tin cans (Figure 12.6). The pattern here is not a simple linear progression; however, the spike in the number of cans used and discarded after 1907 suggests a significant intensification in the use of mass-produced canned goods after this date. While the number of vessels in this sample is small, analysis using the weight of tin can fragments shows a similar increase in the number of tin cans in the deposits dating after 1907. The increased usage of canned goods, as indicated by the artifacts, corresponds closely with the period during which women were intensifying their work by taking in boarders. But in what way was an increasing reliance on mass-produced canned goods related to the process of boarding, women's work, or collective action?

This question can be answered in many ways, and some of the answers

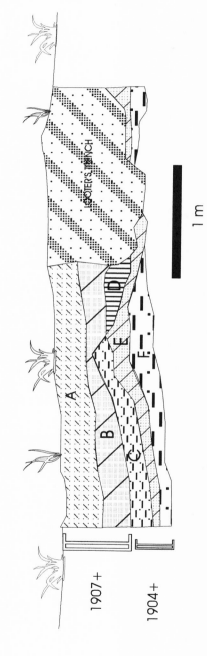

Fig. 12.5. Profile of midden feature.

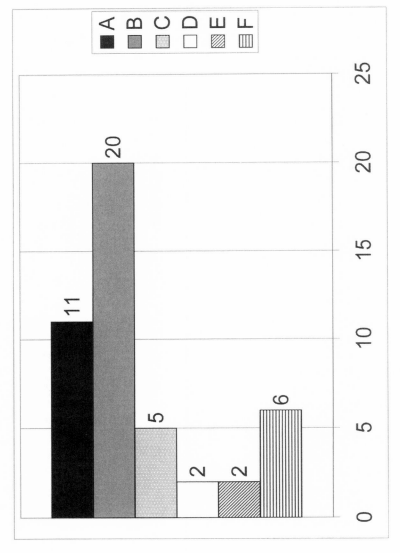

Fig. 12.6. Bar graph showing increase in use of mass-produced canned goods in strata dating after 1907.

are more pragmatic than others. If we think of canned goods as a tool that women used in their domestic productive activities, it is clear that the use of mass-produced food would have been very helpful to women. When women took in boarders, they often doubled the size of their households. The increased workload in washing, cleaning, and hauling water alone was enough to fill the day.

The ability to purchase canned goods was contingent upon women's ability to earn a sufficient amount of money. In the years before World War I, canned food was considered an expensive luxury. A 1902 study by the Colorado Bureau of Labor Statistics showed that while a one-pound can of beef ranged in price from 15–30 cents, fresh beef cost around half that price at 10–15 cents per pound. Beans cost around 20 cents for a three-pound can, while the same quantity of fresh beans cost around 15 cents (CBLS 1902). In a community where the wages were low, the reliance on more expensive canned goods is at first glance puzzling. In 1914 a young girl from one of the coal camps expressed the significance and preference for canned food among mining families when she boasted to a magazine reporter, "I tell you we live high . . . we buy the very best canned goods we can get" (Eastman 1914). Mining families were not wealthy or extravagant, but it is probable that the earnings of women from taking in boarders allowed families to purchase food that was considered healthy, nutritious, and a luxury.

A women's contribution to family income, especially when her work involved domestic labor, is difficult to quantify. The informal nature of boarding relations within a home left few records. It is possible, however, to estimate women's earnings based on data from a comparable occupational group—farm workers, who earned approximately the same as miners did in the early twentieth century. In 1913 a farm worker in Colorado paid $15 per month, or about 50 cents per day, for room and board (USDA Bulletin 1921:8). This amount is consistent with the testimony of oral history informants who grew up in the coal camps. A woman taking in three boarders in 1913 could earn around $540 a year while her husband was making $615 a year in the mines. Clearly, women's economic contributions to their households could be substantial, especially if they took in a large number of boarders.

Women's paid labor in this context was visible because of the extreme intensification of boarding. It is probable, however, that the consumption choices women were making served to downplay their contributions within families and the community. In her study of Guatemalan women, anthropologist Tracy Ellers (2000) shows how income produced by women in female family businesses is often consumed immediately by the family for basic needs, so women's contributions seem less visible and less tangible. At Berwind, boarders probably paid women in cash. That money was then taken to the store and exchanged for food, a basic need of the family. Once the food was consumed and the refuse thrown in a midden, the material manifestations of women's work were made invisible. Therefore, the benefits of women's labor were consumed immediately and completely. Although women's contributions to their families and the working-class community may have been great, it is probable that the magnitude of that contribution was only minimally apparent, in part because of the disposable nature of the material culture that constituted the reproduction of those relations.

In the late nineteenth and early twentieth century, many of the demands of organized labor were based on the idea of a "family wage." This was a highly gendered ideology that asserted that a man should be able to earn enough to support a wife who doesn't work and their children. In this arrangement men are the providers and women and children are the dependents. Working families utilized ideologies of proper gender and family relations in order to demand better wages and decent living conditions. The kinds of work that women chose to do at Berwind did not challenge the basic assumption upon which these expected gendered relations were based. By extending the feminine gendered domestic labor into profit-making ventures, women did not overtly challenge the role of men as providers. The consumption and disposal of mass-produced food products and the disposal of their associated containers served to obfuscate the relations in household economies in which women were playing an increasingly prevalent role. Collective action was possible because of a unity of purpose between people of shared ethnicity and because of a unity of purpose between men and women.

Coffee and Socializing: Women's Friendships

While relations within households reinforced unity among ethnic groups and between men and women, friendships between women who lived in different households often served to transcend ethnic difference. In multiethnic neighborhoods, women held the power to build bridges across ethnic communities and socially constructed racial difference. In the social and physical environment created by the company, these relationships proved to be of vital importance. In their homes, women worked to maintain ethnic traditions through language, food, and ritual, but they also were open to developing friendships with people who did not share their ethnic backgrounds. Friendships between women were often based on the shared experience of domestic responsibility.

Tereza Sykzinch* (names with asterisks in this section were changed to maintain anonymity) was a teenage immigrant from Bulgaria when she arrived in southern Colorado. She had come to help her second cousin Ana Spolk,* who had three Bulgarian boarders living in her four-room house. Two months later, Tereza married Thomas Pecnik,* a miner, and moved to Berwind. Within four years, she had given birth to four children. From the yard of her two-room house where she hung her family's clothes to dry, Tereza could see the home of Mrs. Frieda Elkins,* an African-American woman. Despite the barriers of language and race, Frieda and Tereza developed a close and warm friendship, much of which was built around cooking and food. Tereza had grown up the eldest of five children in Bulgaria. Her father had lost a leg in a factory accident, and she spent most of her adolescent years helping him cut wood in the forest to sell in a nearby village. As a result, she was more skillful with axes and saws than with pots and pans. Every week, Frieda Elkins would come to Tereza's house and teach her how to cook. Tereza's first son, Thomas Pecnik, Jr.,* remembered these days:

> Above all I remember the institution of the Saturdays Mrs. Elkins spent with Mama at our house. The day was devoted to cooking and baking, and that was how Mama learned to bake biscuits, cookies, and pies. The great mystery was how they communicated. Mama knew practically no English, and Mrs. Elkins's background had no connection with Yugoslavia. Yet I remember no difficulties at all. The talk was constant, the laughs were many, the good cheer and warm friendliness were unmistakable. Among the most significant memories of my life, was the evening after one of those Saturdays when Mama said to Papa, "You know, Thomas, today I was observing Mrs. Elkins's hands. I noticed that her palms are as light as my own, and I also discovered that the lines on her hands are nearly identical with mine." It was a stupendous realization of common humanity across superficial racial difference! (Thomas Pecnik, Jr. interview 1998)

Through their friendship, Frieda and Tereza forged ties between their families and across the community. This is just one story of many in which women expressed the importance of their friendships and how they relied on their nearest neighbors for help with child care, childbearing, and some forms of housework. In order to explore further these kinds of relationships between women, I will look at ceramics excavated from the midden and a nearby privy feature that date to the same period. Some of these ceramics, coffee cups in particular, were involved in women's leisure activities, during which they built friendships with other women.

One goal of this archaeological analysis was to find significant patterns in the consumption, use, and deposition of material culture. Patterns are more easily defined in ceramics that exhibit clear decorative differences. While variations in decoration are poked and prodded to expose subtle meanings, plain and undecorated ceramics are generally acknowledged to be part of an assemblage and then are set aside. Likewise, decorated wares that do not fall into clearly identifiable sets are often dismissed. The result is that while patterns in decorated wares are assumed to have meaning, plainness or variety in decoration type is assumed to be meaningless. For those whose goal is merely to identify women, the degree of consistent decoration within an assemblage has sometimes been used as a signal that women were present. The assumption here is that women, more than men, liked pretty things. Although most archaeologists dismiss this kind of view out of hand, it is still assumed that decorated ceramics in sets have the potential to provide greater analytical precision in the exploration of gendered activities than do plain ceramics or assemblages that exhibit a great variety.

Of the ceramics excavated from both the midden and the privy feature in this neighborhood, over one-half were plain (Figure 12.7). Rather than assuming that these ceramics are meaningless, however, the plainness of the ceramics may have been extremely meaningful. Figure 12.7 shows a breakdown of food consumption and service vessels by general decoration types. Roughly, all ceramics fit into three categories: minimally decorated, floral decorated, and Chinese patterns. Minimally decorated ceramics include plain ironstone and those with very simple contours or molding around the rim or handle of the vessel. Floral decorated ceramics include transfer print, decal, and hand-painted wares with general botanical designs. The only Chinese patterned ceramics were inexpensive replicas of willow pattern cups.

A high percentage of plain ceramics were represented in various vessel types associated with food service. Platters, pitchers, serving dishes, nappies, and bowls all exhibited a tendency to be plain. The fact that households used a large proportion of plain tableware can be explained, in part, by a variety of pragmatic issues. Undecorated ironstones were relatively inexpensive, at approximately one-half the cost of decorated wares. The availability of these ceramics by the piece, rather than as sets, was also probably attractive to working families, to whom the cost of a full set of dishes would be a great expense. Heavy white ironstone ceramics were also more durable than finer ceramics. In large households, where meals could include service for 10 or more people, dishes were used, jostled, and washed often.

Given the economic situation of most mining households, it is perhaps predictable that no sets were present. Of all 253 ceramic vessels, only two pairs of matching tea wares could be identified, represented by six vessels. This finding indicates that while households may have had a few matching ceramic vessels, it was more likely for them to buy ceramics by the piece.

With respect to cups and saucers, the ratio of decorated to undecorated wares was much less disproportionate, but plain whiteware was still predomi-

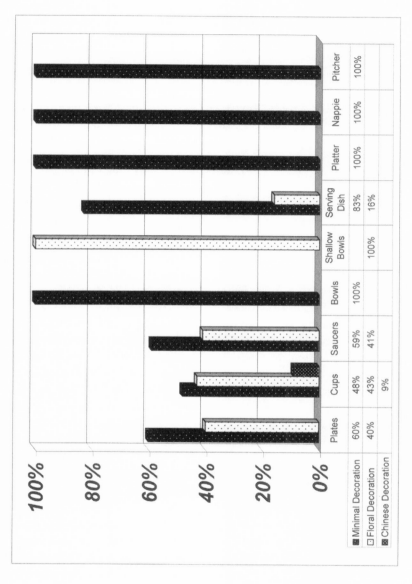

	Plates	Cups	Saucers	Bowls	Shallow Bowls	Serving Dish	Platter	Nappie	Pitcher
■ Minimal Decoration	60%	48%	59%	100%		83%	100%	100%	100%
□ Floral Decoration	40%	43%	41%		100%	16%			
▨ Chinese Decoration		9%							

Fig. 12.7. Bar graph showing plain ceramics by functional category.

nant in these categories (see Figure 12.7). For the most part, the pattern indicated by the decorated vessels in this assemblage was "variety." While some general pattern types were found on various vessels (such as pink roses), the number of different versions of this same basic pattern was astounding. Of 33 cup vessels, 28 could be identified as distinct and different patterns.

In historical archaeology, much attention has focused on the beverage tea and tea wares and their association with middle-class social rituals. In her important study of middle-class consumption patterns of the early and mid-nineteenth century, Diana diZerega Wall (1991, 1994, 2000) uses assemblages from middle-class households to explore how the styles of tea wares were used as a display of family status and to emphasize to those invited to tea the social position of the household. Wall argues that in tea rituals, during which other women were entertained, highly formalized matching tea wares were important in establishing and jockeying for class position. Her study is significant in that she asks several important questions: Under what circumstances was tea consumed? Who were the social actors involved in this activity? What did it mean to the people involved?

Both historic sources and oral history accounts indicate that coffee was a more important beverage than tea at Berwind. Understanding both the plainness and variety of the coffee and tea wares at Berwind involves an appreciation for the ways that coffee was used in particular social situations. Unlike tea, which is associated with formality, ritual, and class, coffee was a beverage that was utilized in informal situations and offered people a way to extend their hospitality and friendship.

In her autobiography, Mary Thomas O'Neal (1971), a Welsh immigrant who lived in the coal camp of Delagua in 1913, emphasized the significance of coffee in the informal get-togethers between herself and her Italian neighbors Sedi Costa and Margo Gorci. These three women became acquainted over a cup of coffee and thereafter shared coffee together almost every day. They developed a relationship of trust and interdependence. If tea parties offered middle-class women a venue for class competition, getting together for coffee offered working-class women at Berwind a venue to build friendly relationships.

The form and decoration of vessels from which coffee was consumed do not represent difference and competition; rather they represent similarity and commonality through an emphasis on plainness. For those vessels that were not plain, variety in decoration was the rule. Even when people were consuming coffee out of vessels that were decorated, it is likely that they were drinking from mismatched cups and saucers. Through variety and variation in the vessel forms, women were extending a vision of commonality and shared experience.

Historians of working-class culture have recently begun to explore the ways in which men's informal relationships have contributed to class consciousness and class action. In his book *Eight Hours for What We Will,* Ray Rosenzweig (1983) argues that working-class leisure activities offered a refuge from the dominant value system of competitive individualism. Through such activities as treating rounds in the saloon, workers created relations of reciprocity that were the basis through which a shared class consciousness could be expressed and carried out. Just as working-class men forged relations through alcohol consumption, working-class women did the same through coffee consumption. By inviting their friends and neighbors into their homes to share cups of coffee, relatively poor women were able to establish bonds of reciprocity and friendship. Highly varied or formalized ceramics would not have been appropriate, given the social reasons for sharing coffee. In neighborhoods in which the Colorado Fuel & Iron Company attempted to separate ethnic groups, women's nearest neighbors often did not share their ethnicity. Thus, friendships between women based on shared domestic responsibilities and shared living situations often crossed ethnic lines.

CONCLUSIONS

While the Colorado Fuel and Iron Company intended to defuse the possibility of workers organizing within the community, they unwittingly created the perfect conditions for the development of social relations that facilitated collective action. By dividing workers on the landscape but allowing women to take in boarders, they merely changed the focus of ethnic organizing from the neighborhood to the household. In multiethnic neighborhoods, women formed friendships that crossed ethnic lines. These relationships, in part, allowed workers from varied and diverse backgrounds to act together based on preestablished bonds of trust and mutual reliance.

In their households women built social relations that made collective action possible. Domesticity within working-class households was distinct from domesticity in middle-class households, and people used their domestic relations to achieve their class-based goals. When miners marched through the streets in 1913, they were fighting not only *for* their homes but *from* their homes. The working-class household, made by the women of Berwind, provided a base from which mining families sustained a challenge to the emerging corporate order.

ACKNOWLEDGMENTS

A predoctoral grant from the Wenner-Gren Foundation for Anthropological Research funded my dissertation research. Many thanks to my advisors and friends LouAnn Wurst, Randy McGuire, and Doug Armstrong who have provided unending help and support through the years. The extraordinarily talented and professional librarians at the Denver Public Library, Western History Department, who have been both friends and coworkers, provided invaluable research assistance. Many thanks also go to my husband, Jason Lapham, who has patiently tolerated my obsession with this project.

Part IV
Making Sense of It All: Commentaries on the Household

13

What Difference Does Feminist Theory Make in Researching Households?

A Commentary

Suzanne Spencer-Wood

INTRODUCTION

Feminist theory and history are essential for fully defining and understanding the household and the family. Feminist critiques have revealed that power dynamics and social agency in households and families have been historically undertheorized because they have been devalued as women's passive domestic sphere subordinate to men's supposedly more important public sphere. Theorizing about the male public/political sphere, as well as male-associated reasoning or epistemology, traditionally has been considered important. Theorizing about the domestic sphere and household gender roles has not been considered important because of the association of households with women's subordinate status. Feminists have critiqued how household archaeology has been devalued because it concerns the domestic sphere that is traditionally identified with women (Spencer-Wood 1992, 1999a:163).

Households and families have been considered ahistorical, with unchanging relationships and repetitive chores that have been considered natural, innate, and therefore not in need of explanation. Historians traditionally viewed men as the makers of a history that required explanation, while women just made babies innately in the same way as they had since the beginning of time. Feminists have critiqued conceptions of the household that are static and universalizing, including the exclusive association of women with the domestic sphere (Moore 1988; Spencer-Wood 1999a:164, 166).

The neglect of household theory supported the uncritical acceptance of the claimed immutable universality of male dominance in families and households as well as in society at large. While men's philosophies and histories focused on the public sphere, feminist theory has historically focused on gender relationships and power dynamics in households in relation to the cultural ideology and larger social structures that construct and enforce inequalities among social groups (Donovan 2001). For instance, feminists have revealed how historic women who performed household chores, whether wives, servants, or slaves, were deprived of legal and human rights and made invisible in male-headed households (Millett 1970:67–69; Spencer-Wood 1999a:163–164).

In this commentary I address how feminist theory and history are related to research in this volume. Some authors use feminist definitions of household and some use feminist history as well. Since most authors address gender, feminist theory has often influenced research questions. This volume covers household issues fundamentally addressed by feminist theory, from gendered division of labor to social agency and power dynamics involved in complex intersections among gender, class, race, and ethnic identities.

I first discuss the influence of feminist theory on the definitions of household used in this volume. Then each theory will be considered in historical order in terms of its contribution to one or more chapters. Each theory has provided new fundamental insights that enhance our understanding of different aspects of households. Further, feminist theories have revealed previously neglected household power dynamics, social agency, and their relationships with larger sociocultural systems.

FEMINIST THEORY IN DEFINITIONS OF HOUSEHOLD

A variety of definitions of household are used here, including some addressing feminist concerns with power dynamics among household members and social agency of subordinate social groups. Most authors use definitions that distinguish household from family and from house sites or dwellings. Definitions consider household composition, life cycle, and functions that group household chores into categories such as production, distribution, consumption, socialization of children, and social reproduction of the labor force. Bonine* (authors' names with asterisks appear in this volume) emphasizes feminist critiques of functional definitions that treat the household as a single social unit and neglect composition and internal social dynamics involved with gender, class, and ethnicity. Anderson* adds feminist research relating gendered division of labor to use of household spaces. Some authors have used postmodern feminist definitions, such as Hendon, Tringham, or Allison, which include conflict among members of households related to differences in gender and, in some cases, ethnicity, class, and age identities (Anderson, Bonine, Galindo, Spencer-Wood).* A couple of authors also emically address prescriptive historic conceptions of gendered power dynamics in households (Brandon, Spencer-Wood).*

A number of authors draw on feminist definitions of household to relate power dynamics between individual household members to inequalities among larger social groups that are legitimated by cultural ideology and social structures. Galindo* and Spencer-Wood* both mention Hendon's point that household power dynamics are politicized because they are connected to the "larger economic and political structure of society" (Hendon 1996:46). Galindo* relates Yanagisako's analysis of kinship as a system carrying larger cultural symbolic meanings to the diversity among households and their inequalities due to differences in members' wealth, religion, nationality, ethnicity, gender, and folk concepts of the "person."

Existing definitions of household have often been used in this volume as starting points to be developed and conceptualized further. Some authors discuss feminist critiques that have revealed problems in ahistorical existing universal definitions. Research addresses the actual complexity and diversity in household structure(s), composition, function, and power dynamics found in different historical situations. One of the major contributions of feminist theory is analysis of the historical situatedness of knowledge and its construction. Feminist standpoint theory reveals the socially situated viewpoint(s) embedded in household definitions developed in this volume at a number of social scales, from the level of individual dwellings to multiple dwellings on ranchos, plantations as complex households, and community households where chores were performed for a number of individual households. The diverse household definitions used in this volume are related to larger sociocultural structures, including ideologies and laws concerning gender, race, and class power dynamics.

HISTORY OF FEMINIST THEORIZING OF HOUSEHOLDS

Feminist historians have traced the roots of women's inequality to misogynist male Greek philosophers who justified the exclusion of women from education and formal politics on the grounds that women were domestic and physical and lacked men's intelligence (Spencer-Wood 1999a:168). Engels (1884) traced the origin of the word *family* to the Latin word *famulus,* which meant domestic slave. The plural *familia* designated the wives, children, and slaves owned by a Roman man (Rossi 1973:480).

Feminist historical research has revealed roots of feminist egalitarian theory dating back to feminist Greek philosophers who argued that women and men were intellectual equals. Greek egalitarian gender theories were overlooked by traditional histories focused on men's philosophies that dismissed women as domestic and intellectually inferior (Spencer-Wood 1999a:168). Feminist historians have recovered women's writings from the fourteenth through the nineteenth centuries that continued to argue that women deserved education because they were as intelligent as men. Feminist writers recorded a long list of women's intellectual achievements back to the Greek philosophers (Lerner 1993).

Feminist historians revealed that men's Enlightenment philosophies argued only that all men were created equal but not women, for whom older principles of *femme couvert* had been codified in law. In English common law, which was used in America, Blackstone's 1754 commentary on the law of coverture makes it clear that, historically, the household's women and children were legally owned as chattel by husbands or fathers. A man legally owned the persons and all the possessions, including earnings, of his wife and children, and could rent them out and take their earnings. Further, men could legally physically chastise their wives and children (Millett 1970:67–69). The sociocultural acceptability of domestic violence was linguistically codified in the "rule of thumb," which specified that a man should not beat his wife with a rod larger than the thickness of a man's thumb. Feminists described the widespread nature of domestic violence that historically resulted in other slang phrases, such as Liverpool's nineteenth-century "kicking districts," where lower-class men were renowned for kicking, trampling, and "purring" wives with hobnailed shoes and clogs (Kolmar and Bartkowski 2000:81).

Brandon* discussed here how white patriarchal dominance on plantations was supported by the doctrine of coverture that gave control of household matters including slaves, wives, and children to the male plantation owner. The brief feminist history in this commentary further reveals that men's legal power to dominate their slaves, wives, and children was absolute by law. The laws of coverture made a plantation the household of the planter because he legally owned not only his slaves but also his wife and children. Brandon* points out that postbellum legal doctrines that recognized women and children as individuals still governed them with state paternalism that created sexist and racist laws. Modern liberal equal-rights feminists continue to critique this legal heritage that provides women with unequal justice today. Modern radical feminist theory argues that state-condoned socially and legally sanctioned violence by men against women fundamentally enforces the subordination of women to men (Donovan 2001:159–160).

Enlightenment Liberal Feminist Theory Argues for Domestic and Public Gender Equality

Democratic revolutions in America and France inspired the rise of liberal egalitarian feminism in America and Europe in the late eighteenth century. Feminists argued against the absolute subjection of wives to their husbands on the grounds that the doctrine of men's natural rights to equality, representative government, life, liberty, and the pursuit of happiness should also apply to women. The Enlightenment philosophy of Utilitarianism was the first of men's philosophies to argue for equality between men and women as necessary to meet the goal of perfecting society by creating the greatest happiness for the greatest number of people. Utilitarian philosophers, liberal egalitarian femi-

nists, and Marxist feminists all revealed and critiqued women's legal and economic status as domestic slaves (Donovan 2001:19–24, 39–41).

Nineteenth-century feminism was stimulated by women's experiences of
unequal treatment as leaders of the abolitionist movement. Male leaders did
not permit female leaders to speak at an abolitionist convention in London in
1840. Female abolitionists discovered that women as well as slaves were legally
denied fundamental human rights (Donovan 2001:36–37). Brandon* pointed
out how nineteenth-century feminists in the northern United States, such as
Elizabeth Cady Stanton, equated the status of women with slaves.

Suffragists, led by Stanton and Susan B. Anthony, worked not only for wom-
en's right to vote but also for their right to divorce abusive husbands, for married women to have property rights, and to change laws that gave men the absolute power of masters over their wives and children. Anthony argued that
"resistance to tyranny is obedience to God." This argument shows how the
feminist justification of resistance to male domination in the household as well
as in the public sphere applied the liberal Enlightenment theory of natural
rights used in the American and French revolutions (Donovan 2001:33–36).

Brandon* contrasts the northern suffragist strategy of analogy between
women and slaves with the southern suffragist argument that enfranchising
white women would cancel out the effect of the Fifteenth Amendment to the
American Constitution, which granted suffrage to African-American men. On
this subject it is important to note that the northern suffrage movement split
over supporting this amendment, because it showed that white male political
leaders had not been persuaded to support female suffrage by the analogy
drawn between slaves and women. Stanton and Anthony felt their support of
African-American suffrage had been betrayed by the exclusion of women from
the Fifteenth Amendment. They made racist arguments against the amendment and led the majority of northern suffragists, who were white, to make
common cause with southern suffragists by the early twentieth century. The
racialization of the suffrage movement, and of feminist liberal theory, differed
not only owing to the regional identity of the South, as Brandon* points out,
but was dynamic and complex in the North, where abolitionism did not eradi-
cate racism (Giddings 1984:66–67).

CULTURAL FEMINIST THEORY AND THE IDEOLOGY
OF WOMAN'S DOMESTIC SPHERE

Cultural feminists, a.k.a. domestic reformers, accepted the dominant gender
ideology identifying men with the public sphere and women with the domestic
sphere, but they argued that women were morally superior to men and therefore should control their domestic sphere (Spencer-Wood*). Important for the

definition of households, cultural feminists defined and elaborated women's household chores to increase the importance of women's roles and thus raise their social status. Many domestic manuals gave advice on producing multi-course Victorian meals that raised women's status by an elaborate display of culinary skills (Wall 1994). The complexity of these meals justified the need for servants or slaves to produce them, usually under the supervision of the wife of the head of the household. Managing servants or slaves also raised a woman's status from being domestic slave of her husband to being a supervisor who directed and controlled a number of servants or slaves.

This cultural feminist perspective increases our understanding of the complex power dynamics in the many volume chapters addressing middle- and upper-class households in urban areas, as well as plantation households (Anderson, Barile, Battle, Bonine, Galindo, Stewart-Abernathy).* (See the section on power dynamics below.) At the same time, in contrast to cultural feminists' new ideology that a woman should control her household as the "sovereign of an empire" (Beecher and Stowe 1985:222), authors here show that male dominance of individual households continued in the United States both in the South (Brandon*) and in the North (Spencer-Wood*).

Cultural feminists theorized that women were innately morally superior to men because women and their domestic sphere were closer to nature and therefore to God than men's capitalistic public sphere that condoned the sins of usury and price gouging. Cultural feminists then theorized that women's domestic sphere of the household was equivalent to a sacred church where women held the high status of ministers. Women were argued to be similar to ministers in achieving status through their self-sacrifice for the good of their flock, identified as a woman's family. Thus cultural feminists raised women's status through an analogy elevating women's housework to be equivalent to men's higher-status public sphere profession of minister. Women's role as minister in the Cult of Home Religion was materially symbolized ideally with a cruciform-shaped house with arched Gothic doors, niches with religious statues, and bucolic religious paintings symbolically depicting the connections among the domestic sphere, nature, and God (Spencer-Wood 1996:418–420).

Pappas* describes cruciform cabins that housed families in a lumber camp, including the family of the assistant superintendent. Insights into the meaning of these cruciform houses is provided by the cultural feminist theorizing of the Cult of Home Religion. Cruciform houses materially symbolized the moralizing influence of wives as ministers of home religion. Thus these houses indicate that the company promoted the superior moral power of women in the Cult of Home Religion as a way of supporting the company's enforcement of moral lives by the lumbermen. So the company hierarchy was not only paternalistic in compelling proper conduct through physical surveillance of single men's cabins, but it was also acting as the maternalistic moral head of the family.

The metaphor of family gendered power-dynamics at the lumber camp in the late nineteenth century was further embodied by the assistant superintendent's cruciform dwelling, symbolizing an analogy to the position of a moral wife to the superintendent. His larger permanent masculine T-shaped dwelling represented the ultimate authority of the male head of the metaphorical family household of the lumber camp. This interpretation fits with the material symbolism of the single men as children, metaphorically justifying more physical and moral regulation of their lives. The company was maternalistic in viewing alcohol as a sinful vice to be prevented. Some of the paternalistic enforcement of proper behavior through reprimand, such as regulating fair dinner servings, also masked cost savings to the company by hierarchical management. Pappas* addressed male hierarchical dominance in the metaphorical household of the lumber camp. However, he is androcentric in neglecting the importance in the family hierarchy of the moral superiority of the maternal role both of wives and of the assistant superintendent, who held the position in the metaphorical family hierarchy of wifely helpmate to the supervisor of the lumber camp.

Pappas* strangely states that gender has received the least research attention, with most studies focused on females, thus opposing gender and women as if women do not have gender and implying that gender research has to include men physically. How can single-sex households not have gender when women and men are cultural concepts constructed in relationship to each other? Women and men perform culturally constructed gender roles, including household chores, whether in single-sex households or mixed-gender households. Kryder-Reid (1994) has demonstrated that single-sex households still must perform mixed-gender household roles. An individual's gender identity is defined in terms of ideal relationships constructed between men's and women's roles in a cultural gender system.

FEMINIST THEORIES OF CHILDHOOD SOCIALIZATION

Since the nineteenth century, feminists have increasingly theorized the household chore of child rearing, which is connected to household composition and life cycle. Cultural feminists theorized in the Cult of Republican Motherhood that women held an exalted position as the innately superior child rearers of tomorrow's leaders (Spencer-Wood 1999a:172). At the same time they argued that child rearing did not occur naturally but required training. Domestic advice manuals increasingly addressed child rearing, and the topic generated separate manuals starting in the late nineteenth century (Ryan 1982:45–70).

Twentieth-century Freudian feminists argued that parents, especially mothers, socialize children into gender roles and unconscious expectations of dominating male behaviors and submissive female behaviors (Donovan 2001:123–125). In this volume, Brandon* analyzed the significance to childhood racial socialization of a doll portraying racial exclusion and connection between white ladies and female African-American slaves. Anderson* and Battle* included child rearing among the house chores commonly performed in individual house yards.

CULTURAL FEMINIST THEORY AND COMMUNITY HOUSEHOLDS

Cultural feminists also argued that women's domestic powers of cooperation and moral suasion were superior to men's hierarchical dominating powers. Women became identified with church-associated moral and communitarian values in the eighteenth century as men were drawn away from the church by the conflicting values of individualistic competition and hierarchy in capitalism (Epstein 1981).

Cultural feminism drew on communitarian socialism in arguing for cooperative housekeeping by women in a community. Communitarian socialist feminists argued for founding communes in which the status of women's housework and men's public work would be equal (Spencer-Wood 1999a:174–175). Cultural feminists further theorized about and created community cooperative households to perform chores for a number of individual households. Through cooperatives, cultural feminists sought to raise the status of housework to that of other public businesses, conflating and combining the domestic and public spheres (Spencer-Wood*).

In municipal housekeeping, feminists theorized towns, cities, countries, and the whole world as households. These domestic reformers argued that the whole world had domestic meaning because individual urban households were inextricably connected to, and dependent on, household chores performed by (1) capitalist businesses that manufactured domestic consumer goods such as foodstuffs and (2) municipal governments that ensured safe food, water supplies, street cleaning, and garbage collection. Reform women argued successfully for their appointment as inspectors of streets, garbage, and factories because women were the housekeepers of the world (Spencer-Wood 1994:180).

MARXIST-FEMINIST THEORIZING OF THE MIDDLE-CLASS FAMILY HOUSEHOLD

Marxist feminists, starting with Engels in 1884, theorized the household in analogy to a workplace in which women were unpaid proletarian workers, while men were the bourgeois owners of the capital and means of production. Marxist feminists attributed women's performance of household chores to the fact that they were forced to trade their domestic and sexual labor for payment in the form of food and housing, which were owned by men. Men by law owned all the property and earnings of their wives and children until the American married women's property acts of the 1850s (Rossi 1973:481–487; Tong 1989:64).

Marxist feminists theorized household gender power dynamics as a class struggle between unpaid proletarian women and bourgeois men—a struggle that is fundamental to the operation of capitalism (Donovan 2001:93). Feminists gendered the domination and resistance Marxist framework, influencing historical archaeologies considering class, racial, and gender power dynamics (Paynter and McGuire 1991).

Barile* analyzed how the Vesey slave rebellion sparked further resistance by Africans to enslavement. White Americans who feared rebellion altered plantation landscapes to increase their security, control, and domination of the slaves and the plantation. Davidson* analyzed how white domination led to the formation of African-American Freedman's Town north of Dallas that provided a community for resisting white domination within the town.

Engels (1884) argued that women's status and power would become equal to men's if women worked at paid professions equivalent to men's professions. Twentieth-century Marxist feminists argued for paid housework (Tong 1989: 50, 54–55), but by 1869 socialist domestic reformers had already advocated that housework should be paid both in the home and in public housekeeping cooperatives (Spencer-Wood*). Subsequently, reform women created a number of middle-class women's public professions that they argued were really domestic, conflating the public and domestic spheres (Spencer-Wood 1994).

POSTMODERN FEMINIST THEORY AND THE HOUSEHOLD

Postmodern feminist theory critiqued previous feminist theories that essentialized women as a monolithic group based on the limited experience of white middle-class women. Postmodern feminists have worked to theorize the complex intersections between social systems of inequality including gender, race, class, and ethnicity. It has been recognized that women of color suffer from racism as well as sexism and often classism. However, feminists have argued that these forms of discrimination are not simply added to each other but interact and reinforce each other as multipliers. Feminists have also analyzed individual identity formation as comprised of intersecting affiliations with a variety of social groups (Spencer-Wood 1995:129–130; 1997; 2001:207).

From the viewpoint of feminist theory, the authors in this volume have taken a postmodern approach in beginning to problematize definitions of the household with case studies that lead to concepts of the diversity in household structure(s), composition, functions, life cycle, and power dynamics. They show

how important it is to theorize the diverse and changing power dynamics between the different genders, races, classes, and ages of household members.

The volume is postmodern in analyzing intersections between race, ethnicity, gender, and/or class, sometimes including power dynamics owing to inequality between social groups. In some chapters power dynamics are analyzed between social groups that made up larger-scale complex households such as plantations (Barile*), ranchos, or community cooperatives, which are also defined as households. Power dynamics involved in complex intersections between gender, class, and race or ethnicity have been analyzed for elite southern urban households (Stewart-Abernathy*), plantations (Battle*), Freedman's Town in north Dallas (Davidson*), a southern household artifact (Brandon*), Spanish colonial ranchos (Bonine, Galindo*), and a company mining town (Wood*). Intersecting gender and class power dynamics are analyzed in a company lumber town (Pappas*) and a community cooperative (Spencer-Wood*). Brandon* is the only author who cited a postmodern feminist theorist, bell hooks. A number of others cited postmodern feminist archaeologists who have theorized the household, including Allison, Hendon, Spencer-Wood, and Tringham.

Pappas* states that "distinctions based on metaphorical family hierarchy suggest deeper symbolic and ideological systems than gender, ethnic, or class based analyses alone can detect." However, the symbolism of family hierarchy cannot be separated from household gender power dynamics that are fundamental to that hierarchy. Class, age, racial, or ethnic inequalities also affect family hierarchy.

FEMINIST STANDPOINT THEORY AND THE SCALE OF HOUSEHOLD DEFINITIONS

Postmodern feminism led to the development of feminist standpoint theory, which analyzes the historically contingent and socially situated power dynamics involved in the construction of knowledge. Standpoint theory developed the postmodern awareness of women's multiple perspectives owing to different class, race, and ethnic identities. This theory analyzes how the researcher's multiple intersecting identities influence the standpoint from which the research is conducted, including the kinds of research questions that are asked or not asked, and the assumptions and concepts used (Hartsock 1987). In this volume Anderson demonstrates a postmodern awareness of who has the power to define a household.

Definitions of household can be analyzed in terms of their standpoint. Feminist theory leads to questions about whose point(s) of view are represented in different household definitions. Who is made invisible by being subsumed in a household definition? Brandon* argues that local analyses of race and gender reveal more information about the fluidity and constant renegotiation of identity construction than is visible in collective analyses at the national level. He points out that most landscape analyses are undertaken at a relatively coarse scale that privileges racial analysis at the expense of gender. He cites Spencer-Wood's (1999a:163) point that women and children disappear in large-scale analyses and argues for analyses at the household level to reveal information about the lives of women and men.

Even at the household level, women, children, and servants or slaves are subsumed and become invisible in the standard historical archaeological practice of using the name of the male head to designate the household or plantation (Spencer-Wood 1991a:236; 1995:118; 1999a:163). This archaeological practice reifies the traditional social practice of wives taking their husbands' names, linguistically representing wives' loss of legal rights in marriage (Spencer-Wood*). Brandon* quotes Elizabeth Cady Stanton's statement that women were like slaves in being given their master's name. Marriage records could be researched to add a wife's maiden name to an archaeological site name, but servants or slaves would still be subsumed and invisible. The prehistoric practice of numbering sites would not privilege any group in naming a site.

Some authors in this volume define households as individual dwellings, which can address the standpoints of different household members in relationship to each other. For instance, middle- and upper-class households of one dwelling or more were probably recognized as a single household by members with kinship relationships (Spencer-Wood, Bonine, Galindo*). Servants or slaves may or may not have considered themselves household members. Servants, as with slaves, performed household chores for their master's family as well as for themselves. They also lived with the family they served, although they were separated in that they were paid for labor and did not eat with the family. Slaves sometimes lived in their master's house, but field slaves were provided separate cabins. On ranchos and New England farms, hired hands housed in the barn or a separate barracks probably did not consider themselves part of the household that took them on to do fieldwork because they lived, ate, and slept in a separate building.

Davidson* takes the viewpoint of African-American freedmen after the Civil War who rented or bought individual houses in north Dallas's Freedman's Town. He further discusses how houses were also workplaces for freedwomen who took in laundry. Individual households are also considered in relationship to each other in a city block rviewed as representative of the community.

Wood* took the viewpoint of miners' wives in analyzing the relationships among household members within and between households, as well as the relationships of the workers' households to the mining company. In contrast,

Pappas* analyzes a lumber company's viewpoint in using the metaphor of family hierarchy to naturalize the camp social organization. Single workers housed in three-man cabins were viewed as children in the metaphorical family hierarchy. Similarly, the term *corporate households* is a company viewpoint on the Boot Mill boardinghouses in Lowell (Beaudry 1989b). *Single-gender nonfamily household* is a more neutral term used by some archaeologists (e.g., Hardesty 1994).

In the eighteenth and nineteenth centuries many institutions were constructed as large houses to symbolize materially a metaphorical family hierarchy by those running the institutions, whether the Magdalene Asylum (De Cunzo 2001) or almshouses (Spencer-Wood 2001). In the second half of the nineteenth century the term *cooperative home* was used by reform women to suggest egalitarian family power dynamics in households of unrelated working women who shared household chores (Spencer-Wood 1987b, 1991a, 1994, 1999a). Kryder-Reid (1994) has shown how mixed-gender family power dynamics were replicated in an all-male monastery.

Southern middle- and upper-class urban households, as well as plantation households, represent the viewpoint of the white owner who owned not only the property but also the buildings and all the people who lived in them. It is likely that the wife and children would see themselves as belonging to the household of the husband/father (Anderson, Barile, Battle, Stewart-Abernathy).* House slaves may also have identified themselves with their master's family household.

Some slaves viewed their own separate dwellings or the kitchen where they slept and ate as their household in contrast to the white owner's separate household. Brandon* in citing bell hooks took the African-American viewpoint that slave households were places of resistance to white domination. This viewpoint seems even more relevant on plantations where slave houses were separated from the planter's house by greater distances (Barile*). Battle* takes the viewpoint of slaves in gendering a variety of household chores for which evidence was excavated around slave cabins on the Jackson plantation.

It is possible that slaves may have viewed the place of their households on plantations in a similar way that wage laborers viewed the relationship of their households to company towns. In both cases the workers' houses were owned by the capitalist profiting from the workers' production. In many instances wage laborers were enslaved by companies that paid wages too low to support family households at the prices charged in the company store. Wage laborers in company towns, similar to tenant farmers on postbellum plantations, were permanently indebted to the white landowner and, therefore, could not legally stop working any more than slaves could refuse to work for their masters. Neither were indebted wage laborers any more free than slaves to leave the houses owned by the company or landowner. However, slaves could be subjected, by law, to more physical punishment than could legally be meted out to wage laborers.

The Berwind massacre analyzed by Wood* shows how early laborers' strikes for living wages were suppressed nearly as violently as the Vesey slave rebellion in Charleston (Barile*), with the difference that male slave leaders of the rebellion were hanged while the striking miners' children and wives were massacred in larger numbers than the miners themselves. Wood's* analysis of the importance of wives' social networks to organizing the workers' strike may explain the indiscriminate attack by strikebreaking militia on the families of miners living in tents.

The Cambridge Cooperative Housekeeping Society was created from the viewpoint of one middle-class housewife. Mapping the individual houses of participants and the cooperative revealed how the viewpoint of the woman who organized the cooperative was expressed through the short distance between her house and the cooperative where she worked hard to make the enterprise a success (Spencer-Wood*).

Anderson* analyzes nested households from the viewpoint of kinship relations among planters linking households on their plantations and neighboring plantations. It is difficult to recover the viewpoints of undocumented slaves as individuals. However, Battle* shows that slave household chores and relationships among household members can be recovered from excavations of activity areas and features around slave houses and in their yards.

HOUSEHOLD POWER DYNAMICS

Postmodern feminist theory addresses power dynamics involved in the complex intersections of gender, class, race, and ethnicity (Spencer-Wood 2001: 207). Power dynamics between social groups and individuals with different complex identities can be represented with a social distance model composed of a set of concentric spheres that are arranged like a hierarchical pyramid when viewed from the side. The top sphere represents the dominant group of elite white men. The next wider sphere surrounding these men would be elite white women. Subsequent concentric spheres at increasing distances from the dominant group would represent middle-class and lower-class white men and women, followed by increasingly darker-skinned racial groups organized by classes and by gender within each class. This model explains why white men have more power over other social groups than do white women, who have class or racial powers over other groups but not the gender powers that are the foundational model for the other hierarchical powers. This model also shows how stereotypes creating discrimination accumulate and multiply with greater social distance from the dominant group (Spencer-Wood 1997).

Anderson's* analytical framework of nested households, in conjunction with the social distance model noted, provides a useful framework for understanding nested layers of intersecting gender and racial power dynamics within and between households at different levels. For instance, in many households white men dominated their wives and children as well as their servants and slaves, all of whom they legally owned as chattel historically. White men, and in some cases African-American men, held power as overseers of field hands or slaves. The white female head of household, whether married, widowed, or divorced, historically dominated children and household servants or slaves, overseeing them in producing food, clean laundry, and housework. While slaves were African American, servants could be lower-class whites, Hispanics, etc. It should be noted that middle- and upper-class African Americans also often had African-American servants and replicated the gender power structure of the white household. If the servants or slaves are considered as a subordinate household, then one can analyze relations of domination and subordination within the servant or slave household, which in many cases were dominated by a male servant or slave.

The analysis of power dynamics includes male domination over women of the same race and class and the addition of race and class power differentials between white men and women and nonwhite servants or slaves. So while white men have the conjunction of three social sources of power over nonwhite working women, white women have only race or class powers over their servants or slaves, since women are the subordinate gender. Women who were wives or heads of household had only class power over servants or slaves of the same racial or ethnic group. From this analysis it is clear that the gendered power of male dominance is a fundamental source of social power that substantially reinforces racial and class powers. In fact, feminists have theorized and provided evidence that gender power dynamics and discrimination are the model for racial and class powers and discrimination. Therefore, gender is foundational to, and strongly reifies, other forms of social power (Spencer-Wood 1997).

Feminists have identified a variety of different types of power in addition to the "power-over" people of domination that has been traditionally considered as the only type of power. French (1985) contrasted destructive power-over that controls others, in contrast to social agency or "power-to" accomplish things and overcome barriers to achieving personal or group goals. She views power-to as the result of community support networks that provide communal resources for individual achievement. Both individual talent and communal resources to nurture that talent are considered essential for an individual's success. In addition, French viewed individual achievement as inherently competitive and thus involving some dominating power-over as individuals compete for limited communal support resources required for individual success (French 1985:505; Tong 1989:100–101).

Archaeologists have used the dichotomy of dominating power-over others to support the status quo versus culturally transformative "power-to" create change (e.g., Shanks and Tilley 1992:129–130). Crumley (1987) critiqued the limited conception of power as hierarchical and added the concept of a heterarchy or plurality of types of power, including not only hierarchical types of ranked power but also lateral and situational types of power usually associated with women. A third form of "powers-with" has often been used by women, as well as "powers-to" (Spencer-Wood 1997).

The plurality of different types of power can be expressed by making each category of power plural, yielding "powers-over," "powers-with," and "powers-to." Powers-over include domination, coercion, brainwashing, intimidation, argumentation, physical and verbal abuse, and physical violence. All these forms of power are directed at the goal of controlling the actions or words of other persons. Powers-with involve relational and group social agency, from persuasion, inspiration, empowerment, negotiation, affiliation, cooperation, and collaboration, to group identity-creation, decision-making, and agreement-generating processes that lead to coordinated group actions. Powers-with is often aimed at resisting and overcoming attempts at domination by individuals or groups using powers-over the resisting social group. Powers-to create change, I would argue, that can occur at the individual social agency level or can be generated using powers-with others in social organizations and movements (Spencer-Wood 1999b:178–180). Powers-to create change at the individual level include consciousness-raising, individual change in fundamental beliefs, and writing, speaking, or singing about those changes, which can be used as powers-with those receiving the message.

It is useful to distinguish these types of powers and to consider how they are interrelated. All types of power have been used by women as well as men, although dominating powers-over have been stereotypically identified with men, while cooperative powers-with have been identified with women. From the above discussion of nested gender power dynamics in households, it is apparent that white women had power-over house servants and slaves who were predominantly female, even though middle-class housewives often worked with their servants or slaves in demanding tasks such as producing thread, cloth, cheese, and complex Victorian meals.

Household definitions express power dynamics. Different levels of household definition facilitate analysis of power dynamics among household members or larger social groups. At the smallest scale of the individual household, it is possible to analyze power dynamics among individual household members. In households defined at the scale of plantation, neighborhood, community, or town, power dynamics are usually analyzed between social groups, losing the diversity in individual interactions. Local variation among social groups is lost in national-scale analyses that address only regional differences in social group identities and interactions.

Household theory and research methods affect the amount of information gained about household power dynamics. To address power dynamics archaeologically, it is necessary to be able to compare different social groups in terms of their spatial relationships and differences in household artifact assemblages. Much early gender research examined changes in gender roles owing to culture contact but not resulting changes in gender power dynamics (e.g., Deetz 1971). Early feminists concerned with household gender power dynamics included Devens (1991), who researched how the fur trade drastically shifted Cree egalitarian gender power dynamics toward male domination. Deagan (1983) analyzed the power of lower-status aboriginal wives or female servants to change foodways in households dominated by male Spanish colonizers. Singleton (1990) provided evidence that slaves had the power to replicate African household architecture and foodways in America despite their enslaved status.

In this volume most authors analyzed spatial relationships among buildings on household landscapes for evidence of the expression of power dynamics in the distance between buildings housing different or similar social groups. Some analyzed the arrangement of buildings determining the amount of surveillance of a subordinate group possible from the house of the dominant social group. Some related spatial arrangements of buildings to control of subordinate social groups by dominant social groups, and some analyzed the importance of proximity among households in organizing resistance to domination (especially Barile, Wood).*

Individual households can be interpreted as sharing "powers-with" other neighboring households of the same race or ethnicity. The proximity between buildings on Texas ranchos, along with similarity of artifacts, led to arguments that two neighboring buildings were occupied by related families or kin groups (Bonine, Galindo).* On the Jackson plantation Battle* analyzed how the shared yard between two slave houses and evidence of activities undertaken there suggested the possibility of sharing of household chores by members of the two households. In the case of southern urban households (Stewart-Abernathy*), the single kitchen building is archaeological evidence of slaves cooking for their master's family and themselves, performing a chore that is often considered fundamental to the definition of a household as a group that cooks and eats together. In this case food was shared, but racial segregation was enforced in the separate spaces in which whites and slaves ate, slept, and lived.

Traditionally, plantations have been considered economic units composed of interrelated households, including the planter's house, overseer's house(s), and slave dwellings. While racial power dynamics have been researched, gender roles and power dynamics have been neglected. Historical archaeologists have often gained information about power dynamics by comparing assemblages or geographical relationships among slave dwellings, overseers' houses, and planters' houses (e.g., Delle 1999; Otto 1984). Some plantation research has shown that slaves were permitted social agency by being entrusted with guns to hunt at least some of their food (Singleton 1990:75). Some planters permitted slaves, in many cases women, to trade at town markets (Franklin 2000).

The degree of powers-over slaves exercised by their white masters varied. Close surveillance was permitted by the proximity of slave dwellings and kitchen to middle- and upper-class urban white southern houses (Stewart-Abernathy*). Barile* discussed a number of plantations where the threat of a male-organized slave rebellion using social agency powers-with slaves in Charleston led to a shift in outlying plantation settlement patterns. Slave houses in proximity to the planter's house were dispersed to more isolated locations on the plantation where they could be watched by an overseer at a safe distance from the planter's house. Slave women's roles were no doubt important but were undocumented. Valuable products and mobile property were moved into storage buildings that were close enough to the planter's house to be kept under surveillance easily.

At the Jackson plantation, Battle* analyzes the distance between slave dwellings and the planter's house to interpret the degree of autonomy given the slaves by the lack of total surveillance of the slave cabins from the planter's dwelling. The relationships between buildings on the landscape showed that the Jacksons did not exert complete dominating powers over the slaves as they did in some Jamaican plantations analyzed by Delle (1999).

A number of authors relate individual households to groups of households within the next larger scale of company household. Pappas* analyzes how company hierarchical powers-over workers was reinforced through architectural differences in houses and their arrangement on the landscape to symbolize the camp as a metaphorical family. Gender power dynamics are addressed indirectly in the comparison of unmarried and married workers' housing.

Wood* documents how a mining company exerted its powers-over workers by separating households of the same ethnic group to prevent workers from organizing. These company powers-over workers were overcome by women's social agency powers-with each other in networking between households and by women's frequent practice of taking in boarders of the same ethnicity to provide additional household income. Wood* further provides oral history documenting egalitarian power relationships between an African-American woman who visited a Hungarian woman in her household every Saturday to teach her cooking. The egalitarian social networks among women in different ethnic groups were instrumental in organizing the strike along ethnic lines and also in linking different ethnic groups in their shared interest. The women's cooperative powers-with each other were essential in the development of resistance to the company hierarchy by the workers as a unified group.

At the scale of community households, greater distances may express less household sharing of powers-with other households. Spencer-Wood* found that distances to the Cambridge Cooperative Housekeeping Society from most members' houses probably contributed to the less powerful participation in the CCHS by women in these households. The social agency of the one housewife who organized the cooperative was not enough to maintain it without participation of other households. However, the social meaning of larger distances depends on the historical context, as is shown in the case of the Spanish colony in Texas, where elite individual families owned both a rancho and a house in town. It seems that physical distance between houses means less when kinship relates the houses than when households are just acquaintances.

CONCLUSION

In this commentary I have analyzed how research case studies in this volume have been influenced by feminist theory and history. Some definitions of household have included feminist concerns for power dynamics and social agency involved in the complex intersections of gender, class, race, and ethnic identities of household members. Further, feminist household definitions have been used that connect division of labor and relationships among household members to culturally constructed and naturalized power dynamics between social groups in the larger culture.

Taken as a whole, this volume addresses power dynamics and social agency between dominating and resisting members of individual households and social groups in large-scale community households. Intersections of gender with class or racial/ethnic power dynamics have been analyzed at the levels of individual households and the complex households of plantations, ranchos, company towns, and community households. This commentary has shown how different points of view or social standpoints (from feminist standpoint theory) are embedded in the different levels of definitions that were most inclusively modeled as "nested" households by Anderson.*

This commentary has discussed that feminist theory has influenced much of the research on power dynamics in this volume. A number of authors take a postmodern feminist approach in researching power dynamics in households connected to the complex intersections of gender, class, race or ethnicity (Anderson, Battle, Brandon, Spencer-Wood, Stewart-Abernathy, Wood).* In some chapters households are analyzed as places maintaining social inequality through division of labor naturalized by ideology and enforced by dominating "powers-over" subordinate groups (e.g., Barile, Pappas, Spencer-Wood, Stewart-Abernathy, Wood).* Some analyzed households as places of cooperative division of labor, including gender and racial socialization of children (Anderson, Battle, Brandon, Bonine, Galindo, Spencer-Wood).* In a few cases subordinate groups' households are shown as places of social agency essential to creating "powers-with" a subordinate group resisting oppression by the dominant group (Battle, Brandon, Wood).* Marxist-feminist theory is relevant to gendered domination and resistance frameworks of analysis (Barile, Brandon citing hooks, Davidson, Stewart-Abernathy)* in historical reform women's arguments that household chores should become businesses (Spencer-Wood*) and in African-American working-class households where women were paid to do laundry from white households (Davidson*). This volume as a whole further relates household inequalities to inequalities socially constructed, ideologically justified, and structurally enforced between social groups in the culture as a whole.

Feminist theory and history can contribute useful interpretive frameworks and context for the historical archaeology of households. Feminists have theorized how gendered power dynamics are fundamental to relationships among household members, their gender roles, and who performs which household chores. Feminists have shown how culturally constructed gender ideology legitimates household power dynamics and unequal division of labor. Feminist theories address how family households socialize children into gender identities, replicating gendered power relationships across generations in both the domestic and public spheres. Postmodern feminist theory is concerned with how social structure and culture are permeated by complex intersections among sexism, racism, and classism.

Feminist theory and history bring understanding of fundamental causes of social inequities and historical processes that created and legitimated those inequities, with the goal of determining how social inequities can be eliminated. Feminists have theorized family households as a fundamental source that maintains, propagates, and naturalizes sociocultural inequalities through processes of socialization and enculturation. At the same time feminists have theorized and researched how women's social agency in households changed societal gender roles, identities, power dynamics, and cultural gender ideology.

14

Doing the Housework

New Approaches to the Archaeology of Households

Mary C. Beaudry

It is far from surprising that questions of how best to identify, study, and interpret households are of sustaining interest and debate among scholars working in virtually all areas of archaeology (for recent examples, see Allison 1999b; Nevett 1999). The contributors to this volume take up "household archaeology" in different ways, approaching and critiquing it from a variety of perspectives, but all agree that the household is a critical social unit and vital medium for understanding innumerable aspects of social life. Indeed, it is within the context of the household, whatever form it may take, that cultural consciousness and notions of personhood are initially forged; households are the primary arena in which "space is experienced and life is lived" (Lefebvre 1971:46).

My own interest in the archaeology of households began in the 1970s and early 1980s, when I was introduced to the notion that historical archaeologists ought to attempt to integrate the approach of the New Social History, which focused on ordinary people and on the history of the family (e.g., Demos 1970; Laslett and Wall 1972; Rabb and Rotberg 1971; Stone 1977) with anthropological studies of the developmental cycle of the domestic group and of households more generally (Goody 1971; Wilk and Rathje 1982; Wilk et al. 1984). By attending to the ways in which architectural and other material remains, especially household refuse (e.g., Rathje and Ritenbaugh 1984) could be interpreted as clues to the life histories of families in the past, archaeologists too could contribute to such studies.

From the outset my interest in the archaeology of households (Beaudry 1984, 1986, 1989a) was strongly situated within the interpretive, contextual strand of anthropological and archaeological thought (e.g., Rabinow and Sullivan 1987), and I remain convinced that archaeologists should strive to excavate household sites in such a way that they can make persuasive links between the life history of sites—stratigraphic sequences and site formation processes—and episodes of household stasis, upheaval, and transformation (Beaudry 1995,

1996, 1999; Simmons et al. 1993). My approach to historical archaeology has always closely attended to "practice," to what people do in their daily lives. I am interested in how close critical attention to the "action contexts" in which material culture was deployed (see, e.g., Beaudry 1995, 1996), and I have always subscribed to a definition of culture as more than just "an abstract order of signs, or relations among signs . . . or the sum of habitual practices." For me, culture is never a closed system; rather, it consists of "polyvalent, potentially contestable messages, images, and actions" and is historically situated (Comaroff and Comaroff 1992:10). I have therefore never felt it necessary to adopt the notion of *habitus* developed by Bourdieu (1977) that many historical archaeologists find useful as an antidote to the definitions of culture that constituted the rationale for the attempts by earlier generations of historical archaeologists to construct grand synthetic narratives or to delineate systemic cultural patterning (e.g., Brandon and Barile, Stewart-Abernathy, this volume).

It is important for archaeologists to take from the interdisciplinary literature on households what is most useful to them and to avoid adopting a single or monolithic definition of "the household"; we encounter so many different sorts of domestic arrangements that there is simply not a "one-size-fits-all" definition that can be of use to us. That is why I am encouraged to see the creativity and originality that these scholars bring to their work on households; all give due consideration to the classics of the secondary literature, but they all adopt a definition of the household that works for the particular context(s) they are investigating and that best suits the goals of their own research. My colleagues and I found in our work on "boardinghouseholds" in Lowell, Massachusetts, for instance, that we could not make use of any traditional definition of household if we were to be successful in interpreting the material remains from boardinghouse backlots. Because they were company-owned businesses operated by "professional" boardinghouse keepers, we characterized the "boardinghouseholds" as *corporate* households, the material residues of which had to be interpreted at a minimum of three different levels of analysis: that controlled by the textile companies; that under the purview of the boardinghouse keeper; and that over which individual boarders had control (Beaudry 1989a:88–89; Beaudry and Mrozowski 1989:57–60; and *contra* Spencer-Wood, this volume, chap. 8). We were forced to consider not just the built environment of the "company city" (e.g., Beaudry 1989c; Beaudry and Mrozowski 1987, 1989, 2001) but also the economics of boardinghouse keeping (e.g., Beaudry and Landon 1988; Landon 1989) as well as the agency and decision-making represented by personal effects and other items purchased by the boarders (e.g., Beaudry et al. 1991; Mrozowski et al. 1986).

Contributors to this volume similarly find it useful to unpack the notion of household in ways that lead to fresh insights into the construction of domestic space and the relationships among members of households and between those who are members and those who are not. I see many themes and potentialities in these essays, but I have chosen to examine only three here, the ones I find most evocative and promising for future research. These themes, as I see them, are Intimacy and Separation; Patriarchy, Spatial Ordering, and Power Relations; and the Subversive Poetics of Housework.

INTIMACY AND SEPARATION

Battle and Stewart-Abernathy both address ways in which households construct "personal landscapes" through differential use and perception of spaces within the domestic compound, spaces that are not part of the house per se. Much as Yentsch et al. (1987) noted that formal gardens serve as outdoor extensions of household space and hence as expressions of household or family identity, Battle notes that slave yards were actively employed for a variety of activities, many related to maintaining the household. But in the context of the field quarter at The Hermitage, these outdoor spaces also afforded a measure of privacy for the enslaved because they did not fall readily under surveillance from the main house. For this reason the enslaved were able to relate to one another in ways of their own choosing.

But separation comes in many forms, some of which hinder rather than permit personal freedom. Stewart-Abernathy reveals how contemporary "preservation" efforts erased the outkitchens from the Washington, Arkansas, townscape in ways that echo the separation more psychological than physical to which those who once worked and dwelt in those kitchens were subjected (cf. Chan 2003). His research reminds us that households are more than "units"; they are complex sites of interaction, intimacy, emotion, and often conflict. It is difficult for the contemporary archaeologist to come to grips with the notion that slaveholding households had within them persons for whom membership in the household was tenuous if acknowledged at all, people who had access to family space and who regularly performed the most intimate tasks of feeding and clothing the family but who were, for most purposes, invisible and largely unacknowledged.

Stewart-Abernathy leads us also to ponder issues of archaeological visibility; historical archaeologists for many years were in despair at the very idea that archaeologists could sort out individual households in towns and cities (see, e.g., Brown 1987; but see also Beaudry 1987; Mrozowski 1984), but highly successful recent projects such as those in New York's Five Points (Yamin 2000) and Sydney's Rocks (Karskens 1999) neighborhoods have, one hopes, silenced the nay-sayers for good. U.S. historical archaeologists have not been very successful to date in developing ways of looking at how enslaved and free Africans and African Americans interacted with others; they prefer to find "isolated" sites (plantation slave quarters, burying grounds) where separation is seen as an aid to archaeological interpretation. In the United States, only a few archaeologists have ventured to consider ways of exploring the everyday lives of slaves (Yentsch 1994; Joseph 2000) and free blacks (Praetzellis and Praetzellis 1992b; Wilkie and Shorter 1997) in urban contexts. Away from plantation settings in which the presence of enslaved Africans is a given, archaeologists have turned most often not to domestic sites and African-American neighborhoods within cities and towns but to communities of the dead, that is, to cemeteries, to study African-American culture (see, e.g., Crist et al. 1995, on the 10th St. First African Baptist cemetery, Philadelphia; HUJMA 1993, on the African Burial Ground, New York; Parrington and Roberts 1990, on the 8th St. First African Baptist cemetery site, Philadelphia; Parrington and Wideman 1986). As a result thousands of African-American graves have been excavated in U.S. cities, yet very few African-American urban homesteads have been investigated; hence little attention has been paid to African-American urban home life, neighborhoods, and communities.

In the United States, urban renewal has been used repeatedly as a means of denying African Americans their rightful place in the history of the cities to which they moved after emancipation or in which their ancestors lived during slavery times (on District Six in Cape Town, Africa, cf. Hall 2000 Malan and van Heyningen 2001). A vivid and heartrending example of this denial of heritage unfolded in Dallas, Texas. In this volume, James Davidson recounts how North Dallas, formerly known as Freedman's Town and once outside the city limits, was established in the late nineteenth century by freed slaves who attempted to move to Dallas but were denied the right to live within the boundaries of the town; by the early twentieth century it was a thriving neighborhood of family homes, businesses, and churches serving black congregations. But as Dallas grew, the city fathers and developers began a long process of removing blacks from their homes. It culminated in a project done in an expressway right of way that went through the Freedman's Cemetery, and this time archaeologists were there in advance of construction—not to work on any of the former residential or retail sites whose buildings were razed but only in the cemetery. In the end over 1,100 African-American graves were excavated, and local archaeologists considered it something of a triumph: they got to study the African Americans who once lived in Freedman's Town as a biological community. But what about the once-vibrant and living community?

Until recently, it seems, archaeologists have been more comfortable dealing with African Americans who have been removed from their daily lives, lives in which they interacted with neighbors and kin and negotiated their identities within the wider community. The separation, or should I say segregation, of death allows archaeologists to make scientific observations on mortality rates, disease, and pathologies brought on by overwork and malnutrition, but it relieves the archaeologist of looking at African Americans as living persons who dealt with the conditions that their remains indicate they suffered and endured. What is more, the removal of the dead of Freedman's Town that accompanied the demolition of block after block of black-owned houses and businesses and even some churches works in a most insidious way to deny in retrospect the community's existence and to deprive its few remaining residents and its former residents the right to their own past. Davidson describes results of efforts initiated recently under the direction Dr. Maria Franklin of the University of Texas at Austin to explore backlots of demolished former homes of African-American residents of a North Dallas neighborhood, and one hopes that the stories of real lives that emerge from this work, which involve an explicit orientation toward African-American households, will help revive at least some portion of this remnant community's links to its own history and identity.

PATRIARCHY, SPATIAL ORDERING, AND POWER RELATIONS

Several essays in this volume (Anderson, Barile, Brandon, Pappas) address issues of the ways in which power relations are reflected in material culture, both within the household and between households and broader societal forces, especially corporations or companies that created "communities" out of whole cloth as a means of having a workforce close at hand. Throughout history the majority of households have been organized around principles arising out of both the reality and ideology of patriarchy. In colonial America this was especially true, and historians have investigated the ways in which court records reveal much about relations between men and women in the seventeenth century (Norton 1996); entries in diaries by such notables as "William Byrd and Thomas Jefferson expressing misogyny" and "patriarchal rage can be used to gain insight on the wider contexts of gender and power in the eighteenth century" (Lockridge 1994).

Pappas's essay reveals in considerable and vivid detail the many ways in which corporate paternalism of the sort based on the traditional model of patriarchy was made manifest in every aspect of the layout, housing, and internal furnishings of the Soap Creek Pass lumber camp. At every level, it seems, the lumber company's efforts to construct a social order that maximized efficiency and reinforced company hierarchy and policies found material expression. Pappas finds only limited evidence of workers' refashioning the material environment to meet personal needs or to express individuality or difference.

Anderson uses the conceptual framework of "nested households" to characterize the interrelatedness of households on plantations in the Bahamas. She notes that while it is possible to delineate specific households based on co-residence, the complicated nature of social relations on the plantation led to a blurring of actual and genetic boundaries among households and their composition. She notes that analysis of plantation households requires a multiscalar approach that takes into account the ways in which the households of the enslaved are "nested" within the wider complex of the plantation household. Anderson's approach in some ways prefigures Barile's conceptualization of the plantation as a whole as a form of household.

Plantations were not company towns but nevertheless were often agricultural/industrial estates whose owners apportioned space in order to maximize profits. In exploring the notion that the plantation as a whole constituted a household of sorts, Barile provides a useful construct for examining the ways in which patriarchy found expression in plantation landscapes. After the Denmark Vesey uprising in South Carolina, many plantations were spatially reordered as the paternalistic "ideal" of the plantation household was supplanted by a more custodial, quasi-militaristic model of social relations on the plantation. The master—the patriarch—no longer masqueraded as *pater familias* of the plantation household but was clearly master over his refashioned dominion.

Brandon's wide-ranging essay explores several topics that he feels must be addressed if historical archaeologists are to succeed in analyzing African-American households in ways that consider the multiple vectors of personal and group identity, combining gender, race, and other aspects of identity construction. He notes that most historical archaeologists have failed to acknowledge that the black family in freedom did not fully subscribe to the patriarchal model of household relations that white families perpetuated. Black consumerism may have been agenda-driven in ways that scholars have only recently acknowledged (Mullins 1999a); black households were places in which children learned the realities of racism and how to resist it.

Bonine's attempts to delineate household composition based on the surviving material evidence and contextual information derived from documentary analysis and Galindo's ethnohistorically grounded study of *rancho* households along the Rio Grande frontier both grapple with issues of the (extended) spatial dimensions of households. Bonine seeks to define a model for the rancho household yet comes quickly to the conclusion that a certain degree of variability must be taken into account and that perhaps separate households operated somewhat differently—and that this might be the reason for the perceived nuances of spatial ordering at several recorded rancho sites. In such instances the historical archaeologist confronts the problem prehistorians face daily: it is exceedingly difficult to reconstruct household demographics and internal dynamics if we do not know for sure who really lived at a site. The situation is made even more difficult when the archaeological evidence seems to indicate multiple domestic compounds in close proximity to one another (in the Outer Hebrides we encountered similar domestic complexes that historians of the Scottish Highlands have dubbed "hamlet clusters"; cf. Beaudry 2000). We are left to wonder what sort of relationships existed among these presumably linked households and usually speculate that the sorts of domestic complexes that Galindo discusses reflect extended family groups who settle near one another for mutual support and protection. Galindo and Bonine both conclude that the rancho households of the Spanish colonial frontier cannot be properly studied in isolation, that the scale of analysis must encompass, at the very least, the broader landscape over which relations of kinship and power were distributed and expressed.

THE SUBVERSIVE POETICS OF HOUSEWORK

In a book with the phrase "household chores" in the title, one might expect far more attention to the sorts of tasks performed within households, but here "housework" is treated explicitly in only two essays (Spencer-Wood, chap. 8, and Wood)—this despite the fact that one is able to point to several recent examples of intense and explicit interest on the part of historians and historical archaeologists in various aspects of "women's work" as it relates to women's roles and constructed identities (Ulrich 1982). These examples include traditional household chores like doing laundry (Richard 2003); milking cows and preparing dairy products as contributions to the household economy (Snow 2003; Yentsch 1991); serving as nurse and healer to family and others (Tannenbaum 2003; Wilkie 1996b); and giving birth and mothering (Ulrich 2003; Wilkie 2003). The majority of the contributors to this volume, it seems, wish—quite justifiably—to avoid getting entangled in the thicket created by archaeologists who insist that we need to develop a "task-orientation" approach that consists of creating two columns, one headed "women's chores" and the other "men's chores" with lists of relevant artifacts and spaces under each. The idea is that once the archaeologists match up their archaeological finds with items listed in the two columns, they have done a gendered household analysis.

It barely needs repeating (cf. Spencer-Wood, this volume, chap. 13) that a too-ready acceptance of the nineteenth-century ideology of separate spheres leads as well to a too-ready reification of that ideology through archaeological analysis. Judith Butler (1999:187) notes that too often identity categories such as gender are taken to be foundational and fixed; she sees gender as a constituted status and notes that too often, despite the advances of feminism over the past decades, "the feminist discourse on cultural construction remains trapped within the unnecessary binarism of free will and determinism." In Spencer-Wood's chapter on the Cambridge Cooperative Housekeeping Society (CCHS) and Wood's essay on women's lives in the Berwind coal camp in Colorado, we see efforts to move away from the constricting framework of gender as constituted, determined, or arbitrary in clear efforts "to locate strategies of subversive repetition enabled by those constructions, to affirm the local possibilities of intervention through participating in precisely those practices of repetition that constitute identity and, therefore, present the immanent possibility of contesting them" (Butler 1999:188).

The women who founded the CCHS, as Spencer-Wood so clearly demonstrates, sought to professionalize housework and to place it on an equivalent footing with wage labor. Their effort involved establishing a dedicated locale at which "housework" could be done outside of the household—and, ironically, it was this very attempt to remove household work from the household sphere that proved the downfall of the enterprise. Spencer-Wood points out with some acerbity that as eager as the women might have been to play active roles in this innovative cooperative housekeeping effort, their husbands, resolute subscribers to the ideology of separate spheres, were unprepared to permit their wives the freedom of movement in the public sphere that their participation required.

Margaret Wood's essay is a well-crafted examination of the ways in which women's "housework" is a form of subversive poetics that serves to constitute relations within the family and among families as well as between the household and the outside world. Archaeologists have overlooked the fact that working-class notions of domesticity differed dramatically from the middle-class ideal of separate spheres that seem to be so readily reflected in the material culture of middle-class households. It is critical, she notes, to examine the material culture of working-class life with this fact in mind (cf. Beaudry 1993:92). Wood's evocation of the informal ritual of exchanging hospitality and forging friendships over a cup of coffee through her analysis of ceramics from the Berwick camp dump struck a familiar chord with me; one of the strongest memories of my childhood spent on military bases in one part of the world or another is the daily morning ritual, usually held around my mother's dinette table, of the *kaffeeklatsch* at which women of different racial and cultural backgrounds shared over seemingly endless cups of coffee the common experiences of womanhood, of being wives and mothers. Wood's analysis shows how in small ways women's activities within the household, by fostering class-based identities and gender-based solidarity across lines of "difference," mediate between "a creative tension and transformative action" (Comaroff and Comaroff 1993:xxix).

FINAL THOUGHTS

The promise and potential of household archaeology is well represented in this volume, and it is heartening to find the range of ideas and insights that the contributors bring to the project of comprehending households and family life through material remains, through houses, through artifacts used in the conduct of everyday life, and through use and perception of space and landscapes. What is most uplifting is to find that young scholars have sought out the human dimension in their research efforts; here we find careful consideration of the contexts in which human lives were lived and the ways in which households in all their forms and variety are hearths at which consciousness and identity are forged. The contributors shun simplistic formulations and rigid definitions; they explore variability and embrace complexity and ambiguity in the intersecting variables of race, class, ethnicity, and gender. They do not see gender as arbitrary and fatal and wholly delimited but as subject to negotiation within the context of household relations. The work that men and women do for others, outside of their own households, is acknowledged as contributing to the maintenance and reproduction of those other households. And the work that women and men do in households—for their own families—is not presented solely as a round of hateful, punitive, and endlessly repetitive chores that offer no satisfaction but as potentially constructive and gratifying and, in some cases, transformative and even subversive.

ACKNOWLEDGMENTS

Thanks to Kerri Barile and Jamie Brandon for inviting me to make a contribution to this volume. I came late to the project (later than I should have!) but am happy to be a part of it.

References

Adams, Natalie P.

    1990   Early African-American Domestic Architecture from Berkeley County, South Carolina. Unpublished Master's thesis, Department of Anthropology, University of South Carolina, Columbia.

Adams, Paul C., Steven Hoelscher, and Karen E. Till (editors)

    2001   *Textures of Place: Exploring Humanist Geographies.* University of Minnesota Press, Minneapolis.

Agee, James, and Walker Evans

    1939   [1988] *Let Us Now Praise Famous Men.* Houghton Mifflin, New York.

Albury, Paul

    1975   *The Story of the Bahamas.* St. Martin's Press, New York.

Alexander, Edward P.

    1996   *Museums in Motion: An Introduction to the History and Functions of Museums.* AltaMira Press, Walnut Creek, California.

Allen, James B.

    1966   *The Company Town in the American West.* University of Oklahoma Press, Norman.

Allison, Penelope M.

    1999a   Introduction. In *The Archaeology of Household Activities,* edited by P. M. Allison, pp. 1–18. Routledge, New York.

    1999b   (editor) *The Archaeology of Household Activities.* Routledge Press, London.

Alonzo, Armando C.

    1998   *Tejano Legacy: Rancheros and Settlers in South Texas, 1734–1900.* University of New Mexico Press, Albuquerque.

Anderson, Nesta J.

    1998   Conversations and Excavations: An Ethnoarchaeological Examination of the African-Bahamian Houseyard. Unpublished Master's thesis, Department of Anthropology, Louisiana State University, Baton Rouge.

Anonymous

    1792   Mapa de la Sierra Gorda y Costa del Seno Mexicano. In *Monumentos para la his-*

toria de Coahuila y Seno Mexicano, Archivo General de la Nación, Cat. 221, Historia, vol. 29, f. 190.

1997   Anthony Overton, Born Entrepreneur. *Issues and Views* (Spring). Electronic document. http://www.issues-views.com/index.php/sect1000/1006, accessed October 6, 2003.

2003   Website on the Federal Reserve Bank of Dallas. Electronic document. www.kpf.com/Projects/federal.htm, accessed October 8, 2003.

n.d.   In Memoriam. Typescript biography of Simon T. Sanders. On file, Southwest Arkansas Regional Archives, Washington, Arkansas.

Aptheker, Herbert

1965   *One Continual Cry: David Walker's Appeal to the Colored Citizens of the World, 1829–1830.* Humanities Press, New York.

1971   On Denmark Vesey. In *American Slavery: The Question of Resistance,* edited by J. Bracey, A. Meier and E. Rudwick, pp. 120–126. Wadsworth Publishing, Belmont, California.

Armstrong, Douglas V.

1983   The "Old Village" at Drax Hall Plantation: An Archaeological Examination of an Afro-Jamaican Settlement. Ph.D. diss., Department of Anthropology, University of California at Los Angeles.

1985   An Afro-Jamaican Slave Settlement: Archaeological Investigation at Drax Hall. In *The Archaeology of Slavery and Plantation Life,* edited by T. A. Singleton, pp. 261–285. Academic Press, Inc., San Diego.

1990   *The Old Village and the Great House: An Archaeological and Historical Examination of Drax Hall Plantation, St. Ann's Bay, Jamaica.* University of Illinois Press, Urbana.

Ashmore, Wendy, and A. Bernard Knapp (editors)

1999   *Archaeologies of Landscape: Contemporary Perspectives.* Blackwell Press, London.

Ashmore, Wendy, and Richard Wilk

1988   Household and Community in the Mesoamerican Past. In *Household and Community in the Mesoamerican Past,* edited by R. Wilk and W. Ashmore, pp. 1–28. University of New Mexico Press, Albuquerque.

Atkinson, Norma P.

1983   An Examination of the Life and Thought of Zina Fay Peirce, an American Reformer and Feminist. Ph.D. diss., Department of Philosophy, Ball State University, Muncie, Indiana.

Austin, Curtis

1990   Archaeologist Avoids Plowing Through History. *Dallas Times Herald,* March 6.

Babson, David W.

1988   *The Tanner Road Settlement: The Archaeology of Racism on Limerick Plantation.* Volumes in Historical Archaeology IV. South Carolina Institute of Archaeology and Anthropology, University of South Carolina, Columbia.

Ball, Edward

1998   *Slaves in the Family.* Farrar, Straus, and Giroux, New York.

Barbassa, Juliana
1998   Trash Heap of History, A Dallas archaeology buff is forced to the sidelines as the city's past makes way for the new arena. *Dallas Observer,* October 8–14.

Bardaglio, Peter W.
1995   *Reconstructing the Household: Families, Sex and the Law in the Nineteenth-Century South.* University of North Carolina Press, Chapel Hill.

Barile, Kerri S.
1999   Causes and Creations: Exploring the Relationship Between Nineteenth Century Slave Insurrections, Landscape, and Architecture at Middleburg Plantation, Berkeley County, South Carolina. Unpublished Master's thesis, Department of Anthropology, University of South Carolina, Columbia.
2004   Race, the National Register, and Cultural Resource Management: Creating a Historic Context for Post-Bellum Sites. *Historical Archaeology* 34(1):90–100.

Barley, M. W.
1961   *The English Farmhouse and Cottage.* Routledge and Kegan Paul, Cambridge, U.K.

Barr, Alwyn
1996   *Black Texas, a History of African-Americans in Texas, 1528–1995.* 2nd edition. University of Oklahoma Press, Norman.

Bassett, Everett
1994   "We Took Care of Each Other Like Families Were Meant To": Gender, Social Organization, and Wage Labor Among the Apache at Roosevelt. In *Those of Little Note: Gender, Race, and Class in Historical Archaeology,* edited by E. M. Scott, pp. 55–80. University of Arizona Press, Tucson.

Beaudry, Mary C.
1984   Archaeology and the Historical Household. *Man in the Northeast* 28:27–38.
1986   The Archaeology of Historical Land Use in Massachusetts. *Historical Archaeology* 20(2):38–46.
1987   Analytical Scale and Methods for the Archaeological Study of Urban Households. Society for Historical Archaeology *Newsletter* 20(1):22–25.
1989a   Household Structure and the Archaeological Record: Examples from New World Historical Sites. In *Households and Communities,* edited by S. MacEachern, D. Archer, and R. Garvin, pp. 84–92. University of Calgary, Calgary, Alberta.
1989b   Introduction. In *Interdisciplinary Investigations of the Boott Mills, Lowell, Massachusetts,* vol. III, *The Boarding House System as a Way of Life,* edited by M. C. Beaudry and S. A. Mrozowski, pp. 1–6. Cultural Resources Management Study No. 21. Division of Cultural Resources, National Park Service, North Atlantic Regional Office, Boston.
1989c   The Lowell Boott Mills Complex and Its Housing: Material Expressions of Corporate Ideology. *Historical Archaeology* 23(1):19–32.
1993   Public Aesthetics versus Personal Experience: Archaeology and the Interpretation of 19th-Century Worker Health and Well Being in Lowell, Massachusetts. *Historical Archaeology* 27(2):90–105.
1995   Scratching the Surface: Seven Seasons Digging at the Spencer-Pierce-Little Farm, Newbury, Massachusetts. *Northeast Historical Archaeology* 24:19–50.

1996   Reinventing Historical Archaeology. In *Historical Archaeology and the Study of American Culture,* edited by L. De Cunzo and B. L. Herman, pp. 473–497. Distributed by University of Tennessee Press, Knoxville, for the Henry Francis Du Pont Winterthur Museum, Winterthur, Delaware.

1999   House and Household: The Archaeology of Domestic Life in Early America. In *Old and New Worlds,* edited by G. Egan and R. L. Michael, pp. 117–126. Oxbow Books, Oxford, U.K.

2000   Who Lived at Airigh Mhuillin? An Exercise in Documentary Archaeology. Paper presented at the annual meetings of the Council for Northeast Historical Archaeology, Halifax, Nova Scotia.

Beaudry, Mary C., and David B. Landon

1988   Domestic Ideology and the Boardinghouse System in Lowell, Massachusetts. Paper presented at the Dublin Seminar for New England Folklife, Durham, New Hampshire.

Beaudry, Mary C., and Stephen A. Mrozowski

1989   Archeology in the Backlots of Boott Units 45 and 48: Household Archeology with a Difference. In *Interdisciplinary Investigations of the Boott Mills, Lowell, Massachusetts,* vol. III, *The Boarding House System as a Way of Life,* edited by M. C. Beaudry and S. A. Mrozowski, pp. 49–82. Cultural Resources Management Study No. 21. National Park Service, North Atlantic Regional Office, Boston.

2001   Cultural Space and Worker Identity in the Company City: Nineteenth-Century Lowell, Massachusetts. In *The Archaeology of Urban Landscapes: Explorations in Slumland,* edited by A. Mayne and T. Murray, pp. 118–131. Cambridge University Press, Cambridge.

Beaudry, Mary C., and Stephen A. Mrozowski (editors)

1987   *Interdisciplinary Investigations of the Boott Mills, Lowell, Massachusetts,* vol. I, *Life in the Boarding Houses: A Preliminary Report.* Cultural Resources Management Study No. 18. National Park Service, North Atlantic Regional Office, Boston.

1989   *Interdisciplinary Investigations of the Boott Mills, Lowell, Massachusetts,* vol. III, *The Boarding House System as a Way of Life.* Cultural Resources Management Study No. 21. National Park Service, North Atlantic Regional Office, Boston.

Beaudry, Mary C., Lauren J. Cook, and Stephen A. Mrozowski

1991   Artifacts and Active Voices: Material Culture as Social Discourse. In *The Archaeology of Inequality,* edited by R. H. McGuire and R. Paynter, pp. 150–191. Blackwell, Oxford.

Beecher, Catharine E.

1841   *A Treatise on Domestic Economy for the use of Young Ladies at Home, and at School.* Marsh, Capen, Lyon, and Webb, Boston. Facsimile of original reprinted (1970) by Source Book Press, New York.

Beecher, Catharine E., and Harriet Beecher Stowe

1985   [1869] *The American Woman's Home; or, Principles of Domestic Science.* Reprinted by Stowe-Day Foundation, Hartford, Connecticut.

Bender, Diane

1967   A Refinement of the Concept of Household: Families, Coresidence, and Domestic Functions. *American Anthropologist* 69:493–504.

Bergman, Peter M. (editor)

1969   *The Chronological History of the Negro in America.* Harper and Row, New York.

Beshoar, Barron

1942   *Out of the Depths: The Story of John R. Lawson, a Labor Leader.* Golden Bell Press, Denver.

Bishir, Catherine W.

2000   Landmarks of Power: Building a Southern Past in Raleigh and Wilmington, North Carolina, 1885–1915. In *Where These Memories Grow: History, Memory and Southern Identity,* edited by W. F. Brundage, pp. 139–168. University of North Carolina Press, Chapel Hill.

Blanton, Richard E.

1994   *House and Households: A Comparative Study.* Plenum Press, New York.

Blassingame, John

1972   *The Slave Community: Plantation Life in the Antebellum South.* Oxford University Press, New York.

1973   *Black New Orleans, 1860–1880.* University of Chicago Press, Chicago.

Bonine, Mindy L.

2001   Households in the Wilderness: An Analysis of Two Spanish Colonial Sites along the Rio Grande, Starr County, Texas. Unpublished Master's thesis, Department of Anthropology, University of Texas, Austin.

Borchert, James

1980   *Alley Life in Washington: Family, Community, Religion and Folklife in the City, 1850–1970.* University of Illinois Press, Urbana.

Bourdieu, Pierre

1973   The Berber House. In *Rules and Meanings: The Anthropology of Everyday Knowledge,* edited by M. Douglas, pp. 98–110. Penguin Books, Harmondsworth, U.K.

1977   *Outline of a Theory of Practice,* Translated by R. Nice. Cambridge University Press, Cambridge.

1993   *The Field of Cultural Production: Essays on Art and Literature.* Edited and introduced by R. Johnson. Columbia University Press, New York.

Boyer, M. Christine

1994   *The City of Collective Memory: Its Historical Imagery and Architectural Entertainments.* MIT Press, Cambridge, Massachusetts.

Bracey, John, August Meier, and Elliott Rudwick (editors)

1971   *American Slavery: The Question of Resistance.* Wadsworth Publishers, Belmont, California.

Brah, Avtar

1996   *Cartographies of Diaspora: Contesting Identities.* Routledge, New York.

Brandon, Jamie C.

2000   Constructions of Race, Class, and Gender in Dallas, Texas, 1870–1930: Views from the Historical and Archeological Records. Paper presented to the 44th annual meeting of the American Studies Association of Texas, Waco.

Brandon, Jamie C., and James Davidson

2002   *The Archaeology of Van Winkle's Mill (3BE413): Where Ozarks and Ozone Meet.*

Arkansas Archeological Survey Research Series. Arkansas Archeological Survey, Fayetteville. In press.

Brandon, Jamie C., James M. Davidson, and Jerry E. Hilliard

2000a   *Preliminary Archeological Investigations at Van Winkle's Mill (3BE413), Beaver Lake State Park, Benton County, Arkansas, 1997–1999.* Report Submitted to Arkansas Department of Parks and Tourism, Little Rock, by the Arkansas Archeological Survey.

2000b   Excavations at the Van Winkle Saw Mill, 1997–1999: Industry, Ethnicity and Landscape in the Ozark Upland South. Paper presented to the annual meeting of the Society for Historical Archaeology, Quebec City.

Braverman, Harry

1998   *Labor and Monopoly Capital.* Monthly Review Press, New York.

Breeden, J. (editor)

1980   *Advice Among Masters: The Ideal in Slave Management in the Old South.* Greenwood Press, Westport, Connecticut.

Brent, Linda

1987   *Incidents in the Life of a Slave Girl, Written by Herself, by Harriet A. Jacobs [1861].* Edited by J. Yellin. Harvard University Press, Cambridge, Massachusetts.

Brigance, Fred

1975   Historical Background of the First Hermitage. Ladies' Hermitage Association and the Tennessee Bicentennial Commission. On file at the Hermitage, Tennessee.

Brooker, Colin

1990   Tabby Structures on Spring Island. In *The Second Phase of Archaeological Survey on Spring Island, Beaufort County, South Carolina: Investigation of Prehistoric and Historic Settlement Patterns on an Isolated Sea Island.* Chicora Foundation Research Series 20, Chicora Foundation, Columbia, South Carolina.

Brown, David

1990   Austin's Buried History: Archaeological Excavations at Convention Center Site Open a New Window on the City's Past. *Heritage,* Publication of the Texas Historical Foundation 8(2):8–11.

Brown, Marley R., III

1987   Issues of Scale Revisited. Society for Historical Archaeology *Newsletter* 20(1):25–27.

Brumfiel, Elizabeth M.

1991   Weaving and Cooking: Women's Production in Aztec Mexico. In *Engendering Archaeology: Women and Prehistory,* edited by J. M. Gero and M. W. Conkey, pp. 224–251. Blackwell, Oxford, U.K.

Brundage, W. Fitzhugh

2000   No Deed But Memory. In *Where These Memories Grow: History, Memory and Southern Identity,* edited by W. F. Brundage, pp. 1–28. University of North Carolina Press, Chapel Hill.

Bull, Elias B.

1979   Historic Preservation Inventory: Berkeley County. Department of Archives and History, Columbia, South Carolina.

Butler, Judith

1999   *Gender Trouble: Gender and the Subversion of Identity.* Routledge, New York.

Butler, Steve

1989   Honoring the Past: Confederate Monuments in Dallas. *Legacies, A History Journal for Dallas and North Central Texas* 1(2):31–36.

Byra, Patti L.

1996   The Contextual Meaning of the 1830s Landscape at Middleburg Plantation, Berkeley County, South Carolina. Unpublished Master's thesis, Department of Anthropology, University of South Carolina, Columbia.

Cady, Edwin H.

1956   *The Road to Realism: The Early Years of William Dean Howells (1837–1885).* Syracuse University Press, Syracuse, New York.

Calhoun, Craig, Edward LiPuma, and Moishe Postone (editors)

1993   *Bourdieu: Critical Perspectives.* University of Chicago Press, Chicago.

Cambridge Cooperative Housekeeping Society (CCHS)

1869   *Prospectus,* October 5. Social Ethics Pamphlet collection, Widener Library, Harvard University, Cambridge, Massachusetts.

Camp & Plant Magazine (C&P)

1902–   Published by Colorado Fuel & Iron Company. On file, Western History and
1909   Genealogy Department, Denver Public Library.

Cande, Kathleen H., and Jamie C. Brandon

1999   *Archaeological Collections Management: Old Washington State Park, Washington, Hempstead County, Arkansas.* Arkansas Archeological Survey, Fayetteville. Submitted to the Arkansas Natural and Cultural Resources Council, Little Rock, Grant no. 98–001.

Cárdenas, Mario A.

1999   José de Escandón, the Last Spanish Conquistador: A Study of Royal Service and Personal Achievement in 18th Century New Spain. Unpublished Master's thesis, Department of History, Texas A&M University, Kingsville.

Casteñada, Carlos E.

1976   *Our Catholic Heritage in Texas, 1519–1936.* Vol. 4. Arno Press, New York.

Chan, Alexandra

2003   The Slaves of Colonial New England: Discourses of Colonialism and Identity at the Isaac Royall House, Medford, Massachusetts, 1732–1775. Ph.D. diss., Boston University. University Microfilms International, Ann Arbor.

Channing, Steven A.

1970   *Crisis of Fear: Secession in South Carolina.* Simon and Schuster Press, New York.

Charleston Courier

1822   *Charleston Courier Daily,* August 12. South Caroliniana Library, Columbia.

Chipman, Donald

1992   *Spanish Texas, 1519–1821.* University of Texas Press, Austin.

Citizens of Charleston

1822   *Memorial of the Citizens of Charleston to the Senate and House of Representatives of* the State of South Carolina. South Carolina Department of Archives and History, Columbia.

City of Cambridge Directories
1863–   On file. Public Library, Cambridge, Massachusetts.
1870

Clark, John W., Jr., and Ana Maria Juarez
1986   *Urban Archaeology: A Culture History of a Mexican-American Barrio in Laredo, Webb County, Texas*, vol. 1. Publications in Archaeology no. 31. State Department of Highways and Public Transportation, Austin.

Clinton, Catherine (editor)
1994   *Half Sisters of History: Southern Women and the American Past*. Duke University Press, Durham, North Carolina.

Cobb, James C.
1984   *Industrialization and Southern Society, 1877–1984*. Dorsey Press, Chicago.
1999   *Redefining Southern Culture: Mind and Identity in the Modern South*. University of Georgia Press, Athens.

Cochran, John H.
1928   *Dallas County: A Record of Its Pioneers and Progress*. Service Publishing Company, Dallas.

Cohen, Lizabeth
1990   *Making a New Deal: Industrial Workers in Chicago, 1919–1939*. Cambridge University Press, New York.

Colorado Bureau of Labor Statistics (CBLS)
1899–   Annual Reports. On file, Government Documents, Denver Public Library.
1913

Comaroff, Jean, and John L. Comaroff
1993   Introduction. In *Modernity and Its Malcontents: Ritual and Power in Post-Colonial Africa,* edited by J. Comaroff and J. L. Comaroff, pp. xi–xxx. University of Chicago Press, Chicago.

Comaroff, John L., and Jean Comaroff (editors)
1992   *Ethnography and the Historical Imagination*. Westview Press, Boulder, Colorado.

Commission on Industrial Relations (CIR)
1916   (McLellan testimony: 6531) CIR Report, U.S. Senate, vol. 9. Government Printing Office, Washington.

Conkey, Margaret W., and Joan M. Gero
1991   Tensions, Pluralities and Engendering Archaeology: An Introduction to Women and Prehistory. In *Engendering Archaeology: Women and Prehistory,* edited by M. Conkey and J. Gero, pp. 3–30. Blackwell Press, Cambridge, U.K.

Condon, Cynthia, Joy L. Becker, Heather J. R. Edgar, James M. Davidson, Jeurena R. Hoffman, Patricia Kalima, Daniel Kysar, Susan Moorhead, Victoria M. Owens, and Keith Condon
1998   *Freedman's Cemetery: Site 41DL316, Dallas, Texas. Assessments of Sex, Age at Death, Stature, and Date of Interment for Excavated Burials.* Report no. 9. Archeology

Studies Program, Environmental Affairs Division, Texas Department of Transportation, Austin.

Coontz, Stephanie
1992   *The Way We Never Were: American Families and the Nostalgia Trap.* Basic Books, New York.

Cooper, Judy Hennessee, Angela L. Tine, Marsha Prior, Charles M. Clow, David Shanabrook, and Ed Salo
2000   *Cultural Resources and Bioarchaeological Investigations at the Dallas Convention Center and Pioneer Cemetery, Dallas, Texas.* Miscellaneous Reports of Investigations Number 205. Geo-Marine, Inc., Plano, Texas.

Corelly, Janet L., Thomas H. Appleton, Jr., Anastasia Sims, and Sandra G. Treadwater (editors)
2000   *Negotiating Boundaries of Southern Womanhood: Dealing with the Powers That Be.* University of Missouri Press, Columbia.

Craton, Michael, and Gail Saunders
1992   *Islanders in the Stream: A History of the Bahamian People.* Vol. 1, *From Aboriginal Times to the End of Slavery.* University of Georgia Press, Athens.

Crist, Thomas J., A. J. Reginald, H. Pitts, Arthur Washburn, John P. McCarthy, and Daniel G. Roberts
1995   *"A Distinct Church of the Lord Jesus": The History, Archaeology, and Physical Anthropology of the Tenth Street First African Baptist Church Cemetery, Philadelphia, Pennsylvania.* John Milner Associates, Philadelphia.

Crumley, Carole L.
1987   A Dialectical Critique of Hierarchy. In *Power Relations and State Formation,* edited by T. C. Patterson and C. W. Gailey. Archeology Division, American Anthropological Association, Washington, D.C.

Dallas, City of
2001   *Annual Report Reinvestment Zone No. 1, State-Thomas Tax Increment Financing District.* City of Dallas Economic Development Department.

Dallas City Council
1982   Abandonment Ordinance #172491. Dallas City Ordinance Books (on microfiche). Dallas City Hall, Dallas, Texas.

Dallas City Directories
1873–   On microfilm, Dallas Public Library.
1910

Dallas County Deed Records
1841–   Microfilm, County Records Building, Dallas.

Dallas Express
        Weekly newspaper. Microfilm on file, Dallas Public Library.

Dallas Gazette
        Newspaper published in Cahawba, Alabama. Microfilm copies on file at Old Cahawba Preservation Project and Park, Selma, Ala.

Dallas Herald
        Weekly newspaper. Microfilm on file, Dallas Public Library.

Dallas Morning News
    Daily newspaper. Microfilm on file, Dallas Public Library.
Dallas Observer
    Weekly newspaper. Microfilm on file, Dallas Public Library.
Dallas Times Herald
    Daily newspaper. Microfilm on file, Dallas Public Library.
Dalleo, Peter T.
  1982   African-Bahamian Origins. *Journal of the Bahamas Historical Society* 4(1):17–19.
  1984   Africans in the Caribbean: A Preliminary Assessment of Recaptives in the Bahamas, 1811–1860. *Journal of the Bahamas Historical Society* 6(1):15–24.
Dambacher, Garnet
  1989   Video interview by Jim Smith. Greater Yosemite Council, Boy Scouts of America, Modesto, California.
Dary, David
  1981   *Cowboy Culture, A Saga of Five Centuries.* Alfred A. Knopf, New York.
Davidson, James M.
  1998   The Old Dallas Burial Ground: A Forgotten Cemetery. *Southwestern Historical Quarterly* 102(2):162–184.
  1999   Freedman's Cemetery (1869–1907): A Chronological Reconstruction of an Excavated African American Burial Ground, Dallas, Texas. Unpublished Master's thesis, department of Anthropology, University of Arkansas, Fayetteville.
  2000   An Archival History of Freedman's Cemetery, Dallas, Texas. In *Freedman's Cemetery: A Legacy of A Pioneer Black Community in Dallas, Texas,* edited by D. E. Peter, M. Prior, M. M. Green, and V. G. Clow, pp. 21–50. Geo-Marine, Inc., Plano, Texas, Special Publication No. 6. Texas Department of Transportation, Environmental Affairs Division, Archeology Studies Program, Report no. 21. Austin.
Davidson, James M., Jerome C. Rose, Myron Gutmann, Michael Haines, Keith Condon, and Cindy Condon
  2002   The Quality of African-American Life in the Southwest Near the Turn of the Twentieth Century. In *The Backbone of History: Health and Nutrition in the Western Hemisphere,* edited by R. Steckel and J. C. Rose, pp. 226–280. Cambridge University Press, New York.
Deagan, Kathleen (editor)
  1983   *Spanish St. Augustine: The Archaeology of a Colonial Creole Community.* Academic Press, New York.
  1996   Colonial Transformation: Euro-American Cultural Genesis in the Early Spanish-American Colonies. *Journal of Anthropological Research* 52(2):135–160.
Deagan, Kathleen, and Jane Landers
  1999   Fort Mose: Earliest Free African-American Town in the United States. In *"I, Too, Am America": Archaeological Studies of African-American Life,* edited by T. Singleton, pp. 261–282. University Press of Virginia, Charlottesville.
DeCunzo, LeAnn
  2001   On Reforming the "Fallen" and Beyond: Transforming Continuity at the Mag-

dalene Society of Philadelphia, 1845–1916. *International Journal of Historical Archaeology* 5(1):19–44.

Deetz, James

1971   *Man's Imprint from the Past; Readings in the Methods of Archaeology.* Little, Brown Press, Boston.

1977   *In Small Things Forgotten: Archaeology of Early American Life.* Doubleday, New York.

1982   Households: A structural key to archaeological explanation. In *Archaeology of the Household: Building a Prehistory of Domestic Life,* edited by R. Wilk and W. Rathje. *American Behavioral Scientist* 25(6):717–724.

1993   *Flowerdew Hundred: The Archaeology of a Virginia Plantation, 1619–1864.* University Press of Virginia, Charlottesville.

Delle, James A.

1999   The Landscapes of Class Negotiation on Coffee Plantations in the Blue Mountains of Jamaica, 1790–1850. *Historical Archaeology* 33(1):136–158.

2000   Gender, Power and Space: Negotiating Social Relations under Slavery on Coffee Plantations in Jamaica, 1790–1834. In *Lines that Divide: Historical Archaeologies of Race, Class and Gender,* edited by J. A. Delle, S. A. Mrozowski, and R. Paynter, pp. 168–201. University of Tennessee Press, Knoxville.

Delle, James A., Stephen A. Mrozowski, and Robert Paynter (editors)

2000   *Lines that Divide: Historical Archaeologies of Race, Class and Gender.* University of Tennessee Press, Knoxville.

Demos, John

1970   *A Little Commonwealth: Family Life in Plymouth Colony.* Oxford University Press, London.

Denton, Mark

1999   Dealing with Late Nineteenth and Early Twentieth Century Sites. *Cultural Resource Management News and Views* 11(1):13–14.

Department of Archives, Bahamas

1991   Aspects of Bahamian History: Loyalists, Slavery and Emancipation, Junkanoo. Ministry of Education, Nassau.

Derry, Linda

1992   Fathers and Daughters: Land Ownership, Kinship Structure, and Social Space in Old Cahawba. In *The Art and Mystery of Historical Archaeology: Essays in Honor of James Deetz,* edited by A. E. Yentsch and M. C. Beaudry, pp. 215–228. CRC Press, Boca Raton, Florida.

DeVaughn, Michael

1987   St. Paul U.M. Church: A Century of Service to Dallas. (Dallas County) *Heritage News,* a Journal Dedicated to the History of North Central Texas. 12(2):16–18.

Devens, Carol

1991   Gender and Colonization in Native Communities: Examining the Historical Record. In *The Archaeology of Gender: Proceedings of the 22nd (1989) Annual Chacmool Conference,* edited by D. Walde and N. D. Willows, pp. 510–515. University of Calgary Archaeological Association, Calgary, Alberta.

Dickens, Roy S., Jr. (editor)

1982   *Archaeology of Urban America, The Search for Pattern and Process.* Academic Press, New York.

Dietler, Michael, and Ingrid Herbich

1998   Habitus, Techniques, Style: An Integrated Approach to the Social Understanding of Material Culture and Boundaries. In *The Archaeology of Social Boundaries,* edited by M. T. Stark. Smithsonian Institution Press, Washington.

Di Leonardo, Micaela

1998   *Exotics at Home: Anthropologies, Others, American Modernity.* University of Chicago Press, Chicago.

DiPaolo Loren, Diana

2000   The Intersection of Colonial Policy and Colonial Practice: Creolization on the Eighteenth-Century Louisiana/Texas Frontier. *Historical Archaeology* 34(3):85–98.

Donley, Linda W.

1982   House Power: Swahili Space and Symbolic Markers. In *Symbolic and Structural Archaeology,* edited by I. Hodder, pp. 63–73. Cambridge University Press, Cambridge.

Donovan, Josephine

2001   *Feminist Theory: The Intellectual Traditions.* 3rd ed. Continuum International Publishing Group, New York.

Douglass, William

1998   The Mining Camp as Community. In *Social Approaches to an Industrial Past,* edited by A. B. Knapp, V. C. Pigott, and E. W. Herbert, pp. 97–108. Routledge Press, London.

Drake, St. Clair, and Horace R. Cayton

1945   [1993] *Black Metropolis: A Study of Negro Life in a Northern City.* University of Chicago Press, Chicago.

Du Bois, W. E. B.

1920   [1999] *Darkwater: Voices from Beyond the Veil.* Dover Press, New York.

1940   [2000] *Dusk of Dawn: An Autobiography of a Race Concept.* Transaction Press, New Brunswick, New Jersey.

1995   *W. E. B. DuBois: A Reader,* edited by D. L. Lewis. Henry Holt, New York.

Eastman, Max

1914   The Nice People of Trinidad. *The Masses* 5, no. 10(38):5–8.

Edgar, Walter

1998   *South Carolina: A History.* University of South Carolina Press, Columbia.

Edwards, Ywone

1998   "Trash" Revisited: A Comparative Approach to Historical Descriptions and Archaeological Analysis of Slave Houses and Yards. In *"Keep your head to the sky": Interpreting African American Home Ground,* edited by G. Gundaker, 245–271. University of Virginia Press, Charlottesville.

Ehrenreich, Barbara, and Deirdre English

1978   *For Her Own Good: 150 Years of the Experts' Advice to Women.* Anchor Press/Doubleday, New York.

Eliot Papers
1860– On file. Harvard University Archives, Cambridge, Massachusetts.
1900

Ellers, Tracy Bachrach
2000 *Silent Looms: Women and Production in a Guatemalan Town*. University of Texas Press, Austin.

Ellison, Ralph
1947 [1995] *Invisible Man*. Vintage Press, New York.

Engels, Frederick
1884 [1942] *The Origin of the Family, Private Property, and the State*. Reprint by International, New York.

Engerrand, Steven W.
1978 Black and Mulatto Mobility and Stability in Dallas, Texas, 1880–1910. *Phylon* 39(3):203–209.

Epperson, Terrence E.
1989 Race and Disciplines of the Plantation. Paper presented at the "Digging the Past: Archaeology and the Black Experience" Conference, Oxford, Mississippi.
1991 Constructed Places/Contested Spaces: Contexts of Tidewater Plantation Archaeology. Paper presented at the Society for Historical Archaeology meeting, Richmond, Virginia.

Epstein, Barbara L.
1981 *The Politics of Domesticity: Women, Evangelism, and Temperance in Nineteenth Century America*. Wesleyan University Press, Middletown, Connecticut.

Farnsworth, Paul
1993 Archaeological Excavations at Wade's Green Plantation, North Caicos. *Journal of the Bahamas Historical Society* 15(1):2–10.
1994 Archaeological Excavations at Promised Land Plantation, New Providence. *Journal of the Bahamas Historical Society* 16(1):21–29.
1996 The Influence of Trade on Bahamian Slave Culture. *Historical Archaeology* 30(4): 1–23.

Faust, Drew Gilpin
1982 *James Henry Hammond and the Old South: A Design for Mastery*. Louisiana State University Press, Baton Rouge.
1996 *Mothers of Invention: Women of the Slaveholding South in the American Civil War*. University of North Carolina Press, Chapel Hill.

Ferguson, Leland
1992 *Uncommon Ground*. Smithsonian Institution Press, Washington, D.C.
1996 Struggling with Pots in South Carolina. In *Images of the Recent Past: Readings in Historical Archaeology*, edited by C. E. Orser, Jr., pp. 260–271. AtlaMira, Walnut Creek, California.

Fitts, Robert K.
1999 The Archaeology of Middle-Class Domesticity and Gentility in Victorian Brooklyn. *Historical Archaeology* 33(1):39–62.

Flannery, Kent (editor)
1976 *The Early Mesoamerican Village*. Academic Press, New York.

Fleming, Sharon E.

1998   Building La Frontera: The Form and Technology of Historic Ranch Architecture in Zapata County, Texas. Unpublished Master's thesis, School of Architecture, Texas Tech University, Lubbock.

Fleming, Sharon E., and Timothy K. Perttula

1999   San José de Corralitos, a Spanish Colonial Ranch in Zapata and Webb Counties, Texas. In *Bulletin of the Texas Archaeological Society,* vol. 70/1999, edited by T. K. Perttula and L. W. Ellis, pp. 395–410. Archaeological Society of Austin.

Flick, David

1995   Losing Ground: Once Vibrant Black Community Succumbs to Migration, Apartments. *Dallas Morning News,* February 12.

Flores, Richard R.

1998   Memory-Place, Meaning, and the Alamo. *American Literary History* 10(3):428–445.

2002   *Remembering the Alamo: Memory, Modernity and the Master Symbol.* University of Texas Press, Austin.

Flynn, Charles L.

1983   *White Land, Black Labor: Caste and Class in Late Nineteenth-Century Georgia.* Louisiana State University Press, Baton Rouge.

Foley, Douglas E.

1995   *The Heartland Chronicles.* University of Pennsylvania Press, Philadelphia.

Foley, Neil

1997   *The White Scourge: Mexicans, Blacks, and Poor Whites in Texas Cotton Culture.* University of California Press, Berkeley.

Foster, Jon M., Roberta S. Greenwood, and Anne Q. Duffield

1988   *Work Camps in the Upper Santa Ana River Canyon.* Report to the Army Corps of Engineers, Los Angeles District, Los Angeles.

Foucault, Michel

1979   *Discipline and Punish: The Birth of the Prison.* Vintage Books, New York.

Fouts, Jarrel

1989   Video interview by Jim Smith. Greater Yosemite Council, Boy Scouts of America, Modesto, California.

Fouts, Merlin

1990   Video interview by Jim Smith. Greater Yosemite Council, Boy Scouts of America, Modesto, California.

Fowler, Bridget

1997   *Pierre Bourdieu and Cultural Theory: Critical Investigations.* Sage Publications, London.

Fox-Genovese, Elizabeth

1988   *Within the Plantation Household: Black and White Women of the Old South.* University of North Carolina Press, Chapel Hill.

Franklin, Maria

1997   Out of Site, Out of Mind: The Archaeology of an Enslaved Virginia Household, 1740–1778. Unpublished Ph.D. diss., Department of Anthropology, University of California, Berkeley.

2000 Critical Reflections and Feminist Perspectives of Race and Gender in Historical Archaeology. Paper presented at the annual meeting of the American Anthropological Association, San Francisco.

2001a Black Feminist-Inspired Archaeology? *Journal of Social Archaeology* 1(1):108–125.

2001b The Archaeological Dimensions of Soul Food: Interpreting Race, Culture and Afro-Virginian Identity. In *Race and the Archaeology of Identity,* edited by C. Orser, pp. 88–107. University of Utah Press, Salt Lake City.

Franklin, Maria, and Garrett Fesler (editors)

1999 *Historical Archaeology, Identity Formation and the Interpretation of Ethnicity.* Dietz Press, Richmond.

Frazer, Bill

1999 Reconceptualizing Resistance in the Historical Archaeology of the British Isles: An Editorial. *International Journal of Historical Archaeology* 3(1):1–10.

Fredrickson, George M.

1971 *The Black Image in the White Mind: The Debate on Afro-American Character and Destiny, 1817–1914.* Harper and Row, New York.

French, Marilyn

1985 *Beyond Power: On Women, Men, and Morals.* Summit Books, New York.

Friedman, Jean E.

1985 *The Enclosed Garden: Women and Community in the Evangelical South, 1830–1900.* University of North Carolina Press, Chapel Hill.

Galindo, Mary J.

1999 An Ethnohistorical Approach to the Marriage, Inheritance, and Settlement Patterns Among Eighteenth-Century Spanish Colonial Settlers of Mier, Tamaulipas, Mexico. Unpublished Master's thesis, Department of Anthropology, University of Texas, Austin.

Garman, James C.

1995 "The New Goree Lot": An African American Cultural Landscape in Bristol, Rhode Island, 1805–1920. Paper presented at the annual meeting of the Society for Historical Archaeology, Washington, D.C.

Garner, John S.

1992 *The Company Town: Architecture and Society in the Early Industrial Age.* Oxford University Press, New York.

Gates, Henry Louis, Jr. (editor)

2002 *The Bondwoman's Narrative, a Novel by Hannah Crafts.* Warner Books, New York.

General Appraisal Company

1968 Appraisement of Soap Creek Pass Camp, July 27. Greater Yosemite Council, Boy Scouts of America, Modesto, California.

Genovese, Eugene D.

1974 *Roll Jordan Roll: The World the Slaves Made.* Random House, New York.

1979 *From Rebellion to Revolution: Afro-American Slave Revolts in the Making of the Modern World.* Louisiana State University Press, Baton Rouge.

George, Eugene

1975 *Historic Architecture of Texas: The Falcon Reservoir.* Texas Historical Commission, Austin.

278 / REFERENCES

Gero, Joan M., and Margaret W. Conkey (editors)
   1991   *Engendering Archaeology: Women and Prehistory.* Basil Blackwell, Oxford.
Gerth, Hans Heinrich, and Charles Wright Mills
   1946   *"From Max Weber": Essays in Sociology.* Oxford University Press, New York.
Gibb, James G., and Julia A. King
   1991   Gender, Activity Areas, and Homelots in the 17th Century Chesapeake Region. *Historical Archaeology* 25(4):109–131.
Giddens, Anthony
   1990   *The Consequences of Modernity.* Stanford University Press, Stanford.
Giddings, Paula
   1984   *When and Where I Enter: The Impact of Black Women on Race and Sex in America.* Bantam Books, New York.
Gilchrist, Roberta
   1999   *Gender and Archaeology: Contesting the Past.* Routledge Press, London.
Gillespie, Michele, and Catharine Clinton (editors)
   1998   *Taking Off the White Gloves: Southern Women and Women Historians.* University of Missouri Press, Columbia.
Gillespie, Susan D.
   2000   Opening Up the House: An Introduction. In *Beyond Kinship: Social and Material Reproduction in House Societies,* edited by R. A. Joyce and S. D. Gillespie, pp. 1–22. University of Pennsylvania Press, Philadelphia.
Gilman, Caroline H.
   1834   *Recollections of a Housekeeper.* Harper and Brothers, New York.
Gilmore, Glenda Elizabeth
   1996   *Gender and Jim Crow: Women and the Politics of White Supremacy in North Carolina, 1896–1920.* University of North Carolina Press, Chapel Hill.
Gilroy, Paul
   1993   *The Black Atlantic: Modernity and Double Consciousness.* Harvard University Press, Cambridge, Massachusetts.
Gitelman, Howard M.
   1988   *The Legacy of the Ludlow Massacre: A Chapter in American Industrial Relations.* University of Pennsylvania Press, Philadelphia.
Glassie, Henry
   1975   *Folk Housing in Middle Virginia: A Structural Analysis of Historic Artifacts.* University of Tennessee Press, Knoxville.
Goldfield, David R.
   1991   Black Life in Old South Cities. In *Before Freedom Came: African-American Life in the Antebellum South,* edited by E. D. C. Campbell, Jr. and K. S. Rice, pp. 123–154. The Museum of the Confederacy, Richmond, Virginia.
González, Esther P.
   1998   *Little Known History of the South Texas Hill Country.* Esther P. González, Rio Grande City, Texas.
Goody, Jack (editor)
   1971   *The Developmental Cycle of the Domestic Group.* Cambridge University Press, New York.

1972   The Evolution of the Family. In *Household and Family in Past Time,* edited by
        P. Laslett and R. Wall, pp. 103–124. Cambridge University Press, Cambridge.

Gordon, Edmund T.

1998   *Disparate Diasporas: Identity and Politics in an Afro Nicaraguan Community.* Uni-
        versity of Texas Press, Austin.

Gordon, Edmund T., and Mark Anderson

1999   The African Diaspora: Toward an Ethnography of Diasporic Identification. *Jour-
        nal of American Folklore* 112:282–296.

Gordon, Fon Louise

1995   From Slavery to Uncertain Freedom: Blacks in the Delta. In *The Arkansas Delta:
        Land of Paradox,* edited by J. Whayne and W. Gatewood, pp. 99–127. University of
        Arkansas Press, Fayetteville.

Gotanda, Neil

1995   A Critique of "our Constitution is Color-Blind." In *Critical Race Theory: The Key
        Writings that Formed the Movement,* edited by K. Crenshaw, N. Gotanda, G. Peller,
        and K. Thomas, pp. 257–275. The New Press, New York.

Graham, Joe S.

1994   *El Rancho in South Texas: Continuity and Change from 1750.* University of North
        Texas Press, Denton.

Gramsci, Antonio

1988   Prison Writings: Hegemony, Relations of Force, Historical Bloc and Passive Revo-
        lution, Caesarism, Fascism. In *An Antonio Gramsci Reader: Selected Writings, 1916–
        1935,* edited by D. Forgacs, 189–221, pp. 246–274. Schocken Books, New York.

Gray, Lewis Cecil

1941   *History of Agriculture in the Southern United States to 1860,* vol. 1. Peter Smith Press,
        New York.

Gray-White, Deborah

1999   *Ar'n't I a Woman? Female Slaves in the Plantation South.* W. W. Norton and Com-
        pany, New York.

Guendling, Randall L.

1992   *Archeological Assessment of the Sanders Block, Old Washington State Park, Hemp-
        stead County, Arkansas.* Arkansas Archeological Survey Sponsored Research Pro-
        gram. Submitted to Arkansas Department of Parks and Tourism, Little Rock.
        Copy on file, Arkansas Archeological Survey, Fayetteville.

Guendling, Randall L., Kathleen. H. Cande, Leslie C. Stewart-Abernathy, and Dawn Novak

2001   *The Archeological Investigation of the Sanders Kitchen, 1981 and 1992, Old Washing-
        ton Historical State Park.* Sponsored Research Program, Arkansas Archeological
        Survey. Grant No. 01–001, A AS Project No. 01–01. Submitted to the Arkansas
        Natural and Cultural Resources Council, Little Rock.

Guendling, Randall L., Kathleen H. Cande, Maria Tavaszi, Leslie C. Stewart-Abernathy, and
        Barbara Ruff

2002   *The Archeological Investigation of the Block Detached Kitchen: The 1982 and 1983
        Arkansas Archeological Society Digs, Old Washington Historic State Park.* Sponsored
        Research Program, Arkansas Archeological Survey. Grant No. 02–002, A AS Proj-

ect No. 02– 01. Submitted to the Arkansas Natural and Cultural Resources Council, Little Rock.

Guerra, Antonio M.

1953   *Mier en la Historia.* New Santander Press, Edinburg, Texas.

Gundaker, Grey

1998   *Signs of diaspora, diaspora of signs: literacies, creolization, and vernacular practice in African America.* Oxford University Press, New York.

Gutman, Herbert

1976a   *The Black Family in Slavery and Freedom, 1750–1925.* Vintage Books, New York

1976b   *Work, Culture, and Society in Industrializing America.* Vintage Books, New York.

Gyory, Andrew

1998   *Closing the Gate: Race, Politics and the Chinese Exclusion Act.* University of North Carolina Press, Chapel Hill.

Hale, Grace Elizabeth

1998   *Making Whiteness: The Culture of Segregation in the South, 1890–1940.* Vintage Press, New York.

Hall, Martin

2000   *Archaeology and the Modern World: Colonial Transcripts in South Africa and the Chesapeake.* Routledge Press, London.

Hammel, E. A., and Paul Laslett

1974   Comparing Household Structure Over Time and Between Cultures. *Comparative Studies in Society and History* 16:73–109.

Haney Lopez, Ian F.

1996   *White by Law: The Legal Construction of Race.* New York Univerity Press, New York.

Hardesty, Donald L.

1988   *The Archaeology of Mining and Miners: A View from the Silver State.* Special Publication 6. Society for Historical Archaeology, Ann Arbor, Michigan.

1994   Class, Gender Strategies, and Material Culture in the Mining West. In *Those of Little Note: Gender, Race, and Class in Historical Archaeology,* edited by E. M. Scott, pp. 129–145. University of Arizona Press, Tucson.

2002   Commentary: Interpreting Variability and Change in Western Work Camps. *Historical Archaeology* 36(3):94–98.

Hareven, Tamara K.

1982   *Family Time and Industrial Time: The Relationship Between The Family and Work in a New England Industrial Community.* Cambridge University Press, New York.

Hareven, Tamara K., and John Modell

1973   Urbanization and the Malleable Household: An Examination of Boarding and Lodging in American Families. *Journal of Marriage and the Family* 35:467–479.

Harris, Cheryl I.

1995   Whiteness as Property. In *Critical Race Theory: The Key Writings that Formed the Movement,* edited by K. Crenshaw, N. Gotanda, G. Peller, and K. Thomas, pp. 276–291. The New Press, New York.

Hart, G.

1992   Imagined Unities: Constructions of the Household in Economic Theory. In *Understanding Economic Processes,* edited by S. Ortiz and S. Lees, pp. 111–129. University Press of America, Lanham, Maryland.

Hartigan, John

1999   *Racial Situations: Class Predicaments of Whiteness in Detroit.* Princeton University Press, Princeton.

Hartle, Donald D., and Robert L. Stephenson

1951   *Archeological Excavations at the Falcon Reservoir, Starr County, Texas.* Manuscript on file, Texas Archeological Research Laboratory, The University of Texas at Austin.

Hartmann, Heidi I.

1974   Capitalism and Women's Work in the Home, 1900–1930. Unpublished Ph.D. diss., Department of History, Yale University, New Haven, Connecticut.

Hartsock, Nancy C. M.

1987   The Feminist Standpoint: Developing the Ground for a Specifically Feminist Historical Materialism. In *Feminism and Methodology,* edited by S. Harding, pp. 157–181. Indiana University Press, Bloomington.

Harvey, David

1990   *The Condition of Postmodernity.* Blackwell Press, Cambridge, U.K.

Hayden, Dolores

1981   *The Grand Domestic Revolution: A History of Feminist Designs for American Homes, Neighborhoods, and Cities.* MIT Press, Cambridge, Massachusetts.

Hazel, Michael V.

1982   The 'Shotgun': Home of Forgotten Dallasites. *Dallas County Heritage News,* fall issue.

Heath, Barbara J.

1999   *Hidden Lives: The Archaeology of Slave Life at Thomas Jefferson's Poplar Forest.* University Press of Virginia, Charlottesville.

Heath, Barbara J., and Amber Bennett

2000   "The little Spots allow'd them": The Archaeological Study of African-American Yards. *Historical Archaeology* 34(2):38–55.

Hendon, Julia A.

1996   Archaeological Approaches to the Organization of Domestic Labor: Household Practice and Domestic Relations. *Annual Review of Anthropology* 25:45–61.

Herman, Bernard L.

1999   Slave and Servant Housing in Charleston, 1770–1820. *Historical Archaeology* 33(3): 88–101.

Hermitage, The

1999   The Hermitage. Brochure, created by The Hermitage, Tennessee.

Hill, Mackie

1988   A Brief History of Middleburg Plantation. Unpublished manuscript. On file, Department of Anthropology, University of South Carolina, Columbia.

Hill, Patricia Evridge
    1996   *Dallas: The Making of a Modern City.* University of Texas Press, Austin.

Hinshaw, Jane
    1979   *The First Hermitage.* The Ladies' Hermitage Association. Hermitage, Tennessee.

Hodder, Ian
    1986   *Reading the Past: Current Approaches to Interpretation in Archaeology.* Cambridge University Press, Cambridge.

Holmes, Maxine, and Gerald D. Saxon (editors)
    1992   *The WPA Dallas Guide and History.* Dallas Public Library and University of North Texas Press, Dallas.

Honerkamp, Nicholas
    1988   Questions that Count in Historical Archaeology. *Historical Archaeology* 22:5–6.

hooks, bell
    1990   *Yearning: Race, Gender and Cultural Politics.* South End Press, Boston.

Hopkins, George M.
    1873   *Atlas of the City of Cambridge, Middlesex County, Massachusetts.* G. M. Hopkins & Co., Philadelphia.

Horkheimer, Max, and Theodor W. Adorno
    1944   [2001] *Dialectic of Enlightenment.* Continuum Press, New York.

Horne, Lee
    1982   The Household in Space: Dispersed Holdings in an Iranian Village. *American Behavioral Scientist* 25:677–685.

Houk, James
    2000   Telephone interview, March 7.

Howard, J. Myrick
    1987   Where the Action Is: Preservation and Local Government. In *The American Mosaic: Preserving a Nation's Heritage,* edited by R. E. Stipe and A. J. Lee, pp. 114–144. United States Committee, International Council on Monuments and Sites. Preservation Press, Washington, D.C.

Howard University and John Miller & Associates (HUJMA)
    1993   *Research Design for Archeological, Historical, and Bioanthropological Investigations of the African Burial Ground (Broadway Block), New York, N.Y.* Howard University, Washington, D.C., and John Milner Associates, Inc., New York.

Hudson, Larry E. (editor)
    1994   *Working Toward Freedom: Slave Economy in the American South.* University of Rochester Press, Rochester, New York.

Hugh-Jones, Stephen
    1995   Inside-Out and Back-to-Front: The Androgynous House in Northwest Amazonia. In *About the House: Lévi-Strauss and Beyond,* edited by J. Carsten and S. Hugh-Jones, pp. 226–252. Cambridge University Press, Cambridge.

Hughs, Arrie, Jr., and Deborah Fridia
    1990   North Dallas: Freedman's Town/Stringtown/Deep Ellum. In *African American Families and Settlements of Dallas: On the Inside Looking Out,* edited by M. McKnight, pp. 23–26. Black Dallas Remembered, Inc., Dallas.

Hungry Wolf, Adolf
  1978   *Rails in the Mother Lode.* Darwin Publications, Burbank, California.
Ignatiev, Noel
  1995   *How the Irish Became White.* Routledge Press, New York.
Jackson, Jack
  1986   *Los Mesteños: Spanish Ranching in Texas, 1721–1821.* Texas A&M University Press, College Station.
Jacobson, Matthew Frye
  1998   *Whiteness of a Different Color: European Immigrants and the Alchemy of Race.* Harvard University Press, Cambridge, Massachusetts.
James, William H.
  1988   *Exuma: The Loyalist Years, 1783–1834.* Privately published.
Jameson, Fredric
  1981   *The Political Unconscious: Narrative as a Socially Symbolic Act.* Cornell University Press, Ithaca, New York.
  1991   *Postmodernism or The Cultural Logic of Late Capitalism.* Duke University Press, Durham, North Carolina.
January, Alan F.
  1977   The South Carolina Association: An Agency for Race Control in Antebellum Charleston. *South Carolina Historical Magazine* 78(3):191–201.
Johnson, Howard
  1991   *The Bahamas in Slavery and Freedom.* Ian Randle Publishers, Ltd., Kingston, Jamaica.
  1996   *The Bahamas from Slavery to Servitude.* University Press of Florida, Gainesville.
Johnson, Randal
  1993   Pierre Bourdieu on Art, Literature, and Culture. In *The Field of Cultural Production: Essays on Art and Literature,* edited and introduced by R. Johnson, pp. 1–25. Columbia University Press, New York.
Johnson, Rossiter, and John H. Brown (editors)
  1904   *The Twentieth Century Biographical Dictionary of Notable Americans.* Plimpton Press, Boston.
Jones, H. Lawrencie
  1997   Personal communication, Chesapeake, Virginia.
Jones, Jacqueline
  1985   *Labor of Love, Labor of Sorrow: Black Women, Work, and the Family from Slavery to the Present.* Harper and Row, New York.
Jones, Oakah L.
  1996   *Los Paisanos: Spanish Settlers on the Frontier of New Spain.* University of Oklahoma Press, Norman.
Jones, Robbie
  2001   Personal communication, architectural historian, Hermitage, Tennessee.
  2002   *The First Hermitage Historic Structures Report.* On file at The Hermitage.
Jordan, Terry G.
  1978   *Texas Log Buildings: A Folk Architecture.* University of Texas Press, Austin.

Jordan, Winthrop D.

1974   *The White Man's Burden: Historical Origins of Racism in the United States.* Oxford University Press, Oxford.

Joseph, Joe W.

2000   Archaeology and the African-American Experience in the Urban South. In *Archaeology of Southern Urban Landscapes,* edited by A. L. Young, pp. 109–126. University of Alabama Press, Tuscaloosa.

Joyner, Charles

1984   *Down by the Riverside: A South Carolina Slave Community.* University of Illinois Press, Urbana.

Jurney, David H., and Susan L. Andrews (editors)

1994   *Archaeological Investigations at 41DL279, Site of the John F. Kennedy Exhibit, Dallas County Administration Building, Dallas, Texas.* Report prepared by Archaeology Research Program of Mercyhurst Archaeological Institute, Mercyhurst College, Erie, Penn., for Southern Methodist University and the Dallas County Historical Foundation.

Jurney, David H., Jackie McElhaney, and Donald Payton

1987   *Archaeological Resources Impact Analysis Technical Memorandum, P310 State Street Station and City Place Station.* Report submitted to Parsons, Brinckerhoff, Centec, Inc./DeLeuw, Cather & Company by Archaeology Research Program, Institute for the Study of Earth and Man, Southern Methodist University, Dallas.

Kaplan, Temma

1982   Female Consciousness and Collective Action: The Case of Barcelona, 1910–1918. *Signs: Journal of Women in Culture and Society* 7(3):545–566.

Karskens, Grace

1999   *Inside the Rocks: The Archaeology of a Neighbourhood.* Hale & Iremonger, Sydney.

Kearney, Belle

1903   The South and Woman Suffrage. *NAWSA Convention Minutes,* New Orleans, March 15–25.

Kimbal, Justin F.

1927   *Our City—Dallas: A Community Civics.* Kessler Plan Association of Dallas. Dallas, Texas.

Kimmel, Richard H.

1993   Notes on the Cultural Origins and Functions of Sub-Floor Pits. *Historical Archaeology* 27(3):102–113.

Knapp, A. Bernard, and Wendy Ashmore

1999   Archaeological Landscapes: Constructed, Conceptualized, Ideational. In *Archaeologies of Landscape: Contemporary Perspectives,* edited by W. Ashmore and A. B. Knapp, pp. 1–32. Blackwell Publishers, London.

Kolmar, Wendy, and Frances Bartkowski (editors)

2000   *Feminist Theory: A Reader.* Mayfield, London.

Kramer, Carol

1982   Ethnographic Households and Archaeological Interpretation: A Case from Iranian Kurdistan. *American Behavioral Scientist* 25(6):663–675.

Kreiger, Alex D., and Jack T. Hughes

1950 *Archaeological Salvage in Falcon Reservoir Area: Progress Report No. 1*. National Park Service and the University of Texas at Austin. Manuscript on file, Center for American History, The University of Texas at Austin.

Kryder-Reid, Elizabeth

1994 "With Manly Courage": Reading the Construction of Gender in a Nineteenth-Century Religious Community. In *Those of Little Note: Gender, Race and Class in Historical Archaeology*, edited by E. M. Scott, pp. 97–114. University of Arizona Press, Tucson.

Lack, Paul D.

1982 An Urban Slave Community: Little Rock, 1831–1862. *Arkansas Historical Quarterly* 41(3):258–287.

Landon, David B.

1989 Domestic Ideology and the Economics of Boardinghouse Keeping. In *Interdisciplinary Investigations of the Boott Mills, Lowell, Massachusetts*, vol. III, *The Boarding House System as a Way of Life*, edited by M. C. Beaudry and S. A. Mrozowski, pp. 37–47. Cultural Resources Management Study No. 21. Division of Cultural Resources, National Park Service, North Atlantic Regional Office, Boston.

Laslett, Peter

1972 Introduction: The History of the Family. In *Household and Family in Past Time*, edited by P. Laslett and R. Wall, pp. 1–89. Cambridge University Press, Cambridge.

Laslett, Peter, and Richard Wall (editors)

1972 *Household and Family in Past Time*. Cambridge University Press, Cambridge.

Laurence, R., and A. Wallace-Hadrill (editors)

1997 Domestic Space in the Roman World: Pompeii and Beyond. *Journal of Roman Archaeology Supplement* 22. Portsmouth, Rhode Island.

Lawrence, Susan

1999 Towards a Feminist Archaeology of Households: Gender and Household Structure on the Australian Goldfields. In *The Archaeology of Household Activities*, edited by P. M. Allison, 121–141. Routledge, London.

Leacock, Elanor B.

1983 Interpreting the Origins of Gender Inequality: Conceptual and Historical Problems. *Dialectical Anthropology* 7(4):263–285.

Lebsock, Suzanne

1984 *The Free Women of Petersburg: Status and Culture in a Southern Town, 1784–1860*. W. W. Norton, New York.

Lees, William B.

1980 *Limerick, Old and In the Way: Archaeological Investigations at Limerick Plantation*. Anthropological Studies no. 5. Occasional Papers of the Institute of Archaeology and Anthropology. University of South Carolina, Columbia.

Lefebvre, Henri

1971 *The Production of Space*. Blackwell Publishers, London.

LeMaster, Carolyn G.

1994 *A Corner of the Tapestry: A History of the Jewish Experience in Arkansas, 1820–1990s*. University of Arkansas Press, Fayetteville.

Leone, Mark P.

1984   Interpreting Ideology in Historical Archaeology: Using the Rules of Perspective in the William Paca Garden in Annapolis, Maryland. In *Ideology, Power, and Prehistory,* edited by D. Miller and C. Tilley, pp. 25–35. Cambridge University Press, Cambridge.

1995   Historical Archaeology of Capitalism. *American Anthropologist* 97:2.

Leone, Mark P., and Barbara Little

1993   Artifacts as Expressions of Society and Culture: Subversive Genealogy and the Value of History. In *History from Things: Essays on Material Culture,* edited by S. Lubar and W. D. Kingery, pp. 160–181. Smithsonian Institution Press, Washington, D.C.

Lerner, Gerda

1993   *The Creation of Feminist Consciousness: from the Middle Ages to Eighteen-seventy.* Oxford University Press, Oxford.

Lévi-Strauss, Claude

1982   *The Way of the Masks.* Translated by S. Modelski. University of Washington Press, Seattle.

1987   *Anthropology and Myth: Lectures, 1951–1982.* Translated by R. Willis. Blackwell, Oxford.

Levinson, Sanford

1998   *Written in Stone: Public Monuments in Changing Societies.* Duke University Press, Durham, North Carolina.

Limón, José E.

1998   *American Encounters: Greater Mexico, the United States and the Erotics of Culture.* Beacon Press, Boston.

Littlefield, Daniel

1981   *Rice and Slaves: Ethnicity and the Slave Trade in Colonial South Carolina.* University of Illinois Press, Urbana.

Lockridge, Kenneth

1994   *On the Sources of Patriarchal Rage: The Commonplace Books of William Byrd and Thomas Jefferson.* New York University Press, New York.

Loewen, James W.

1999   *Lies Across America: What Our Historic Sites Get Wrong.* Touchstone, New York.

Lofton, John

1964   *Insurrection in South Carolina: The Turbulent World of Denmark Vesey.* Antioch Press, Yellow Springs, Ohio.

Long, Priscilla

1991   *Where the Sun Never Shines: A History of America's Bloody Coal Industry.* Paragon House, New York.

1996   The 1913–1914 Colorado Fuel and Iron Strike, with Reflections on the Causes of Coal-Strike Violence. In *United Mine Workers of America: A Model of Industrial Solidarity?* edited by J. S. M. Lasett, pp. 345–369. Pennsylvania State University Press, University Park.

Lucas, Jonathan III

   1822   *General Order Citing Regulations for the Conduct of Troops during an Insurrec-
            tion*. Governor's Message Enclosure. General Assembly Papers, no. STo828. South
            Carolina Department of Archives and History, Columbia.

Lyons, Julie

   1992   Brown Jesus (and other tales from the projects): Fifty Years at Roseland Homes.
            Dallas Observer (August 6), 18–25.

Malan, Antonia, and Elizabeth van Heyningen

   2001   Twice Removed: Horstley Street in Cape Town's District Six, 1865–1982. In *The
            Archaeology of Urban Landscapes: Explorations in Slumland*, edited by A. Mayne
            and T. Murray, pp. 39–56. Cambridge University Press, Cambridge.

Malone, Ann

   1992   *Sweet Chariot: Slave Family and Household Structure in Nineteenth-Century Loui-
            siana*. University of North Carolina Press, Chapel Hill.

Malone, Dumas (editor)

   1934   *Dictionary of American Biography*, s.v. Charles Peirce. Scribner's Sons, New York.

Maniery, Mary L.

   2002   Health, Sanitation, and Diet in a Twentieth-Century Dam Construction Camp: A
            View from Butt Valley, California. *Historical Archaeology* 36(3):69–84.

Margolis, Eric

   1985   Western Coal Mining as a Way of Life: An Oral History of the Colorado Coal
            Miners to 1914. *Journal of the West* 24:1–115.

Massey, Doreen

   1994   *Space, Place and Gender*. University of Minnesota Press, Minneapolis.

Mayne, Alan, and Tim Murray (editors)

   2001   *The Archaeology of Urban Landscapes: Explorations in Slum Land*. Cambridge Uni-
            versity Press, New York

McCarthy, Felicia

   2002   Poor vs. Poorer: Plans for an Expanded Roseland Homes Spark a Protest in a
            Working Class Neighborhood Near Cityplace. *Dallas Observer*, February 24.

McGovern, George S., and Leonard F. Guttridge

   1972   *The Great Coalfield War*. Houghton Mifflin Co., Boston.

McGuire, Randall H.

   1992   *A Marxist Archaeology*. Plenum Press, New York.

McGuire, Randall H., and Robert Paynter (editors)

   1991   *The Archaeology of Inequality*. Blackwell Publishers, Oxford.

McGuire, Randall H., and Paul Reckner

   2002   The Unromantic West: Labor, Capital, and Struggle. *Historical Archaeology* 36(3):
            44–58.

McKee, Larry

   1992a   *Summary Report on the 1991 Field Quarter Excavation*. The Ladies' Hermitage As-
            sociation, Hermitage, Tennessee.

   1992b   Reinterpreting the Construction History of the Service Area of the Hermitage

Mansion. In *Text-Aided Archaeology,* edited by B. J. Little, pp. 161–176. CRC Press, Boca Raton, Florida.

1995   The Earth Is Their Witness. *Sciences* 35(2):36–41.

1999   Food Supply and Plantation Social Order: An Archaeological Perspective. In *"I, Too, Am America": Archaeological Studies of African-American Life,* edited by T. Singleton, pp. 218–239. University Press of Virginia, Charlottesville.

McKee, Larry, and Jillian Galle

2000   *Summary Report on the First Hermitage Excavation.* The Ladies' Hermitage Association, Hermitage, Tennessee.

McKnight, Mamie (editor)

1990   *African American Families and Settlements of Dallas: On the Inside Looking Out.* Black Dallas Remembered, Inc., Dallas.

McLaurin, Melton A.

1987   *Separate Pasts: Growing Up White in the Segregated South.* University of Georgia Press, Athens.

McMurry, Sally A.

1988   *Families and Farmhouses in Nineteenth Century America: Vernacular Design and Social Change.* Oxford University Press, New York.

Meadows, Karen

1999   The Appetites of Households in Early Roman Britain. In *The Archaeology of Household Activities,* edited by P. M. Allison, pp. 101–120. Routledge, London.

Medearis, Mary (editor)

1976   *Washington, Arkansas: History on the Southwest Trail.* Etter Printing Co., Hope, Arkansas.

Mier Church Baptism Records

1989   *Mier church baptism records, 1767–1880.* Vols. 1–4. Spanish American Genealogical Society, Corpus Christi, Texas.

Mier Church Death Records

1989   *Mier church death records, 1767–1903.* Vols. 1, 2. Spanish American Genealogical Society, Corpus Christi, Texas.

Mier Church Marriage Records

1989   *Mier church marriage records, 1767–1925.* Vols. 1, 2. Spanish American Genealogical Society, Corpus Christi, Texas.

Miller, George L.

1991   A Revised Set of CC Index Values for Classification and Economic Scaling of English Ceramics from 1787 to 1880. *Historical Archaeology* 25:1–25.

Miller, Randall M. (editor)

1990   *"Dear Master"—Letters of a Slave Family.* University of Georgia Press, Athens.

Millett, Kate

1970   *Sexual Politics.* Doubleday, Garden City, New York.

Mintz, Sidney W.

1974   *Caribbean Transformations.* Aldine Publishing, Chicago.

Mintz, Steven, and Susan Kellogg

1988   *Domestic Revolutions: A Social History of American Family Life.* The Free Press, New York.

Mitararchi, Sylvia W.

1978   Melusina Far Peirce: The Making of a Feminist. Unpublished manuscript, Rad-
        cliffe Institute Working Paper, Radcliffe College, Cambridge, Massachusetts.

Mitchell, Don

1996   *The Lie of the Land: Migrant Workers and the California Landscape.* University of
        Minnesota Press, Minneapolis.

2000   *Cultural Geography: A Critique.* Blackwell Publishers, Oxford.

Momyer, Frank

1990   Video interview by Jim Smith. Greater Yosemite Council, Boy Scouts of America,
        Modesto, California.

Monday, Jane C., and Betty B. Colley

1997   *Voices from the Wild Horse Desert: The Vaquero Families of the King and Kenedy
        Ranches.* University of Texas Press, Austin.

Montejano, David

1987   *Anglos and Mexicans in the Making of Texas, 1836–1986.* University of Texas Press,
        Austin.

Montgomery, Donald R.

1980   Simon T. Sanders, Public Servant. *Arkansas Historical Quarterly* 39(2):159–168.

1981a   A History of Block 32 in Washington, Arkansas. Old Washington Historical Re-
        search Report on file, Old Washington Historical State Park, Washington, Arkan-
        sas. Copy on file, Arkansas Archeological Survey, Russellville.

1981b   A Chronology of Events in the History of Washington, Arkansas. Old Washing-
        ton Historical Research Report on file, Old Washington Historical State Park,
        Washington, Arkansas. Copy on file, Arkansas Archeological Survey, Russellville.

Moore, Henrietta L.

1988   *Feminism and Anthropology.* University of Minnesota Press, Minneapolis.

1994   *A Passion for Difference.* Indiana University Press, Bloomington.

1996   *Space, Text and Gender.* Guilford Press, New York.

Mrozowski, Stephen A.

1984   Prospects and Perspectives on an Archaeology of the Household. *Man in the
        Northeast* 27:31–49.

Mrozowski, Stephen A., Grace H. Ziesing, and Mary C. Beaudry

1986   *Living on the Boott: Historical Archaeology at the Boott Mills Boardinghouses in
        Lowell, Massachusetts.* University of Massachusetts Press, Amherst.

Mullins, Paul R.

1999a   *Race and Affluence: An Archaeology of African America and Consumer Culture.*
        Klewer Academic Press, New York.

1999b   Race and the Genteel Consumer: Class and African American Consumption,
        1850–1930. *Historical Archaeology* 33(1):22–38.

1999c   "A Bold and Gorgeous Front": The Contradictions of African America and Con-
        sumer Culture. In *Historical Archaeologies of Capitalism,* edited by M. Leone and
        P. Potter, pp. 169–193. Klewer Academic Press, New York.

2001   Racializing the Parlor: Race and Victorian Bric-a-Brac Consumption. In *Race and
        the Archaeology of Identity,* edited by C. Orser, pp. 158–176. University of Utah
        Press, Salt Lake City.

Myres, Sandra L.

1969   *The Ranch in Spanish Texas, 1691–1800.* Texas Western Press, El Paso.

Nelson, Sarah M.

1997   *Gender in Archaeology: Analyzing Power and Prestige.* AltaMira, Walnut Creek, California.

Netting, Robert McC.

1982   Some Home Truths on Household Size and Wealth. *American Behavioral Scientist* 25:641–661.

1993   *Smallholders, Households: Farm Families and the Ecology of Intensive, Sustainable Agriculture.* Stanford University Press, Stanford, California.

Netting, Richard, and Richard Wilk

1984   Households: Changing Forms and Functions. In *Households: Comparative and Historical Studies of the Domestic Group,* edited by R. Netting, R. Wilk, and E. Arnould. University of California Press, Berkeley.

Netting, Robert M., Richard R. Wilk, and Eric J. Arnould (editors)

1984   *Households: Comparative and Historical Studies of the Domestic Group.* University of California Press, Berkeley.

Nevett, Lisa C.

1999   *House and Society in the Ancient Greek World.* Cambridge University Press, Cambridge.

Nixon, Lucia

1994   Gender Bias in Archaeology. In *Women in Ancient Societies: An Illusion of the Night,* edited by S. Fischler, L. Archer, and M. Wyke, pp. 1–23. Routledge Press, New York.

Noel-Hume, Ivor

1978   *A Guide to Artifacts of Colonial America.* 2nd ed. Alfred A. Knopf Press, New York.

Norton, Mary Beth

1996   *Founding Mothers & Fathers: Gendered Power and the Forming of American Society.* Alfred A. Knopf, New York.

Novak, Dawn

2001   *Urban Farmstead Meat Utilization at Old Washington: The Sanders Kitchen.* Paper presented at the annual meeting of the Arkansas Archeological Society, Hot Springs.

O'Brien, John T.

1978   Factory, Church, and Community: Blacks in Antebellum Richmond. *Journal of Southern History* 44:509–536.

O'Brien, Michael J.

1984   *Grassland, Forest, and Historical Settlement: An Analysis of Dynamics in Northeast Missouri.* University of Nebraska Press, Lincoln.

O'Neal, Mary T.

1971   *Those Damn Foreigners.* Minerva Books, Hollywood, California.

O'Neill, Colleen

1993   Domesticity Deployed: Gender, Race, and the Construction of Class Struggle in the Bisbee Deportation. *Labor History* 34 (Spring–Summer):256–273.

Orser, Charles E.

1988   *The Material Basis of the Postbellum Tenant Plantation: Historical Archaeology in the South Carolina Piedmont.* University of Georgia Press, Athens.

1996   *A Historical Archaeology of the Modern World.* Plenum Press, New York.

1998   The Challenge of Race to American Historical Archaeology. *American Anthropologist* 100:661–668.

2001   (editor) *Race and the Archaeology of Identity.* University of Utah Press, Salt Lake City.

Orser, Charles E., and Brian M. Fagan

1994   *Historical Archaeology.* HarperCollins College Publishers, New York.

Otto, John S.

1984   *Cannon's Point Plantation, 1794–1860: Living Conditions and Status Patterns in the Old South.* Academic Press, New York.

Pader, Ellen J.

1993   Spatiality and Social Change: Domestic Space in Mexico and the United States. *American Ethnologist* 20(1):114–137.

Pan, Denise

1994   Peace and Conflict in an Industrial Family: Company Identity and Class Consciousness in a Multi-Ethnic Community, Colorado Fuel and Iron's Cameron and Walsen Coal Camps, 1913–1928. Unpublished Master's thesis, Department of History, University of Colorado, Denver.

Papanikolas, Zeese

1982   *Buried Unsung: Louis Tikas and the Ludlow Massacre.* University of Nebraska Press, Lincoln.

Parrington, Michael, and Daniel G. Roberts

1990   Demographic, Cultural, and Bioanthropological Aspects of a Nineteenth-Century Free Black Population in Philadelphia, Pennsylvania. In *A Life in Science: Papers in Honor of J. Lawrence Angel,* edited by J. E. Buikstra, pp. 138–170. Center for American Archaeology, Campsville, Illinois.

Parrington, Michael, and Janet Wideman

1986   Acculturation in an Urban Setting: The Archaeology of a Black Philadelphia Cemetery. *Expedition* 28(1):55–62.

Parton, James

1850   Remembering the Hermitage. On File at The Hermitage, Hermitage, Tennessee.

Patten, M. Drake

1997   Cheers of Protest? The Public, the *Post* and the Parable of Learning. *Historical Archaeology* 31(3):132–139.

Paynter, Robert, and Randall H. McGuire

1991   The Archaeology of Inequality: Material Culture, Domination and Resistance. In *The Archaeology of Inequality,* edited by R. Paynter and R. H. McGuire, pp. 1–27. Blackwell Publishers, Oxford.

Peirce, Melusina F.

1864   *The World.* July 11. New York.

1868   Cooperative Housekeeping II. *Atlantic Monthly* 22 (December).

1869a   Cooperative Housekeeping IV. *Atlantic Monthly* 23 (136) (February).

1869b   *The World.* July 10. New York.

1872   *Report of the Cambridge Co-operative Housekeeping Society.* Press of John Wilson and Son, Cambridge, Massachusetts.

1884   *Cooperative Housekeeping: How Not to Do It and How to Do It, a Study in Sociology.* James R. Osgood, Boston.

1918   *New York, a Symphonic Study.* Neale Publishing Co., New York.

Peirce, Sarah Mills

1869   Letter to Benjamin Mills Peirce, Septemeber 11. Charles S. Peirce Papers, Houghton Library, Harvard University, Cambridge, Massachusetts.

Perttula, Timothy K., James B. Boyd, Sergio A. Iruegas, and Bo Nelson

1999   Archeological Investigations at Area I, the Cabaseño Ranch (41ZP79), Falcon Reservoir. In *Bulletin of the Texas Archaeological Society,* vol. 70/1999, edited by T. K. Perttula and L. W. Ellis, pp. 327–338. Texas Archaeological Society.

Peter, Duane

2000   The Freedman's Cemetery Project. In *Freedman's Cemetery: A Legacy of a Pioneer Black Community in Dallas, Texas,* edited by D. E. Peter, M. Prior, M. M. Green, and V. G. Clow, pp. 1–19. Geo-Marine, Inc., Plano, Texas, Special Publication No. 6. Texas Department of Transportation, Environmental Affairs Division, Report No. 21. Austin.

Peter, Duane E., Marsha Prior, Melissa M. Green, and Victoria G. Clow (editors)

2000   *Freedman's Cemetery: A Legacy of a Pioneer Black Community in Dallas, Texas.* Geo-Marine, Inc., Plano, Texas, Special Publication No. 6. Texas Department of Transportation, Environmental Affairs Division, Archeology Studies Program, Report No. 21. Austin.

Pitman, William, Leslie McFaden, and George Miller

1987   Laboratory Manual of the Office of Archaeological Excavation. Department of Archaeology, Colonial Williamsburg Foundation, Williamsburg, Virginia.

Pland, Richard

2000   Telephone interview, February 20.

Powers, Bernard E.

1994   *Black Charlestonians: A Social History, 1822–1885.* University of Arkansas Press, Fayetteville.

Poyo, Gerald E.

1996   *Tejano Journey, 1770–1850.* University of Texas Press, Austin.

Praetzellis, Adrian, and Mary Praetzellis

1992a   Faces and Facades: Victorian Ideology in Early Sacramento. In *The Art and Mystery of Historical Archaeology: Essays in Honor of James Deetz,* edited by A. E. Yentsch and M. Beaudry, pp. 75–99. CRC Press, Ann Arbor, Michigan.

1992b   *"We Were There, Too": Archaeology of an African-American Family in Sacramento, California.* Cultural Resources Facility, Anthropological Studies Center. Sonoma State University, Rohnert Park, California.

2000   Mangling Symbols of Gentility in the Wild West. *American Anthropologist* 103(3): 645–654.

Preston, Samuel H., and Michael R. Haines
  1991   *Fatal Years: Child Mortality in Late Nineteenth-Century America.* Princeton University Press, Princeton.
Prince, Robert
  1993   *A History of Dallas: From a Different Perspective.* Nortex Press, n.p.
Prior, Marsha, and Terry Anne Schulte
  2000a   Early Presence of African Americans in Dallas and Dallas County. In *Freedman's Cemetery: A Legacy of A Pioneer Black Community in Dallas, Texas,* edited by D. Peter, M. Prior, M. Green, and V. G. Clow, pp. 57–68. Geo-Marine, Inc., Plano, Texas, Special Publication No. 6. Texas Department of Transportation, Environmental Affairs Division, Archeology Studies Program, Report No. 21. Austin.
  2000b   Freedman's Town/North Dallas: The Convergence and Development of an African American Community. In *Freedman's Cemetery: A Legacy of A Pioneer Black Community in Dallas, Texas,* edited by D. Peter, M. Prior, M. Green, and V. G. Clow, 69–116. Geo-Marine, Inc., Plano, Texas, Special Publication No. 6. Texas Department of Transportation, Environmental Affairs Division, Archeology Studies Program, Report No. 21. Austin.
Pulsipher, Lydia
  1990   They Have Saturdays and Sundays to Feed Themselves: Slave Gardens in the Caribbean. *Expedition* 32(2):24–33.
  1993a   Changing Roles in the Life Cycles of Women in Traditional West Indian Houseyards. In *Women and Change in the Caribbean: A Pan-Caribbean Perspective,* edited by J. Momsen, pp. 50–64. Ian Randle, London.
  1993b   He Won't Let She Stretch She Foot: Gender Relations in Traditional West Indian Houseyards. In *Full Circles: Geographies of Women over the Life Course,* edited by C. Katz and J. Monk, pp. 107–121. Routledge, London.
  1994   The Landscapes and Ideational Roles of Caribbean Slave Gardens. In *The Archaeology of Garden and Field,* edited by N. F. Miller and K. L. Gleason, pp. 202–221. University of Pennsylvania Press, Philadelphia.
Rabb, Theodore K., and Robert I. Rotberg (editors)
  1971   *The Family in History: Interdisciplinary Essays.* Harper & Row, New York.
Rabinow, Paul, and William M. Sullivan
  1987   *Interpretive Social Science: A Second Look.* University of California Press, Berkeley.
Rapoport, Amos
  1969   *House Form and Culture.* Prentice-Hall, Inc., Englewood Cliffs, New Jersey.
Rathje, William L., and Cheryl K. Ritenbaugh (editors)
  1984   Household Refuse Analysis: Theory, Method, and Applications in Social Science. *American Behavioral Scientist* 28(1) (Special Issue).
Remini, Robert
  1977   *Andrew Jackson,* vol. 1, *The Course of American Empire, 1767–1821.* Johns Hopkins University Press, Baltimore.
Richard, Maureen
  2003   Washing Household Linens and Linen Clothing in 1627 Plymouth. In *Women's Work in New England, 1620–1920,* edited by P. Benes, pp. 10–21. The Dublin Semi-

nar for New England Folklife Annual Proceedings 2001, vol. 26. Boston University Scholarly Publications, Boston.

Richter, William L.
1969   Slavery in Baton Rouge, 1820–1860. *Louisiana History* 10 (Spring):125–145.

Roberts, Diane
1994   *The Myth of Aunt Jemima: Representations of Race and Region.* Routledge, London.

Robinson, W. B.
1979   Colonial Ranch Architecture in the Spanish-Mexican Tradition. *Southwestern Historical Quarterly* 83(2):123–150.

Roediger, David R.
1991   *The Wages of Whiteness: Race and the Making of the American Working Class.* Verso Press, London.
1994   *Towards the Abolition of Whiteness: Essays on Race, Politics and Working Class History.* Verso Press, London.

Rosenzweig, Roy
1983   *Eight Hours for What We Will: Workers and Leisure in an Industrial City, 1870–1920.* Cambridge University Press, Cambridge.

Rossi, Alice S. (editor)
1973   *The Feminist Papers.* Bantam, New York.

Royston, Mrs. C. E.
1912   *History of Hempstead County, Arkansas during the War Between the States.* Typescript on file, Southwest Arkansas Regional Archives, Washington, Arkansas.

Ruff, Barbara L.
1985   *Analysis of the Vertebrate Fauna from Feature 14 (3HE236–19), Washington, Arkansas.* Report submitted to the Arkansas Archeological Survey, Fayetteville. Copies available from the Arkansas Archeological Survey, Fayetteville.

Ryan, Mary P.
1982   *The Empire of the Mother: American Writing about Domesticity, 1830–1860.* Haworth Press, New York.
1990   *Women in Public: Between Banners and Ballots, 1825–1880.* Johns Hopkins University Press, Baltimore.

St. John's Parish Vestry
1753–   Vestry Minutes for St. John's Parish, Berkeley County. South Carolina Archives
1853   and History Center, Columbia. Microfilm reel PR4.

St. Thomas and St. Dennis Parish Census Records
1820–   Census (Microfilm). South Carolina Department of Archives and History, Co-
1840   lumbia.

Salley, A. S.
1936   Some Early Simons Records. *South Carolina Historical Magazine* 37(1):142–150.

Samford, Patricia
1996   Archaeology of African-American Slavery and Material Culture. *William and Mary Quarterly* 53(1):87–114.

Sanborn Fire Insurance Company Maps
1899–   Microfilm. On file, Dallas Public Library, Dallas, Texas.
1941

Sánchez, Mario L.

1994   *A Shared Experience: The History, Architecture and Historic Designations of the Lower Rio Grande Heritage Corridor.* Texas Historical Commission, Austin.

Sánchez-Eppler, Karen

1993   *Touching Liberty: Abolition, Feminism and the Politics of the Body.* University of California Press, Berkeley.

Sanford, Douglas W.

1999   Landscape, Change, and Community at Stratford Hall Plantation: An Archaeological and Cultural Perspective. *Quarterly Bulletin of the Archeological Society of Virginia* 54(1):2–19.

Saunders, Gail

1983   *Bahamian Loyalists and Their Slaves.* Macmillan, London.

Saunders, Hartley C.

1991   *The Other Bahamas.* Bodab Publishers, Nassau.

Savage, Kirk

1997   *Standing Soldiers, Kneeling Slaves: Race, War, and Monument in Nineteenth-Century America.* Princeton University Press, Princeton.

Saxton, Alexander

1971   *The Indispensable Enemy: Labor and the Anti-Chinese Movement in California.* University of California Press, Berkeley.

Schiffer, Michael B.

1987   *Formation Processes of the Archaeological Record.* University of Utah Press, Salt Lake City.

Schofield, Ann

1983   Rebel Girls and Union Maids: The Woman Question in the Journals of the AFL and IWW, 1905–1920. *Feminist Studies* 9(2):335–358.

Schulte, Terry Anne, and Marsha Prior

2000   Epilogue. In *Freedman's Cemetery: A Legacy of a Pioneer Black Community in Dallas, Texas,* edited by D. Peter, M. Prior, M. Green, and V. G. Clow, pp. 191–196. Geo-Marine, Inc., Plano, Texas, Special Publication No. 6. Texas Department of Transportation, Environmental Affairs Division, Archeology Studies Program, Report No. 21. Austin.

Schuyler, Robert L. (editor)

1982   Urban Archaeology in America. *North American Archaeologist* 3(3).

Schwartz-Cowan, Ruth

1983   *More Work for Mother: The Ironies of Household Technology from the Open Hearth to the Microwave.* Basic Books, Inc., New York.

1992   The "Industrial Revolution" in the Home: Household Technology and Social Change in the 20th Century. In *Domestic Ideology and Domestic Work,* edited by N. Cott, pp. 375–397. History of Women in the United States: Historical Articles on Women's Lives and Activities, vol. 4. K. G. Saur, New York.

Scott, Elizabeth M.

1994   Through the Lens of Gender: Archaeology, Inequality and Those "of Little Note." In *Those of Little Note: Gender, Race and Class in Historical Archaeology,* edited by E. M. Scott, pp. 1–24. University of Arizona Press, Tucson.

1997   "A Little Gravy in the Dish and Onions in a Tea Cup": What Cookbooks Reveal About Material Culture. *International Journal of Historical Archaeology* 1(2):131–155.

Scott, Francis J.

1937   *Historical Heritage of the Lower Rio Grande: An Historical Record of Spanish Exploration, Subjugation and Colonization of the Lower Rio Grande Valley and the Activities of José Escandón, Count of Sierra Gorda, Together with the Development of Towns and Ranches Under Spanish, Mexican and Texas Sovereignties, 1747–1848.* Naylor Company, San Antonio.

Scott, James

1990   *Dominance and the Arts of Resistance.* Yale University Press, New Haven.

Sebesta, Edward H.

2002   web site: http://www.templeofdemocracy.com/index.htm, accessed October 26, 2003.

Shackel, Paul A.

1996   *Culture Change and the New Technology: An Archaeology of the Early American Industrial Era.* Plenum Press, New York.

2001a   (editor) *Myth, Memory and the Making of the American Landscape.* University Press of Florida, Gainesville.

2001b   Introduction: The Making of the American Landscape. In *Myth, Memory and the Making of the American Landscape,* edited by P. A. Shackel, pp. 1–16. University Press of Florida, Gainesville.

Shanks, Michael, and Christopher Tilley

1992   *Reconstructing Archaeology: Theory and Practice.* Routledge Press, London.

Silliman, Stephen Walter

2000   Colonial Worlds, Indigenous Practices: The Archaeology of Labor on a 19th Century California Rancho. Unpublished Ph.D. diss., Department of Anthropology, University of California, Berkeley.

Simmons, David, Myron O. Stachiw, and John Worrell

1993   The Total Site Matrix: Strata and Structure at the Bixby House. In *Practices of Archaeological Stratigraphy,* edited by E. C. Harris, M. R. Brown III, and G. J. Brown, 181–197. Academic Press, New York.

Simons, Robert B.

1954   *Thomas Grange Simons III: his forebears and relations.* R. L. Bryan Co., Columbia, South Carolina.

Singleton, Theresa

1990   The Archaeology of the Plantation South: A Review of Approaches and Goals. *Historical Archaeology* 24(4):70–77.

1999a   An Introduction to African-American Archaeology. In *"I, Too, Am America": Archaeological Studies of African-American Life,* edited by T. Singleton, pp. 1–17. University Press of Virginia, Charlottesville.

1999b   (editor) *"I, Too, Am America": Archaeological Studies of African-American Life.* University Press of Virginia, Charlottesville.

Singleton, Theresa, and Mark Bograd

2000   Breaking Typological Barriers: Looking for the Colono in Colonoware. In *Lines*

That Divide: Historical Archaeologies of Race, Class, and Gender, edited by J. Delle, S. Mrozowski, and R. Paynter, pp. 3–21. University of Tennessee Press, Knoxville.

Sirigo, John

1936   *The Official Guide Book, Texas Centennial Exposition.* Centennial Central Exposition, Dallas.

Smith, Paul

1978   Domestic Labor and Marx's Theory of Value. In *Feminism and Materialism,* edited by A. Kuhn and A. Wolpe, pp. 109–125. Routledge Press, London.

Smith, Samuel

1976   *An Archaeological and Historical Assessment of the First Hermitage.* Division of Archaeology, Tennessee Department of Conservation, Nashville.

Smith, Thomas H.

1986   Old City Park's Mission: Feeding the Human Spirit. (Dallas County) *Heritage News, a Journal Dedicated to the History of North Central Texas.* 11(4):21–24.

Snow, Pamela J.

2003   Increase and Vantage: Women, Cows, and the Agricultural Economy of Colonial New England. In *Women's Work in New England, 1620–1920,* edited by P. Benes, pp. 22–39. The Dublin Seminar for New England Folklife Annual Proceedings 2001, vol. 26. Boston University Scholarly Publications, Boston.

Sobel, Mechal

1987   *The World They Made Together: Black and White Values in Eighteenth Century Virginia.* Princeton University Press, Princeton, New Jersey.

Soja, Edward W.

1989   *Postmodern Geographies: The Reassertion of Space in Critical Social Theory.* Verso Press, London.

South, Stanley

1977   *Methods and Theory in Historical Archaeology.* Academic Press, New York.

1988   Whither Pattern? *Historical Archaeology* 22(1):25–28.

Spencer-Wood, Suzanne

1984   Status, Occupation and Ceramic Indices: A 19th Century Comparative Analysis. *Man in the Northeast* 28:87–110.

1987a   (editor) *Consumer Choice in Historical Archaeology.* Plenum Press, New York.

1987b   A Survey of Domestic Reform Movement Sites in Boston and Cambridge, c. 1865–1905. *Historical Archaeology* 21(2):7–36.

1987c   Introduction. In *Consumer Choice in Historical Archaeology,* edited by S. M. Spencer-Wood, pp. 1–24. Plenum Press, New York.

1991a   Towards a Feminist Historical Archaeology of the Construction of Gender. In *The Archaeology of Gender: Proceedings of the 22nd [1989] Chacmool Conference,* edited by D. Walde and N. D. Willows, pp. 234–44. University of Calgary Archaeological Association, Calgary, Alberta.

1991b   Toward an Historical Archaeology of Domestic Reform. In *The Archaeology of Inequality,* edited by R. McGuire and R. Paynter, pp. 231–286. Blackwell Publishers, London.

1992   A Feminist Agenda for Non-sexist Archaeology. In *Quandaries and Quests: Visions of Archaeology's Future,* edited by L. Wandsnider, pp. 98–114. Southern Illinois University Press, Carbondale.

1994   Diversity in 19th Century Domestic Reform: Relationships Among Classes and Ethnic Groups. In "*Those of Little Note": Race and Class in Historical Archaeology,* edited by E. M. Scott, pp. 175–208. University of Arizona Press, Tucson.

1995   Toward the Further Development of Feminist Historical Archaeology. *World Archaeological Bulletin* 7:118–136.

1996   Feminist Historical Archaeology and the Transformation of American Culture by Domestic Reform Movements, 1840–1925. In *Historical Archaeology and the Study of American Culture,* edited by L. A. De Cunzo and B. L. Herman, pp. 397–446. Winterthur Museum and University of Tennessee Press, Knoxville.

1997   Feminist Inclusive Theory: Crossing Boundaries in Theory and Practice. Paper invited for Feminism on the Frontier, 4th Australian Women in Archaeology Conference, Cairns, July 3–5.

1999a   The World Their Household: Changing Meanings of the Domestic Sphere in the Nineteenth Century. In *The Archaeology of Household Activities: Gender Ideologies, Domestic Spaces and Material Culture,* edited by P. M. Allison, pp. 162–189. Routledge, London.

1999b   Gendering Power. In *Manifesting Power: Gender and the Interpretation of Power in Archaeology,* edited by T. L. Sweely, pp. 175–183. Routledge, London.

2001   What Difference Does Feminist Theory Make? In *The Archaeology of Nineteenth Century Institutions for Reform,* edited by S. M. Spencer-Wood and S. Baugher. Journal Issue of *International Journal of Historical Archaeology* 5(1).

2002   Personal communication, August 5.

Stansell, Christine

1995   Women, Children and the Use of the Streets: Class and Gender Conflict in New York City, 1850–1860. In *Women's America: Refocusing the Past,* edited by L. K. Kerber and J. S. De Hart, pp. 129–141. Oxford University Press, New York.

Starobin, Robert S.

1970   *Denmark Vesey: The Slave Conspiracy of 1822.* Prentice-Hall, Englewood Cliffs, New Jersey.

1971   Denmark Vesey's Slave Conspiracy of 1822: A Study in Rebellion and Repression. In *American Slavery: The Question of Resistance,* edited by J. Bracey, A. Meier, and E. Rudwick, pp. 142–157. Wadsworth Publishers, Belmont, California.

State Inspector of Mines (SIM)

1911   State Inspector of Mines Annual Report. On file, Denver Public Library, Government Documents. Denver.

Steinbeck, John

1939   [1986] *The Grapes of Wrath.* Penguin Books, New York.

Stewart-Abernathy, Leslie C.

1982   The Sanders Kitchen Site: A Preliminary Report of Excavations at 3HE236–32. Copy on file at Arkansas Archeological Survey, Russellville.

1986a   Urban Farmsteads: Household Responsibilities in the City. *Historical Archaeology* 20(2):5–15.

1986b   The Block House Piers: A Contribution to the Archeological Underpinning of Historic Preservation in Washington, Arkansas. Report submitted to the Arkansas Department of Parks and Tourism. Copy on file at Arkansas Archeological Survey, Russellville.

1987   Reconnaissance to the Hempstead House Site (3HE236-200), Washington, Arkansas. Report submitted to Arkansas State Archeologist, copy on file at Arkansas Archeological Survey, Russellville.

1988   Queensware in a Southern Store: Perspectives on the Antebellum Ceramics Trade from a Merchant Family's Trash in Washington, Arkansas. Six-panel poster session with paper presented at annual meeting of the Society for Historical Archaeology, Reno.

1992   Separate Kitchens and Intimate Archeology: Constructing Urban Slavery on the Antebellum Cotton Frontier in Washington, Arkansas. Paper presented at the annual meeting of the Society for American Antiquity, Pittsburgh, Pennsylvania.

1999   From Famous Forts to Forgotten Farmsteads: Historical Archaeology in the Mid-South. In *On Beyond Zebree, Papers in Honor of Dan and Phyllis Morse*, edited by R. Mainfort, 225–244. University of Arkansas Press, Fayetteville.

n.d.   The Sanders and Block Kitchens (3HE236-32 and 3HE236-19), Washington, Arkansas. Manuscript on file, Arkansas Archeological Survey, Russellville.

Stewart-Abernathy, Leslie C., and Barbara L. Ruff
1989   A Good Man in Israel: Zooarchaeology and Assimilation in Antebellum Washington, Arkansas. *Historical Archaeology* 23(2):96–112.

Stine, Linda F., Melanie Cabek, and Mark Groover
1996   Blue Beads as African-American Cultural Symbols. *Historical Archaeology* 30(3): 9–75.

Stine, Linda F., Martha Zierden, Lesley M. Druker, and Christopher Judge (editors)
1997   *Carolina's Historical Landscape: Archaeological Perspective*. University of Tennessee Press, Knoxville.

Stone, Lawrence
1977   *The Family, Sex and Marriage in England, 1500–1800*. HarperCollins, New York.

Stoney, Samuel G.
1938   *Plantations of the Carolina Low Country*. Dover Publishers, New York.

Strasser, Susan
1982   *Never Done: A History of American Housework*. Random House, New York.

Tannenbaum, Rebecca J.
2003   The Housewife as Healer: Medicine as Women's Work in Colonial New England. In *Women's Work in New England, 1620–1920*, edited by P. Benes, pp. 160–169. The Dublin Seminar for New England Folklife Annual Proceedings 2001, vol. 26. Boston University Scholarly Publications, Boston.

Taylor, Orville W.
1958   *Negro Slavery in Arkansas*. Duke University Press, Durham, North Carolina.

Texas Archeological Research Laboratory
n.d.   Site files. J. J. Pickle Research Center, The University of Texas at Austin.

Thomas, Brian
    1998   Power and Community: The Archaeology of Slavery at the Hermitage Plantation. *American Antiquity* 63(4):531–552.

Thomas, Brian, Larry McKee, and Jennifer Bartlett
    1995   Summary Report on the 1995 Hermitage Field Quarter Excavation. Report on file at The Hermitage, Hermitage, Tennessee.

Thomas, Julian
    2001   Archaeologies of Place and Landscape. In *Archaeological Theory Today,* edited by I. Hodder, pp. 165–186. Polity Press, Cambridge, U.K.

Thomas, J. E., and J. M. Adovasio, with contributions by J. Stabler, D. C. Dirkmaat, C. L. Pedler, D. H. Jurney, R. W. Moir, A. G. Quinn, and D. R. Pedler
    1996   *The Texas Capital Extension Archaeological Project.* Report prepared for 3D/ International, Inc., and Ford, Powell & Carson, Inc. Mercyhurst Archaeological Institute, Mercyhurst College, Erie, Pennsylvania.

Tijerina, Andres
    1998   *Tejano Empire: Life on the South Texas Ranchos.* Texas A&M University Press, College Station.

Tjarks, Alicia V.
    1974   Comparative Demographic Analysis of Texas, 1777–1793. *Southwestern Historical Quarterly* 77:291–338.

Tong, Rosemarie
    1989   *Feminist Thought: A Comprehensive Introduction.* Westview Press, Boulder.

Tricentennial Celebration Committee
    1970   Berkeley County, South Carolina: Celebrating 300 years of Sovereign Statehood, 1670–1970. Pamphlet. Berkeley County, South Carolina.

Trieber, Jacob
    1911   Legal Status of Negroes in Arkansas Before the Civil War. *Publications of the Arkansas Historical Association* 3:175–183.

Tringham, Ruth
    1988   Households, Housefuls and Archaeological House Remains: Social Archaeology at a Microscale. Paper presented to the 21st Chacmool Conference, Calgary, Alberta.
    1990   Conclusion: Selevac in the Wider Context of European Prehistory. In *Monumenta Archaeologica,* vol. 15, edited by R. Tringham and D. Krstick, 567–615. UCLA Institute of Archaeology, Los Angeles.
    1991   Households with Faces: The Challenge of Gender in Prehistoric Architectural Remains. In *Engendering Archaeology,* edited by J. M. Gero and M. W. Conkey, pp. 93–131. Blackwell, Cambridge, U.K.

Trinkley, Michael
    1988   *Archaeological Testing of Six Sites on Hilton Head Island, Beaufort County, South Carolina.* Chicora Research Series 13. Chicora Foundation, Columbia, South Carolina.
    1990a   *The Second Phase of Archaeological Survey on Spring Island, Beaufort County, South*

Carolina: Investigation of Prehistoric and Historic Settlement Patterns on an Isolated Sea Island. Chicora Research Series 20. Chicora Foundation, Columbia, South Carolina.

1990b *Archaeological Excavations at 38BU96, a Portion of Cotton Hope Plantation, Hilton Head Island, Beaufort County, South Carolina.* Chicora Research Series 21. Chicora Foundation, Columbia, South Carolina.

Trinkley, Michael, Debi Hacker, and Natalie Adams

1992 *Plantation Life in the Piedmont: A Preliminary Examination of Rosemont Plantation, Laurens County, South Carolina.* Chicora Research Series 29. Chicora Foundation, Columbia, South Carolina.

Trouillot, Michel-Rolph

1995 *Silencing the Past: Power and the Production of History.* Beacon Press, Boston.

Ulrich, Laurel Thatcher

1982 *Good Wives: Image and Reality in the Lives of Women in Northern New England, 1650–1750.* Oxford University Press, New York.

2003 Women's Travail, Men's Labor: Birth Stories from Eighteenth-Century New England. In *Women's Work in New England, 1620–1920,* edited by P. Benes, pp. 170–183. The Dublin Seminar for New England Folklife Annual Proceedings 2001, vol. 26. Boston University Scholarly Publications, Boston.

Upton, Dell

1988 White and Black Landscapes in Eighteenth Century Virginia. In *Material Life in Early America, 1600–1800,* edited by R. B. St. George. Northeastern University Press, Boston.

U.S. Department of Agriculture (USDA)

1921 Bureau of Markets and Crop Estimates, Bulletin 30, November. On file, Denver Public Library, Government Documents, Denver.

U.S. Department of Labor

1925 Home Environment and Employment Opportunities of Women in Coal-Mine Workers' Families. U.S. Department of Labor, Women's Bureau, Washington, D.C.

U.S. Federal Census

1900 Microfilm. On file, Dallas Public Library, Dallas.

1910 Official Census of the United States, 1910. On file, Denver Public Library, Government Documents, Denver.

Van Bueren, Thad M.

2002 Struggling with Class Relations at a Los Angeles Aqueduct Construction Camp. *Historical Archaeology* 36(3):28–43.

Veltre, Douglas W., and Allen P. McCartney

2002 Russian Exploitation of Aleuts and Fur Seals: The Archaeology of Eighteenth- and Early-Nineteenth-Century Settlements in the Pribilof Islands, Alaska. *Historical Archaeology* 36(3):8–17.

Vesey Trial Papers

1822 *Court Proceedings and Testimony Regarding the Vesey Rebellion.* Governor's Message Enclosure. Papers number ST0828. South Carolina Archives and History Center, Columbia.

Vlach, John Michael

1993   *Back of the Big House: The Architecture of Plantation Slavery.* University of North Carolina Press, Chapel Hill.

Wade, Peter

1996   *Race and Ethnicity in Latin America.* Pluto Press, London.

Wade, Richard C.

1964   *Slavery in the Cities: The South 1820–1860.* Oxford University Press, New York.

1971   The Vesey Plot: A Reconsideration. In *American Slavery: The Question of Resistance,* edited by J. Bracey, A. Meier, and E. Rudwick, pp. 127–141. Wadsworth Publishers, Belmont, California.

Walde, Dale, and Noreen D. Willows (editors)

1991   *The Archaeology of Gender, Proceedings of the 22nd [1989] Annual Chacmool Conference.* University of Calgary Archaeological Association, Calgary, Alberta.

Walker, Lester

1981   *American Shelter: An Illustrated Encyclopedia of the American Home.* Overlook Press, Woodstock, New York.

Wall, Diana diZerega

1991   Sacred Dinners and Secular Teas: Constructing Domesticity in Mid-Nineteenth Century New York. *Historical Archaeology* 25(4):69–81.

1994   *The Archaeology of Gender: Separating the Spheres in Urban America.* Plenum Press, New York.

2000   Family Meals and Evening Parties: Constructing Domesticity in Nineteenth-Century Middle-Class New York. In *Lines that Divide: Historical Archaeologies of Race, Class and Gender,* edited by J. A. Delle, S. A. Mrozowski, and R. Paynter, pp. 109–141. University of Tennessee Press, Knoxville.

Walton, Anthony

1996   *Mississippi: An American Journey.* Vintage Press, New York.

Walz, Robert

1953   Arkansas Slaveholdings and Slaveholders in 1850. *Arkansas Historical Quarterly* 12(1):38–73.

Washington, Booker T.

1907   [1970] The Economic Development of the Negro Race Since its Emancipation. In *The Negro in the South,* pp. 43–76. University Books, New York.

Washington, Minerva, Community Elder

1998   Personal communication, Hermitage, Tennessee.

Washington Telegraph

n.d.   Historic Newspaper, on file, Southwest Arkansas Regional Archives, Washington, Arkansas.

Watanabe, John M.

1992   *Maya Saints and Souls in a Changing World.* University of Texas Press, Austin.

Waterson, R.

1995   Houses and Hierarchies in Island Southeast Asia. In *About the House: Lévi-Strauss and Beyond,* edited by J. Carsten and S. Hugh-Jones, pp. 47–68. Cambridge University Press, Cambridge.

Weir, Robert

1983   *Colonial South Carolina: A History.* KTO Press, Millwood, New York.

Westmacott, Richard

1992   *African-American Gardens and Yards in the Rural South.* University of Tennessee Press, Knoxville.

Whayne, Jeannie M.

1996   *A New Plantation South: Land, Labor, and Federal Favor in Twentieth-Century Arkansas.* University of Virginia Press, Charlottesville.

White, Deborah Gray

1985   *Ar'n't I a Woman? Female Slaves in the Plantation South.* W. W. Norton and Co., New York.

White, Dena D.

1984   Slavery in Hempstead County, Arkansas. Unpublished Honors thesis, Department of History, Ouachita Baptist University, Arkadelphia, Arkansas. Copy on file Southwest Arkansas Regional Archives, Washington, Arkansas.

White, Shane, and Graham White

1998   *Stylin': African American Expressive Culture from Its Beginnings to the Zoot Suit.* Cornell University Press, Ithaca.

Wilk, Richard R., and Wendy Ashmore (editors)

1988   *Household and Community in the Mesoamerican Past.* University of New Mexico Press, Albuquerque.

Wilk, Richard R., and Robert M. Netting

1984   Households: Changing Forms and Functions. In *Households: Comparative and Historical Studies of the Domestic Group,* edited by R. M. Netting, R. R. Wilk, and E. J. Arnould, pp. 1–28. University of California Press, Berkeley.

Wilk, Richard, and William Rathje

1982   Household Archaeology. *American Behavioral Scientist* 25(6):617–639.

Wilk, Richard R., Robert McC. Netting, and Eric J. Arnould (editors)

1984   *Households: Comparative and Historical Studies of the Domestic Group.* University of California Press, Berkeley.

Wilkie, Laurie

1996a   House Gardens and Female Identity on Crooked Island. *Journal of the Bahamas Historical Society* 18:33–39.

1996b   Medicinal Teas and Patent Medicines: African-American Women's Consumer Choices and Ethnomedical Traditions at a Louisiana Plantation. *Southeastern Archaeology* 15(2):119–131.

2000a   *Creating Freedom: Material Culture and African American Identity at Oakley Plantation, Louisiana, 1840–1950.* Louisiana State University Press, Baton Rouge.

2000b   Culture Bought: Evidence of Creolization in the Consumer Goods of an Enslaved Bahamian Family. *Historical Archaeology* 34(3):10–26.

2003   *Archaeology of Mothering: An African-American Midwife's Tale.* Routledge, New York.

Wilkie, Laurie A., and George W. Shorter, Jr.

1997   *Lucretia's Well: An Archaeological Glimpse of an African-American Midwife's House-*

hold. University of Southern Alabama Archaeological Monograph 11. University of Southern Alabama Archaeology Facility, Mobile.

Williams, Charleen M.

1951   *The Old Town Speaks: Washington, Hempstead County.* Anson Jones Press, Houston.

Williams, Eric E.

1971   *From Columbus to Castro: The History of the Caribbean, 1492–1969.* Harper & Row, New York.

Williams, Lyle W.

1982   *Ranches and Ranching in Spanish Texas.* American Press, Boston.

Williams, Patricia

1979   *A Guide to African Villages in New Providence.* Public Records Office, Nassau.

Williams, Raymond

1973   *Country and City.* Oxford University Press, Oxford.

1977   *Marxism and Literature.* Oxford University Press, Oxford.

Wilson, Madison

1992   Personal communication, Washington, Arkansas, September 26.

Witsell, Evans, & Rasco P. A., Historic Planners, and Arkansas State Parks

1985   *Master Plan for Old Washington Historic State Park.* Arkansas Division of Parks and Tourism, Little Rock.

Woodward, C. Vann

1974   [1955] *The Strange Career of Jim Crow.* 3rd rev. ed. Oxford Press, New York.

Yamin, Rebecca (editor)

2000   *Tales of Five Points: Working-Class Life in Nineteenth-Century New York.* Vol. 1, *A Narrative History and Archeology of Block 160.* U.S. General Services Administration, New York.

Yamin, Rebecca, and Karen Bescherer Metheny (editors)

1996   *Landscape Archaeology: Reading and Interpreting the American Historical Landscape.* University of Tennessee Press, Knoxville.

Yanagisako, Sylvia Junko

1979   Family and Household: The Analysis of Domestic Groups. *Annual Review of Anthropology* 8:161–205.

Yans-McLaughlin, Virginia

1971   *Family and Community: Italian Immigrants in Buffalo, 1880–1930.* Cornell University Press, Ithaca.

Yentsch, Anne Elizabeth

1991   Engendering Visible and Invisible Ceramic Artifacts, Especially Dairy Vessels. In *Gender in Historical Archaeology,* edited by D. J. Seifert. *Historical Archaeology* 25(4):132–155.

1994   *A Chesapeake Family and Their Slaves: A Study in Historical Archaeology.* Cambridge University Press, Cambridge.

Yentsch, Anne, and Mary C. Beaudry

2001   American Material Culture in Mind, Thought, and Deed. In *Archaeological Theory Today,* edited by I. Hodder, pp. 214–240. Polity Press, Cambridge, U.K.

Yentsch, Anne E., Naomi Miller, Barbara Paca, and Dolores Piperno
  1987 Archaeologically Defining the Earlier Garden Landscapes at Morven: Preliminary Results. *Northeast Historical Archaeology* 16:1–29.
Young, Amy L. (editor)
  2000 *Archaeology of Southern Urban Landscapes.* University of Alabama Press, Tuscaloosa.
Yuhl, Stephanie E.
  2000 Rich and Tender Remembering: Elite White Women and an Aesthetic Sense of Place in Charleston, 1920s and 1930s. In *Where These Memories Grow: History, Memory and Southern Identity,* edited by W. F. Brundage, pp. 227–248. University of North Carolina Press, Chapel Hill.

Contributors

Nesta Anderson is a Ph.D. candidate in the Anthropology Department at the University of Texas, Austin, specializing in African Diaspora archaeology in the Caribbean and southeastern United States. She is also a project archaeologist at Hardy, Heck, Moore, Inc., in Austin.

Kerri S. Barile is a principal investigator at SWCA Environmental Consultants in Austin, Texas, where she specializes in historical archaeology and architectural history in the mid-Atlantic region, the southeastern United States, and Texas. In her spare time, she is a Ph.D. candidate at the University of Texas at Austin.

Whitney Battle is a Ph.D. candidate in the African Diaspora Graduate Program in Anthropology and is affiliated with the Center for African and African American Studies, University of Texas, Austin. Her research interests include African Diaspora studies, historical archaeology, and black feminist theory.

Mary C. Beaudry is associate professor of archaeology and anthropology at Boston University. Her research interests in historical and industrial archaeology include comparative colonialism, archaeology of households, farms, and landscapes, and contextual analysis of small finds.

Mindy Bonine is a project archaeologist at Ecological Communications Corporation in Austin, Texas, where she specializes in historic and prehistoric archaeology in Texas, Oklahoma, and the Southwest.

Jamie C. Brandon is a visiting instructor in the Anthropology Department at the University of Arkansas, Fayetteville, and project-specific archeologist with the Arkansas Archeological Survey, specializing in historical archaeology, historical collective memory, and the archaeology of the African Diaspora in the American South.

James M. Davidson is a Ph.D. candidate in the Department of Anthropology at the University of Texas at Austin. His research interests are historic mortuary archaeology, the archaeology of the African Diaspora, and folklore studies.

Maria Franklin is assistant professor in the Department of Anthropology and the Center for African and African American Studies at the University of Texas at Austin. Her research interests include historical archaeology, the African Diaspora, and the ethics and politics of archaeology, race, gender, and feminist studies.

Mary Jo Galindo is a Ph.D. candidate in the Department of Anthropology at the University of Texas at Austin, where she specializes in the ethnicities and archaeology of eighteenth-century Spanish colonial rancho households along the Rio Grande Valley.

Efstathios I. Pappas is a Ph.D. student in the Department of Anthropology at the University of Nevada, Reno. Focusing in historical archaeology, his research interests include industrial labor populations and the rise of the industrial order in nineteenth- and twentieth-century America.

Suzanne Spencer-Wood is associate professor of anthropology and director of women's studies at Oakland University, as well as Associate at the Peabody Museum of Archaeology and Ethnology at Harvard University. In 1987 she wrote the first feminist article published in *Historical Archaeology,* and she is considered one of the pioneers of feminist historical archaeology.

Leslie C. "Skip" Stewart-Abernathy is a station archeologist for the Arkansas Archeological Survey, based at Arkansas Tech University in Russellville, where he is responsible for both prehistoric and historic cultural resources in 11 counties. He is also an associate professor of anthropology at the University of Arkansas at Fayetteville.

Margaret Wood is assistant professor of anthropology at Washburn University in Topeka, Kansas. Her teaching and research interests include historical archaeology, labor history, social inequality, gender, nationalism, and class and social change in early-twentieth-century communities.

Index

racism, 10, 75, 85, 199, 204–5, 207, 239, 253, 259
rancho, 15, 17–19, 25–27, 31, 179, 237, 244–5, 250, 252, 259–60
Reconstruction, 67, 76, 89, 100–1, 105, 199, 201–5
resistance, 197, 259
Rio Alamo, 28, 183
Rio Grande, 15, 17–18, 25, 27–29, 183
Robert E. Lee Memorial Foundation, 2

Sabine Fields plantation, 114–6
Saint Paul United Methodist Church, 88, 102, 106
San Antonio, Texas, 3, 77. *See also* Texas
segregation, 72, 135, 200–1, 206, 250, 257
separate spheres, 10, 203, 235, 243, 260–1
Sierra Nevada Mountains, 11, 162
Skull Creek Plantation. *See* Cotton Hope Plantation
slave(s)/slavery, 37, 47–48, 50–51, 53, 54–58, 59–60, 67–69, 72–74, 89, 101, 113–4, 121, 126–7, 130, 133, 142, 149, 154–5, 201, 204, 236, 238–9, 240, 242, 245–6, 250–1, 256; community, 9, 33, 37, 39, 47, 49, 50; dwellings, 9, 48; experience of, 33; family, 9, 36, 38, 40; housing, 38; labor, 38; material aspects of, 38; quarters, 10, 123–4, 126–9, 133–5, 257; representation of, 33; urban, 55–8, 60; workers, 36, 40, 126
Smithsonian Institution, 18
Soap Creek Pass, 11, 162–3, 172–3, 258
Socioeconomic status. *See* class
South, Stanley, 3–5
South Carolina, 68, 122, 128, 133–5, 136, 259
space, 9, 11, 17, 20, 26, 43–44, 47–49, 55, 63, 109–11, 117–8, 122, 135, 146, 161–2, 167, 175, 181, 201, 209, 222, 254, 256, 262; consumer, 205; contested, 43, 69; dwelling, 48; empty, 48; female-controlled, 47, 141, 201; gendered, 1; household, 9, 117; interior, 20; outdoor, 26, 47; private, 167, 175; shared, 9, 110–1; social, 49, 130; symbolic, 6. *See also* garden; patio; yard
spatial analysis, 10, 11, 36, 99, 250, 259. *See also* landscape(s), analysis
spatial distribution, 163
spatial location, 11
spatial map, 10

spatial separation, 9, 12, 36, 51, 61–63, 66–67, 69, 72–73, 135, 206, 250, 256
Spanish American Genealogical Society, 185
Spanish colonial, 11, 15, 17–18, 25–27, 31, 179, 185, 195–6, 244, 252, 260; government, 31, 179; household, 11, 31, 185; influence, 31; rancho, 15, 17–19, 25–27, 31, 237, 244–5, 250, 252, 259–60; settlements, 17; sites, 18
Starr County, Texas, 10, 18, 28. *See also* Texas
Stoney's Plantation. *See* Fairfield Plantation
Stratford Hall, 2–3
subsistence, 3–4, 15. *See also* cooking; food preparation

Tamaulipas, 15, 179, 185, 195. *See also* Mexico; Nuevo Santander
Tennessee, 33–34
Texas, 3, 26, 76–77, 79, 85, 250, 252; north, 76; south, 15, 25, 29, 31; border(lands), 17, 183. *See also* Mexico
Texas Archeological Research Laboratory, 18, 86
Troupe, Alexander M., 86, 105

United Mine Workers of America, 217
University of South Carolina, 126
University of Texas at Austin, 18, 86, 101–2, 105, 179, 258
urban farmstead, 56, 64, 68, 72–73

Van Winkle's Mill, 207–9
Vesey, Denmark, 10, 68, 131–7, 243, 247, 259

War for Mexican Independence, 26
War of 1812, 37
washerwomen, 56 *see also* laundress; laundry
Washington, Arkansas, 9, 51–74, 207, 256; *See also* Arkansas; Hempstead County, Arkansas
Westmoreland County, Virginia, 2

yard(s), 10, 27, 36, 43, 47–51, 55, 104, 111, 117–8, 133, 165, 242, 247; backyard, 36, 51, 103, 167, 255; courtyard, 27; houseyard, 117–8

Zapata County, Texas, 28, 179, 185
Zapata, town of, 18, 183